TRANSFORMING ARCHAEOLOGY

Transforming Archaeology

Activist Practices and Prospects

EDITED BY

Sonya Atalay, Lee Rains Clauss,
Randall H. McGuire, and John R. Welch

Walnut Creek, CA

Left Coast Press, Inc.
1630 North Main Street, #400
Walnut Creek, CA 94596
http://www.LCoastPress.com

ISBN 978-1-61132-961-2 hardback
ISBN 978-1-61132-962-9 paperback
ISBN 978-1-61132-963-6 institutional eBook
ISBN 978-1-61132-759-5 consumer eBook

Library of Congress Cataloging-in-Publication Data

Transforming archaeology : activist practices and prospects / edited by Sonya Atalay, Lee Rains Clauss, Randall H. McGuire, and John R. Welch.
    pages cm
  Includes bibliographical references and index.
  ISBN 978-1-61132-961-2 (hardback : alk. paper)—
  ISBN 978-1-61132-962-9 (pbk. : alk. paper)—
  ISBN 978-1-61132-963-6 (institutional ebook)—
  ISBN 978-1-61132-759-5 (consumer ebook)
  1. Archaeology—Methodology.   2. Archaeology—Philosophy.   3. Social archaeology.
4. Environmental archaeology.   5. Interdisciplinary research.   I. Atalay, Sonya, 1968– .
  CC80.T73 2014
  930.1—dc23
                                                                    2013049754

Printed in the United States of America
∞™ The paper used in this publication meets the minimum requirements of American National Standard for Information Sciences—Permanence of Paper for Printed Library Materials, ANSI/NISO Z39.48–1992.

Cover design by Piper Wallis

Contents

Chapter 1   7
   Transforming Archaeology
   Sonya Atalay, Lee Rains Clauss, Randall H. McGuire,
   and John R. Welch

Chapter 2   29
   Betwixt and Between: Archaeology's Liminality and Activism's
   Transformative Promise
   Lee Rains Clauss

Chapter 3   45
   Engaging Archaeology: Positivism, Objectivity, and Rigor in
   Activist Archaeology
   Sonya Atalay

Chapter 4   61
   Situating Activism in Archaeology: The Mission of Science the Activist
   Affect, and the Archaeological Record
   Quetzil E. Castañeda

Chapter 5   91
   "We Have Met the Enemy and It Is Us": Transforming Archaeology
   through Sustainable Design
   John R. Welch and Neal Ferris

Chapter 6   115
   Working Class Archaeology
   Randall H. McGuire

Chapter 7   133
   Reconciling Inequalities in Archaeological Practice and
   Heritage Research
   George P. Nicholas

Chapter 8   159
    Transforming the Terms of Engagement between Archaeologists and
        Communities: A View from the Maya Region
        Patricia A. McAnany

Chapter 9   179
    From the Bottom Up: Transforming Communities with
        Public Archaeology
        M. Jay Stottman

Chapter 10   197
    Activating Archaeology
        K. Anne Pyburn

Chapter 11   215
    Beyond Archaeological Agendas: In the Service of a
        Sustainable Archaeology
        Neal Ferris and John R. Welch

Chapter 12   239
    Archaeologists as Activists, Advocates, and Expert Witnesses
        T. J. Ferguson

Index   255

About the Editors   265

Chapter 1

Transforming Archaeology

Sonya Atalay, Lee Rains Clauss,
Randall H. McGuire, and John R. Welch

In this second decade of the twenty-first century, many archaeologists have become tired of the polemical war that ended the twentieth century. They have grown weary of the jousts between the champions of reflexivity and the defenders of positivism, and of the constant skirmishing over what we can know and how we can know it. Increasingly, archaeologists just want to get on with it and do archaeology. The contributors in this volume, however, seek to disrupt both the polemical battle and the complacency of those who would hammer their swords into trowels so that they can dig their square holes in peace. In discussing these points, the contributors to this volume repeatedly came back to a key question. Like Panameno and Nalda (1978) more than thirty-five years earlier, we ask: "Archaeology for whom?" In different parts of the world (see Figure 1.1 on page 21), using varied approaches and methods and in their own voices, each of the authors in this volume came to a similar response: "For those who see archaeology as a way to create collective benefits."

To bring that vision to reality, we argue that archaeology must be transformed—not updated, rehabilitated, or reformed—but altered in elemental ways. This transformation is not encapsulated in the creation of a new theoretical approach or by merely employing more sophisticated and complex methodologies to know the world. Instead, we see the need to change central aspects of the conception and character of the discipline to address new purposes and fresh aspirations that

Transforming Archaeology: Activist Practices and Prospects, edited by Sonya Atalay, Lee Rains Clauss, Randall H. McGuire, and John R. Welch, 7–28. © 2014 Left Coast Press, Inc. All rights reserved.

transcend the interests of professional archaeologists and that advance something other than the welfare of academic departments or cultural resource management/archaeological resource management (CRM/ARM) firms. We are issuing a call—hopeful and practical—to refit archaeology to serve the pressing present needs of communities outside of our discipline. As we look to the future, we want to see archaeology transformed into a practice that is not only acceptable to communities but also useful and perhaps even necessary in our contemporary world. There is much at stake, and we challenge ourselves and other archaeologists to make archaeology a way and a means for taking care of our planet and of one another—a tool for activism in the world.

We are not the first or only archaeologists to call for activism. In the late 1970s and early 1980s, scholars in Latin America and Europe mobilized archaeology in pursuit of progressive political goals (McGuire 2008, 51–98). Latin Americans sought to build a social archaeology around Pameno and Nalda's (1978) question of "archaeology for whom?" In Germany, archaeologists and other activists excavated the headquarters of the Gestapo in the dark of night, often returning to dig out what the city government had backfilled the day before (Topography of Terror Foundation 2005; Rürup 2008). We also find our inspiration in the work of archaeologists who sought to build archaeologies by and for indigenous peoples around the world (Dowdall and Parrish 2003; Gnecco and Ayala 2011; Layton 1989; Nicholas and Andrews 1997; Silliman 2008; Smith and Wobst 2005; Smith, Morgan, and van Meer, 2003; Watkins 2000; Wobst 2010). Building on these earlier efforts, we bring a distinctively North American perspective to activism and archaeology. We raise the call for activism in the context of a dying polemical debate over science and relativism. Most importantly, we seek to transform the discipline, not just create an activist niche in archaeology (Silverman and Ruggles 2007; Stottman 2010).

Our call for transformation is not a heedless provocation, but the result of a serious and careful assessment of the practice of archaeology today. Archaeology has always possessed great power. However, it has often wielded much of its weight at the expense and to the detriment of living peoples. More to the point, except in rare instances of private expeditions, the entire archaeological enterprise is publicly owned and funded. What better reason for archaeology to exist than to meet the needs of people. We agree with Schmidt (2005) that much of our discipline's potential to apply information from the past to positively affect the present has been underutilized. In the chapters that follow, the authors discuss and demonstrate ways that archaeology can realize its potential beyond the confines of "studying the past." For many, this includes reversing the rationale for archaeology: transforming it from narrowly academic and regulatory practices into an activist tool that draws on the discipline to address politics and real-world problems in the present. Archaeology as activism rejects the choice between science and critique, and instead embraces the cognitive dissonance of deploying both archaeological science and critical archaeology to serve the interests of communities in the world.

What We No Longer Want to See in Archaeology

Archaeology needs disruption because when pursued as top-down, researcher-driven, or government-mandated practice, it can (and all too often does) disenfranchise people from their heritage in real and powerful ways (McAnany and Parks 2012; Pyburn, this volume). Too often, practicing archaeology under prevailing current principles and precepts disconnects people from their past through highly constrained knowledge production, interpretation, and dissemination processes that are, with few exceptions, dictated by and meaningful to archaeologists and archaeologists alone. Archaeologists, perhaps unwittingly although at times quite intentionally, act in paternalistic ways to claim authority and dominion over all or part of other people's heritage. This is particularly visible when the archaeological record is framed as global cultural heritage or requisitely part of a universal human heritage that must be shared equally by all.

The Society for American Archaeology (SAA) identifies stewardship as the central principle of archaeological ethics (Lynott and Wylie 1995). The principle springs from a declaration that archaeological materials are a public trust that should be used to benefit all people, and from an assertion that archaeologists are the stewards of these materials. As stewards, archaeologists are both caretakers of, and advocates for, archaeological materials. The SAA principles recognize that various groups within the "public" may have differing interests in archaeological materials, and they charge archaeologists to address these interests. Even though the SAA principles argue that no one person or group should have exclusive access or control of archaeological resources, they clearly privilege archaeologists as the managers and specialists who must advocate the scientific study and preservation of archaeological materials. Yet, stewards are servants—they work for somebody. Who do archaeologists work for? The SAA principles incorporate a long-standing position in American archaeology: that the archaeological record is a public trust, and that archaeologists are stewards for that public (Groarke and Warrick 2006). But who is that public, and how did they choose archaeologists to be the stewards of their heritage? Zimmerman (1995, 66) suggests that we start by recognizing that a diversity of valid interests exists (and have always existed) in the past, and that, as such, we should assert that "All people are stewards of the past." We concur, adding that archaeologists also share responsibilities as stewards of the present.

Assuming a self-appointed, sole stewardship role over the archaeological record, creating knowledge for knowledge's sake, and foregrounding data over people, all contribute to larger contemporary problems. For example, archaeology is often used for cultural authentication and the gatekeeping of ethnic and gender identities (Clauss 2007). Furthermore, the discipline supports a flawed class structure in its demarcation of CRM/ARM archaeology versus academic archaeology. As Welch and Ferris (this volume) and Ferris and Welch (this volume) point out, archaeology also perpetuates and benefits from an extraction-consumption paradigm within societies struggling toward greater sustainability, collective responsibility, and balanced reciprocity in all its interactions with the environment and other people. And, as previously remarked, the discipline continues to contribute to nationalist agendas, racial inequality, colonialism, and globalization in many countries around the world (McDavid 2002; McNiven and Russell 2005; Wobst 2010; Zimmerman 2006).

Unfortunately, these acts of disenfranchisement have become the status quo in much of the way archaeology is practiced. In response, there has been a growing literature that reflects upon, and dissects, this process of disenfranchisement (Cojti-Ren 2006; Gnecco and Hernandez 2008; Lilley 2009; McAnany and Parks 2012; McNiven and Russell 2005; Moser et al. 2002; Welch and Riley 2001; Wobst 2010). Yet, overall, these discussions have been relegated to the margins of the field, and as a result, the problematic aspects of archaeology persist (Clauss, this volume). So although some individual archaeologists have come to question their role as stewards, and many of them have changed the way they engage with communities outside the discipline, we don't see evidence that the majority of practitioners recognize and acknowledge the problematic ways that the practice of archaeology subjugates those outside the profession or that this aspect of the discipline requires alteration. Although there is movement toward greater collaboration and community-oriented practice, we haven't yet experienced an overarching shift, a *sea change* in the way archaeology, as a profession, is practiced.

At least part of the reason for this reluctance may be that the literature detailing the ways archaeology is oppressive tends to focus on critique rather than pragmatic solutions, more on theory than practice. And although critique is necessary for identifying problems, it often does little to create pathways by which the problematic aspects of a discipline can be challenged to the point of change. To truly and lastingly transform archaeology, we think it is time to move beyond critique. Thus, what we offer in this volume is forward looking and solution oriented. The chapters presented here collectively propose that archaeologists act individually, and in concert, to employ and apply activist perspectives, methods, and subject expertise to craft a better world.

We remain aware of the need to critique archaeology, yet our goal is not simply to tear it down. Instead, we are working to model the move from critique to action. Our aim for this volume is to provide readers with glimpses of areas in which archaeology is being transformed (see chapters in this volume by McGuire, McAnany, Nicholas, Stottman, and Pyburn). We offer plans for actions that will further transform the discipline (see chapters in this volume by Clauss, Atalay, Ferris and Welch, and Welch and Ferris) and we consider carefully the implications of such a fundamental transformation (Atalay, Castañeda, Pyburn, and Ferguson). Moreover, the chapters that follow offer a discourse on archaeological practices that reflect and support the needs of communities.

Beyond Critical Archaeology

Archaeologists have demonstrated that for all of archaeology's inadequacies and missteps, the discipline can be used in the service of communities to achieve their objectives and address social issues and concerns (Atalay 2012; Little 2002; McAnany et al. 2013; Sabloff 2008; Shackel and Chambers 2004; Stottman 2010). The contributors to this volume agree. And although most archaeologists assert that archaeology *can* assist communities, the authors of this volume advocate that it *must*. We argue that archaeology is poised to contribute, systematically although seldom exclusively, to serving the needs and interests of nonarchaeological communities. Furthermore, the authors and editors view archaeology performed solely for the advancement of the discipline or obligatory compliance with regulations as misguided, needlessly wasteful of public trust and financial resources, and often more harmful than beneficial. Thus our ultimate goal is to transform much of archaeology into a practice that, at its core, serves communities in the present and with long-term considerations for the future.

For at least two decades, archaeologists have realized the situated nature of archaeological knowledge and the capability of archaeology to do good or ill for social interests. Many have applied this realization through critical archaeologies based in postmodernism (Hodder 1999; Meskell 2002), feminism (Conkey and Spector 1984; Gilchrist 1999), Marxism (McGuire 1992a; Patterson 2003), and decolonizing or indigenous theory (Atalay 2006; Lydon and Rizvi 2010; Nicholas 2006; Smith 1999; Smith and Jackson 2006; Smith and Wobst 2005). Critical archaeology is a form of intellectual activism that analyzes the political nature of knowledge content and production by highlighting the intersubjectivity of archaeological research (see Castañeda, this volume). For some, an important point of departure is to acknowledge and demonstrate the ways that doing archaeology can perpetrate violence on communities (McDavid 2002; McNiven and Russell 2005; Wobst 2010). Others champion the promise of a future made better through applications of ethical, engaged, and community-based archaeologies (Atalay 2006, 2012; Dawdy 2010; Little 2002; McGuire 2008; Moser et al. 2002; Rizvi 2008; Rossen 2006, 2008; Schmidt 2006; Schmidt and Patterson 1995; Silliman and Dring 2008; Zimmerman 2006). This important work has laid foundations for archaeology's transformation by championing subaltern groups and deconstructing power.

These calls for supporting subaltern communities and deconstructing power, however, have prompted a backlash that questions the idea of archaeology in service of communities, specifically indigenous communities. Robert McGhee (2008) and Daryl Stump (2013) question the legitimacy and efficacy of archaeology in the service of communities. In their assumption that only science can produce factual observations about the past, these critics dismiss thirty years of scholarship on the situated nature of science. They further argue that doing archaeology in support of communities necessitates the adoption of perspectives that are incommensurate with the archaeologists' conception of reality and the use of essentialized notions of community identity that perpetuate harmful stereotypes of people. As proponents of critical archaeology point out, these authors assert that only one correct interpretation of the past can exist. Such a belief precludes their comprehension of a critical multivocality in which numerous perspectives and values are brought together to enlarge our shared understanding of the past (Atalay 2006, 2008; Castañeda, this volume; Colwell-Chanthaphonh et al. 2010; Colwell-Chanthaphonh 2013).

Holtorf (2009) and McGhee (2008) also have voiced concerns about archaeology in the service of communities as an entry point for pernicious nationalism. We are concerned about nationalistic uses of archaeology as well. However, we recognize that archaeology is not and never has been objective or apolitical (Castañeda, this volume; McGuire 2008; Silverman and Ruggles 2007). Archaeology has long been (ab)used by governments, nation-states, and academic archaeologists to direct and concentrate benefits and powers in the hands and pockets of narrow constituencies. We see it as problematic to take this power away from *people* in locales in which it is already utilized by their governments, oftentimes in ways that are against their wishes and damage their heritage. In fact, we do not need to look to the oft-cited case of Nazi Germany for nation-state uses of archaeology (Arnold 2006). We can look in our own backyard.

The government of the United States has historically and consistently used archaeology and historic preservation legislation to disenfranchise Native American communities and to support a materialist and capitalist society (McGuire 1992b; McManamon 2003). In many ways, in the United States, archaeology continues to serve a gatekeeping function over Native American cultural heritage simply because of the centralization of power that exists and the fact that state and national government agencies control much of the archaeology practiced within the country. These links are obvious from any review of the history of government archaeology. So although archaeology's connections to government in the United States may not be as overt as in some countries, they are still unmistakably political and contribute to a particular agenda (Ferris and Welch, this volume; Welch and Ferris, this volume). Howard Zinn (2002) reminds us, "You can't be neutral on a moving train." Archaeologists—even those focused on seemingly apolitical analyses such as Paleolithic scraper typologies or chert sourcing—may advance national and industrial agendas, most fundamentally in the context of preserving and celebrating "our shared national heritage" (see Pyburn, this volume). Again, for whose benefit?

There are also critiques of community-based archaeology related to scientific rigor (McGhee 2008; Stump 2013). It is our position that research carried out with communities need not and should not entail relaxation of essential scientific standards (McGuire 2008; Welch, Lepofsky, and Washington 2011a). Hale (2006) speaks directly to this point in his discussion of activist anthropology scholarship, arguing the need to reclaim what it means to conduct rigorous research across all domains of anthropology. Atalay's chapter in this volume considers this within the context of archaeology. She argues that engaged and activist scholarship should be first about doing rigorous research, but that it should also be done in partnership with communities, not simply archaeology for the sake of archaeology or intellectual curiosity. Furthermore, we would suggest that epistemic injustice, a concept detailed in the work of Miranda Fricker (2007), should be central to discussions of rigor, questions concerning who holds "valid" knowledge, and assessments of the risks and rewards of democratizing knowledge (Atalay 2012; Fortmann 2008). Ultimately, we believe that the positivist-realist critics of community-centered archaeology fail to recognize power relations in the construction of the past. In doing so, they also fail to answer this volume's central question about archaeology's motivations and beneficiaries.

Community archaeology, public archaeology, collaborative archaeology, engaged archaeology, and indigenous archaeology all recognize the moral imperatives and practical benefits of collaborations with people outside of archaeology. These approaches have produced theoretically important critiques and they encourage archaeologists to be concerned about and responsive to contemporary society. However, the daily practice of archaeology has yet to truly transform at national and global scales (see Castañeda, this volume). To achieve revolutionary change requires that archaeologists transform both how we "think" archaeology and how we "do" archaeology. We also must give constant attention to how the benefits of archaeology are delineated and distributed.

Our interests center not in dismantling academic or CRM/ARM archaeologies, but in moving all or most archaeologies toward matters of practical interest and away from narrowly theoretical or compliance-focused discourses. We advocate for an archaeology that has dual loyalties to communities of archaeologists and to communities of nonarchaeologists who value the past and welcome opportunities to harness archaeology to address contemporary social, economic, and political concerns. Critique is, of course, necessary to challenge hegemonic knowledge systems and to legitimate participation by communities in the creation of knowledge. However, using critique to dismiss scientific knowledge may be counterproductive to the goals of political struggle or social movement. A transformative archaeology does not need to disentangle critique and science but rather to do both—that is, to deploy scientific method in tandem with rigorous critique (Atalay, this volume). As this volume illustrates, activists within archaeology use cultural critique, but also the language and methods of science, to invoke the authority of science to defend the legitimacy of nonarchaeological communities' rights and the results of our work.

For this reason, we place archaeology squarely amid the tensions between academic ideals and practical politics with dual commitments to critical scholarly production and to the principles and practices of people who struggle beyond the academic setting. These dual commitments transform our research methods—from the formulation of research questions to the dissemination of results. They require collaboration, dialogue, and types of accountability that conventional methods can, and regularly do, ignore (Atalay 2012). This can be a tense and uncomfortable place. Staying in it requires a constant mediation and attention to multiple responsibilities—those we have to the communities we partner with and aim to serve; as well as those we have as scholars, professionals, community members, and actors engaged in contemporary social and political struggles. As the chapters that follow demonstrate, when we engage in archaeology as activism and/or practice activism within archaeology, we often find ourselves in complex situations in which we are asked to choose one set of priorities over another. This book offers no one-size-fits-all solution to such dilemmas, but in such situations we return to the same familiar question to guide our approach: archaeology for whom?

In advocating for a transformed archaeology, however, we do not wish to develop another niche approach to archaeology. We do not aspire to lay out or prescribe a set of practices that are relevant only to specific groups or audiences or merely set forth a new methodology. Rather, we hope to contribute to a transformation in the way *all* archaeologists think about and practice their crafts. We argue that archaeologists should generate new knowledge and theoretical insights, but that these activities should be an outgrowth of the needs of nonarchaeological communities. In other words, the new knowledge that archaeologists produce should have usefulness and transformative implications; at the same time, such knowledge should be produced via active involvement with nonarchaeological communities and their concerns.

Such a radical departure from the prevailing goals of the majority of archaeological practice, not surprisingly, requires rethinking the role of archaeology within society. Ultimately, a transformed archaeology—a discipline focused on doing research with, by, and for nonarchaeological communities—is an archaeology that no longer presumes intrinsic value to the public; no longer bestows the title of "subject expert" upon its practitioners; and no longer gives primacy to the thrill of discovery or data accumulation over human rights. Instead, recognizing archaeology's tremendous potential to bring about positive change in peoples' lives, as well as its historical shortcomings in achieving such social relevance, the contributors to this volume endeavor to practice and promote the many ways in which archaeology can contribute to community-wide capacity-building, empowerment, restoration, and revitalization. The chapters that follow demonstrate various current efforts to do so.

The Transforming Archaeology Collective

The authors in this volume have interacted with one another for more than a decade on collaborative research projects and in various sessions at Society for American Archaeology (SAA), American Anthropological Association (AAA), World Archaeological Congress (WAC), and other professional meetings. During this time, we have found loci of intersection among ourselves and others. These intersections are multiple and varied. Some of the common threads are the application and evaluation of multiple narratives (Dongoske, Aldenderfer, and Doehner 2000; Ferguson and Colwell-Chanthaphonh 2006; Franklin and Paynter 2010; Silliman 2008; Swidler et al. 1997); the need to "remodel the master's house" (Atalay 2004, 2008); archaeological ethics (Atalay et al. 2009; Castañeda and Matthews 2008; Colwell-Chanthaphonh and Ferguson 2004; Hodder 2002; McGuire 1994, 2003; Nicholas and Hollowell 2006, 2007; Pyburn 2003a, 2003b; Pyburn and Wilk

1997; Zimmerman 2006; Zimmerman, Vitelli, and Hollowell-Zimmer 2003); the consideration of how archaeology and archaeologists can affect descendant communities' identities and vitalities (Atalay 2012; Parks and McAnany 2007; Welch and Ferguson 2007; Welch et al. 2011b); and recognition that archaeology could do more to become socially relevant and responsive to extra-archaeological communities' needs and concerns regarding the discipline (Welch 2000; Welch and Riley 2001). Indigenous archaeology was a common theme for many of these sessions (Atalay 2006; Nicholas 2011; Phillips and Allen 2010; Watkins 2000), yet through our engagements and conversations, we found similar lines of thought outside of indigenous archaeology. We found that within the overlapping realms of CRM/ARM and academia, and among archaeologists working in different parts of the world, the need to transform archaeological practice in active ways was a shared concern.

Based on this realization, we brought multiple colleagues from diverse backgrounds together to talk directly about both the transformative role that archaeology can adopt through activism, as well as the ways archaeology itself can be transformed through activism within the discipline. In spring 2011, we organized an SAA session titled "On the Edge of (a) Reason: Archaeology, Activism, and the Pursuit of Relevance" to primarily discuss the theory and practices encompassed in "activist archaeology." Our aim was to bring together a group of those who were already moving archaeology in new directions and who had experiences confronting the complex ethical and theoretical conundrums that such a shift in praxis entails. We realized then and want to emphasize here that the list of invitees for that session could have included many more names. There is a substantive history of activist archaeology—numerous archaeologists have sought and are seeking to transform the discipline, and many more are employing archaeology to positively transform the world (e.g., Hamilakis and Duke 2007; Little 2009; Little and Shackel 2007; Little and Zimmerman 2010; McGuire 2008; Pyburn 2007; Saitta 2007; Zimmerman, Singleton, and Welch 2010).

Our "activist archaeology" SAA session then led to an intensive Amerind Foundation Seminar. In March 2013, the Amerind Foundation generously hosted twelve participants from the original SAA symposium for four days. During that time, the authors in this volume conferred, debated, and ruminated about what we would like to see archaeology become and how we can contribute, both individually and as a group, to transforming our shared discipline. We wrestled with such questions as "What, precisely, do we want to change?"; "Do we have a shared vision of what a transformed archaeology would be?"; "What are our hopes and aims for the discipline moving forward?"; "How can we best build, implement, and encourage a transformed archaeology?"; and "What are the challenges that we must face and the obstacles we anticipate having to overcome?" In the end, a central point shone through: "We want more from archaeology and we think our profession can and should do more in the world." This volume reflects those deliberations and is the culmination of our shared insights about, and commitments to, a transformed archaeology.

What We Want the World to Be Like

Our time at the Amerind allowed us to reflect on desired futures at disciplinary and global scales. We carefully considered if and how archaeology could contribute to that vision. Such reflection is essential to any call to action, the legitimacy of which is grounded in moral, theoretical, and ideological foundations. Specifically, our call to action recognizes the challenges of putting refined theories and best intentions into practice with communities.

We recognize that "communities" are seldom resolved entities, unified in their desires and dreams, immutable in their constituencies, or coherent in their identities. As is the case with all other human social constructs, communities are always in process, poorly bounded, and full of internal contradictions. Individuals are normally members of multiple communities and they form, manipulate, and perform identities within and between them. These processes invariably transform communities, making boundaries and membership dynamic and fluid over various temporal, social, and geographical scales. Finally, each community exists in relationship to other communities with their own interests and different abilities to realize those interests. Conflicts, collaborations, and clashes between these communities transform them all.

Members of a community share a lived experience and common interests as a result of that experience. However, members of a community do not participate equally in that lived experience. Power relations exist within, between, and among communities. Almost without exception, these result in inequalities, inequities, and various forms of oppression. Alienation, therefore, may exist both between communities and within communities. For these reasons, an emancipation that confronts oppressive relations within and between communities cannot be fully successful if it ignores alienations of class, gender, sexuality, and so on.

Recognizing these inherent complexities in communities, our consideration of the social contexts for archaeological practice begins with the identification of the communities involved, their interests, their internal relations and their relationships with other communities. Each of the contributors to this volume has struggled with the vagaries, dynamics, and contradictions of the communities with which we work. These struggles informed our most pertinent discussions, leading us to the concepts and ideals upon which we believe archaeology should be built. We offer them as bases for ongoing discussions of desired futures, not as a way to limit or narrowly focus transformative archaeologies.

Social and environmental justice: We want to see a world in which social justice and environmental justice are ever-present datum points for orienting archaeological planning and decision making. In this view, it is not only humans that benefit and are considered but also the totality of our connections to plant and animal life, as well as landscapes and bodies and courses of water across the planet. We want to confront alienation and individualistic thinking and replace it with collaborative decision making that helps strengthen and renew our relationships with each other as global citizens. This involves building solidarity with one another as well as establishing and nurturing new connections (Clauss, this volume; McGuire, this volume).

Equity: Working toward equity is a key component of social justice, and archaeology can and should contribute in positive ways toward achieving equity. We recognize that equity and equality are different concepts with different implications. Equality relates to division and uniform distribution, whereas equity suggests that each party should be treated as their needs require. Equality focuses on matched inputs, and equity focuses on just and equal results. Others have detailed the complexity involved in deciding to work for equity versus equality (Cook and Hegtvedt 1983; Konow 2003; Konow, Saijo, and Akai 2009). Despite these challenges, we think that just social change happens only when equity is among the guiding principles.

Knowledge democratization: Central to this vision and to the concept of social justice is the idea that the entire archaeological process, from research design to field methods and from data analysis and interpretation to knowledge dissemination and mobilization, must be democratized. Contrary to Stump's (2013, 282) critique, our call for a democratization of knowledge is not just rhetoric. Rather, we wish to enlarge the discipline's commitments and practice. Democratization is about diversity and participation in contrast to the power of interpretation (Atalay 2012; Fortmann 2008). Archaeological projects should be developed, from the start, with communities affected by and interested in the places and topics to be studied. Projects should include a detailed plan for how the knowledge that is produced will be curated and shared in culturally appropriate ways (Atalay 2012; Atalay, this volume). By working directly in partnership with communities to consider the research questions and archaeological projects that are relevant, archaeologists become facilitators for studying, understanding, and interpreting the past in ways that people in the present find relevant, compelling, and most of all, useful (Atalay 2012; Pyburn, this volume; Stottman, this volume).

Sovereignty: We also believe that enacting sovereignty for indigenous peoples is crucial and we look to the UN Declaration on the Rights of Indigenous Peoples (UNDRIP), finally endorsed by the United States and Canada in 2010, as an important guiding framework for ensuring and protecting the sovereignty of indigenous peoples. A close read of the UNDRIP reveals several points of intersection with archaeology. Most central is the recognition that indigenous peoples have the right to control their own cultural heritage. Also important is the protection of intellectual property, which intersects with archaeology in important ways (Nicholas, this volume; Nicholas and Bannister 2004; Nicholas et al. 2010). Doing archaeology in partnership with indigenous peoples can be a useful capacity-building tool that assists communities in building or flexing their sovereignty (McAnany, this volume; Welch et al. 2006).

Respect and Trust: Both concepts are foundational for human interactions. Our work as archaeologists must build upon foundations that uphold these essential attributes of good relationships while fostering them in our engagements with communities outside of archaeology (Colwell-Chanthaphonh and Ferguson 2004;

Zimmerman 2005). The respect we point to must occur at the *human* scale, with individuals and communities. This means taking the time necessary to listen and seek to understand and act upon the needs and interests expressed by community partners and other interested parties (see Atalay, this volume; Clauss, this volume; Ferguson, this volume; Welch et al. 2011a).

Sustainability: Perhaps sustainability is at this point more an aspirational goal than a foundational principle; nonetheless, when we consider transforming archaeology in order to foster more just and equitable practices, we want those practices to be viable beyond the lifespan of our individual careers. We envision archaeologies that both model sustainability on a disciplinary scale and contribute to sustainability on a global scale (Ferris and Welch, this volume; Welch and Ferris, this volume). Certainly, scientific practices evolve and adapt to changing times to suit the needs of the society. Archaeology is hardly immune to this mutability. But the foundational concepts we put forward here, and which we hope to build upon, are stated with the long-term sustainability of the discipline in mind—a longevity that we believe will occur only when all those within the discipline, as individuals and collectively through our professional organizations, work in partnerships that transcend archaeology (Parks and McAnany 2011). We want to be clear that a call for sustainability within archaeology does not mean that people and communities are of a lesser concern than our discipline's self-maintenance. Quite the contrary, in fact. We envision transforming archaeology so that it places first priority on people and community needs and measures its success by how well it makes itself useful to those outside the discipline.

These foundational concepts provide the interlocking timbers of a robust framework for archaeological practices and prospects dedicated to continuous reflexivity and expansive engagement with nonarchaeologists and the issues and concerns they have about the past and how they want it to matter today and in the future. But our vision is more than a wistful romantic dream. The transformation we seek within archaeology is not born of naive desires to create a better world. Barbara Little (2010, 155) notes, and we agree, that it is important for archaeologists to take seriously the privileges of our positions in order to contribute in a positive way to our world. We aspire to harness the transformative power of collective learning that invariably emerges through good-faith listening and cooperative acting. After all, the well-being of communities and of archaeology is connected in significant ways. Both stand to benefit if we transform archaeology and rebuild it as a collaborative and community-centered practice.

How Do We Pursue This Desired Future? Activism!

How are we to achieve the transformation we have outlined for archaeology? First, like any other form of activism, it requires starting from a point of personal engagement. Few if any broadly beneficial social or communal processes or products are contingent on archaeologists; it is up to archaeologists to pursue engagements with and become involved in change. However, even if the work involved in creating benefits for communities is archaeocentric, it must not become egocentric (Clauss, this volume; Ferguson, this volume). This can sometimes be a challenge in academia, in which ideas are the currency, and individual production and ownership of ideas is the norm. Comparable issues arise in CRM/ARM, in which success is intimately tied to efficiency, expediency, and cost effectiveness—goals that are often at odds with collaborative endeavors with communities. To be sure, transforming archaeology in these environments is challenging. It is, nonetheless, possible.

A commitment to making change through activist interventions is the key. Largely because changes in institutions and practices are contingent on individual actions, micro- and macro-level leadership within institutions is the surest activist path to closing gaps between desired futures and the present. Critical masses of individual and institutional commitments must be built. Additionally, participating with others to actively transform archaeology and make it relevant in the world requires both internal and external foci. Thus, in this volume, we advocate for taking up the principles of activism in two ways: using activism as a tool to transform archaeology and using archaeology as a tool to transform and build a better world.

Such transformation is generally contingent on strategic goals and plans. Specifically, our goals at this point include:

- Opening archaeology's institutional infrastructure to allow for change;
- Fostering safe spaces for the expression of alternative opinions and practices;
- Rededicating archaeological practice to collective learning and capacity building at project, program, community, disciplinary, and societal scales; and
- Crafting archaeological projects and programs to harness the discipline's intrinsic potential to integrate hand-heart-mind thinking, acting, and learning within and across social categories.

As for strategic plans, we intend, through this volume and our respective and collective works, to continue to illustrate how archaeological places, projects, perspectives, and data can and are bringing about change both within archaeology and across diverse, extra-academic contexts. We know the world is a moving target and that our plans and tactics must accordingly be modified in continuous and dynamic response to extradisciplinary needs and interests. We want readers to understand that we do not claim that any of the approaches or answers provided here are more than good ways to move forward given the political, financial, and conceptual limitations of the circumstances. However, we do see this volume as an important step: a call to action and an invitation for students and colleagues to become involved and help frame follow-up plans for transforming archaeology over the course of lifetimes and careers. This volume is also a request for further dialogue within our discipline on how to collectively act to transform archaeology.

Volume Organization

As this book illustrates, there are numerous sites of engagement within archaeology—geographical, social, and conceptual spaces in which activism can be used to transform the discipline into a proactive, service-oriented, community-based endeavor. Activism within archaeology has no geographical or sociopolitical bounds. And, as witnessed in several of the volume's chapters, activism by archaeologists and through archaeology can take on many different forms. In some instances, archaeology is used as a tool for a community's activism-oriented aims. In others, the activism occurs within the discipline to change the fundamental structures of why, how, and for/by whom we do archaeology.

And although this diversity of approach can be liberating, it can also create ambiguity with regards to how someone might enter into this transformative work and then create successful practices to sustain it. It is for these reasons that most of us have been approached, at some point in our careers, by those seeking to know more about activism within and through archeology. This book is for them; we structured the chapters so that they provide details on the authors' entry into activism as well as a discussion of methods.

Each chapter begins with a biographical sketch of the author to provide some background on each person and his/her entry into activism. This is because, as noted previously, all true activism begins with and is sustained by personal commitments and distinct senses of purpose. The biographical statements aim to give our readers insights into those commitments, what sparked them, and how they developed and were put into action. In the case of the two coauthored chapters, the biographical sketch focuses on the first author.

At the close of each chapter, the reader will find a short methodological essay. These brief vignettes provide insight into some of the guidelines and practices each of us has found particularly salient in our efforts to transform archaeology and the world beyond.

It is through these descriptions of personal forays into activism, examples of activism within archaeology being practiced in various locations throughout the world, and discussions of the ethics and methods of a transformed and transformative archaeology, that we hope to educate and enlist. It is also our desire that this volume will encourage and support our fellow sojourners on the transformative path. And, finally, it is our hope that our contribution to the topic of activism within archaeology will engender more substantial, equitable, and sustainable engagement between the discipline's practitioners and the nonarchaeological communities we work within and directly (and indirectly) affect. We hope the book's success will be judged less on the number of scholarly citations received and more on the intellects and imaginations liberated from the shackles of an inward-looking and self-serving archaeology. Our discipline can do more and better, and we offer our words, thoughts, and deeds in service to collective aspirations for just and equitable uses of archaeological places, data, and practices.

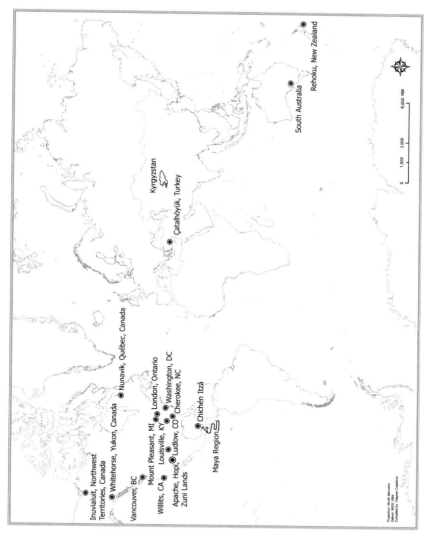

Inuvialuit, Northwest
Territories, Canada

Whitehorse, Yukon, Canada

Nunavik, Québec, Canada

Vancouver, BC

Mount Pleasant, MI

London, Ontario

Willits, CA

Louisville, KY

Washington, DC

Apache, Hopi, Ludlow, CO

Cherokee, NC

Zuni Lands

Chichén Itzá

Maya Region

Kyrgyzstan

Çatalhöyük, Turkey

South Australia

Rehoku, New Zealand

0   1,500   3,000   6,000 KM

Projection: World Mercator
Datum: WGS 1984
Compiled by Clayton Crawford

Figure 1.1   World Map with locations mentioned in this volume.

Acknowledgments

This book is the final product of a three-year-long engagement among the contributors to this volume. Engagements are often filled with a complex blend of excitement, bewilderment, wonderment, trepidation, frustration, and camaraderie. Ours was no exception. In recognition of this fact, the coeditors of this book would like to thank each of the contributing authors for their professionalism and perseverance during our literary journey and their dedication to our shared goal of seeing archaeology transformed. We also recognize that this volume is the direct result of a 2013 Amerind Foundation Advanced Seminar. The authors are indebted to Dr. John Ware for his belief in our vision and support of our mission. We thank the Amerind Foundation staff for the hospitality showered upon us during our time in Dragoon. We truly appreciate the insight, recommendations, and constructive critique offered by our four anonymous peer reviewers and Dr. Thomas Patterson. Our final manuscript was greatly bettered by each of their thoughtful examinations. Clayton Crawford of Simon Fraser University must be credited for deftly transforming a list of widely dispersed place and region names into the world map featured in the introduction. We thank Mitch Allen and the team at Left Coast Press for their interest in our manuscript and their decisive and timely guidance throughout the publication process.

REFERENCES

Arnold, Bettina. 2006. "'Arierdämmerung': Race and Archaeology in Nazi Germany." *World Archaeology* 38(1): 8–31.

Atalay, Sonya. 2004. *Multiple Voices for Many Ears in Indigenous Archaeological Practice.* Washington, DC: Society for American Archaeology.

———. 2006. "Indigenous Archaeology as Decolonializing Practice." *American Indian Quarterly* 30(3 & 4): 280–310.

———. 2008. "Multivocality and Indigenous Archaeologies." In *Evaluating Multiple Narratives: Beyond Nationalist, Colonialist, and Imperialist Archaeologies,* edited by Junko Habu, Clare Fawcett, and John M. Matsunaga, 29–44. New York: Springer.

———. 2012. *Community-Based Archaeology: Research with, by, and for Indigenous and Local Communities.* Berkeley: University of California Press.

Atalay, Sonya, Chip Colwell-Chanthaphonh, Edward Jolie, Paula Lazarus, Janet Levy, Dorothy Lippert, Dru McGill, Mark Oxley, Anne Pyburn, Nick Shepherd, Alison Wylie, and Larry Zimmerman. 2009. "An Open Letter to the SAA Membership: Ethics." *Archaeological Record* 9(2): 4–5.

Castañeda, Quetzil E., and Christopher N. Matthews, eds. 2008. *Ethnographic Archaeologies: Reflections on Stakeholders and Archaeological Practices.* Lanham, MD: AltaMira Press.

Clauss, Lee Rains. 2007. "Identity Crisis: The Archaeology of Indigenousness and Ethnicity in 21st Century America." Paper presented at the 72nd Annual Society for American Archaeology Meeting, Austin, TX.

Cojti-Ren, Avexnim. 2006. "Maya Archaeology and the Political and Cultural Identity of Contemporary Maya in Guatemala." *Archaeologies: Journal of the World Archaeological Congress* 2(1): 8–19.

Colwell-Chanthaphonh, Chip. 2013. "Comment to Daryl Stump's 'On Applied Archaeology, Indigenous Knowledge, and the Usable Past.'" *Current Anthropology* 54(3): 285–286.

Colwell-Chanthaphonh, Chip, and T. J. Ferguson. 2004. "Virtue Ethics and the Practice of History: Native Americans and Archaeologists Along the San Pedro Valley of Arizona." *Journal of Social Archaeology* 4(1): 5–27.

Colwell-Chanthaphonh, Chip, T. J. Ferguson, Dorothy Lippert, Randall H. McGuire, George P. Nicholas, Joe E. Watkins, and Larry. J. Zimmerman. 2010. "The Premise and Promise of Indigenous Archaeology." *American Antiquity* 75(2): 228–238.

Conkey, Margaret W., and Janet Spector. 1984. "Archaeology and the Study of Gender." *Advances in Archaeological Method and Theory* 7: 1–38.

Cook, Karen S., and Karen A. Hegtvedt. 1983. "Distributive Justice, Equity, and Equality." *Annual Review of Sociology* 9: 217–241.

Dawdy, Shannon Lee. 2010. "Clockpunk Anthropology and the Ruins of Modernity." *Current Anthropology* 51(6): 761–793.

Dongoske, Kurt E., Mark S. Aldenderfer, and Karen Doehner, eds. 2000. *Working Together: Native Americans and Archaeologists.* Washington, DC: Society for American Archaeology.

Dowdall, Katherine M., and Otis O. Parrish. 2003. "A Meaningful Disturbance of the Earth." *Journal of Social Archaeology* 3(1): 99–133.

Ferguson, T. J., and Chip Colwell-Chanthaphonh. 2006. *History Is in the Land: Multivocal Tribal Traditions in Arizona's San Pedro Valley.* Tucson: University of Arizona Press.

Fortmann, Louise. 2008. "Introduction: Doing Science Together." In *Participatory Research in Conservation and Rural Livelihoods,* edited by Louise Fortmann, 1–17. Oxford, UK: Wiley-Blackwell.

Franklin, Maria, and Robert Paynter. 2010. "Inequality and Archaeology." In *Voices in American Archaeology,* edited by Wendy Ashmore, Dorothy Lippert, and Barbara Mills, 131–159. Washington, DC: Society for American Archaeology.

Fricker, Miranda. 2007. *Epistemic Injustice: Power and the Ethics of Knowing.* Oxford, UK: Oxford University Press.

Gilchrist, Roberta. 1999. *Gender and Archaeology: Contesting the Past.* London: Routledge.

Gnecco, Cristobal, and Patricia Ayala, eds. 2011. *Indigenous Peoples and Archaeology in Latin America.* Walnut Creek, CA: Left Coast Press.

Gnecco, Cristobal, and Carolina Hernandez. 2008. "History and its Discontents: Stone Statues, Native Histories, and Archaeologists." *Current Anthropology* 49(3): 439–466.

Groarke, Leo, and Gary Warrick. 2006. "Stewardship Gone Astray? Ethics and the SAA." In *The Ethics of Archaeology: Philosophical Perspectives on Archaeological Practice,* edited by Chris Scarre and Geoffrey Scarre, 163–177. Cambridge, UK: Cambridge University Press.

Hale, Charles. 2006. "Activist Research v. Cultural Critique: Indigenous Land Rights and the Contradictions of Politically Engaged Anthropology." *Cultural Anthropology* 21(1): 96–120.

Hamilakis, Yannis, and Phillip Duke, eds. 2007. *Archaeology and Capitalism: From Ethics to Politics.* Walnut Creek, CA: Left Coast Press.

Hodder, Ian. 1999. *The Archaeological Process: An Introduction.* Oxford, UK: Basil Blackwell.

———. 2002. "Ethics and Archaeology: The Attempt at Çatalhöyük." *Near Eastern Archaeology* 65: 174–82.

Holtorf, Cornelius. 2009. "A European Perspective on Indigenous and Immigrant Archaeologies." *World Archaeology* 41(4): 672–681.

Konow, James. 2003. "Which Is the Fairest One of All? A Positive Analysis of Justice Theories." *Journal of Economic Literature* 41: 1186–1237.

Konow, James, Tatsuyoshi Saijo, and Kenju Akai. 2009. "Morals and Mores? Experimental Evidence on Equity and Equality." Mimeo. Los Angeles: Loyola Marymount University.

Layton, R., ed. 1989. *Conflict in the Archaeology of Living Traditions: One World Archaeology.* London: Routledge.

Lilley, Ian. 2009. "Strangers and Brothers? Heritage, Human Rights, and Cosmopolitan Archaeology in Oceania." In *Cosmopolitan Archaeologies*, edited by Lynn Meskell, 48–67. Durham, NC: Duke University.

Little, Barbara J., ed. 2002. *Public Benefits of Archaeology.* Gainesville: University Press of Florida.

Little, Barbara J. 2009. "Forum: What Can Archaeology Do for Justice, Peace, Community and the Earth?" *Historical Archaeology* 43(4): 115–119.

———. 2010. "Epilogue." In *Archaeologists as Activists: Can Archaeologists Change the World?*, edited by M. Jay Stottman, 154–158. Tuscaloosa: University of Alabama Press.

Little, Barbara J., and Paul A. Shackel, eds. 2007. *Archaeology as a Tool of Civic Engagement.* Lanham, MD: AltaMira Press.

Little, Barbara J., and Larry J. Zimmerman. 2010. "In the Public Interest: Creating a More Activist, Civically-Engaged Archaeology." In *Voices in American Archaeology*, edited by Wendy Ashmore, Dorothy Lippert, and Barbara Mills, 131–159. Washington, DC: Society for American Archaeology.

Lydon, Jane, and Uzma Rizvi, eds. 2010. *Handbook of Postcolonial Archaeology.* Walnut Creek, CA: Left Coast Press.

Lynott, Mark J., and Alison Wylie, eds. 1995. *Ethics in American Archaeology: Challenges for the 1990s.* Special Report. Washington, DC: Society for American Archaeology.

McAnany, Patricia A., and Shoshaunna Parks. 2012. "Casualties of Heritage Distancing: Children, Ch'orti' Indigeneity, and the Copán Archaeoscape." *Current Anthropology* 53(1): 80–107.

McAnany, Patricia A., Sarah M. Rowe, Israel Quic Cholotio, Evelyn Caniz Menchú, and Jose Mendoza Quic. 2013 (under review). "Mapping Indigenous Self-Determination." *International Journal of Applied Geo-Spatial Research,* Special Issue on "Geospatial Technologies and Indigenous Community Engagement."

McDavid, Carol. 2002. "Archaeologies that Hurt; Descendants that Matter: A Pragmatic Approach to Collaboration in the Public Interpretation of African-American Archaeology." *World Archaeology* 34(2): 303–314.

McGhee, Robert. 2008. "Aboriginalism and the Problems of Indigenous Archaeology." *American Antiquity* 73(4): 579–597.

McGuire, Randall H. 1992a. *A Marxist Archaeology.* Orlando, FL: Academic Press.

———. 1992b. "Archaeology and the First Americans." *American Anthropologist* 94(4): 816–836.

———. 1994. "Do the Right Thing." In *Reckoning with the Dead*, edited by Tamara Bray, 180–184. Washington, DC: Smithsonian Institution.

———. 2003. "Forward." In *Ethical Issues in Archaeology*, edited by Larry J. Zimmerman, Karen D. Vitelli, and Julie Hollowell-Zimmer, vii–ix. Lanham, MD: AltaMira Press.

———. 2008. *Archaeology as Political Action.* Berkeley: University of California Press.

McManamon, Francis P. 2003. "Archaeology, Nationalism, and North America." In *The Politics of Archaeology and Identity in a Global Context,* edited by Susan Kane, 115–137. Boston: Archaeological Institute of America.

McNiven, Ian, and Lynette Russell. 2005. *Appropriated Pasts: Indigenous Peoples and the Colonial Culture of Archaeology.* Lanham, MD: AltaMira Press.

Meskell, Lynn. 2002. "The Intersections of Identity and Politics in Archaeology." *Annual Review of Anthropology* 31: 279–301.

Moser, Stephanie, Darren Glazier, James E. Phillips, Lamya Nasser el Nemr, Mohammed Saleh Mousa, Rascha Nasr Aiesh, Susan Richardson, Andrew Conner, and Michael Seymour. 2002. "Transforming Archaeology through Practice: Strategies for Collaborative Archaeology and the Community Archaeology Project at Quseir, Egypt." *World Archaeology* 34(2): 220–248.

Nicholas, George P. 2006. "Decolonizing the Archaeological Landscape: The Practice and Politics of Archaeology in British Columbia." *American Indian Quarterly* 30(3/4): 350–380.

Nicholas, George P., ed. 2011. *Being and Becoming Indigenous Archaeologists.* Walnut Creek, CA: Left Coast Press.

Nicholas, George P., and Thomas Andrews, eds. 1997. *At a Crossroads: Archaeology and First Peoples in Canada.* Burnaby, Canada: Archaeology Press, Simon Fraser University.

Nicholas, George P., and Kelly P. Bannister. 2004. "Copyrighting the Past? Emerging Intellectual Property Rights Issues in Archaeology." *Current Anthropology* 45(3): 327–350.

Nicholas, George P., Catherine Bell, Rosemary Coombe, John R. Welch, Brian Noble, Jane Anderson, Kelly Bannister, and Joe Watkins. 2010. "Intellectual Property Issues in Heritage Management, Part 2: Legal Dimensions, Ethical Considerations, and Collaborative Research Practices." *Heritage Management* 3(1): 117–147.

Nicholas, George P., and Julie Hollowell. 2006. "Intellectual Property Issues in Archaeology: Addressing the Needs of a Changing World through Negotiated Practice." Plenary address presented at the Cultural Heritage & Indigenous Cultural &Intellectual Property Rights Conference. 5th World Archaeological Congress Intercongress, Burra, Australia.

———. 2007. "Ethical Challenges to a Postcolonial Archaeology." In *Archaeology and Capitalism: From Ethics to Politics,* edited by Yannis Hamilakis and Phillip Duke, 59–82. Walnut Creek, CA: Left Coast Press.

Panameno, Rebeca, and Enrique Nalda. 1978. "Arqueología, Para Quien?" *Nueva Antropología* 12: 111–124.

Parks, Shoshaunna, and Patricia A. McAnany. 2007. "Reclaiming Maya Ancestry." In *Look Close, See Far: A Cultural Portrait of the Maya,* edited by Bruce T. Martin, 17–26. New York: George Braziller.

———. 2011. "Heritage Rights and Global Sustainability via Maya Archaeology." *Anthropology News* 52(5): 27.

Patterson, Thomas C. 2003. *Marx's Ghost: Conversations with Archaeologists.* Oxford, UK: Berg.

Phillips, Caroline, and Harry Allen, eds. 2010. *Bridging the Divide: Indigenous Communities and Archaeology in the 21st Century.* Walnut Creek, CA: Left Coast Press.

Pyburn, K. Anne. 2003a. "What Are We Really Teaching in Archaeological Field Schools?" In *Handbook of Archaeological Ethics,* edited by Larry J. Zimmerman, Karen D. Vitelli, and Julie Zimmer, 213–223. Lanham, MD: AltaMira Press.

———. "Archaeology for a New Millennium: The Rules of Engagement." 2003b. In *Archaeologists and Local Communities: Partners in Exploring the Past,* edited by Linda Derry and Maureen Molloy, 167–184. Washington, DC: Society for American Archaeology.

———. 2007. "Archaeology as Activism." In *Cultural Heritage and Human Rights,* edited by Helaine Silverman and D. Fairchild Ruggles, 172–183. New York: Springer.

Pyburn, K. Anne, and Richard Wilk. 1997. "Ethics." In *Archaeological Research, Oxford Companion to Archaeology,* edited by Brian Fagan, 206–207. Oxford, UK: Oxford University.

Rizvi, Uzma. 2008. "Decolonizing Methodologies as Strategies of Practice: Operationalizing the Postcolonial Critique in the Archaeology of Rajasthan." In *Archaeology and the Postcolonial Critique,* edited by Matthew Liebmann and Uzma Z. Rizvi, 109–128. Lanham, MD: AltaMira Press.

Rossen, Jack. 2006. "New Vision in the Cayuga Heartland of Central New York." In *Cross-Cultural Collaboration: Native Peoples and Archaeology in the Northeastern United States,* edited by Jordan E. Kerber, 250–264. Lincoln: University of Nebraska.

———. 2008. "Field School Archaeology, Activism, and Politics in the Cayuga Homeland of Central New York." In *Collaborating at the Trowel's Edge: Teaching and Learning in Indigenous Archaeology,* edited by Stephen W. Silliman, 103–121. Tucson: University of Arizona.

Rürup, Reinhard, ed. 2008. *Topography of Terror: Gestapo, SS and Reich Main Security Office on Wilhelm-and Prinz-Albrecht-Straβe: A Documentation* (translated by Karen Margolis and Pamela E. Selwyn). Berlin: Stiftung Topographie des Terrors.

Sabloff, Jeremy A. 2008. *Archaeology Matters: Action Archaeology in the Modern World.* Walnut Creek, CA: Left Coast Press.

Saitta, Dean. 2007. *The Archaeology of Collective Action.* Gainesville: University Press of Florida.

Schmidt, Peter R. 2005. "Using Archaeology to Remake History in Africa." In *Making Alternative Histories: The Practice of Archaeology and History in Non-Western Settings,* edited by Peter R. Schmidt and Thomas C. Patterson, 119–148. Santa Fe, NM: School of American Research.

———. 2006. *Historical Archaeology in Africa: Representation, Social Memory, and Oral Traditions.* Lanham, MD: AltaMira Press.

Schmidt, Peter R., and Thomas C. Patterson, eds. 1995. *Making Alternative Histories: the Practice of Archaeology and History in Non-Western Settings.* Santa Fe, NM: School of American Research.

Shackel, Paul A., and Erve J. Chambers, eds. 2004. *Places in Mind: Public Archaeology as Applied Anthropology.* New York: Routledge.

Silliman, Stephen W. 2008. "Collaborative Indigenous Archaeology: Troweling at the Edges, Eyeing the Center." In *Collaborating at the Trowel's Edge: Teaching and Learning in Indigenous Archaeology,* edited by Stephen W. Silliman, 1–24. Tucson: University of Arizona.

Silliman, Stephen W., and Katherine H. Sebastian Dring. 2008. "Working on Pasts for Future: Eastern Pequot Field School Archaeology in Connecticut." In *Collaborating at the Trowel's Edge: Teaching and Learning in Indigenous Archaeology,* edited by Stephen W. Silliman, 67–87. Tucson: University of Arizona.

Silverman, Helaine, and D. Fairchild Ruggles, eds. 2007. *Cultural Heritage and Human Rights.* New York: Springer.

Smith, Claire, and Gary Jackson. 2006. "Decolonizing Indigenous Archaeology: Developments from Down Under." *American Indian Quarterly* 30(3/4): 311–349.

Smith, Claire, and H. Martin Wobst, eds. 2005. *Indigenous Archaeologies: Decolonising Theory and Practice.* New York: Routledge.

Smith, Laurajane, Anna Morgan, and Anita van der Meer. 2003. "The Waanyi Women's History

Project: A Community Partnership Project, Queensland, Australia." In *Archaeologists and Local Communities: Partners in Exploring the Past,* edited by Linda Derry and Maureen Malloy, 147–166. Washington, DC: Society for American Archaeology.

Smith, Linda Tuhiwai. 1999. *Decolonizing Methodologies: Research and Indigenous Peoples.* New York: Zed Books-University of Otago.

Stottman, M. Jay, ed. 2010. *Archaeologists as Activists: Can Archaeologists Change the World?* Tuscaloosa: University of Alabama Press.

Stump, Daryl. 2013. "On Applied Archaeology, Indigenous Knowledge, and the Usable Past." *Current Anthropology* 54(3): 268–298.

Swidler, Nina, Kurt E. Dongoske, Roger Anyon, and Alan S. Downer, eds. 1997. *Native Americans and Archaeologists: Stepping Stones to Common Ground.* Lanham, MD: AltaMira Press.

Topography of Terror Foundation. 2005. "Foundation Topography of Terror in Berlin: New Exhibition and Documentation Center," accessed July 11, http://www.topographie.de/en.

Watkins, Joe E. 2000. *Indigenous Archaeology: American Indian Values and Scientific Practice.* Lanham, MD: AltaMira Press.

Welch, John R. 2000. "The White Mountain Apache Tribe Heritage Program: Origins, Operations, and Challenges." In *Working Together: Native Americans and Archaeologists,* edited by Kurt E. Dongoske, Mark Aldenderfer, and Karen Doehner, 67–83. Washington, DC: Society for American Archaeology.

Welch, John R., Mark Altaha, Doreen Gatewood, Karl Hoerig, and Ramon Riley. 2006. "Archaeology, Stewardship, and Sovereignty." *The SAA Archaeological Record* 6(4): 17–20, 57.

Welch, John R., and T. J. Ferguson. 2007. "Putting Patria into Repatriation: Cultural Affiliations of White Mountain Apache Tribe Lands." *Journal of Social Archaeology* 7: 171–198.

Welch, John R., Dana Lepofsky, and Michelle Washington. 2011a. "Assessing Collaboration with the Sliammon First Nation in a Community-Based Heritage Research and Stewardship Program." *Archaeological Review from Cambridge* 26(2): 171–190.

Welch, John R., Dana Lepofsky, Megan Caldwell, Georgia Combes, and Craig Rust. 2011b. "Treasure Bearers: Personal Foundations for Effective Leadership in Northern Coast Salish Heritage Stewardship." *Heritage and Society* 4(1): 83–114.

Welch, John R., and Ramon Riley. 2001. "Reclaiming Land and Spirit in the Western Apache Homeland." *American Indian Quarterly* 25(1): 5–12.

Wobst, H. Martin. 2010. "Indigenous Archaeologies: A Worldwide Perspective on Human Materialities and Human Rights." In *Indigenous Archaeologies: A Reader on Decolonization,* edited by Margaret Bruchac, Siobhan M. Hart, and H. Martin Wobst, 17–28. Lanham, MD: AltaMira Press.

Zimmerman, Larry J. 1995. "Regaining Our Nerve: Ethics, Values, and the Transformation of Archaeology." In *Ethics in American Archaeology: Challenges for the 1990s,* edited by Mark J. Lynott and Alison Wylie, 64–67. Washington, DC: Society for American Archaeology.

———. 2005. "First, Be Humble: Working with Indigenous Peoples and Other Descendant Communities." In *Indigenous Archaeologies: Decolonizing Theory and Practice,* edited by Claire Smith and H. Martin Wobst, 301–314. London: Routledge.

———. 2006. "Liberating Archaeology, Liberation Archaeologies, and WAC." *Archaeologies* 2: 85–95.

Zimmerman, Larry J., Courtney Singleton, and Jessica Welch. 2010. "Activism and Creating a Translational Archaeology of Homelessness." *World Archaeology* 42(3): 443–454.

Zimmerman, Larry J., Karen D. Vitelli, and Julie Hollowell-Zimmer, eds. 2003. *Ethical Issues in Archaeology.* Lanham, MD: AltaMira Press.
Zinn, Howard. 2002. *You Can't Be Neutral on a Moving Train: A Personal History of Our Times.* Boston: Beacon.

Chapter 2

Betwixt and Between
Archaeology's Liminality and Activism's Transformative Promise

Lee Rains Clauss

As a child growing up in the American South, parented by avid readers of history and surrounded by Civil War battlefields, early settler log cabins, and Woodland-era mounds, it came as no surprise to my family when I announced that I would be pursuing an education in historic preservation. I had a great appreciation for public history and sought to develop this interest by learning all that I could about historic architecture, local history research, museums, and art history. As I was particularly interested in the interpretation and preservation of precontact histories and sites, I also undertook a minor in archaeology.

It was while sitting in those introductory archaeology classes that my career path was decided. In these courses, my professors dutifully presented the development of American archaeology, which necessitated the requisite discussions of the "myth of the moundbuilder"—a perspective described by my instructors and textbook authors as an early antiquarian misunderstanding born of armchair archaeology and overt racism. Earnestly believing that this national myth was but a passing, long-disproven interpretation of the moundbuilders and their descendants, I was quite shocked when I saw this same myth appear, albeit cloaked, in advanced archaeology courses and readings. Although the semantics had changed, Southeastern archaeology's preoccupation with collapse, abandonment, failed civilization, and the mysterious "vacant quarter" appeared to me as nothing more than a modern, academicized perpetuation of that same old myth. Furthermore, I

Transforming Archaeology: Activist Practices and Prospects, edited by Sonya Atalay, Lee Rains Clauss, Randall H. McGuire, and John R. Welch, 29–44. © 2014 Left Coast Press, Inc. All rights reserved.

was disturbed to discover that harm, identical to that which had befallen Native peoples at the hands of the moundbuilder myth, continued in the present—even in the post-NAGPRA generation. Archaeology, with its historical ties to nation building and the appropriation of property and heritage it requires, still disenfranchises the indigenous peoples of America and their descendants from their history—both in terms of physical ownership and access to cultural landscapes and material remains, as well as the historical interpretations of and imbuement of value to these tangible heritage resources.

Fortunately, the disillusionment that normally follows such a discovery was thwarted by my burgeoning knowledge of historic preservation and federal Indian law. To my mind, the passage of the Native American Graves Protection and Repatriation Act (NAGPRA), the 1992 amendments to the National Historic Preservation Act (NHPA), and Executive Orders 13007 and 13175 permitted archaeology to be practiced in ways that no longer mandated the titles "expert" and "steward" to be reserved for the discipline's practitioners. It occurred to me that restitution for Native communities could be achieved via this new regulatory language and that archaeology could be decolonized while simultaneously being employed to advance tribal sovereignty and cultural revitalization. This revelation necessitated a response and, for me, begat a personal responsibility. At that moment, I endeavored to become a professional archaeologist and heritage law expert so that tribal governments might find me a useful tool in their navigation of the national historic preservation program. Thus, my activism within the discipline began with my education, which was developed based on a steadfast dedication to an archaeology performed in the service of descendant communities.

> Even if you're on the right track, you'll get run over if you just sit there.
> —Will Rogers

After more than a decade of working within regulatory archaeology, often in the employ of indigenous communities, I began to perceive an inexplicable anxiousness within myself concerning the trajectory of American archaeology. I now know this incompletely attributable concern was born of two different, yet related, circumstances.

For one, from 2005–2011, I found myself increasingly disillusioned by the waves of publications self-described as new, unique, and sophisticated approaches to public archaeology, community-based archaeology, or engaged archaeology. My disappointment with these offerings sprang from a nefarious trend in archaeological discourse—archaeologists conflating mere consultation with communities with actual collaboration. Additionally, the general tone in most professional meetings seemed to support my suspicion that in archaeology's quest for respect as a rigorous scientific endeavor, the discipline had actually made itself less relevant. To quote Einstein (1941), "A perfection of means, and a confusion of aims, seem[ed] to be our main problem." I began to fear that we were coming full circle back to antiquarianism—granted, an incredibly sophisticated form of the beast, but antiquarianism nonetheless. Furthermore, within my work for indigenous communities, I started to notice that numerous federal and state agency–employed archaeologists were beginning to take the position that additional growth and refinement regarding work for (and with) communities were unnecessary. Taken altogether, a troublesome position was solidifying: we, as a discipline, had arrived at an enlightened state of collaboration sufficient enough to satisfy legislative requirements, disciplinary ethical mandates, and external community interests.

Secondly, I worried that although I knew archaeology had most certainly *not* arrived, I did not readily know the path by which archaeology would achieve the social relevance I sought. I did, however, have a vision of what I wished the discipline to ultimately become: an archaeology that embraces its political nature and harnesses its ability to be a thoroughly engaged, authentically collaborative endeavor with the ultimate goal of serving nonarchaeological, community-based needs.

Even though armed with a distinct aspiration, I remained unable to eruditely fix nomenclature and methodology to this "other" archaeology. In the midst of my frustration, I happened upon the work of a Franciscan friar named Richard Rohr. In a narrative on sacred space, Rohr states that

> Limina is the Latin word for threshold, the space betwixt and between. It is when you have left the 'tried and true' but have not yet been able to replace it with anything else. It is when you are finally out of the way. It is when you are in between your old comfort zone and any possible new answer. It is no fun. [Yet] everything genuinely new emerges in some kind of liminal space. (Rohr 2002)

Rohr's words were revelatory. The anxiousness and frustration I was experiencing were to be expected, even necessary. Both the discipline and I were, and still are, in a liminal space. Archaeology, I have concluded, is on the threshold of achieving something with great promise and I am on the cusp of grasping, intellectually and practically, a vital new direction for the discipline.

Probing the Depths of the Liminal Space

For all this musing, however, I initially did not know what to call my desired type of archaeology or how to differentiate it from other alternative approaches that had made inroads in the discipline. And despite my desperation to name it, thereby shifting it from its uncomfortably tenuous liminal space to a more tangible, knowable place, I found this archaeology to be a moving target (Stottman 2010).

Interestingly, as I researched my idea about a service-oriented, socially responsible, and collaborative archaeology, a literature search revealed that its transitional nature is not due to the fact that it had never before been articulated. On the contrary, it is a type and mode of archaeology that other scholars—in a perfect example of independent intellectual innovation—have been talking about and undertaking at various levels for nearly twenty years (Little and Shackel 2007; Little and Zimmerman 2010; McGuire 2008; McNiven and Russell 2005; Pyburn 2009; Pyburn and Wilk 1995; Sabloff 2008; Shackel and Chambers 2004; Tilley 1989; Welch et al. 2006; Wood 2002; Zimmerman 2000; Zimmerman, Singleton, and Welch 2010). Instead, I discovered that this brand of archaeology's reluctance to be easily categorized, and ultimately realized, results from multiple entwined layers of liminality that have existed within the discipline for decades.

The hallmarks of this in-between condition, initially developed by van Gennep (1960) and Turner (1967, 1969), are evident within the discipline. The requisite calls for the dismantling of established structures and/or the reversal of hierarchies have gone forth (Atalay 2006; Lydon and Rizvi 2010; Rizvi 2008a, 2008b; Smith 1999; Smith and Wobst 2005; Tilley and Shanks 1987; Zimmerman 1994), and, as expected, have resulted in discomfort. As generally described and predicted by Horvath, Thomassen, and Wydra (2009), there has been a noticeable discordance about the present aims of archaeology and an unnerving anxiousness about its future (Clark 1998; Kohl 1993; McGee 2008, 2010; Mason 2000; Meighan 1994; Murray 1993; Stark 1993; Stump 2013). Fortunately, however, liminality is not wholly destructive—it can be constructive as well. As Turner adeptly noted, the withdrawal from norms permits a period of self-reflexivity and scrutiny that often leads to the formation of new values and behaviors that can lead to significant social change (Thomassen 2006, 2009). Thus, instead of the despair that normally accompanies a loss of self and one's orientation, a hope began to grow … perhaps archaeology can finally become, not just of interest to the public, but truly relevant to society.

My optimism became tempered, however, when I realized that my vision for such an archaeology is being undermined by the very process of transition that will ultimately bring it forth. Even though liminal periods are defined as temporary conditions, the liminality that exists within archaeological practice appears to be persistent. More specifically, I have noticed in my professional practice, and in my recent literature review referenced previously, that the discipline is enduring over two decades of dislocation by continuing to live betwixt and between (1) materialism and humanism; (2) self-absorption versus service; (3) tradition versus transformation; and what I would eventually come to understand as (4) reform versus revolution.

This incessant displacement was inexplicable until I read Thomassen's (2009) references to Turner's (1967, 1969) and Szakolczai's (2000) work that explained how a liminal phase can become fixed or permanent. According to these scholars, this "fixed liminality" is often the deleterious result of society-level liminal situations in which no preprescribed ritual or ceremony master exists to guide the participants from separation to reintegration. And of even greater concern is the realization that in such circumstances, the lack of leadership and structure often results in mimesis, or imitation, and a protracted mimetic rivalry (Szakolczai 2009).

I then applied Szakolczai's (2000) modes of permanent liminality and their neces-sary imitative processes to archaeology. Based on this analysis, I hypothesized that if the discipline is indeed mired in a fixed liminal state, one or all of the following will be found true: archaeologists will (1) endlessly prepare to separate from the norm, but never actually achieve secession; (2) continuously perform roles based on old rivalries without ever reconciling the disparate worldviews; and/or (3) incessantly reproduce dominant behaviors in the midst of supposed transformation. As I com-pared each of these potentialities with the reality of today's American archaeology, I recognized that all of them sound—and feel—eerily familiar.

The Nature of an Ersatz Archaeology

The realization that the socially relevant, service-oriented archaeology I embrace and want to expand is stuck in a fixed liminal state—that by its very nature castrates the ability for the new ideas to ever displace the old—discouraged me. Armed with Tennyson's admonition to "lose myself in action, lest I wither in despair," however, I resolved to explore the shackles that bind archaeology in perpetual liminality and, thus, disciplinary stagnation.

I chose to conduct this liberation from liminality by first attempting to unravel our discipline's burgeoning lexicon of specialized brands or types of archaeology that had appeared in post-processualist discourse. My reasoning for doing so stemmed from my suspicion that the near-synonymous-sounding approaches such as applied archaeology, action archaeology, postcolonial archaeology, public archaeology, community archaeology, participatory archaeology, and civically engaged archaeology might indeed be breeding the very kind of confusion that would quite easily keep archaeology from completing any truly powerful and meaningful transformation.

A very thorough review of the contemporary literature on these various ar-chaeologies culminated in two unshakable conclusions: (1) there is currently no consistency as to the definitions or proper usages of such niche archaeolo-gies; and (2) the vast majority of them have little to contribute to the sort of discipline-level change I see as a way forward. After all, in my work with indig-enous communities, postcolonial archaeology is viewed as a misnomer at best and a politically correct ruse at worst. Action archaeology is but an antiquated synonym for applied archaeology and its precursor, applied anthropology. And, references to "public," "participatory," or "engaged" archaeologies are most often muddled contrivances. After all, every type of archaeology employs some level of engagement and participation with the public. However, to suggest that the majority of these niche archaeologies are not elitist (of a top-down approach), propagandist, or self-serving (at the discipline level) would be to mischaracterize the objectives, methods, and outcomes of many projects espoused as engaged or participatory (LaSalle 2010).

Furthermore, it became alarmingly apparent that in archaeologists' quest to lay hold of the inherent power of naming, they had not only permitted their own marginalization within the discipline but also unwittingly contributed to and perpetuated archaeology's state of fixed liminality. Not only does the taxonomic morass I described create a kind of theoretical paralysis but it also begets a confused methodology. Many of these niche approaches not only permit but also encourage archaeologists to plan and conduct research based on the regrettably ubiquitous belief that there is a collaborative spectrum. Unfortunately, this view allows collaboration to take the form of an "add and stir" approach (Atalay 2012, 56), which can result in "collaborative drift" (Welch, Lepofsky, and Washington 2011, 179). For example, as McAnany (this volume) so poignantly explains, "[A] community's provision of field laborers, cooks, launderers, and house cleaners for archaeological projects should not be confused with a collaborative community of practice in which community members and archaeologists share in the design, execution, and benefits of research." In my experience working with indigenous communities in the United States, this "value added archaeology," which often confuses notification with consultation, consultation with collaboration, and silence with approval, does little to change the status quo of archaeology or its research subjects. Instead, it perpetuates many of the elements of traditional archaeology that continue to cause inequalities. Dawdy (2009) and Boast (2011) rightly note that much of archaeology billed as being conducted for the public interest is really public relations archaeology, and often what is referred to as "community archaeology" is really neocolonialism in disguise. In other words, didactic projects that merely include elements of public education and tout the virtues of outreach are most often neocolonialist perpetrators and perpetuators—examples of what Fricker (2007) might describe as "epistemic injustice."

Ultimately, my distillation of the nomenclature resulted in an opinion that there are really only two types of contemporary archaeology. One is characterized by archaeologists who view and use the discipline as a self-serving, all-encapsulating purpose, means, and end. This type of archaeology is fundamentally hierarchical, authoritarian, and exclusionary. Moreover, this traditional form of the discipline views work with communities as obligatory, reactive, and ephemeral. The other type of archaeology—one that is championed by the authors in this volume—is characterized by archaeologists who view and use the discipline as a tool to address the many nonarchaeological, community-defined, or socially constructed issues of contemporary concern. It is fundamentally democratized, holistic, and inclusive. This is an archaeology in the service of nonarchaeological "others" that regards work with these communities as purposeful, collaborative, and restorative.

Based on this understanding, I concluded that neither the permanent separation born of perpetual naming nor the proliferation of mimetic acts that reference change while reproducing old paradigms would ensure the completion of our passage through the ambiguous margin. There would be only one way out of our discipline's fixed liminal state: activism within archaeology.

From Imitation to Transformation:
Creating Archaeology Anew

To my mind, there are two basic faces of activism within archaeology: an archaeology for activism and activism for archaeology. First, an "archaeology for activism" refers to the use of archaeological theories, methods, and data to support the needs of a nonarchaeological community in ways that the community delineates as valuable and appropriate. An excellent contemporary example of this type of activism within archaeology is what is often referred to as "indigenous archaeology" (Atalay 2006, 2008; Bruchac, Hart, and Wobst 2010; Dongoske 2000; Nicholas 2011; Silliman 2008; Smith and Wobst 2005; Swidler, et al. 1997; Watkins and Ferguson 2005). And although the term "indigenous archaeology" is sparingly used in this volume, several of this book's authors provide salient examples of work with various descendant communities from British Columbia (Nicholas, this volume) to Belize (McAnany, this volume) to Kyrgyzstan (Pyburn, this volume). Additionally, McGuire (this volume; 2008) and Stottman (this volume; 2010) illustrate how archaeologists can engage, respectively, in activism with labor unions and historically disadvantaged, impoverished communities in the United States. Activism within corporate and regulatory archaeology is also presented. The two coauthored chapters by Ferris and Welch (this volume) argue that cultural resource management/archaeological resource management (CRM/ARM) must be transformed from an irresponsible extraction and consumption process to a sustainable one and from a practice that permits only the most cursory levels of legalistic compliance to one that requires truly collaborative approaches that result in holistic incorporations of places, values, and people. Furthermore, Ferguson (this volume), Nicholas (this volume), and Atalay (this volume) illustrate how service to, and collaboration with, communities often necessitates the expansion of archaeologists' traditional roles to include skills such as advocacy, expert witness testimony, cultural geography and ethnography, and a working knowledge of intellectual property rights and multigenerational trauma.

The other form of activism I noted—"activism for archaeology"—refers to internal activism. Such activism within the discipline seeks to exact fundamental structural change. The objectives of internal activism include challenging ethics codes, research priorities, curriculum, and professional standards and qualifications. Specifically, to thoroughly transform archaeology into the type of community-based, service-oriented science to which I have herein referred, I would suggest the following:

- archaeological education must be revolutionized from its most basic curricular elements—such as the very definition of archaeology—to the advanced training of a truly multidisciplinary scholar;
- professional ethics, qualifications, and standards of practice must be updated to reflect respect for human rights over the rights of science, the primacy of people over data, and the inherent value of community-driven, collaborative research; and

- archaeological research must be altered to democratize all forms of knowledge production, access, and interpretation; as well as to revisit disciplinary concepts of control, ownership, and stewardship with a renewed commitment to social justice.

Based on this dualistic description of activism within archaeology, it is apparent that in order to achieve the foundational shift I seek, change must be imparted to every domain of archaeological practice. In other words, I agree with Haber (2012, 58) that archaeology must be thoroughly undisciplined as "the framework of archaeology itself—that is, its basic subject matter and method—recapitulates coloniality."

Despite the broad and varied ways in which activism within archaeology must be accomplished, however, there is a consistent set of theoretical, ethical, and methodological guidelines to guide the transformation. With regard to theory, a transformation within archaeology builds from a foundation in Marxist, feminist, critical, and indigenous archaeologies. Emphases on human agency, self-reflexivity, multivocality, power structures, and democratization of knowledge all serve as guideposts (Atalay 2006, 2008; Castañeda, this volume; Gaventa 1993; Leone, Potter, and Shackel 1987; Lydon and Rizvi 2010; Shanks and Tilley 1987; Tilley 1989; Trigger 2006; Smith 1999). Furthermore, activism within the discipline has much to gain from applied anthropology. The applied anthropological work of Tax (1958), Chambers (1989), van Willigen (1986), and Hale (2008) have been particularly instructive in my practice, especially in their dispensation of advice on the proper role of anthropologists working within communities and the professional ethics surrounding advocacy and self-determination.

Applied anthropology also provides a basic foundation for the kinds of methods one can employ when conducting archaeological work in the service of others (Downum and Price 1999). Additionally, collaborative archaeology (Colwell-Chanthaphonh and Ferguson 2008; Silliman 2008), participatory action research (Robinson 1996), ethnographic archaeology (Castañeda and Matthews 2008) and community-based participatory research (Atalay 2012) provide directly applicable methods for a transformed archaeology. Personally, I have found that a blend of multiple ideologies, applied anthropology's aims, and community-based participatory research's ethics and methodologies culminate in the creation of useful philosophical and operational guidelines for the archaeology I practice and advocate.

Echoing and building upon the work of some of my esteemed colleagues (Atalay 2012; Colwell-Chanthaphonh and Ferguson 2004; Kuwanwisiwma 2008; McNiven and Russell 2005; Mills et al. 2008; Silliman 2008; Smith 2007; Welch, Lepofsky, and Washington 2011; Zimmerman 1995, 2005), I envision archaeology, once transformed, as a science that

1. seeks to serve and build capacity within nonarchaeological communities before and above oneself, one's peers, and/or the discipline;

2. participates with these communities via the creation of authentic partnerships, with "partnership" defined as a truly collaborative, equitable, and mutually respectful relationship between two parties that cocreate, share, and benefit from all aspects of a project;

3. operates using ethics that (1) value the knowledge, skills, and history of the community as being, at the very least, coequal to that of the archaeologist; and (2) foreground the community's contemporary concerns and needs over obligations to the data; and

4. acknowledges that research is not apolitical or socially neutral, and that, as such, one must be committed to the community in which one has been invited to work and assist, as requested, in the community's efforts to exact social change and social justice.

Finally, I would be remiss if I did not clarify that these guidelines do not constitute or recommend the creation of new theory or field methods, but rather signal the need for a marked shift in ideology. To be sure, the theoretical challenges archaeology has undergone in the last twenty years must be credited for placing archaeology in its current liminal state. However, it is obvious that even the most polemical rhetoric cannot complete the discipline's transformation. Furthermore, based on my own experiences within and observations of American archaeological practice over the last fifteen years, I have found that shifts in praxis born of political correctness, sociopolitical expediency, and/or intellectual trendiness do not have the resolute sense of purpose or unwavering perseverance required to successfully move archaeology across the liminal threshold. It is for these reasons that, as Haber (2012) so insightfully noted, we must move beyond epistemology and methodology to fundamentally altered metaphysics and ethics if we are to ever truly transform archaeology.

Trading Reform for Revolution

At the outset of my chapter, I described archaeology today as existing within a liminal state. Throughout my subsequent discussion regarding the transformation of archaeology, I have striven to move the discipline out of its current ambiguity and bifurcation—at least with regard to definitions and ideologies. Whether archaeology will ever truly be transformed, however, depends on the discipline's willingness to trade reform for revolution.

Such a distinction is not mere semantics. Reform and revolution differ quite significantly from one another based on the nature and magnitude of the change that is planned or underway. To my mind, reform within archaeology will only ever seek to alter the externalities of our practice—a way of changing some seemingly outdated or objectionable aspect of the discipline without really disturbing archaeology's core goals and objectives. Furthermore, reform will always take the form of timely approaches, trendy methodologies, and enlightened yet optional ethics—but holistic, lasting change will remain elusive. And, unfortunately, reformist archaeologists, even at their best, will never achieve anything beyond accidental activism. Revolution, on the other hand, is much more radical. It seeks to change the internalities of our practice—our most fundamental understandings of what archaeology can, and therefore should, be. A revolution within archaeology regards nothing as sacrosanct—even the very definition of archaeology is taken under review and renegotiated. And, what's more, revolutionary archaeologists recognize that social relevance and value are not achieved via happenstance, but rather through passionate yet thoughtful intentionality of action.

As the authors in this volume illustrate, such an activist revolution is not a utopian ideal, but a process already underway within the individual and collective practice of some archaeologists. Despite unsettling epistemological and methodological shifts, professional restrictions, and personal tribulations, we believe the transformation of archaeology to be not only worthwhile but also a requisite responsibility. So vital is the task that we have diligently worked to not offer a diatribe on the ills of archaeology, but to provide encouragement and an agenda about how to assist archaeology in completing its metamorphosis. Our aim has been to crystallize the means by which archaeology can be forever transformed. And in doing so, we aspire to move beyond the transformative potential of our individual endeavors to create communitas—the critically massed agent of change required to fully affect our activism and finally unleash archaeology from its fixed liminality.

In the end, I am hopeful that this book will contribute to the radical conversion of the discipline to which I have dedicated myself. Whether I will ever see this all-encompassing alteration, I do not think is currently or even imminently knowable. I am of the mind that, ultimately, only history will be able to make that determination. As history unfolds, however, I believe activist-minded archaeologists should work to engender our desired revolutionary end. We have a responsibility to continually bring clarity to the ideals of a transformed and transformative archaeology, to effectively and convincingly champion its merits, and to build capacity for its continued practice within new generations of archaeologists. It is in these ways, every day, we can enthusiastically proclaim "vive la révolution!"

Considering Methods: Cognitive Change as a Catalyst for Successful Community Partnerships

For me, transforming the practice of archaeology must necessarily begin with a personal transformation at the conceptual level. I find this to be particularly salient because many archaeologists' collaborations with communities, including my own, require the archaeologist to act as an advocate and/or activist on behalf of a community. Based on advocacy and activism conducted alongside Apache, Cherokee, and Pomo communities, my most sage advice is that such delicate and nuanced roles must be undertaken with the following guidance well-ensconced in one's mind:

1. Accept that archaeology is inherently political and reckon with the truth that every archaeologist works on behalf of something, whether it be the advancement of the discipline, an agency or organization, one's career, or a community. Furthermore, acknowledge that every archaeologist advocates for the discipline in some regard—whether it's the perpetuation of the status quo or disruption to the norm.

2. Understand that when you permit yourself to work on behalf of or alongside a community, archaeology must be relegated to the status of "tool" and no longer be regarded as a right of science, a public entitlement, or an expert's worldview. You, the archaeologist, must willingly become an instrument, and your discipline must become a means to a community's ends. Additionally, know that working with a community may place you at odds with the larger archaeological community. Accept that you cannot serve two masters and address this probable ethical conundrum within your worldview at the outset of your work.

3. Recognize that the role of advocate and/or activist on behalf of a community is not a self-appointed position (see Ferguson, this volume). This is "by invitation only" work. And once you accept that invitation, never forget that you are operating within a host/guest relationship (McNiven and Russell 2005).

4. Be prepared to elucidate the potential for community-based archaeology to assist with identity construction and maintenance, capacity building, and cultural revitalization and preservation. However, do not impose your personal agenda upon the community. Collaborative work with communities is, first and foremost, about the advancement of their rights and the strengthening of their sovereignty. Whether your career is advanced in the process must not be your primary concern.

5. Endeavor to fully understand what is required to protect and perpetuate the sovereignty practiced by the community you serve. Recognize that your role must never hinder, compromise, limit, or usurp a community's sovereignty (see Ferguson, this volume). Understand that there is a fine line, but a significant difference between the offering of requested council versus the provision of directives, and between illuminating decision points versus making decisions. It is crucial that an archaeologist collaborating with a community not overstep his/her authority, especially when a community may offer undeserved and inappropriate power to you out of a response to epistemic injustice, insufficient education, and disenfranchisement.

6. Be respectful of and consistently abide by a community's culturally appropriate internal processes related to leadership, decision making, communication, reciprocity, and confidentiality. Even when invited to interact

with a community as an advocate and/or activist, understand that rapport and trust are not always automatic or permanent. Your relationship with the community must be developed over time and renegotiated, as necessary, when power structures, personnel, and community priorities change.

7. Be acutely aware of any marginalization being perpetuated or created within the community due to historic and/or modern monolithic conceptions of communities (see McAnany, this volume; Pyburn, this volume). Be careful to not romanticize the nature of the community or its individual members. Furthermore, be cautious in how you define and delineate "community" to not give undue or culturally inappropriate primacy to one segment of the heterogeneous population over, or in lieu of, others.

9. Ready yourself for the possibility of a long-term commitment, but also be prepared for either temporary or unexpectedly truncated interactions (see Stottman, this volume). To this end, be flexible in your approach, be cautious of setting overly ambitious goals, be transparent and honest about your limitations as well as the discipline's, and interact with the community based on integrity, not obligation or sentimentality.

10. Champion confidentiality, protect intellectual property, and guard against misappropriation of community knowledge (see Nicholas, this volume). Require appropriate assurances, permits, and informed consent. Disallow research that is not properly vetted by the community. Ensure that the community has editorial rights in the production of written, oral, and/or visual media. Encourage communities to author or coauthor reports and presentations. Promote the equitable distribution of professional accolades and personal gain that might be accrued through work with the community.

Acknowledgments

Although words cannot fully convey my deep respect and admiration for the communities in which I have been honored to work, I do want to express my gratitude to the White Mountain Apache Tribe, the Eastern Band of Cherokee, and the Sherwood Valley Rancheria of Pomo for the invitation to work alongside their communities in the protection, preservation, and promotion of their cultural heritage, as well as their peoples' health and well-being. You all have kept me centered, yet ever vigilant. I also wish to thank my venerable family for their unwavering support of my passion and my person. Thanks for letting me fly.

REFERENCES

Atalay, Sonya. 2006. "Indigenous Archaeology as Decolonializing Practice." *American Indian Quarterly* 30(3 & 4): 280–310.

———. 2008. "Multivocality and Indigenous Archaeologies." In *Evaluating Multiple Narratives: Beyond Nationalist, Colonialist, and Imperialist Archaeologies,* edited by Junko Habu, Clare Fawcett, and John M. Matsunaga, 29–44. New York: Springer.

———. 2012. *Community-Based Archaeology: Research with, by, and for Indigenous and Local Communities.* Berkeley: University of California.

Boast, Robin. 2011. "Neocolonial Collaboration: Museum as Contact Zone Revisited." *Museum Anthropology* 34(1): 56–70.

Bruchac, Margaret, Siobhan Hart, and H. Martin Wobst, eds. 2010. *Indigenous Archaeologies: A Reader on Decolonization.* Walnut Creek, CA: Left Coast Press.

Castañeda, Quetzil E., and Christopher N. Matthews, eds. 2008. *Ethnographic Archaeologies: Reflections on Stakeholders and Archaeological Practices.* Lanham, MD: AltaMira Press.

Chambers, Erve J. 1989. *Applied Anthropology: A Practical Guide.* Long Grove, IL: Waveland Press.

Clark, Geoffrey A. 1998. "NAGPRA: The Conflict Between Science and Religion, and the Political Consequences." *Society for American Archaeology Bulletin* 16(5): 22–25.

Colwell-Chanthaphonh, Chip, and T. J. Ferguson. 2004. "Virtue Ethics and the Practice of History: Native Americans and Archaeologists Along the San Pedro Valley of Arizona." *Journal of Social Archaeology* 4(1): 5–27.

Colwell-Chanthaphonh, Chip, and T. J. Ferguson, eds. 2008. *Collaboration in Archaeological Practice: Engaging Descendant Communities.* Lanham, MD: AltaMira Press.

Dawdy, Shannon Lee. 2009. "Millennial Archaeology: Locating the Discipline in the Age of Insecurity." *Archaeological Dialogues* 16(2): 131–142.

Dongoske, Kurt E., Mark S. Aldenderfer, and Karen Doehner, eds. 2000. *Working Together: Native Americans and Archaeologists.* Washington, DC: Society for American Archaeology.

Downum, Christian E., and Laurie J. Price. 1999. "Applied Archaeology." *Human Organization* 58(3): 226–239.

Einstein, Albert. 1941 (September 28). "The Common Language of Science." Broadcast recording for the Science Conference, London.

Fricker, Miranda. 2007. *Epistemic Injustice: Power and the Ethics of Knowing.* New York: Oxford University Press.

Gaventa, John. 1993. "The Powerful, the Powerless, and the Experts: Knowledge Struggles in an Information Age." In *Voices of Change: Participatory Research in the United States and Canada,* edited by Peter Park, Mary Brydon-Miller, Budd L. Hall, and Ted Jackson, 21–40. Westport, CT: Bergin and Garvey.

Haber, Alejandro F. 2012. "Un-Disciplining Archaeology." *Archaeologies* 8(1): 55–66.

Hale, Charles R., ed. 2008. *Engaging Contradictions: Theory, Politics, and Methods of Activist Scholarship.* Berkeley: University of California Press.

Horvath, Agnes, Bjørn Thomassen, and Harald Wydra. 2009. "Introduction: Liminality and Cultures of Change." *International Political Anthropology* 2(1): 3–4.

Kohl, Phillip L. 1993. "Limits to a Post-processual Archaeology (or, the Dangers of a New Scholasticism)." In *Archaeological Theory: Who Sets the Agenda?,* edited by Norman Yoffee and Andrew Sherrat, 13–19. Cambridge, UK: Cambridge University Press.

Kuwanwisiwma, Leigh J. 2007. "Collaboration Means Equality, Respect, and Reciprocity: A Conversation about Archaeology and the Hopi Tribe." In *Collaboration in Archaeological Practice: Engaging Descendant Communities,* edited by Chip Colwell-Chanthaphonh and T. J. Ferguson, 151–170. Lanham, MD: AltaMira Press.

La Salle, Marina J. 2010. "Community Collaboration and Other Good Intentions." *Archaeologies* 6(3): 401–422.

Leone, Mark P., Parker B. Potter Jr., and Paul A. Shackel. 1987. "Toward a Critical Archaeology." *Current Anthropology* 28(3): 283–302.

Little, Barbara J., and Paul A. Shackel, eds. 2007. *Archaeology as a Tool of Civic Engagement.* Lanham, MD: AltaMira Press.

Little, Barbara J., and Larry J. Zimmerman. 2010. "In the Public Interest: Creating a More Activist, Civically-Engaged Archaeology." In *Voices in American Archaeology,* edited by Wendy Ashmore, Dorothy Lippert, and Barbara Mills, 131–159. Washington, DC: Society for American Archaeology.

Lydon, Jane, and Uzma Rizvi, eds. 2010. *Handbook of Postcolonial Archaeology.* Walnut Creek, CA: Left Coast Press.

McGhee, Robert. 2008. "Aboriginalism and the Problems of Indigenous Archaeology." *American Antiquity.* 73(4): 579–597.

———. 2010. "Of Strawmen, Herrings, and Frustrated Expectations." *American Antiquity* 75(2): 239–243.

McGuire, Randall H. 2008. *Archaeology as Political Action.* Berkeley: University of California Press.

McNiven, Ian, and Lynette Russell. 2005. *Appropriated Pasts: Indigenous Peoples and the Colonial Culture of Archaeology.* Lanham, MD: AltaMira Press.

Mason, Ronald J. 2000. "Archaeology and Native North American Oral Traditions." *American Antiquity* 65(2): 239–266.

Meighan, Clement. 1994. "Burying American Archaeology." *Archaeology* 47(6): 64, 66, 68.

Mills, Barbara, Mark Altaha, John R. Welch, and T. J. Ferguson. 2008. "Field Schools Without Trowels: Teaching Archaeological Ethics and Heritage Preservation in a Collaborative Context." In *Collaborating at the Trowel's Edge: Teaching and Learning in Indigenous Archaeology,* edited by Stephen W. Silliman, 25–49. Tucson: University of Arizona Press.

Murray, Tim. 1993. "Communication and the Importance of Disciplinary Communities: Who Owns the Past?" In *Archaeological Theory: Who Sets the Agenda?,* edited by Norman Yoffee and Andrew Sherrat, 105–116. Cambridge, UK: Cambridge University Press.

Nicholas, George P., ed. 2011. *Being and Becoming Indigenous Archaeologists.* Walnut Creek, CA: Left Coast Press.

Pyburn, K. Anne. 2009. "Practicing Archaeology—As If It Really Matters." *Public Archaeology* 8(2–3): 161–175.

Pyburn, K. Anne, and Richard R. Wilk. 1995. "Responsible Archaeology Is Applied Anthropology." In *Ethics in American Archaeology: Challenges for the 1990s,* edited by Mark J. Lynott and Alison Wylie, 71–76. Washington, DC: Society for American Archaeology Press, Washington, D.C.

Rizvi, Uzma. 2008a. "Decolonizing Methodologies as Strategies of Practice: Operationalizing the Postcolonial Critique in the Archaeology of Rajasthan." In *Archaeology and the Postcolonial Critique,* edited by Matthew Liebmann and Uzma Z. Rizvi, 109–128. Lanham, MD: AltaMira Press.

———. 2008b. "Conclusion: Archaeological Futures and the Postcolonial Critique." In *Archaeology and the Postcolonial Critique,* edited by Matthew Liebmann and Uzma Rizvi, 197–204. Lanham, MD: AltaMira Press.

Robinson, Michael P. 1996. "Shampoo Archaeology: Towards a Participatory Action Research Approach in Civil Society." *The Canadian Journal of Native Studies* XVI(I): 125–138.

Rohr, Richard. 2002 (January). "Grieving as Sacred Space. *Sojourner,* accessed August 8, 2012, http://sojo.net/magazine/2002/01/grieving-sacred-space.

Sabloff, Jeremy A. 2008. *Archaeology Matters: Action Archaeology in the Modern World.* Walnut Creek, CA: Left Coast Press.

Shackel, Paul A., and Erve J. Chambers, eds. 2004. *Places in Mind: Public Archaeology as Applied Anthropology.* New York: Routledge.

Shanks, Michael, and Christopher Tilley. 1987. *Social Theory and Archaeology.* Cambridge, UK: Polity Press.

Silliman, Stephen W. 2008. "Collaborative Indigenous Archaeology: Troweling at the Edges, Eyeing the Center." In *Collaborating at the Trowel's Edge: Teaching and Learning in Indigenous Archaeology,* edited by Stephen W. Silliman, 1–24. Tucson: University of Arizona.

Smith, Claire. 2007. "The Ethics of Collaboration: Whose Culture? Whose Intellectual Property? Who Benefits?" In *Collaboration in Archaeological Practice: Engaging Descendant Communities,* edited by Chip Colwell-Chanthaphonh and T. J. Ferguson, 171–199. Lanham, MD: AltaMira Press.

Smith, Claire, and H. Martin Wobst, eds. 2005. *Indigenous Archaeologies: Decolonising Theory and Practice.* New York: Routledge.

Smith, Linda Tuhiwai. 1999. *Decolonizing Methodologies: Research and Indigenous Peoples.* New York: Zed Books.

Stark, Miriam. 1993. "Re-fitting the 'Cracked and Broken Façade': The Case for Empiricism in Post-processual Ethnoarchaeology." In *Archaeological Theory: Who Sets the Agenda?,* edited by Norman Yoffee and Andrew Sherrat, 93–104. Cambridge, UK: Cambridge University Press.

Stottman, M. Jay, ed. 2010. *Archaeologists as Activists: Can Archaeologists Change the World?* Tuscaloosa: University of Alabama Press.

Stump, Daryl. 2013. "On Applied Archaeology, Indigenous Knowledge, and the Usable Past." *Current Anthropology* 54(3): 268–298.

Swidler, Nina, Kurt E. Dongoske, Roger Anyon, and Alan S. Downer, eds. 1997. *Native Americans and Archaeologists: Stepping Stones to Common Ground.* Lanham, MD: AltaMira Press.

Szakolczai, Arpad. 2000. *Reflexive Historical Sociology.* London: Routledge.

——. 2009. "Liminality and Experience: Structuring Transitory Situations and Transformative Events." *International Political Anthropology* 2(1): 141–172.

Tax, Sol. 1958. "The Fox Project." *Human Organization* 17(1): 17–19.

Thomassen, Bjørn. 2006. "Liminality." In *Encyclopedia of Social Theory,* edited by Austin Harrington, Barbara L. Marshall, and Hans-Peter Müller, 322–323. London: Routledge.

——. 2009. "The Uses and Meanings of Liminality." *International Political Anthropology* 2(1): 5–27.

Tilley, Christopher. 1989. "Archaeology as Socio-political Action in the Present." In *Critical Traditions in Contemporary Archaeology: Essays in the Philosophy, History, and Socio-Politics of Archaeology,* edited by Valerie Pinsky and Alison Wylie, 104–116. Cambridge, UK: Cambridge University Press.

Tilley, Christopher, and Michael Shanks. 1987. *Re-Constructing Archaeology: Theory and Practice.* Cambridge, UK: Cambridge University Press.

Trigger, Bruce G. 2006. *A History of Archaeological Thought,* 2nd ed. Cambridge, UK: Cambridge University Press.

Turner, Victor W. 1967. "Betwixt and Between: The Liminal Period in Rites de Passage." In *The Forest of Symbols,* 23–59. Ithaca, NY: Cornell University Press.

———. 1969. *The Ritual Process: Structure and Anti-structure.* Chicago: Aldine Press.

van Gennep, Arnold. 1960. *The Rites of Passage.* Chicago: University of Chicago Press.

van Willigen, John. 1986. *Applied Anthropology: An Introduction.* South Hadley, MA: Bergin and Garvey.

Watkins, Joe, and T. J. Ferguson. 2005. "Working with and Working for Indigenous Communities." In *Handbook of Archaeological Methods,* Vol. 2, edited by D. G. Herbert Maschner and Christopher Chippendale, 1372–1406. Lanham, MD: AltaMira Press.

Welch, John R., Mark Altaha, Doreen Gatewood, Karl Hoerig, and Ramon Riley. 2006. "Archaeology, Stewardship, and Sovereignty." *The SAA Archaeological Record* 6(4): 17–20, 57.

Welch, John R., Dana Lepofsky, and Michelle Washington. 2011. "Assessing Collaboration with the Sliammon First Nation in a Community-Based Heritage Research and Stewardship Program." *Archaeological Review from Cambridge* 26(2): 171–190.

Wood, Margaret C. 2002. "Moving Towards Transformative Democratic Action through Archaeology." *International Journal of Historical Archaeology* 6(3): 187–198.

Zimmerman, Larry J. 1994. "Sharing Control of the Past." *Archaeology* 47(6): 65, 67–68.

———. 1995. "Regaining Our Nerve: Ethics, Values, and the Transformation of Archaeology." In *Ethics in American Archaeology: Challenges for the 1990s,* edited by Mark J. Lynott and Alison Wylie, 64–67. Washington, DC: Society for American Archaeology.

———. 2000. "A New and Different Archaeology." In *Repatriation Reader: Who Owns American Indian Remains?,* edited by Devon A. Mihesuah, 294–306. Lincoln: University of Nebraska Press.

———. 2005. "First, Be Humble: Working with Indigenous Peoples and Other Descendant Communities." In *Indigenous Archaeologies: Decolonizing Theory and Practice,* edited by Claire Smith and H. Martin Wobst, 301–314. London: Routledge.

Zimmerman, Larry J., Courtney Singleton, and Jessica Welch. 2010. "Activism and Creating a Translational Archaeology of Homelessness." *World Archaeology* 42(3): 443–454.

Chapter 3

Engaging Archaeology
Positivism, Objectivity, and Rigor in Activist Archaeology

Sonya Atalay

My professional life is one of an engaged scholar. As an indigenous woman (Anishinabe-Ojibwe) and an anthropologist, I feel a strong responsibility to my home community and to multiple professional communities (archaeologists, anthropologists, and Native and Indigenous Studies scholars). A main goal of my scholarship is to contribute to the project of reconfiguring the discipline of archaeology; that is, to the project of forging more collaborative, community-based archaeological practices rather than ones that are seen outside of academia as usurping the cultural heritage of others. To be effective and sustainable, this type of transformative work does not stop with academic publications and what is usually considered "research." I feel this work must also include service within professional associations and innovative and collaborative teaching in order to institutionalize the changes in a way that is systemic and long term. For me, this scholarly service has been another form of activist work.

As a PhD student, I went to Çatalhöyük, Turkey to study early farming households, particularly the foodways and cooking practices during the transition from hunting and gathering to farming. Çatalhöyük's 9,000-year-old mound site provides an amazingly rich and well-preserved window into daily life. My dissertation focused on the use and meaning of thousands of clay balls that I demonstrated were used for boiling food in skins and baskets prior to the use of pottery. Throughout my fieldwork, and particularly while living in rural Turkish villages as a Fulbright scholar, I found that I simply could not, and ethically felt I should not, separate the contemporary people and communities still living in those villages from the material culture and landscapes I was studying. I wondered if village residents had questions about Çatalhöyük. Were they concerned about having 100+ foreign archaeologists regularly wandering into their village, asking questions and taking photographs? Çatalhöyük's nomination for the UNESCO World Heritage list would certainly bring more tourists and development. I wondered how local residents perceived the nomination and what impacts—positive and negative—it would have on their daily lives.

I am acutely aware of the troubling, often painful experiences indigenous peoples face when research is done without community collaboration. Similar concerns are relevant for the rural poor in Turkish villages, and for other descendent and local communities who maintain connections with the places and remains that archaeologists study. We see a growing interest in community collaboration within archaeology, yet the methods, theories, ethics, and on-the-ground practices lag behind those collaborative ideals. My primary research focus has been to improve our understanding in each of these areas, and I have done so by engaging in a wide range of community-based archaeology projects in Native North America and Turkey. My work intersects with activism in multiple ways. First, all the community-based research projects I have chosen to become involved with each encompasses an aspect of social justice: this includes efforts to reclaim ancestral remains, ensuring that local communities have a meaningful role in archaeo-development and heritage tourism efforts, and ensuring that descendent communities have access to their sacred sites and a prominent voice in the interpretation of cultural landscapes. Second, but equally important, I actively work to facilitate long-term change within the academy (archaeology, in particular) so that the infrastructure (funding, tenure and promotion reviews, human subjects protocols, etc.) supports, encourages, and rewards scholarship that is done with, by, and for communities. And I see my work as a teacher and a mentor as an important part of activism because it is through those focused efforts that the next generation of scholars emerges. It's my hope that those of you reading this will continue to strengthen the pursuit of social justice and to produce new knowledge that improves our world.

—⚭—

It is not just about universal truths—though these do matter—but about producing truth in particular contexts and making knowledge useful in particular projects.
—*Craig Calhoun, president, Social Science Research Council (2008, xxi)*

Multiple Meanings of Engagement and Activist Anthropology

Engagement in its multiple forms is currently a popular concept in academia. Campuses seek to engage with the world beyond the walls of the ivory tower. Scholars frame their research as "engaged scholarship" and point to the myriad ways they are engaged with communities.

Such is the case in numerous social science and humanities fields; primary among them is the work of anthropologists. A special edition of *Current Anthropology* from October 2010 focused specifically on "Engaged Anthropology" and highlighted case studies, benefits, and dilemmas. The American Anthropological Association (AAA) demonstrates its commitment to "engagement" through efforts it has made to define, discuss, and support engaged anthropology and scholars who conduct it. According to the AAA (2013), engaged anthropology is "committed to supporting social change efforts that arise from the interaction between community goals and anthropological research." The AAA Anthropology and Environment Society (2013) produces an "Engagement Blog" that highlights anthropological and other social science research aimed at addressing social and environmental problems. Academic tenure and promotion resources are also provided on its website, including guidelines for assessing anthropologists and anthropology programs whose focus is "in the realm of practicing, applied, public interest, and engaged anthropology."

In this chapter, I consider the breadth of engaged practices within archaeology, particularly the forms of activist archaeology. I chose the title "Engaging Archaeology" after reading Charles Hale's (2008a) edited volume, *Engaging Contradictions: Theory, Politics, and Methods of Activist Scholarship*. I found the work of many authors in that volume inspiring and thought provoking. Of particular interest to me were the points raised about the role of objectivity and rigor within scholarly research, most notably how those concepts can and should be reclaimed by "activist" scholars. Through discussions with the contributors to this volume and in reading the growing literature on engaged research and scholarship, several points stand out about academic "engagement." First, is just how widespread the interest in academic engagement with communities is. What was perhaps most surprising is that it is not only individual scholars from social science and humanities disciplines (the usual suspects, in many ways) where these discussions and efforts are taking place. I found numerous efforts at my own campus and other university campuses to become more "engaged" with those outside of academia, and the same is true for other scholarly professional associations. This is evidenced through a growing number of national programs such as Campus Compact (http://www.compact.org) and The Carnegie Foundation for the Advancement of Teaching's Community Engagement Classification (2013). In the "Presidents' Declaration on the Civic Responsibility of Higher Education" (Ehrlich 1999, 1), presidents of public and private colleges and universities call for increased engagement of students and faculty, and they "challenge higher education to become engaged, through actions and teaching, with its communities." Wittman and Crews (2012, 2–3) report on the positive impact of community engagement, focusing on "collaboration and reciprocity, which lead to democratic partnerships among campuses and communities" and how such partnerships are essential to what they call "engaged learning economies."

As someone who is deeply committed to conducting research in partnership with communities, I see this as a positive turn within the academy. However, I also have concerns. One of my primary apprehensions is with how "engagement" is defined. Engagement is used to refer to everything from sharing research results with those outside academia to hosting a science summer camp to increase STEM learning, or it can mean research conducted with, by, and/or for community partners. The same definitional issue is found in reference to "collaborative" research or "community-based research" (Clauss, this volume). Not only are many names used to refer to this type of approach (action research, participatory action research, CBPR, etc.) but too often these words are also labels that scholars place on their work without recognizing that the meanings and practices associated with these forms of research are specific and distinct. There is a wide and growing scholarly literature on specific methods, theories, and practices. For example, I have seen scholars refer to their work as "community-based" simply because they observe and interview people in community settings to gather research data. By that definition, a vast majority of anthropological research would be "community-based." That is far from how the term is used among practitioners of a CBPR methodology who expect that "community-based" research is designed and carried out in partnership with community members who are coresearchers in the process.

My point here is that definitions matter, and grounding one's practice within a theoretical framework is important so that we can understand who is engaging with whom, to what degree, and for what purpose. I am not interested in creating definitions of engagement, or community-based research, or activism as a form of exclusivity, or as a way of telling people that their work does not count as "engaged" or activist or whatever other terms we might come up with. On the contrary, I think multiple readings and broad definitions that are inclusive help us to build allies, and that a broad base is needed to achieve the changes that we want to see within the academy and the world beyond it. However, I do worry that as we build bridges within the academy, we run the risk of taking the potency away from community-based research—a point I will come back to later.

With regard to carving out space and actively making change within the academy, in reading Hale's (2008a) edited volume titled *Engaging Contradictions: Theory, Politics, and Methods of Activist Scholarship* I realized and came to appreciate the multiple ways that the book title could be read. For me, these multiple readings signified the range of meanings and work that surrounds engagement, activism, and activist scholarship as a subject of study within the academy. I chose the title "Engaging Archaeology" for this paper to signal and bring to the foreground the multiple and varied locations in which our engagement and actions as archaeologists are needed. So although this chapter focuses in a theoretical sense about how rigor and objectivity can (and should) be part of our discussions of engagement and activism in archaeology, I also want to point, at least briefly, to the other ways that activism and archaeology encounter one another in the practices and lives of archaeologists.

The first, and perhaps most obvious, relates to the impact archaeology can have (and I would argue that it should have) in the contemporary world—that is, archaeology should be engaging. If we are doing our jobs well, we should produce scholarship that is accessible by and of interest to people outside of academia. Archaeologists have done an impressive job of bringing archaeological interpretations to "the public" broadly, as well as to descendent and local communities that have connections to the sites and materials under investigation (Stottman, this volume). The academic literature in this area of public archaeology, or what is often termed "outreach," continues to expand and is moving in exciting new directions, particularly through the use of digital media.

As the introduction to this volume points out, archaeologists can intersect with activism at several levels. Archaeologists can use archaeology as a tool to bring about changes in the contemporary world. Several of the chapters in this volume (see McAnany, McGuire, Nicholas, and Pyburn) discuss case studies in which the authors engage in archaeological research that directly contributes to social change efforts.

Archaeology and activism also intersect when archaeologists become activists within the discipline and work to bring about changes within the profession of archaeology—a point discussed extensively by Castañeda (this volume). This form of activism is one I hoped to draw attention to by using the title "Engaging Archaeology." Some archaeologists who see archaeology's primary goal, or at least one of its key roles, as being an agent for social change in the world outside of archaeology have also actively chosen to engage at the national and international level to interrupt and alter the way archaeology is practiced. I see this form of activism as an important component of my own work. It is one of my goals to help move the discipline toward a practice that places descendent and local communities at the core and makes choices that actively nurture our most vital relationships—those with everyday people whose heritage we are so privileged to study.

Arguably, the most critical part of this type of activist practice involves building, improving upon, and institutionalizing the processes of community-based research within our universities, granting agencies, and professional organizations. The goal of engaging archaeology in this manner is to ensure that partnerships with descendent and local communities become the norm and are simply viewed as a "way of working" in archaeology.

Another form of engaged scholarship involves conducting archaeological research that demonstrates the inequalities in the past and the ways those inequities impact our present world. Maguire's chapter in this volume provides an excellent example of such research. Here, in his other work (McGuire 2008; Larkin and McGuire 2009; McGuire and Paynter 1991; McGuire and Reckner 2003; McGuire and Walker 1999) and in the scholarship of other archaeologists (Camp 2011; Paynter 1989; Saitta 2007; Saitta, Walker, and Reckner 2006; Zimmerman, Singleton, and Welch 2010), we see the powerful role that archaeology can play in identifying social inequality in the ancient past and in not-so-distant times, as well.

I see at least one more way in which archaeologists intersect with engagement and activism—by conducting archaeological research that studies activist and social change movements. The importance of this form of activist anthropology was foregrounded for me in a recent discussion on the UMass Amherst campus. In May 2013, Charles Hale, Arturo Escobar, and Jeff Juris were invited guests in a forum titled "Challenges for Activist Ethnography." I came to the forum expecting to hear about the scholars' research *as* activists; that is, conducting research that helped transform the world through action. I was surprised to hear each of the speakers use the term "activist" as a subject rather than as an adjective. That is, the speakers primarily discussed their experiences conducting ethnographic research in which activist movements and activists were the subjects of study.

I had understood "activist ethnography" in a way that placed the anthropologist in the role of activist, as someone conducting transformative scholarship. I anticipated anthropologists engaged in action research aimed at social justice; something akin to the "activist scholarship" detailed in Sudbury and Okazawa-Rey's (2009) edited volume or the examples of "feminist activist ethnography" included in Craven and Davis (2013). Harrison (2013) describes the dual forms of such activist scholarship as a "discursive practice and mobilizing tool" aimed to "disrupt and dislodge the prevailing neoliberal regime of truth," including work in public policy. Although the "Challenges for Activist Ethnography" workshop was not what I had initially expected, the forum was intensely interesting and deeply thought provoking. I found three topics particularly interesting. First, I noted the unexpected ways in which ethnographic research on activist movements encounters and must face some of the same challenges within the academy as those who conduct activist scholarship (research that aims to bring about social change). This relates directly to issues of objectivity and scholarly rigor, both points I focus on throughout the remainder of this paper.

The second point I found interesting is that the three speakers who were studying activist movements each described their uneasiness with calling themselves "activists." I was particularly intrigued by Charles Hale's point that he didn't feel qualified to call himself an activist. This point is of particular interest because it was also central to our discussion during our time preparing this volume at Amerind. Many of the contributors to this volume did not think of themselves as activists. Several (Pyburn and Welch, who both discuss this in their respective chapters in this volume) considered their activism not as something purposefully planned, but as accidental. I am not prepared to attempt an analysis of this or to consider what this means about our ideas regarding activism. Rather, the point I want to make is that when combined with our lengthy discussions at Amerind about activism and the concern that many participants in the seminar had with even using the term "activist," there appears to be an uneasiness scholars have with seeing ourselves (or maybe it is simply labeling ourselves) as activists. This is something I hope those reading this volume will ponder. Do you feel comfortable calling yourself an activist? Perhaps this is generational? Or it may be something else altogether.

It's a topic worthy and in need of further consideration as we deliberate the most appropriate and effective ways to actively transform our discipline.

The third point of interest for me at the "Challenges for Activist Ethnography" forum was that the speakers seemed to feel somewhat comfortable thinking of their work as activism. The guests at the forum did acknowledge more readily their role as activists within academia—as scholars working within the discipline to facilitate change in the way anthropology is conducted and what is considered valuable scholarship.

I left the forum that day wondering about yet another meaning of the term "activist archaeology." I wondered if there had yet been any archaeological research conducted on activist movements. I found myself wondering what an archaeologist's gaze might uncover about those activities. What would the material signature of the "Arab Spring" look like, and how could archaeological research contribute to our knowledge about this and other social movements? I was thrilled to find that this form of "activist archaeology" has been conducted in several locations, and a growing literature exists on the topic (Badcock and Johnston 2009; Harrison and Schofield 2009; Schofield 2009). Most interesting, perhaps, in this area is an award-winning session by three Columbia graduate students at the 2012 Theoretical Archaeology Group (TAG) conference. Their session, "The Archaeology of Contemporary Protest Movements" and the accompanying blog (http://ows-archaeology.blogspot.com/) focuses on archaeological analysis of the Occupy Wall Street protests, the Arab Spring, and riots in the UK.

Defining Activist Scholarship

I want to turn now to focus on how archaeological scholarship can be used in an activist way to improve conditions in the world. I want to begin by briefly considering the broader area and definition of "activist scholarship." For Hale (2008b, 4), "Activist scholars work in dialogue, collaboration, alliance with people who are struggling to better their lives." He also notes that activist scholarship "embodies a responsibility for results that these 'allies' can recognize as their own" (Hale 2008b, 4). Applying this to archaeology specifically, I agree that activist archaeology *does* involve conducting research *with* people on projects that directly impact their lives, but I would suggest caution in thinking of "activist archaeology" as something only for those "in struggle." Or perhaps we need to broaden our definition of what that means. Activist archaeology is not only about doing research on activists or with those who are considered "oppressed" communities. I would argue that it can involve research in partnership with any number of groups. What is central is that the archaeology matters both to archaeologists and those they are working with; it aims to improve lives, and is research communities help define and design.

This point deserves further consideration, but perhaps more than precise definitions, it is more productive to follow Hale's approach to *till a field, not fill a container*—that is, aim for our discussion and the research we do to produce fertile ground for further activist scholarship rather than being overly concerned with confining definitions. Certainly, there is a long tradition of activist scholarship in other disciplines that can help us better understand what activist archaeology is or might become (Brown and Strega 2005; Collins 2012; Craven and Davis 2013; Sudbury and Okazawa-Rey 2009). At this juncture, and looking to the future, I see four things that are needed in the area of activist archaeology: 1) we need a survey of the current landscape and scope of practice; 2) we need to place these practices within a theoretical framework; 3) we need to work to bring about institutional and structural changes in our practice at the national and global level, particularly in cultural resource management and archaeological resource management (see Welch and Ferris, this volume; Ferris and Welch, this volume); and 4) we must consider how to best retool the archaeology curriculum so that students gain useful training within a transformed archaeological practice (see Pyburn, this volume).

One useful distinction is to consider that "activist archaeology" is not necessarily synonymous with "applied anthropology." Taking previously known archaeological data and applying it can be within the realm of activism, particularly if improving public policy goals are primary aims of the research. The activist archaeology I hope to see involves a global transformation in the way research is *practiced* so that "democratization of knowledge" (Fortmann 2008) is at the core of archaeology and what archaeologists are trained to do. Once transformed, nonarchaeologists become central figures in the process of creating new knowledge. Working in partnership with nonarchaeologists who are impacted by the research becomes a way of *doing* science. I want to be clear that this is not a reframing to simply increase public archaeology or outreach-education programs. I agree with Calhoun (2008, xvii) who points out that "giving social science more public importance is a matter of choosing important problems for research, not simply finding more effective means of communicating existing disciplinary knowledge (good though that may be)."

While conventional science accepts the world as it is and works to produce knowledge within it, *activist* scholarship calls the very nature of how knowledge is produced into question. It seeks to *critique* that process—to understand why our existing "frameworks of knowledge" are not as useful as they could be and to demonstrate how things could be different. Through the very practice of doing activist archaeology research, we raise questions such as these: Why is archaeology practiced the way it is? How could it be otherwise? Calhoun rightly notes that this "involves both the production and mobilization of knowledge," or what Lutz and Neis call "making and moving knowledge" (2008). I have argued this point strongly within the context of archaeology specifically (Atalay 2012).

Positivism, Objectivity, and Rigor

Activist scholar and anthropologist Charles Hale argues that "Any attempt to make the case for activist scholarship runs directly up against objections, encapsulated in three powerful words: positivism, objectivity and rigor" (Hale 2008b, 8). Here I consider Hale's argument, placing it within the context of *archaeology,* using examples from community-based participatory research projects with which I am involved.

Feminist and critical theorists have detailed problematic aspects of positivist approaches, and indigenous scholars explain the hegemonic and oppressive effects of using an objective, value-free process for understanding the world. These critiques are not new to archaeology. Hale (2008b) argues that it's neither necessary nor advisable to fully dismiss positivist approaches. Rather, activist scholars should follow a "strategic duality" to *deconstruct* positivism—point out the problems with it and then *reclaim* it.

Hale's argument for reclaiming objectivity makes sense for activist archaeology. Here's why: Often, in talking about community-based research, engaged, activist or transformative scholarship, ethics, and so on, we find ourselves "preaching to the choir." To convince skeptical colleagues, arguments are most productively framed in the language of science to demonstrate that archaeology in partnership with descendent, nondescendent, and local communities is actually still about doing science. But it involves re-adjusting power (im)balances so that others have the opportunity to engage in the practice of making new knowledge. The process of knowledge production is *democratized,* as we question who the "valid knowers" are, to use Louise Fortmann's (2008) terminology, and why other knowledge forms are excluded.

For Hale, there is more "subversive potential" in reclaiming words of power than in outright, dismissing critiques of positivism and objectivity—he is likely right. But framing activist research as "rigorous science" isn't just a strategy; it is an accurate assessment. Hearing from indigenous peoples and witnessing exploitative research practices within anthropology and archaeology, I became convinced there are ways of doing research that are not harmful but rather contribute to community well-being. The National Congress of American Indians Policy Research Center provides guidance with training and papers on an approach called "community-based participatory research" or CBPR. And, for the past eleven years, I have set out to understand how CBPR can be effectively applied to archaeology. During this time, I have partnered with indigenous and nondescendent communities on five CBPR projects. I have tried to pinpoint the challenges and determine what doesn't work—in hopes of developing a rigorous methodology for conducting archaeology with communities on projects they choose, that will benefit them, and in which they are active participants in all stages from planning to sharing research results (Atalay 2012).

To be sure, doing community-based research in partnership with communities is about doing science—and doing it well. No one wants the most reliable research more than the communities that I'm partnering with. For example, those in the Saginaw Chippewa Indian Tribe's Ziibiwing Center want the very best archaeological research possible to demonstrate cultural affiliation with the ancestors held by the University of Michigan, Indiana University, and Harvard University, and by others in museums around the world. This research matters to Anishinabe people, to tribal communities, and to Ziibiwing—and they insist it is done well, following strict scholarly protocols. Similarly, at the Flint Stone Street site, where an inadvertent discovery during construction turned up hundreds of ancestral remains in traditional Anishinabe homelands, the Ziibiwing Center wanted the public to know undeniable *truths* about that site—the remains found were not European, nor were they from a battle of fighting tribes. The bodies were mostly women and children, from a habitation site, demonstrating long-standing ties of the Anishinabek to that region. Demonstrating these facts in a definitive way matters—and, in both cases, it would be detrimental for my community partners to undermine the idea that some knowable truths can be found through science.

This is not to say that only archaeological data counts as real and knowable. Hale, Fortmann, and others demonstrate that the "situated knowledge" argued for by Haraway (1988) is "more insightful, complete and accountable" because it considers the sociopolitical context within which research is created. So although it is important for activist archaeologists to critique objectivity, pointing out how its misuse leads to the disenfranchisement of indigenous forms of knowledge, we must then reclaim what Hale refers to as a "positioned objectivity" (following feminist theory)—noting that there is *no value-free position* from which a fully objective and detached ideal scholar stands.

Finally, methodological rigor is another concept that I argue activist archaeologists need to reclaim. Methodological rigor is often linked to a scholar's ultimate control over the research process (Hale 2008b). Within a CBPR paradigm, part of reclaiming methodological rigor involves pointing out the "epistemic injustice," as used by Miranda Fricker (2009) and extreme privilege that scholars who do conventional research hold in having ultimate control over the research process and sole authority to interpret results (Nicholas, this volume).

Not only do some communities want rigorous *archaeological* research but many also have their own strict standards for ensuring that knowledge is properly cared for and transferred to the next generation. This is particularly relevant in indigenous contexts in which knowledge is in danger of being lost. In our *midewiwin* traditional spiritual society, multiple people are charged with learning traditional scroll teachings and associated songs. There is a strict protocol for obtaining this knowledge, and rules for replicating it, to ensure that it is preserved properly— not lost, diluted, or practiced incorrectly. Great value is placed on knowing these teachings correctly *in the language*. In the case of the Sanilac petroglyph site in which several hundred petroglyphs cover a large stone outcrop, it is critical that the teachings associated with those petroglyphs are passed down properly. An annual summer solstice ceremony is held to ensure that the teachings are preserved by four generations of women—during which time the petroglyphs are cleaned and teachings are given in the language. In a community-based research project on intellectual property, I am partnering with the Saginaw Chippewa Indian tribe to protect those teachings while sharing them in culturally appropriate ways. This process of knowledge reproduction involves a great deal of methodological rigor.

Within a place of "positioned objectivity," oral histories and teachings at the Sanilac site are important. They are truth and are combined with other archaeological truths about the site to give a more complete knowledge and understanding of the world. These are points I detail further when describing the concept of "braiding knowledge" (Atalay 2012). In the Sanilac project, we would not argue against truth—there are accurate and knowable interpretations of those petroglyphs. Conventional archaeology has failed to obtain such knowledge and at times actively works to disenfranchise and exclude those who carry and act as careful stewards of that knowledge. Part of an activist archaeology involves demonstrating the historical processes that led archaeologists to discount some forms of knowledge in the name of objectivity.

As Calhoun points out, activist scholarship is not an argument against truth or for an anything-goes relativism (Calhoun et al. 2008). But it is an argument for seeing science as a historical process. I agree with Calhoun, Hale, and others—activist scholars need to offer truth, but at the same time demonstrate that "truths are often highly contextual and conditional, ... not statements of absolute and unvarying causal relationships" (xviii–xix). Archaeology offers *real* knowledge, but it is *incomplete*. At the Sanilac petroglyph site, there is much we know from an archaeological perspective, but the meaning of the petroglyphs as used by present-day Anishinabe and passed down from our ancestors also provides valid and important truths. Through community-based research we are braiding together these forms of knowledge while also protecting it from exploitation.

Activist archaeologists can reclaim the process of "making and moving knowledge" using a more egalitarian and reciprocal mode of knowledge production to do research *with* communities—research that matters and improves our world. We need not sacrifice methodological rigor to do so.

The Future

In conclusion, I want to consider the future of activist archaeology. We still need a great deal more discussion about what activist archaeology is and what it could be. We need to consider how our discipline can support such scholarship at the national and international level. We can work through our professional organizations, such as the Society for American Archaeology (SAA), the American Anthropological Association (AAA), the World Archaeological Congress (WAC), and the National Association of Tribal Historic Preservation Officers (NATHPO); in our universities, academic departments, and tribal and local communities; and at the level of individual research. It seems particularly important that we consider how to teach community-based research and incorporate activist archaeology into the curriculum (Pyburn, this volume) so that young scholars entering the profession who see a world they want to engage with and make better have the opportunity to do so *as* archaeologists.

Considering Methods: Participatory Planning in Community-Based Research

After working with communities on multiple CBPR projects, I strongly advocate for researchers and community partners to use participatory planning to develop a research design that includes a knowledge mobilization plan. Participatory planning allows all partners to be substantively involved in developing an action plan, and this foundational involvement helps ensure the long-term success of, and a positive outcome for, the project because all partners have "buy in" at the outset. Furthermore, within a participatory planning model, those working together take time to define "success." Together they consider what success will look like and how it will feel. This creates a sense of ownership over research results that in turn facilitates the flow of benefits and knowledge to the appropriate communities (e.g., descendent or local community members; archaeologists and other researchers; tribal, state, and government agencies; nongovernmental organizations [NGOs]; and diverse public audiences).

In participatory planning, research partners decide how to approach the research process, set timelines, and determine how the work will be divided and what will be done by whom. Archaeologists are familiar with developing a research design (either alone or as part of a collaborative team). The difference in working with community partners is that many people are involved, often with different levels of knowledge; a wide range of experiences; and sometimes very different goals, timelines, and methods of working. Participatory planning can be one highly effective strategy for developing a research plan that includes everyone in the process and gives all involved a voice and substantive input. It can also be an effective team-building strategy.

My first experience with participatory planning began in 2011 during a planning session for the ezhibiigaadek asin Sanilac petroglyph intellectual property project that I am conducting with a team of community member coresearchers from the Ziibiwing Center of Anishinabe Culture and Lifeways in Mt. Pleasant, Michigan. Ziibiwing is a community-based organization that is funded by and serves the Saginaw Chippewa Indian Tribe of Michigan. Previously, we have partnered on numerous CBPR projects ranging from repatriation research to heritage management and planning (Atalay 2012).

Our current petroglyph project involves Ziibiwing staff, tribal spiritual advisors, tribal members, and elders. Each of us brings different knowledge and experience to the project, and we want to utilize that rich knowledge base effectively. At the project's outset, Shannon Martin, Ziibiwing's director, suggested a participatory planning session to develop a research action plan for the project because she'd had success with the method on several tribal initiatives. As Martin explained it, the participatory planning process was productive for Ziibiwing because it fits with Anishinabe core tribal values and was similar to the way we make decisions and work with each other in a tribal context. For example, it not only allows but also expects that each person will contribute ideas to the process. It calls on participants to define success in their own terms. And it allows those who participate time to reflect on the core values that inform the research.

In brief, our process started with developing a Victory Circle. During this time, all team members were asked to consider, "What kinds of things are we going to see, hear, and feel that let us know we have achieved success in this project?" Ideas were offered by all participants and color coded on large sticky notes that were posted around the room. We considered the community strengths and weaknesses that would help or hinder us in reaching success. We thought carefully about the core tribal values that needed to be at the center to inform all steps in the research process. We discussed the risks and pitfalls and even the things that worried, frightened, or concerned each research partner.

At the end of a 2-day working session, our research team had a clear action plan in hand. A piece of each of us was within that plan, and we could each see ourselves and our community values and goals within it. We developed common language that would help us remain on the same page as we moved forward through the research process. We also developed a sense of shared purpose through the participatory planning. All these aspects made the big work of "research" and some of the challenges of working in partnership more manageable. A critical component of this process, particularly for projects that have a research focus, is that partners include a knowledge mobilization plan in their research design and that they consider and build-in periodic assessment times. After all, the *process* of working together—work that involves creating a plan, discussing who should know about the results, considering appropriate ways for different "audiences" to learn about the research, and openly sharing expectations and tangible measures of success—is just as important (perhaps more so) as the research design that is developed.

REFERENCES

American Anthropological Association. 2013. "What is Anthropology?" accessed December 2, 2013, http://www.aaanet.org/about/whatisanthropology.cfm.

American Anthropological Association, Anthropology and Environment Society. 2013. "Engagement Blog," accessed December 2, 2013, http://www.aaanet.org/sections/ae/index.php/category/engagement-blog/.

Atalay, Sonya. 2012. *Community-Based Archaeology: Research with, by, and for Indigenous and Local Communities.* Berkeley: University of California Press.

Badcock, Anna, and Robert Johnston. 2009. "Placemaking through Protest: An Archaeology of the Lees Cross and Endcliffe Protest Camp, Derbyshire, England." *Archaeologies: Journal of the World Archaeological Congress* 5(2): 306–322.

Brown, Leslie, and Susan Strega, eds. 2005. *Research as Resistance: Critical, Indigenous, and Anti-Oppressive Approaches.* Toronto: Canadian Scholars' Press.

Calhoun, Craig. 2008. "Foreword: Engaging Contradictions: Theory, Politics, and Methods of

Activist Scholarship." In *Engaging Contradictions: Theory, Politics, and Methods of Activist Scholarship,* edited by Charles R. Hale, xiii–xxv. Berkeley: University of California Press.

Camp, Stacey Lynn. 2011. "Materializing Inequality: The Archaeology of Tourism Laborers in Turn-of-the-Century Los Angeles." *International Journal of Historical Archaeology* 15: 279–297.

Carnegie Foundation for the Advancement of Teaching. 2013. "Classification Description: Community Engagement Elective Classification," accessed December 2, 2013, http://classifications.carnegiefoundation.org/descriptions/community_engagement.php.

Collins, Patricia Hill. 2012. *On Intellectual Activism.* Philadelphia: Temple University Press.

Craven, Christa, and Dána-Ain Davis, eds. 2013. *Feminist Activist Ethnography: Counterpoints to Neoliberalism in North America.* Lanham, MD: Lexington Books.

Ehrlich, Thomas. 1999. "Presidents' Declaration on the Civic Responsibility of Higher Education," accessed December 2, 2013, http://www.compact.org/resources-for-presidents/presidents-declaration-on-the-civic-responsibility-of-higher-education/signatories/.

Fortmann, Louise. 2008. "Introduction: Doing Science Together." In *Participatory Research in Conservation and Rural Livelihoods,* edited by Louise Fortmann, 1–17. Oxford, UK: Wiley-Blackwell.

Fricker, Miranda. 2007. *Epistemic Injustice: Power and the Ethics of Knowing.* Oxford, UK: Oxford University Press.

Hale, Charles R., ed. 2008a. *Engaging Contradictions: Theory, Politics, and Methods of Activist Scholarship.* Berkeley: University of California Press.

———— 2008b. "Introduction." In *Engaging Contradictions: Theory, Politics, and Methods of Activist Scholarship,* edited by Charles Hale, 1–30. Berkeley: University of California Press.

Haraway, Donna. 1988. "Situated Knowledges: The Science Question in Feminism and the Privilege of Partial Perspective." *Feminist Studies* 14(3): 575–599.

Harrison, Faye. 2013. "Forward: Navigating Feminist Activist Ethnography." In *Feminist Activist Ethnography: Counterpoints to Neoliberalism in North America,* edited by C. Craven and D. Davis, ix–xv. New York: Lexington Books.

Harrison, Rodney, and John Schofield. 2009. "Archaeo-Ethnography and Auto-Archaeology: Introducing Archaeologies of the Contemporary Past." *Archaeologies: Journal of the World Archaeological Congress* 5(2): 185–209.

Larkin, Karin and Randall H. McGuire, eds. 2009. *The Archaeology of Class War.* Boulder: University of Colorado Press.

Lutz, John Sutton, and Barbara Neis, eds. 2008. *Making and Moving Knowledge: Interdisciplinary and Community-Based Research in a World on the Edge.* Montreal: McGill Queens University Press.

McGuire, Randall H. 2008. *Archaeology as Political Action.* Berkeley: University of California Press.

McGuire, Randall H., and Robert Paynter, eds. 1991. *The Archaeology of Inequality.* Oxford, UK: Blackwell.

McGuire, Randall H., and Paul Reckoner. 2003. "Building a Working Class Archaeology: The Colorado Coal Field War Project." *Industrial Archaeology Review* 25(2): 83–95.

McGuire, Randall H., and Mark Walker. 1999. "Class Confrontations in Archaeology." *Historical Archaeology* 33(1): 159–183.

Paynter, Robert. 1989. "The Archaeology of Equality and Inequality." *Annual Review of Anthropology* 18: 369–399.

Saitta, Dean. 2007. *The Archaeology of Collective Action.* Gainesville: University Press of Florida.

Saitta, Dean, Mark Walker, and Paul Reckner. 2006. "Battlefields of Class Conflict: Ludlow Then and Now." *Journal of Conflict Archaeology* 1: 197–213.

Schofield, John. 2009. "Peace Site: An Archaeology of Protest at Greenham Common Airbase." *British Archaeology* 104: 44–49.

Sudbury, Julia, and Margo Okazawa-Rey, eds. 2009. *Activist Scholarship: Antiracism, Feminism, and Social Change.* Boulder, CO: Paradigm.

Wittman, Amanda, and Terah Crews. 2012. "Engaged Learning Economies: Aligning Civic Engagement and Economic Development in Community-Campus Partnerships. Boston: Campus Compact," accessed December 2, 2013, http://www.compact.org/wp-content/uploads/2012/01/Engaged-Learning-Economies-White-Paper-2012.pdf.

Zimmerman, Larry J., Courtney Singleton, and Jessica Welch. 2010. "Activism and Creating a Translational Archaeology of Homelessness." *World Archaeology* 42(3): 443–454.

Chapter 4

Situating Activism in Archaeology

The Mission of Science, the Activist Affect, and the Archaeological Record

Quetzil E. Castañeda

At the end of an archaeology field school directed by John Henderson in 1983, in the Sula Valley, Honduras, I was impressed by the comment of a graduate student staff member. In a discussion of the Central American politics of that era, he stated that he would not be an ethnographer or do ethnography in the Maya world. He asserted that the ethical risk of doing harm to Maya peoples was too great. In contrast, he claimed that archaeology was "safe"; that archaeology could not hurt or do harm, for example, to eighth-century Maya. Although that seemed reasonable, it certainly did not acknowledge that doing archaeology, like doing ethnography or any other social science, is always political; it is in fact political action (Castañeda 1996; McGuire 2008). Following the field school, I had plans to reunite with my cousins in Guatemala. I was forced to reroute my travels to Belize, Yucatán, Chiapas, and Oaxaca because of the Guatemalan civil war. Later, I learned that two of my cousins were disappeared by the military.

I write this biographic sketch only days after Guatemalan "[j]udges sentenced Rios Montt to 80 years in prison on Friday [May 13, 2013] after finding him responsible for deliberate killings by the armed forces of at least 1,771 members of the Maya Ixil population during his 1982–83 rule" (McDonald 2013). This was precisely the year that I would have visited Guatemala and most likely initiated a research career in Guatemala. Instead, in my travels to Maya archaeological sites, I became intellectually and ethically engaged

Transforming Archaeology: Activist Practices and Prospects, edited by Sonya Atalay, Lee Rains Clauss, Randall H. McGuire, and John R. Welch, 61–90. © 2014 Left Coast Press, Inc. All rights reserved.

with questions not only of anthropological moralism and ethnographic ethics but also the politics of archaeology. In these wanderings, the offhand comment by the graduate student continued to trouble me as thoroughly wrong-headed, self-servingly naïve, and dangerous.

As a teenager, I had been enthralled with the Maya during family visits to relatives in Mexico and Guatemala. After these trips, I began to follow the lead of my brother Omar, who took classes on the Maya at Indiana University. While he converted his search for identity via Maya mythos in his "attack-dog fiction" (Castañeda 1993), I became fascinated with Maya archaeology. I read translations of the Chilam Balam of Chumayel and stalked the F1435 stacks in the Indiana University Wells Library. My mother's Guatemalan nationalism led me, however, to be disturbed by the seemingly empty and somewhat contradictory assertions in archaeology books about "Mexican influence" on the pre-Columbian Maya. These factors converged to create my long-lasting interest in the political implications and motivations of archaeological knowledge, discourse, and interpretations. My "rambles in Yucatán" (Norman 1843) in the summer of 1983 allowed me to connect this ongoing concern for the politics of archaeological representation to the in situ politics of knowledge production; that is, with the politics on the ground of archaeological research projects. What are the effects, consequences, and transformations in local and regional society? How does archaeology collaborate with the tourism industry and the state in creating "the past" as a lived-in landscape and living imaginary? How does archaeology work to produce and make the past part of our everyday life?

These questions, which continue to provoke me, emerge from my personal history. This history has shaped my ethics of questioning anthropology and my use of anthropology to question the world. At times, these ethics have taken shape as a "chip on my shoulder" or an affect of indignation, but it has always guided my interventions in archaeology as a space of engagement and as an institution to be changed and improved.

—∞—

The Vocations of Activism: Introduction

This chapter explores ways to insert subjectivity, ethnography, and history into the very doing of archaeology as a way to make it a better science (see Hale 2008, 8). By "better science," I refer to the criteria of rigor, objectivity, and ethical values of science. There is no doubt that subjectivity, ethnography, and history are problems, methods, and approaches that have always been an integral part of archaeology. Nonetheless, in the history of archaeology, there have been significant differences and changes in how they are envisioned and operate within archaeological practice. Building on archaeological scholarship of the last twenty years, I argue for specific roles and ways of using subjectivity, ethnography, and history in archaeology. I first create a four-part typology of activism based in concepts of vocation, callings, affect, and interpellation. I often use activist archaeology as the relevant example of one of these types (vocational activism). Second, I argue that the sociological dimensions of archaeology must be understood as part of the archaeological record. I provide a strategic plan for the systematic and objectivist ethnographic documentation of these sociohistorical aspects of archaeology. In my argument for this vision and plan for archaeology, I do not appeal to activism, but rather to base it on science, specifically ethical imperatives and values of objectivity and methodological rigor that are hallmarks of science.

Discussions of activism in academia are primarily concerned with the relationship of the activist scholar with groups in need of help or with whom activists collaborate in the resolution of issues of social justice (e.g., Hale 2008; Checker and Fishman 2004; Craven and Davis 2013; Stottman 2011; Sudbury and Okazawa-Rey 2009). This dominant focus derives from the entrenched assumption that activism is about action and that most academic work, which is primarily thinking, theorizing, and analyzing, is politically sterile, at best, or reactionary at worst (e.g., Hale 2006). Contra this ideological perspective, Glick Schiller (2011) defines one type of activist scholarship as the theoretical-conceptual analyses and research that contributes to political action by working to change cultural ideas, assumptions, and beliefs. This chapter, if it is activist scholarship, fits this conception of activism as outlined by Glick Schiller. The task of this chapter is to analyze the fundamental relationship of the activist to oneself and to one's profession. I ground my discussion by situating activist archaeology in a series of four ideal types of intersecting and overlapping modes of activism and associated activists (see Figure 4.1): professional activism (professional

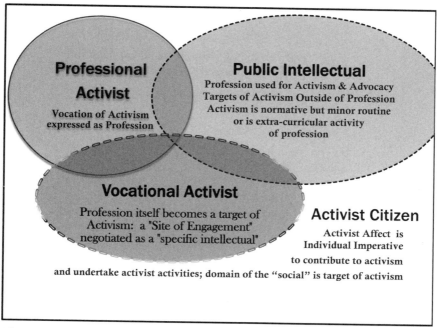

Figure 4.1   Ideal types of activism and activists.

activist), citizen activism (activist citizen), public activism (public intellectual), and vocational activism (specific intellectual). These are best explained in pairs.

The first two types correspond to commonly understood ideas of activism and activists. Private citizens, first type, donate voluntarily their time, labor, skills, money, and so on to increase the collective "good" and social well-being, regardless of how the cause is labelled in terms of political orientations (right/left, conservative, or liberal/progressive, etc.). Professional activism, second type, is conducted by persons who earn a salary for their work in these same areas to which other citizens volunteer their time, money, and labor. In both professional and citizen activism, the causes and commitments, for example, to social justice, rights, health, environment, law, democratic participation, advocacy, and so on are the sites of engagement. Regardless of the sociological shape or substance of these sites of engagement, for example, whether these are institutions, laws, communities, political processes, social problems, or cultural beliefs, these targets of desired change are external to the activist citizen and activist organizations that employ professional activists. In both of these cases, there is no confusion or overlap between the targets and sites of activism, on the one hand, and the activists and their sociological location from which they engage the problems that need to be addressed.

The second two ideal types of activism have more complicated relationships between the agents of activism, their motivations and goals, problems or targets of change, sites of engagement, and modes or forms of action. In both the third and fourth types, the work of activism is embedded in and conducted as part of or in relationship to a professional occupation that is not essentially understood in any normal, popular, or social sense as activism, advocacy, or public policy work. The third type corresponds to the notion of intellectual and specifically to the notion of public intellectual (e.g., Bauman 1989; Glick Schiller 2011) that has emerged in contemporary culture and scholarship. It can also be understood in relation to the idea of "general intellectual," that is discussed by Bourdieu as a type that contrasts to Foucault's notion of the "specific intellectual" (1980). My fourth type of activism, what I call "vocational activism," is conceptualized and modeled on Foucault's concept of the specific intellectual. The third and fourth types of activism are based on and consist of ways professionals (in our case, academics, scholars, and specifically archaeologists) put their profession, expertise, and practices in the service of communities, social justice, defense of rights, restitution of heritage, social movements, increased democratic participation, advocacy, and so on. Again, these contributions to the collective good, as envisioned by the activist, can correspond to "left," "right," or other more radical political orientations and beliefs.

In the third type (public intellectual), activism consists of the person using and putting the profession (skills, expertise, and institutional leverage) in the service of social causes in ways that exceed the "normal" and culturally defined, proper scope of operations of the profession. There is a range of possibilities here. Sometimes this activism can appear to simply be citizen activism if the person does not actually put the profession (as resource, expertise, tools) in the service of a cause, but simply makes public arguments in the name of the cause (more or less using professional expertise as the basis or legitimization of this advocacy). Noam Chomsky is an example: his public activism is not salaried work paid by his university and it mostly has an arbitrary, if any, connection to linguistics.

In other situations, professional activism is a normative but minor part of the profession. There are a number of professions that have formally designated activist activities and obligations as a routine, but restricted domain within the profession. Consider, for example, that the practices of law and medicine include *pro bono* or volunteer work for disenfranchised, marginalized, or low-income persons. Volunteer tourism can be both citizen activism and professional activism when professionals such as dentists, lawyers, or doctors create travel groups precisely as a way to provide their services to economically marginalized communities in the global south. The significant diagnostic of this ideal type is that the targets of change and sites of engagement of this activism are external to the profession: the profession is a tool used to address problems, but it is not among the problems that are targets of change.

In contrast, to the extent that public intellectuals also work to change their professional vocation (i.e., the social institution, practices, political-economic organization, and cultural functioning in society or its values and norms), the activism manifests as a distinct ideal type of a fourth kind: the site of engagement is the profession itself, and the targets of change also include the practices, thinking, and institutions of the vocation. To my mind, this vocational activism is best conceptualized in terms of the political engagement theorized by Foucault as a specific intellectual (1980).

The literature on activist and engaged anthropology (Atalay, this volume; Craven and Davis 2013; Glick Schiller 2011; Hale 2006, 2008; Low and Merry 2010; Stottman 2010) is primarily concerned with activism in the third sense of public activism of the scholar-academic performing as a public intellectual. This literature emerges as a discussion of how to do academic work in such a way that it has immediate relevance or approximate use for some public constituency that in one way or another has a stake or connection to the research. Thus, the concept of activism in this literature is predominantly understood in the sense of action that addresses particularly tangible and sociohistorically situated issues versus the more abstract task of changing beliefs, worldviews, ways of thinking, and scholarly paradigms as exemplified by public intellectuals such as Franz Boas, W.E.B. DuBois, and Edward Said. In this context, the recurrent and underlying questions for this activist-scholar literature are: How can academics put their academic expertise in the service of marginalized or disenfranchised communities? How can this way of doing scholarly work, which seeks to loudly represent and proclaim itself as activism, be routinized as normative habit and routine practice by definition? I provide my own answers to these questions indirectly by addressing other issues about activism.

Specifically, in this chapter, I prioritize activism that also targets or seeks transformation of the profession from within which one does activism (cf. Clauss, this volume; McGuire, this volume). The idea of occupying the establishment forms of thinking and doing to change the academic profession and discipline, in addition to the world "out there," outside of the university, is an idea that has been elaborated in different ways by a variety of traditions of social theory, e.g., feminism, critical race theory, poststructuralism, and postcolonialism (i.e., the idea of decolonization). These strategies of epistemological politics have played a fundamental role in transforming academia: the core tactic and premise of these epistemological strategies, which is to occupy and change from "within" a discipline of knowledge production, can be found in different specific theories and models, such as Haraway's situated knowledges (1988), Hale's reclaiming positivism (2008), DeCerteau's "making do" (1984), and Foucault's specific intellectual (1980).

There are three parts to this chapter. The first part situates archaeology in activism by discussing activism as a calling, that is, as a vocation of archaeology that goes "against the grain" of the profession. I use the concept of vocational activism to introduce the significance and role of ultimate values in forging activism within archaeology. I introduce the Foucaultian concept of specific intellectual as a model of the activist archaeologist. In the second part of the chapter, the idea of archaeology as historiography is reviewed in order to differentiate the idea of "making history" from "constructing the past." The distinction is crucial for my argument because it allows me to specify the site and target of my activist engagement with archaeology. In the third section, I argue for the integration of ethnography in archaeological research based on an ethical imperative to document the ways in which archaeology "makes history." I also propose a scientific change in or, better, addition to, the conceptualization and assumption of the archaeological record. This vision of using ethnography is distinguished from other forms (i.e., ethnographic archaeology and archaeological ethnography) and is premised on an understanding of archaeology as historiography.

On Activist Affect and Imperatives: Archaeology as Vocation

In this section I situate activism as a vocation within archaeology. The dictionary definition of "vocation" includes three meanings: a) an occupation or profession; b) the call or calling from an external, "higher" (more powerful), source, e.g., God or capitalism, that summons and draws a person to an occupation or activity that is culturally designated as being among the most ethical or moral good, or alternatively the most evil and bad; and c) the "gift" of intrinsic capabilities, subjective predilections, inherent qualities, or natural talent that calls, compels, or motivates an individual (from within) to take on a specific profession, role, job, burden, or life trajectory that may or may not have any claim to moral righteousness, but provides ethical virtue to the person for fulfilling the person's inner destiny or personal capacity. Each of these three callings not only motivates but also guides and shapes action; thus, vocations entail or are moral or ethical imperatives. I use vocation and interpellation in all three senses, however, so as to disambiguate my meaning; I tend to use profession in the first sense and vocation and inter-pellation in the second meaning of an external calling. With regard to the third or internal calling, I also use other terms, such as gift, hailing, interpellation, imperative, affect, and "chip" (as in chip on the shoulder) to focus attention on specific aspects of activism.

Conflicts and Contradictions: Interpellation, Calling, Vocation, Gift

One way to theorize vocation as profession is by analogy with Althusser's (1971) notion of interpellation. This concept holds that the state apparatus hails or calls individuals in multiple overlapping ways; in turning to hear the call, individuals accept the identification as a citizen and accede to the legitimacy and authority of the state to govern over its citizens. Similarly, science as a professional vocation is a disciplinary institution that calls individuals to assume and abide by defined roles, identities, and normative (ethical) frameworks of behavior, thinking, and attitudes. This interpellation or hailing takes the tangible form of professional training. Training is not only the disciplinization of our activities as researchers; it entails shaping and molding (at least aspects of) our subjectivity and subject positioning (including eth-ics, vested interests, values, beliefs, and identities) as individuals. In order to achieve our personal career goals, we seek to become successful "citizens" of academia; and as proper "academic citizens," we reproduce in our routine practices the economic, ideological, political, and social structures, processes that shape and give content to our subject position as a professional. This is unavoidable. My point is not to call this domination by way of analogy to Althusser's concept of the State Apparatus and ideology. Rather I want to establish that regardless of how we might experience it (as liberating, oppressive, valuable, banal, dull, or nerdy, etc.) by heeding the interpella-tion (vocational calling) of academia (as well as our own employment inclinations), we develop multifaceted vested interests in maintaining the academic institution, the university system, and our specific disciplinary profession.

Thus, perceived threats to the archaeological institution, including its normative operations of thinking and doing, through which individual archaeologists attain self and professional substantiation can fuel what Leone (2010; cf. Castañeda 2010, 350–352; Maca 2010) analyzed as fear and anger. Nonetheless, vocational activism (Figure 4.1) does question, challenge, and work to change accepted standards of operation of one's profession. Here it is crucial to differentiate between the kinds or degrees of change that might be advocated. New theoretical traditions or frameworks that advocate for paradigmatic change establish themselves by asserting the need to change the discipline. The specific targets of change are the thinking and doing of the profession (theory, methods, and topics or issues that should be studied). Further, these changes that are sought after via activism as well as by paradigmatic shifts in the discipline are always moralized or morally coded as ethically "good" ways of research and engagement with the world (see Castañeda 2005; Pels 1999; Pels and Salemink 2000). This is the case with the archaeologies subsequent to the post-processual movement that inaugurated a whole new investigation and analyses of ethics in archaeology (see Fleuhr-Lobban and Price 2003; Scarre and Scarre 2006; Zimmerman, Vitelli, and Hollowell-Zimmer 2003); that is to say, the move toward post-postprocessualist archaeologists who are concerned with stakeholders and descendent communities position themselves as morally superior to competing schools of archaeology Thus, it is vital to understand in what ways activism advocates or works for change in the profession by defining the profession itself as a site of engagement and target of change. To what extent are calls for change minor-routine, reformist, transformative, or radically destructive?

In other words, the essential questions to ask of activism in archaeology are these: To what extent is the intellectual movement to formulate and establish activist archaeology yet another attempt to create one more commodity form or brand of academic archaeology within the institutional (i.e., political and economic) contexts of the profession in which scholars are required to develop original research, lengthy publication records, ongoing funding success, and networks of like-practicing scholars? Is activist archaeology just reproducing the academic commodities market or is it seeking to actually accomplish a transformation of the commodities that academic archaeologists produce in order to remain an academic archaeologist? This issue was raised in the conference from which this volume was generated. There was consensus that activist archaeology should not be positioned as yet another intellectual fad or careerist movement that would join the ongoing proliferation of types of socially oriented academic archaeologies: collaborative, community, public, participatory, action, indigenous, ethnographic, postmodern, post-postprocessual, feminist, Marxist, etc. (e.g., Atalay 2012; Colwell-Chanthaphonh and Ferguson 2008; Larkin and McGuire 2009; Smith and Wobst 2005; Silliman 2008; Watkins 2001).

Regardless of our or anyone else's statements or desires in this regard, there is nonetheless the real risk that all this movement toward activist archaeology will only result in and can only just be another archaeological brand of academic commodity with a determinate half-life necessary for career building. As a way to avoid this, many at the conference not only suggested that it would be counterproductive to define what methods would be diagnostic of activist archaeology but also eschewed giving this movement a label that would insert this way of doing archaeology into the academic marketplace of ideas and careers.

What would make this movement toward activism in archaeology different? Archaeological activism cannot be citizen or professional activism, but can be the public activism of public intellectuals. To my mind, what would make this activism all the more valuable and worthwhile concerns precisely *how the profession is approached as a site of engagement and positioned as a target of change.* The degree to which this is actualized is the degree to which this archaeological activism becomes the fourth type of vocational activism. Intellectual movements seek to gain traction in the field by changing the central debates of the discipline in terms of one or another combination of theory, methods, and research issues. Here it is necessary to confront the issue of vested interests. Once we heed the (internal and external) call of the vocation (interpellation and personal imperative), we become invested in the perpetuation of the profession—that is, archaeology as a profession and as an institution, as well as the institution of academia (university system) that supports it. To what extent and in what ways can we actually work to change the profession, current debates, and practices? Answers to this problem require not a theory but multiple theoretical frameworks that allow for the ongoing creation of new understandings and analyses of *what archaeology is in terms of how it operates not simply as a field of study or discipline but also as a profession, institution, and cultural apparatus.* In other words, activist archaeology, I argue, is dependent upon the continual production of new theoretical understandings and analyses of how archaeology is embedded in the sociohistorical fabric of society in a historical dynamic.

It is certainly the case that a rich literature began to emerge in the 1990s that directly engages these issues of the sociopolitical history of archaeology and the problem of analyzing what archaeology is in the sense of a contemporary sociopolitical and cultural institution. Initially, these studies focused on the relationship between archaeology and nationalism and colonialism. But this corpus of work needs to be continually expanded to include new ethnographic, historical, and sociological analyses of what archaeology is in the world. For example, areas of work that have hardly been investigated include archaeology in relationship to tourism, including archaeological research projects and field schools as tourism (Castañeda 1996; Duke 2007; Walker and Carr 2013); the political economy and cultures of archeological field schools (Edgeworth 2006); the sociohistorical effects of archaeological research in communities (Breglia 2006; Castañeda 1996, 2003a, 2009); and the archaeological imaginary expressed in popular culture produced through the mass media, the university, and academic research (Holtorf 2005, 2007; Schablitsky 2007). The conceptualization and theorization of what archaeology is as a field of study, discipline, profession, and institution must be grounded in continually new and nuanced analyses and social theories in order to be the basis of activist archaeology.

Recognition of this point leads to the understanding that the vocational activism of activist archaeology exists on a series of irreducible tensions between the elements of vocation. Not only is there a friction between the external and internal calling of the vocation, which has two aspects, but there is also a conflict, also dual, within the subject position of the activist between the activist affect and the vocational imperative.

On the one hand, the vocation of a profession disciplines the individual to conform to the properly designated ways of thinking and doing. On the other hand, there is the internal calling derived from our individual predilections, natural talents, and capabilities, which in turn derive from our personal biographies. Clearly, archaeologists who undergo the training of professionalization have done so because they have "the gift" (aptitude, inclination, skills) to do this vocation. If we ignore the very real everyday traumas of academic life, we can say that these two vocations can converge in an idealized harmony.

However, the activist has another conflicting gift—inclination and aptitude—that compels, calls, and motivates him or her to work against the vocation ("against the grain" of the normative profession and its designated ways of thinking, doing, acting, and operating). This activist affect can take a variety of forms, such as indignation at injustices, empathy for marginalized groups, a drive for social justice, identity-based alliances and commitments, and so on that are enabled, created, or furthered by the profession (on affect, see Clough 2007; Mazzarella 2010). Sometimes this affective gift works like a "chip on the shoulder" to resolutely resist, critique, and reject (yet not completely) one or more aspects of the vocation. Here then is a conflict within the individual between vested interests and capabilities calling in doing the profession on one side, and the activist calling not simply to use the profession for social justice but to also change perceived negative dimensions of the profession on the other side. But always the activist affect functions as an imperative to take action, in large or small ways, against the norm, against the routine, against one's own disciplinary vocation, and against the established functioning of archaeology as an institution, discipline, research practice, interpretation of the past, or understanding of the world. In short, archaeology itself is part of the problem that the activist archaeologist targets in order to improve the world. But further, this activist must also develop creative, uniquely individual, and productively positive ways to negotiate an internal conflict between the activist imperative to transform the profession and the activist's own investment in and conviction to the vocation.

How ever these conflicts are experienced, recognized, or expressed, they must be negotiated. They create a split in the subject positioning of the activist that is analogous to the idea of "double consciousness" proposed by W. E. B. DuBois. This idea has been developed in distinct ways by diverse postcolonial, indigenous, feminist, Marxist, and poststructuralist critics as a double strategy to insert political agendas into the accepted hegemonic languages of belonging to a minority group within a larger community of identity, whether they be communities of science, nation, gender/sex, or race. For example, Hale (2008) conceives of occupying positivism and Atalay (this volume) advocates a dual strategy of using the rhetoric, language, and methods of science to propose, conduct, and report sociological-oriented archaeology. Although I am in support of such dual thinking, my point is rather along the original identitarian lines of DuBois: this split entails a conflict between two identities that cannot be united or unified into a single identity. The activist archaeologist is a minority identity within an encompassing identity as archaeologist. This irreconcilable dual identity creates an ongoing negotiation of an internal conflict and a tension between oneself and the predominant mode of the profession. The recognition that you are and are not part of the group, that you are being watched by others and yourself, is fraught and uneasy. It is the location and underlying psychological condition of the activist affect that motivates action toward change.

This point is crucial. It means that each activist has to identify what aspects of the institution of archaeology are troublesome for their unique self, based on their situated knowledges forged at the intersections of different networks of power, knowledge, and status. Although experiential knowledge is the basis for this identification, it is not in itself sufficient for taking and planning action; it is not sufficient to create activism. To "fix"—repair, reform, transform—this aspect, the archaeologist needs, to reiterate, a robust sociological analysis of what archaeology is, not as a field of study but as a sociocultural institution embedded in the social fabric of everyday life. In order to develop analyses that ground effective action *against the grain* of archaeology, the activist requires more than this understanding and more than just an experiential knowledge of the profession. Thus, *this is not a call for reflexivity* (but neither is this an argument against reflexivity; e.g., Handler 2005; Hodder 2003). The activist requires theoretical tools and frameworks with which to continue to develop ethnography-based sociopolitical analyses of what archaeology is, not simply as a field of study or discipline, but as an institution that exists and operates in the world.

Activism can really be designed and conducted only in direct relation to socio-historically specific issues and problems situated in particular sites of engagement, including the profession as a site and target of change. The issue I raise here concerns how the activist engagement with a specific community is or is not represented as a universal issue of humanity. As illustrated by Calhoun's (2008) invocation of a Foucaultian analysis of activism and the activist role in social science, the concept of the "specific intellectual" (Foucault 1980) is a useful model for thinking about activism in archaeology. The determination of what is to be done is based on the activist's analysis of where and how they as an individual are located within the disciplinary grid of the profession, the political economy of the institution, and the functioning of archaeology in collective culture. The specific intellectual or vocational activist has an ethical calling, not only to do *some thing* in the world outside of the profession but also in terms of changing the profession. Yet the imperative to work "against the grain" (change the profession) is caught in specific disciplinary constraints of knowledge and institutional grids of power within which the activist works. As well, their own personal investment in the profession as a career, lifestyle, and institution can place enormous constraints and limitations on activism, which at times are so strong that activism is completely reduced to what might be called posturing and posing.

Universal Humanity, Science Jingoism, Activist Efficacy

There is yet another sense in which going against the grain of what I have called vocational activism causes a split in an individual's ethical motivations and sensibility. In this discussion so far, the definition of "positive" change has remained unquestioned and presupposed. This is the space of values in which exists a fraught relationship between the vocations of science and of politics. Max Weber's analysis of these two vocations succinctly expresses the modernist idea of science as requiring a dispassionate or neutral attitude to avoid the imposition not only of biases and distortions of subjectivity but also the introduction of (the researcher's) personal values or ultimate values in the analysis of social realities. The vision of science as value free (and especially as free of ultimate values) is a specific culturally constructed vision created at the end of the nineteenth century, but that really was consolidated and hegemonic in the aftermath of World War II. It is associated with the idea that scientists, especially social scientists, need only produce facts that are useful and to be used by others, such as policy-makers and politicians. This vision of value-free science has been intensely debated and discarded by Marxists, feminists, and postcolonial and indigenous thinkers. However, perhaps the most important critic of this vision of science in the United States of America from the end of the nineteenth century to the mid-twentieth century was the Progressive social science movement associated with Dewey's pragmatism (Bannister 1987; Hyatt 1990; Ross 1979, 1991; Smith 1994). Unlike this earlier critique from the group that Bannister (1987) calls the purposive school, the critiques of science from the 1980s and later tend to dismiss the ultimate values, or axiology, that grounds the moralism of science by analyzing it as ideology. The task of this section is not to dismiss the scientistic axiology of science's ultimate values, but rather to understand the slippage between the universal and the specific in axiologies of science.

The 1902 articles of incorporation of the Carnegie Institution of Washington (CIW, known since 2007 by its legal alias the Carnegie Institution for Science) provide, in my view, a quintessential and succinct statement of the mission and ultimate values of science: "[T]o encourage in the broadest and most liberal manner, investigation, research and discovery [in any field], and the application of knowledge to the improvement of mankind" (CIW 1904, section 2; Castañeda 2005, 2012).[1] This vision of science was commonly shared by the emergent social scientists of early twentieth century; it was a presupposed assumption of both those scholars who viewed science as an objectivist tool for creating facts useful for the engineering of society and those who viewed scholarship as a moral science that only had meaning if derived from and guided by values and a moral vision of a better society (Bannister 1987; Hyatt 1990; Karl 1974; Reingold 1972; Ross 1991; Smith 1994).

This vision and mission was tacitly accepted in, and became more pervasive, during the post-World War II ascendance of, objectivist social science modeled on physical sciences. There is no need to rehearse the history of debates over the nature of science; instead what is important about this vision is that the production of knowledge (whether or not it is conceived as cumulative and progressive) is construed as an ongoing, open-ended task essentially for its own sake but legitimized by the claim to benefit humanity. In other words, the production of truth or truths is the teleological endpoint and justification of the scientific production of knowledge (i.e., "investigation, research and discovery" in any field defined in terms of epistemological-rational truth). The criterion by which to determine the significance and contribution of truth-knowledge as science is expressed in the phrase "improvement of mankind." But what is this "mankind" that is presented as the ultimate value and benefactor of science, that is, of the scientific production of truth and knowledge? This phrasing refers to a cultural notion of a generalized, universal humanity as if what is humanity and what counts as mankind is self-evident. Mankind means an all-inclusive collectivity that transcends by encompassment and inclusion any and all specific sociocultural groups and all individual human beings. In this way the "improvement of mankind" is posited as the ultimate, unique value and universal, unitary criterion to which truth, and thus the activities of scientists, must be evaluated and assessed (see also Castañeda 2005, 2006, 2012; Castañeda and Mathews 2013). This ultimate value is reiterated and clarified in the first Society for American Archaeology (SAA) Principle of Archaeological Ethics that defines stewardship as "both caretakers of and advocates for the archaeological record for the benefit of all people" (SAA 1999, 283). The key words are "all people."

On the surface of these meanings, there would seem to be no contradiction, conflict, or tension between science values and activist values, or doing science and doing activism. The conflict and contradiction exists because of the sociohistorical shaping and cultural construction of the meaning of the words and phrases. We are endlessly bombarded in contemporary culture by films, novels, news, and everyday experience in which the rights of an individual or a minority group are placed in opposition to the rights and benefits of the collective whole. On the one hand, the individual or subgroup is excluded from the benefits to which, on principle, they have a rightful claim. On the other hand, the benefits that are, on principle, to be shared by everyone are, in fact, only received by a definitive and select minority group. Activism, by working to ameliorate and remediate such situations, becomes identified with the interests and values of sub-groups versus that of the whole; activism appears partisan. This common, popular identification, however, is a mistake, as the values of activism are actually not opposed to or in conflict with the values of improving mankind or doing science for the benefit of all people.

Thus the conflict between activist ethics and the scientistic morality of science must be worked through. The morality of activist archaeology does not, in the first instance, hold universal truth-knowledge for a generalized humanity as the primary ethical principle (e.g., Calhoun 2008, xxi). Instead, the activist ethic has among its ultimate value the interests of historically particular, situated sociological groups or communities in relation to particular issues in historically specific contexts. This sociological ethic (versus universal scientific moralism) is shared by the majority of new types of archaeologies—social, public, indigenous, collaborative, community, Marxist, feminist, postcolonial—that seek to put archaeology in the service of historically specific descendent stakeholder groups with whom archaeologists work.

This is the crux of a deep-seated conflict (whether or not it is acknowledged) within activism and activists, as well as the reason why many science-minded social scientists disparage activist, engaged, or applied social science. The view from Max

Weber is that putting the service of one's science profession to specific groups is a corruption of the ultimate value of science. Activism can often be the introduction of situated, partial, contextual truths, and knowledges in science moralism that, in contrast, are based on the ideal of universal truths. What is the status of this conflict *for the activist* between these two ethical imperatives?

It has been demonstrated over and again in various fields that the drive to create science has always been defined implicitly and explicitly as a nationalist agenda conducted under or within an idealized ultimate value of the improvement of a universal humanity. The nationalist foundations of science are only sometimes concealed; mostly, they are hidden in plain sight. It is not evident only in Nazi science. Consider, for example, that "the National Science Foundation [NSF] is an independent federal agency created by Congress in 1950 to promote the progress of science; to advance the national health, prosperity, and welfare; to secure the national defense" (National Science Foundation n.d.). It should not be surprising that this clearly nationalist vision of science is the mission of the NSF given the history of science in the United States of America. In the early nineteenth century there had been a movement to create science in explicit competition with the nationalist sciences of European countries. In particular, efforts extended more than 100 years to establish governmental funding and institutional support of science and research in the United States, such as what finally emerged with national academies of scientists and later the NSF (Castañeda 2005; Lagemann 1989; Madsen 1967, 1969; Reingold 1972, 1979; Woodward 1915, 1917).

Furthermore, the intellectual architect of the NSF was Vannevar Bush (1990), who essentially directed, supervised, or oversaw the science and research development before, during, and after World War II, including the Manhattan Project. In the 1941 CIW President's Report, Bush clearly expressed the deeply interdependent imperatives and intertwined ideals of nationalism and science:

> The urge to do something for humanity, by improving its knowledge of its environment, is so allied to the urge to do something definite to protect one's country from aggression that all scientific effort responds to the stimulus ... For the scientist whose talents apply directly to the means by which a nation defends itself, the way is glaringly clear. *He may well regret deeply that his efforts, so long devoted to an altruistic ideal embracing the whole of mankind, become limited for a time to a narrower national aim.* But he shares in that primal joy that comes from intense group effort in defense of his home, sublimated it is true, but just as real as though he stood at the mouth of a cave with a few strong men of the clan armed with stone axes against a hostile world. (Bush 1941, 4–5)

It seems clear that the ethical lament about the intermingling of nationalism and science is only a false pretense for ranting jingoism. First, this quote illustrates that nationalist values and agendas inhere in and are camouflaged by appeals to universal humanity as the ultimate value that defines the moral groundwork of science. Second, in terms of ultimate values, the activist imperative to work for specific communities (which are either subnational or transnational; i.e., within or across nation-state boundaries) is, therefore, not categorically or morally different from the science moralism that places (positivist and neopositivist) science in the service of a national community. Both hold "less-than" universal social collectivities as the ultimate moral or ethical criteria to assess benefits of knowledge and truth.

Third, nonetheless, the interests and needs of historically specific stakeholder groups are construed as "going against the grain" of the interests, values, and goals of a national community that have been asserted to be identical to those of "universal humanity." Thus, the (sociological) science agenda of serving humanity by attending to specific subnational groups in historically particular situations is implicitly construed or presupposed as politics (biased, value-laden, subjective, unscientific or corrupted science, without rigor, etc.). In contrast, when the national agenda is imminent or embedded in the very institution of science, social science generally or archaeological science specifically in the service of a national agenda is construed as and perceived to be value-free, neutral, and objective.

In the interwar period of the US, this science jingoism needed to be concealed and ideologically obfuscated in this way. World War I and World War II enabled the presidents of the CIW, Ralph Woodward (1904–1920) and Vannevar Bush (1939–1955), to drop this façade and quite explicitly celebrate the conversion of science generally and of all the CIW research departments to explicitly nationalist war agenda. Woodward, for example, was very proud of the fact that even the CIW archaeologist Sylvanus Morley was doing covert espionage: "Amongst other men who have been called from the Institution into the Government we have one man who is serving as a spy. He is an archaeologist, and archaeology puts up a very fine camouflage for that business" (Woodward 1917, 694; Boas 1919; Castañeda 2005, 2010; Darnell 1998, 261–265; Harris and Sadler 2005; Price 2000, 2001). In peacetime, the science values of universal humanity are able to camouflage nationalist interests without much trouble. I view the conflicts over the Native Graves Protection and Repatriation Act (NAGPRA) and related issues of whether archaeological heritage belongs in the first instance to descendent communities or to a national community posing as universal humanity as evidence of this ideological flipping. How is it that nationalist communities can be the covert (at times overt) reference to the concept of "universal humanity" while other subnational or transnational communities are blocked from being viewed as the legitimate reference, signified, and expression of the universal? I believe this is a crucial site of activist intervention.

In this context, it is possible to invert the emphasis given in a comment by Calhoun who says that academic activism " is not just about universal truths—though these do matter—but about producing truth in particular contexts and making knowledge useful in particular projects" (2008, xxi). Indeed, activist scholarship is manifestly about and ethically committed to placing the profession to use in historically particular situations. But, given the core ethical concept of activism that I have discussed, the crucial task—in order to create more effective action—is rather to express how situated knowledges speak objectively to express "universal truths" that are relevant and beneficial for all peoples or humanity in general. The crux of the matter is that the situated truths of sociohistorical locations are made to disclose and transcend the situations of their production to reveal truths of more "global" scope, specifically to contribute to the "improvement of mankind" in the most inclusive sense. Highly relevant to this issue is Mignolo's (2000) questioning of how some nationalist projects have the force of "global history" while others remain "local designs." The imagined universalism created in, by, and for science serves national agendas (in which are also articulated transnational corporate and neocolonial interests), yet this valorization of national communities is concealed and masked in an ideology of producing truths of and for universal humanity. Activist archaeology must also speak its truths for, about, and in terms of these ultimate criteria of scientific relevance and value. When activist scholarship can successfully position its work as beneficial not just to specific groups but to humanity in general then the political partisanism that objectivist-empirical minded science has attached to activism can be overcome.

There are, therefore, two different tasks: not only politicize science by revealing its hidden biases and vested interests, but depoliticize activism by emphasizing its (sociological) objectivity and universalism. On the one hand, historical and ethnographic research can work to reveal how specific national communities (or other more restricted collectivities) operate as the hidden criteria of scientific value and beneficiaries of this imagined universalism. On the other hand, activist archaeologists must strive to reveal and accentuate the universal truths imminent and embedded within the situated knowledges and sites of engagement with which they work. In point of fact, it might be necessary or more efficacious to accentuate the universal value, meanings, and implications over and above the immediate specific situation, even if or despite the urgency of or for a local community. There is an important principle that must guide the work of activist scholarship, specifically activist archaeology. There are no universal truths except those that exist in situated, historically particular contexts. These truths can take many forms given the specificity of the archaeological research; for example, truths related to social justice; human, cultural, and ownership rights; heritage; environment; inclusive democratic participation; and so on. These are truths that "speak" about what it is to be human as individuals, in communities, and as a generalized humanity (see Geertz 1973).

Occupy Science Moralism

The vocational activism of archaeology takes science as a site of engagement and target of change. The point that I prioritize is that activist archaeologists must not only occupy positivism and objectivity (see Atalay, this volume) but also reclaim and reconvert the moralism of science. There is no doubt that activist and other types of committed sociological-oriented archaeologies have been proposing and practicing different ultimate values and ethical frameworks for archaeological science (e.g., Colwell-Chanthaphonh and Ferguson 2007; Scarre and Scarre 2006; Watkins 2001; Zimmerman, Vitelli, and Hollowell-Zimmer 2003). The activist imperative calls us to also do our work in terms of the ultimate value that has been established for and by modernist (positivist, objectivist) science and its current neopositivist empirical expressions. To reiterate, I have identified this as the "improvement" or benefit of humanity-in-general *as an all-inclusive collectivity, as social communities, and as humans.* The activist has an ethical imperative *to occupy* the implicit moral superiority of science and through this action reclaim and transform the ultimate values of science.

In point of fact, the formation of North American (specifically U.S.) anthropology has always had within it an "activism" that did not or has not called itself activism. This drive to put anthropology to the immediate service of society in terms of both scientific knowledge and applied action is evident in all varieties of national traditions in a variety of guises that range from social engineering and applied anthropology to Romanticist motives. The label of activism has been mostly eschewed in order to be more effective in occupying universal and scientific truths. This is one hugely important aspect of the legacy of Boas's work: the operational understanding that anthropological production of knowledge has direct practical relevance for human groups, at times perhaps even greater practical benefit if and when presented in the universalist, objectivist, positivist, and rigorous terms of science.

The idyllic possibility of successful occupation and transformation of science values, positivism, and objectivity, however, raises the question that can be posed only as a concluding and troubling comment to this section: does activism—or specifically the vocational activism of archaeologists—wither away in the age of profound and thorough decolonization? I would say "no," given that there are always persons with a double consciousness of their social positioning in the world and whose subjectivity is forged with an activist affect to go against the grain. Whatever transformed vision of archaeology is achieved through activism, it is by definition going to be hegemonic and thereby provoke in some as of yet unknown others the activist affect and imperative to change and transform it in some unknown ways. For me, it is a scary vision to think that a predetermined endpoint to activism can be advocated.

Affect and Effects: What Does Archaeology Do in the World?

The subjectivity of the activist affect, the particular location of the activist in the profession-discipline, and the specificity of the sociohistorical problems that the activist engages are three (among other possible) factors that point to an inherent openness to what should be considered activism. As recognized by the contributors to this volume and by others on this topic (e.g., Calhoun 2008), attempts to define or preestablish discrete methods, strategies, objectives, targets, and tactics as diagnostic of "activist archaeology" would be a premature foreclosure of this openness. Methodological recipes for activism could very well limit effectiveness and ability to achieve goals. Such exclusive conceptualizations or focus on the identification with what Clauss (this volume) calls "value-added" labels could also lead, as recognized by a number of contributors to this volume, to a routinization of activism as another type of "new" archaeological practice in the academic marketplace. This risk suggests that there are ways of doing "activism" that do not fit a prefigured master model. Similarly, there must be ways of engaging issues without self-identifying or promoting the work (methods, analyses, or concepts) as activism (i.e., but which might be ascribed the label) that might just be as or more effective in instituting desired changes. This returns us again to the question and issue of values. We each have subjective values (constituted by myriad community belongings) that call us to work toward the realization of ultimate values.

In this context, I define my own contribution to activist archaeology not as activism but as "normative" scholarship that engages the problem of "what is this field of study?" that forms part of my vocation (anthropology). I am and am not an archaeologist; or I am, but not in the professionally accepted conventional sense. What I offer, therefore, is not an overt expression of how to use archaeology for the purpose of attaining a measurable increase of social justice for persons or communities outside of the profession. But I am an anthropologist who is deeply concerned with what archaeology is and what it does. This is the chip on my shoulder. I offer a vision of modifying the conceptualization of what archaeology is in order to change what it does. This can be considered activism by those who want to define it, according to the analytical framework I proposed previously or indeed by other criteria. Either way, I am not invested in the label of activism, but am concerned that it might get in the way of accomplishing objectives.

What is significant for me is that my ethical affect calls me to engage the question of *what does archaeology actually do in the world.* What are its effects, consequences, ramifications, implications, and experiences for persons, communities, society, cultures, and humanity? To define the chip on my shoulder, complaint, goal, or motivation in the most basic terms: I want archaeologists to actively participate in the production of knowledge that can allow for these questions to be answered. This requires archaeologists to document, to the greatest extent possible, any and all possible sociological and experiential dimensions in and through which their archaeological research occurs; and to document the ongoing lived experiential interactions, routines, everyday life, and sociological contexts through which research exists, that is, is enabled, constrained, and actualized. This is not simply my subjective ethical imperative that I want archaeologists to assume or that I impose on individuals. It is also not simply an ethical imperative from the perspective of the multiple forms of what I call sociological archaeologies, that is, those archaeologies that prioritize sociological communities. Rather, I argue that *it is a mandate of science to do this work of ethnographic documentation of the archaeological processes of research.* There are two senses in which this is a mandate of science. First, it is a mandate that we do more objective, rigorous, and systematic research on the processes that lead to the production of knowledge via a given science. Second, in order for archaeology to contribute to the improvement of mankind (including all subgroupings), it is an ethical imperative that we know the effects, implications, and consequences of archaeology—from the most individually unique effect to the most broad and encompassing consequences.

In the remainder of this chapter, I present an argument that advocates for a modification of the core concept of the "archaeological record." Significantly this concept is a philosophical principle that operates to ground and stabilize archaeology as a discipline and profession. It does so by providing a theoretical and a material reality to the analytical objects of study around which archaeology as an academic field of study has been historically created, shaped, and structured. The concept of archaeological record is both a metatheoretical assumption of the profession and a crucial ultimate value within archaeological axiology (i.e., system of values). Specifically, I argue first that the sociological and experiential dimensions of the processes of archaeological research must be included within the disciplinary and scientific notion of archaeological record. Second, I point out that the implications of this assumption and presupposition constitute an ethical imperative to ethnographically document these processes—regardless of the type or nature of the collaborative or scientific qualities of an archaeological project. Third, in the methodological conclusion, I propose specific guidelines of what I argue should be documented and how.

The Archaeological Record: Objectivity and the Ethical Mandates of Science

How can the ongoing sociological dimensions and historical contexts of research be understood as objects of study within the very conduct of archaeological research? I argue that the sociological and experiential dimensions of archaeological research must be considered as *a component of the archaeological record* (cf. Bacon 2010; Patrik 1985). This is a different argument than what has been developed by socially oriented archaeologies such as represented in the World Archaeological Congress in new collaborative, community, ethnographic, public, and indigenous archaeologies (e.g., Atalay 2012; Colwell-Chanthaphonh and Ferguson 2008; Larkin and McGuire 2009; Smith and Wobst 2005; Silliman 2008; Watkins 2001). For example, as presented by Herrera and Hollowell (2007) in their synthesis of the revisions of the WAC Code of Ethics, all the sociological dimensions illustrated in the "Circling Chart of Ethical Responsibilities" are conceived as ethical responsibilities. I advocate that these be first conceptualized as part of the archeological record, that is, as data of archaeological research.

The concept of the "archaeological record" in archaeology is no doubt a key topic of debate; my aim is to further problematize and rethink what should be considered a part of it. In general, there is a narrow-restricted and an inclusive-open definition. The narrow concept, on the one hand, strictly speaking, refers to the systems of material and tangible objects that are construed to be "from the past"; these objects from the past are the objects of analysis by which archaeologists construct the past. Thus, included in this restricted-minimalist concept is a secondary series of objects created by the archaeologists in the mapping, measuring, sorting, coding, archiving, documenting, and arranging of the materiality of the past. It includes all the field notes, plans, measurements, drawings, photographs, maps, visual modeling, documents, representations, and other intangible understandings that archaeologists *actively create* as the means by which to constitute data in order to construct the past in interpretative explanations and narratives. A more radically inclusive concept, on the other hand, encompasses other types of immaterial objects. For example beliefs, folklore, cultural ideas, memories, and narratives related to the objects of the past can be conceptualized, as in the WAC Code of Ethics (Herrera and Hollowell 2007), as an integral component of the archaeological record.

In addition to these series of primary and secondary material objects, on the one hand, and intangible cultural objects, on the other, is a third series of elements that can be understood as an inherent component of the archaeological record. The tangible, ongoing, lived experiences, actions, ideas, and choices of researchers, collaborators, and stakeholders that take place in situated interactions involving archaeologists, collaborators, authorities, communities, stakeholders, funders, institutions, and other agents are what I refer to as the sociohistorical dimensions of research. These dimensions, which are the necessary sociological conditions of interaction and contexts for research to be conducted, are the actual processes in which archaeological data, knowledge, and information are constituted, shaped, created, and known. The argument I make is that these aspects of archaeological research must be considered an essential and integral component of the archaeological record. It is the scientific mandate of objectivity, rigor, systematicity, and positivist control over knowledge production that dictates that these sociological dimensions must be conceived and treated as part of the archaeological record.

It is incontrovertible that the production of knowledge in archaeology occurs in sociological processes and has irreducible sociological dimensions. The social process of research is something that every archaeologist is acutely aware of, and project directors seek to manage, negotiate, and manipulate it as part of normal routine operations. I call this function of control the administrative management or the governmentality of research. However, I am stating not only that this aspect of research be understood as social process but also that the sociological dimensions that exceed this management issue be construed in this manner. These "unmanageable" sociological dimensions (not simply the managed social process of doing research) demand rigorous documentation just as variations in soil, landscape, and artifacts do, for example.

This is not a plea for reflexivity. This is a plea for better science and more ethical science. It would be better science to take account of the conditions that shape if not determine the production of knowledge. It would be more ethical science according to the actually existing ultimate values of science and the particular disciplinary values of archaeology. The existing archaeological codes of ethics of different associations of professionals and academics have continued to reiterate that the core ethical mandate or principle of archaeology is the responsibility to preserve and conserve the archeological record (e.g., SAA 1999, 283). If taken seriously and rigorously, the implications of conceptualizing the sociological dimensions of archaeological processes as part of the archaeological record are profound and wide-ranging. Archaeologists would, therefore, be morally obliged to design effective ways by which their research projects integrate strategies for investigating and documenting the social processes and sociological dimensions of research.

If archaeology is a science, we have as our ethical mandate the improvement of mankind through better science. This holds whether the science is "soft-raw" humanities, "medium-rare" social science, or hard-cooked "science-y" science. Is it not the case, therefore, that we have as our moral obligation to know how it actually really and immediately contributes to the benefit of humanity and the improvement of collective life? It seems obvious that our science values ethically oblige us to create knowledge of this type. After twenty or more years of grasping the idea that archaeology is in fact of this world, that it is a sociohistorical and political institution embedded in and affecting the world we live in, we actually have very little understanding of what archaeology does in the immediate reality of where research occurs, or even elsewhere.

We have *impoverished sociological-scientific knowledge* of what archaeology does and what it accomplishes in the lives of the persons and communities involved in archaeology on the ground. The focus on (the politics of) archaeological discourses, interpretations, and representations, and the ethics of practices have left us wholly ignorant and unable to answer questions regarding its effects, consequences, and meaning for humans in general and for specific groups. It would be better science and better ethics to have increasing knowledge and grounded evidence of what is the real, historical, and sociological significance of what archaeology is and does in the world. I advocate here a small but far-reaching suggestion by which answers to these questions can begin to be formulated, and thus through which we can better grasp why and how archeology is a part of the world in which we live. There are two aspects to the scientific and ethical imperative I advocate:

First, *produce ethnographic documentation of the sociological dimensions of archaeological projects as an integral component of the archaeological research design.*

Second, *create a permanent archive of the historical and ethnographic documentation of an archaeological research project conceived and valorized as an intrinsic constituent of the archaeological record.*

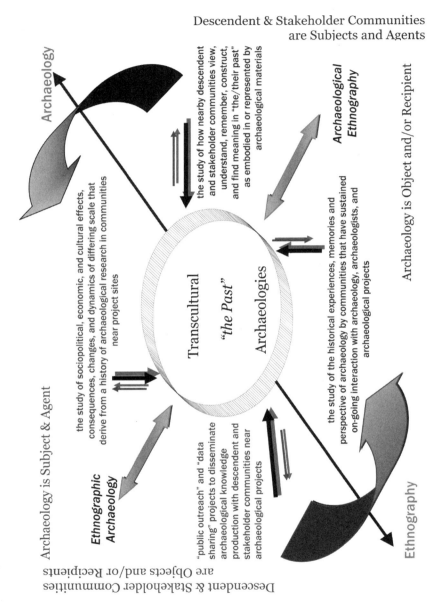

Figure 4.2   Conceptual map of archaeology and ethnography relationships.

Methodological Guidelines for the Ethnographic and Historical Documentation of Archaeological Research

The ethnographic turn in archaeology covers a broad array of research initiatives and includes a confusing array of rubrics. The use of ethnography that is advocated here is not a replacement or substitution for or improvement on these other modes of ethnographic archaeology (e.g., see Castañeda 2008, 2009a, 2009b; Castañeda and Mathews 2013; Castañeda and Matthews 2005, 2008; Edgeworth 2003, 2006; Matthews 2010; Hamilakis and Anagnostopoulos 2009a, 2009b; Meskell 2005; Mortensen and Hollowell 2009). In an irreducible sense, all these wide-ranging uses of ethnography are "optional," in that their use is based on the research design created by project directors that specifies how and why ethnography is to be used and the specific role it plays in the research objectives (see Figure 4.2). The methodological strategies proposed here are not considered to be optional, but rather foundational and essential; they do not change according to the type, mode, form, theory, practice, or research objectives of archaeological projects: *the goal to create a permanent archive of the historical and ethnographic documentation of an archaeological research project conceived and valorized as an intrinsic part of the archaeological record.*

What are the sociological dimensions of research and how should they be documented? My discussion begins with an elaboration on the idea of the archive and then turns to the brief identification of strategies and targets of documentation.

The Ethnographic Archive

With regard to the archive, there are two points to clarify. First, the goal of this documentation is not publication but the production of an archival record. This is simultaneously an ethical practice of writing history, not a path to publishing objectives, and a scientific mandate that prioritizes systematic application of rigorous methodologies in the same manner that one expects comprehensive and meticulous cataloguing of artifacts. The creation of the documentary archive must be conducted in the same manner in which the stone, ceramic, soil, or architectural specialist on the project is systematically constituting a complete analytical archive of materials, regardless of whether the specialist will later produce an article, thesis, dissertation, or book. Similar to these other specialist tasks of creating the archaeological record as a documentary archive, there is great potential for immediately producing journal articles and books based on the creation of the historical archive. This potential for publication as an expression of the production of scientific knowledge may, in fact, be fundamental in the immediate future in order to convince grant review committees of the scientific essence and urgency of this task; in other words, this potential is what will secure legitimacy as an inherent scientific process of archaeology, legitimate funding, and therefore enable research labor to be devoted to this task. The crucial point here is that this documentation is not to be conceived as a special add-on research that results in specific publication, but rather as an intrinsic, inherent component of the project as a whole that will result in a diversity of publications. This archival record is composed of field notes and other ethnographic research materials that can and should be used in the support of multiple different publications. But the archive of materials is not publishable in whole, just as one would not publish the entire set of drawings of all the shards, stone, and other artifacts that are excavated in a site. The ethical value of this documentary work and resulting archive is that it is created always with the logic that it must be useable for someone, anyone else, who could make use of the archive in the future to analyze the meaning, experience, ramifications, and effects of archaeology there in that place. The scientific value of this documentary ethnography is that it is a mechanism for increased systematic documentation of the knowledge that is produced in the processes of archaeological research.

Second, the documentation must be coherently organized and systematically designed for researchers both within and external to the project to access and retrieve information. This archive must, therefore, be thoroughly conceptualized in advance in order to attend to the physical and logistic issues of storage, access, retrieval, and analysis. The archive would consist of ethnographic field notes (of all types), digital images, video recordings, audio recordings, and collections of ethnographic artifacts (e.g., brochures, books, and objects). A formalized plan for indexing must necessarily be created, as well as the allocation of labor for successful archiving. All these technological and archival dimensions must be carefully planned in advance (and submitted as part of research grants) in order to secure the necessary funding to ensure the satisfaction of these open access objectives.

Targets and Strategies of Documentation

The documentation of archaeological research projects can be divided into the following five domains of inquiry: institution, process and practice, event and activities, network and interactions, and contexts and dynamics.

1. Institution
An archaeological project must have a monographic description for each year of the project. It would build on and extend what is already described in a long research proposal such as that for the NSF. It would include extended sociological profiles of all team members, including contracted laborers, consultants, suppliers, and other collaborators; funding sources, allocations, and cycles of support; formal staff structures, administration, and informal organization of authority; and descriptions of the physical, social, and temporal aspects of the "archaeology camp," including the organization and social basis of project logistics. A core description would be

composed at the onset of the project; documentation and description of the changes in personnel, funding, locations, objectives, and so on would occur every year.

2. Social Process and Practice of Research
This documentary strategy builds on and extends what would be conventionally included in a field report submitted to an oversight committee, whether a community, funder, or governmental organization. A field report focuses on the research processes and practices that lead to determinate results. The description advocated here would include the sociological dimensions of those processes that would otherwise be excluded from such a report. It would include documentation of the nature and quality of the social relationships in and through which research is conducted. There is conceptual overlap of this category with the following; the key criterion that differentiates this focus is the idea of the sociological processes that enable, constrain, contain, shape, and substantiate the research process and practices. This is a project-focused description and documentation.

3. Event Diary and Activities
Documentation of events and activities builds on the description of the temporal structures of the project and its research calendar, projected and actual. The key criteria that determine relevance for description are time/temporality and subject-based actions. Temporal structures of activities extend beyond formal calendars to also include temporal organization of routine practices, periodically recurrent events, and unique occasions that can be divided into direct research, social (non-research), and social (indirect research) activities. Documentation of events and activities are structured as a multi-subject diary that includes an accounting of activities in spaces outside and beyond the project camp and research sites. Examples could range from birthday parties for team members and meetings with staff, workers, or community members to the administrative management of routine issues or crisis problems.

4. Social Network and Interactions
Documentation of this domain builds on the sociological profiles of team members and all ancillary personnel. Profiles must extend significantly beyond academic resumes and work credentials to include personal background, histories, work experiences, professional contacts, and connections. Relevant sociological information would vary according to the person's location in the project. Descriptions of team members, for example, would include age, gender, degrees, goals, courses, funding sources, family and class backgrounds, teachers, and other relevant nonacademic connections. Portraits of local personnel would include their social networks in communities. This social network analysis provides context for documenting the modes, forms, and nature of social interactions that occur in the research process.

5. Sociohistorical Contexts and Ethnographic Dynamics
Documentation of contexts is conceptually expansive and elastic. This domain includes historical and ethnographic portraits of the home-base community or

regional communities that are involved in archaeology as stakeholders; or from which collaborators, workers, supplies, permissions, and information are secured; or that provide sites of down-time diversion and nonresearch social interactions. Portraits are monographic descriptions that range from the geographic-statistical (environment, population sizes, etc.) of present-day communities and accounts of cultural, political, and economic history to ethnographic descriptions of the sociological landscape (forms and modes of social organization, social institutions, authority structures, economic sectors, class and ethnic composition, power brokers, and leaders, etc.). Documentation of this domain is a systematicization of information, knowledge, and understanding of the archaeologists who work in this region, further enlarged and enriched by additional research, both in location and through literature research. This documentation can be assembled, modified, and added to throughout the life history of an archaeological project. It should be considered an ongoing task of writing an open-ended ethnographic encyclopedia of the sociocultural locations in which archaeological research occurs.

One may also note that these are guidelines, not a methodological recipe. The near-limitless range of types of archaeological research by itself would exclude specification of exact data to be collected in order to retain generalizability. These guidelines are wide ranging and imply a serious additional labor to the process of doing archaeological research. Some of the recommendations build on writing tasks that are already required of archaeologists and/or further extend and document base knowledge that is necessary for archaeologists to be able to craft a fundable project. Other recommendations would require the efforts of one or more dedicated team members, preferably with significant training in ethnographic methods based in any social science discipline (not necessarily just cultural anthropology!). The actualization of these guidelines would require a major conceptual overhaul of what is considered routine archaeological research practice, the disciplinary assumption of what the archaeological record is, and an understanding of ultimate values in archaeology.

Acknowledgments

I would like to express my gratitude to the editors of the volume for their support and friendship. I am indebted to Sonya Atalay and Lee Rains Clauss for the original invitation to participate in this project. In turn, the reader is indebted to Randy McGuire, whose comments forced me to throw away the first version of this chapter and start from scratch. To John Welch, in whom I discovered a kindred soul, I thank you for your friendship and support in this process. Thanks as well to Tim Knowlton, who was generous enough to read this work in progress and help me think through revisions. I owe Tim Wallace, Christine Preble, and Edy Dzidz for their support and inspiration in thinking through this text. Finally, to Ahmed Khanani and Bogdan Popa, you have my most pre- (and post-) linguistic appreciation for "awakening" my gnosis about affect theory.

NOTE

1. It is significant for several reasons that the creation of this nonprofit organization was based on an act of the 58th Congress and that U.S. President Theodore Roosevelt, along with the Speaker of the House and President of the Senate, signed the CIW into existence.

REFERENCES

Althusser, Louis. 1971, "Ideology and Ideological State Apparatuses." In *Lenin and Philosophy and Other Essays,* 127–186. New York: Monthly Review Press.
Atalay, Sonya. 2012. *Community-Based Archaeology: Research with, by, and for Indigenous and Local Communities.* Berkeley: University of California Press.
Bacon, Kelli. 2010. "The Preservation of Archaeological Records and Photographs." PhD diss., Department of Anthropology, University of Nebraska.
Bannister, Robert C. 1987. *Sociology and Scientism.* Chapel Hill: University of North Carolina Press.
Bauman, Zygmunt. 1989. *Legislators and Interpreters.* London: Polity Press.
Boas, Franz. 1919. "Scientists as Spies." *The Nation* 108: 797.
Breglia, Lisa C. 2006. *Monumental Ambivalence.* Austin: University of Texas Press.
Bush, Vannevar. 1941. "President's Report." In *Yearbook No. 40 (1939–40).* Washington, DC: Carnegie Institution of Washington.
———. 1990 [1945]. *Science: The Endless Frontier.* Washington, DC: National Research Foundation.
Calhoun, Craig. 2008. "Foreword." In *Engaging Contradictions: Theory, Politics, and Methods of Activist Scholarship,* edited by C. Hale, xiii–xxv. Berkeley: University of California Press.
Carnegie Institution of Washington (CIW). 1904. "Articles of Incorporation of the Carnegie Institution of Washington," accessed July 15, 2013, http://carnegiescience.edu/sites/www.ciw.edu/files/articles_of_incorporation.pdf.
Castañeda, Omar S. 1993. *Remembering to Say Mouth or Face.* Boulder: University of Colorado and Fiction Collective Two.
Castañeda, Quetzil E. 1996. *In the Museum of Maya Culture.* Minneapolis: University of Minnesota Press.
———. 2003a. "New and Old Social Movements." *Ethnohistory* 50(4): 611–642.
———. 2003b. "Stocking's Historiography of Influence: Boas, Gamio, and Redfield at the Cross 'Road to Light.'" *Critique of Anthropology* 23(3): 235–262.
——— 2005. "The Carnegie Mission and Vision of Science: Institutional Contexts of Maya Archaeology and Espionage." *Histories of Anthropology Annual* 1: 37–74.
———. 2006. "Ethnography in the Forest: An Analysis of Ethics in the Morals of Anthropology." *Cultural Anthropology* 21(1): 125–145.
———. 2008. "The 'Ethnographic Turn' in Archaeology." In *Ethnographic Archaeologies,* edited by Q. E. Castañeda and C. N. Matthews, 25–62. Lanham, MD: AltaMira Press.
———. 2009a. "Notes on the Work of Heritage in the Age of Archaeological Reproduction." In *Archaeologies and Ethnographies,* edited by Lena Mortensen and Julie Hollowell, 109–119. Gainesville: University Press of Florida.
——— 2009b. "The 'Past' as Transcultural Space: Using Ethnographic Installation in the

Study of Archaeology." Y. Hamilakis and A. Anagnostopoulos, guest editors. *Public Archaeology* 8(2–3): 262–282.

———. 2010. "'Conjunctivitis': Notes on Historical Ethnography, Paradigms, and Social Contexts of Archaeology." In *Prophet, Pariah, and Pioneer,* edited by Allan L. Maca, Jonathan E. Reyman, and William J. Folan, 333–356. Boulder: University Press of Colorado.

———. 2012. "The Neo-Liberal Imperative of Tourism: Rights and Legitimization in the UNWTO Global Code of Ethics." *Practicing Anthropology* 34(3): 47–51.

Castañeda, Quetzil E., and Jennifer P. Mathews. 2013. "Archaeological Meccas of Travel: Exploration, Protection, Exploitation." In *Tourism and Archaeology: Sustainable Meeting Grounds,* edited by Neil Carr and Cameron Walker, 37–64. Walnut Creek, CA: Left Coast Press.

Castañeda, Quetzil E., and Christopher N. Matthews. 2005. "The Public Meanings of the Archaeological Past: Sociological Archaeology and Archaeological Ethnography," accessed June 15, 2013, http://www.osea-cite.org/WGWorkshop/WGWFinal_Report.php.

Castañeda, Quetzil E., and Christopher N. Matthews, eds. 2008. *Ethnographic Archaeologies: Reflections on Stakeholders and Archaeological Practices.* Lanham, MD: AltaMira Press.

Checker, Melissa, and Maggie Fishman, eds. 2004. *Local Actions: Cultural Activism, Power, and Public Life in America.* New York: Columbia University Press.

Clough, Patricia T. 2007. "Introduction." In *Affective Turn,* edited by P. T. Clough, 1–33. Durham, NC: Duke University Press.

Colwell-Chanthaphonh, Chip, and T. J. Ferguson. 2008. *Collaboration in Archaeological Practice: Engaging Descendant Communities.* Lanham, MD: AltaMira Press.

Craven, Christa and Dána-Ain Davis, eds. 2013. *Feminist Activist Ethnography.* Plymouth, UK. Lexington Books.

Darnell, Regna. 1998. *And Along Came Boas: Continuity and Revolution in Americanist Anthropology.* Philadelphia: John Benjamins Publishing.

DeCerteau, Michel. 1984. *The Practice of Everyday Life.* New York: Columbia University.

Duke, Phillip. 2007. *The Tourist Gaze, the Cretan Glance.* Walnut Creek, CA: Left Coast Press.

Edgeworth, Matt. 2003. *Acts of Discovery.* Oxford, UK: Archaeopress.

Edgeworth, Matt, ed. 2006. *Ethnographies of Archaeological Practice.* Lanham, MD: AltaMira Press.

Fleuhr-Lobban, Carolyn, and David Price, eds. 2003. *Ethics and the Profession of Anthropology.* Lanham, MD: AltaMira Press.

Foucault, Michel. 1980. "Truth and Power." In *Power/Knowledge,* 109–133. New York: Vintage.

Geertz, Clifford. 1973. "The Impact of the Concept of Culture on the Concept of Man." In *The Interpretation of Cultures,* 33–54. New York: Basic Books.

Glick Schiller, Nina. 2011. "Scholar/Activists and Regimes of Truth: Rethinking the Divide Between Universities and the Streets." *Transforming Anthropology* 19(2): 162–164.

Hale, Charles R. 2006. "Activist Research v. Cultural Critique: Indigenous Land Rights and the Contradictions of Politically Engaged Anthropology." *Cultural Anthropology* 21(1): 96–120.

———. 2008. "Introduction." In *Engaging Contradictions: Theory, Politics, and Methods of Activist Scholarship,* edited by C. Hale, 1–28. Berkeley: University of California Press.

Hamilakis, Yannis, and Aris Anagnostopoulos. 2009a. "What Is Archaeological Ethnography?" *Public Archaeology: Archaeological Ethnographies* 8(2–3): 65–87.

———. 2009b. *Archaeological Ethnographies.* Cambridge, UK: Maney Publishing.

Handler, Richard. 2005. "A Dangerously Elusive Method." In *Ethnographic Archaeologies: Reflections on Stakeholders and Archaeological Practices,* edited by Q. E. Castañeda and C. Matthews, 95–118. Lanham, MD: AltaMira Press.

Haraway, Donna. 1988. "Situated Knowledges: The Science Question in Feminism and the Privilege of Partial Perspective." *Feminist Studies,* 14(3):575–599.

Harris, Charles H., and Louis R. Sadler. 2005. *The Archaeologist Was a Spy: Sylvanus G. Morley and the Office of Naval Intelligence.* Albuquerque: University of New Mexico Press.

Hyatt, Marshall. 1990. *Franz Boas, Social Activist.* New York: Praeger.

Herrera, Alexander, and Julie Hollowell. 2007. "The Process Is the Outcome." *Archaeologies* 3(3): 384–389.

Hodder, Ian. 2003. "Archaeological Reflexivity and the 'Local' Voice." *Anthropological Quarterly,* 76(1): 55–69.

Holtorf, Cornelius. 2005. *From Stonehenge to Las Vegas: Archaeology as Popular Culture.* Lanham, MD: AltaMira Press.

———. 2007. *Archaeology Is a Brand!: The Meaning of Archaeology in Contemporary Popular Culture.* Walnut Creek, CA: Left Coast Press.

Karl, Barry D. 1974. *Charles E. Merriam and the Study of Politics.* Chicago: University of Chicago Press.

Lagemann, Ellen C. 1989. *Politics of Knowledge.* Middletown, CT: Wesleyan University Press.

Larkin, Karin and Randall H. McGuire, eds. 2009. *The Archaeology of Class War: The Colorado Coalfield Strike of 1913–1914.* Boulder: University Press of Colorado.

Leone, Mark P. 2010. "Walter Taylor and the Production of Anger in American Archaeology." In *Prophet, Pariah, and Pioneer,* edited by Allan L. Maca, Jonathan E. Reyman, and William J. Folan, 315–330. Boulder: University Press of Colorado.

Low, Setha M., and Sally Engle Merry. 2010. "Engaged Anthropologies: Diversity and Dilemmas." *Current Anthropology* 51(Supp. 2): S203–S226.

Maca, Allan L. 2010. "Then and Now: W. W. Taylor and American Archaeology." In *Prophet, Pariah, and Pioneer,* edited by Allan L. Maca, Jonathan E. Reyman, and William J. Folan, 3–56. Boulder: University Press of Colorado.

Madsen, David. 1967. *The National University.* Detroit: Wayne State University Press.

———. 1969. "Daniel Coit Gilman at the Carnegie Institution of Washington." *History of Education Quarterly* 9: 154–186.

Matthews, Christopher N. 2008. "The Location of Archaeology." In *Ethnographic Archaeologies,* edited by Q. E. Castañeda and C. N. Matthews, 157–182. Lanham, MD: AltaMira Press.

———. 2010. *Archaeology of American Capitalism.* Gainesville: University Press of Florida.

Mazzarella, William. 2010. "Affect: What Is it Good for?" In *Enchantments of Modernity,* edited by Saurabh Dube, 291–309. London: Routledge.

McDonald, Mike. 2013. "Guatemala Government Must Apologize After Rios Montt Verdict: Judge," Reuters, accessed May 13, http://www.reuters.com/article/2013/05/13/us-guatemala-riosmontt-idUSBRE94C13V20130513.

McGuire, Randall H. 2008. *Archaeology as Political Action.* Berkeley: University of California Press.

Meskell, Lynn. 2005. "Archaeological Ethnography." Archaeologies 1(1): 81–100.

Mignolo, Walter. 2000. *Local Histories Global/Designs.* Princeton, NJ: Princeton University Press.

Mortensen, Lena, and Julie Hollowell, eds. 2009. *Ethnographies and Archaeologies.* Gainesville: University Press of Florida.

National Science Foundation. N.d. http://www.nsf.gov/about/. Accessed September 6, 2013.

Norman, Benjamin Moore. 1843. *Rambles in Yucatán.* New York: J. & H. G. Langley.

Patrik, Linda E. 1985. "Is There an Archaeological Record?" *Advances in Archaeological Method and Theory* 8: 27–62.

Pels, Peter. 1999. "Professions of Duplexity: A Prehistory of Ethical Codes in Anthropology." *Current Anthropology* 40(3): 101–136.

Pels, Peter, and Oscar Salemink. 2000. "Introduction: Locating the Colonial Subjects of Anthropology." In *Colonial Subjects: Essays on the Practical History of Anthropology,* edited by Peter Pels and Oscar Salemink, 1–52. Ann Arbor: University of Michigan Press.

Price, David. 2000. "Anthropologists as Spies" *The Nation* Vol. 271, Number 16, 24-27, November 20.

———. 2001 " 'The Shameful Business': Leslie Spier On The Censure Of Franz Boas" *HAN* (2):9-12.

Reingold, Nathan. 1972. "American Indifference to Basic Research: A Reappraisal." In *Nineteenth-Century American Science,* edited by George H. Daniels, 38–62. Evanston, IL: Northwestern University Press.

———. 1979. "National Science Policy in a Private Foundation: The Carnegie Institution of Washington." In *The Organization of Knowledge in Modern America, 1860–1920,* edited by Alexandra Oleson and John Voss, 313–341. Baltimore, MD: Johns Hopkins University Press.

Ross, Dorothy. 1979. "The Development of the Social Sciences." In *The Organization of Knowledge in Modern America, 1860–1920,* edited by Alexandra Oleson and John Voss, 107–138. Baltimore, MD: Johns Hopkins University Press.

———. 1991. The Origins of American Social Science. Cambridge: Cambridge University Press.

Scarre, Chris, and Geoffrey Scarre, eds. 2006. *The Ethics of Archaeology.* Cambridge, UK: Cambridge University Press.

Schablitsky, Julie, ed. 2007. *Box Office Archaeology.* Walnut Creek, CA: Left Coast Press.

Silliman, Stephen W. 2008. *Collaborating at the Trowel's Edge.* Tucson: University of Arizona Press.

Smith, Claire, and H. Martin Wobst, eds. 2005. *Indigenous Archaeologies: Decolonising Theory and Practice.* New York: Routledge.

Smith, Mark C. 1994. *Social Science in the Crucible.* Durham: Duke University Press.

Society for American Archaeology. 1999 [1996] Eight Principles of Archaeological Ethics. In *The Ethics of Cultural Property,* edited by P. M. Messenger, 283–285. Albuquerque: University of New Mexico Press.

Stottman, M. Jay, ed. 2010. *Archaeologists as Activists: Can Archaeologists Change the World?* Tuscaloosa: University of Alabama Press.

Sudbury, Julia, and Margo Okazawa-Rey. 2009. *Activist Scholarship: Antiracism, Feminism, and Social Change.* New York: Paradigm.

Walker, Cameron, and Neil Carr, eds. 2013. *Tourism and Archaeology: Sustainable Meeting Grounds.* Lanham, MD: AltaMira Press.

Watkins, Joe. 2001. *Indigenous Archaeology: American Indian Values and Scientific Practice.* Lanham, MD: AltaMira Press.

Woodward, Robert S. 1915. "President's Report." In *Yearbook No. 14 (1914–15).* Washington, DC: Carnegie Institution of Washington.

———. 1917. "President's Report." *Minutes of the Meeting of the Board of Trustees.* Washington, DC: Carnegie Institution of Washington.

Zimmerman, Larry J., Karen D. Vitelli, and Julie Hollowell-Zimmer, eds. 2003. *Ethical Issues in Archaeology.* Lanham, MD: AltaMira Press.

Chapter 5

"We Have Met The Enemy And It Is Us"

Transforming Archaeology through Sustainable Design

John R. Welch and Neal Ferris

Excavating My Activism (John R. Welch)

A minor epiphany arrived, circa 2000, as I pondered a question my boss, Ben Nuvamsa, asked me when he found me at my desk hours after the office had closed: "Why do you work so hard?" At the time, I was employed in Arizona by the U.S. Bureau of Indian Affairs (BIA), to serve as both the BIA's Fort Apache Agency archaeologist and the White Mountain Apache Tribe's historic preservation officer (THPO). I originated the BIA position in 1993 and the THPO function in 1996. Recognition that the Tribe was unable to provide the financial and technical support for rehabilitating sites and perpetuating traditions to serve the interests of tribal members led me, in 1998, to set up the Fort Apache Heritage Foundation as a tribally chartered nonprofit. Perhaps needless to say, the three jobs kept me out of the bars (mostly).

Busy for sure, but whither my zeal? No simple answer to Ben's question came to mind, but I had been listening to the Austin Lounge Lizards (1995), so quipped that life requires extra time and effort when you're not very bright. I may have also mumbled something

Transforming Archaeology: Activist Practices and Prospects, edited by Sonya Atalay, Lee Rains Clauss, Randall H. McGuire, and John R. Welch, 91–113. © 2014 Left Coast Press, Inc. All rights reserved.

about the importance of proving that archaeologists could add value to Indian Country without carting away artifacts and leaving behind holes of various sorts and sizes. The truth was that the question stumped me.

I like getting to the bottom of things (an archaeologist even out of the hole), so the next time Ben's question came to mind, I spun around from my desk in the Fort Apache and Theodore Roosevelt School National Historic Landmark to gaze out the window for some self-excavation. Why was I putting in unpaid hours, days, and weeks to help the Tribe protect threatened sacred sites, repatriate human remains and cultural items, and rehabilitate historic structures (Welch 1997, 2000; Welch and Riley 2002; Welch and Brauchli 2010; Welch, Riley, and Nixon 2009)? What was driving my energetic advocacy on behalf of the Tribe and the Tribe's cultural resources? The answer I came up with distills to two factors: congenital and romantic.

Congenital first. I share with many people of Irish descent, and other members of historically oppressed populations, a predisposition to righteous indignation and to campaigning against abusers of authority and privilege. My parents, both of whom had great grandparents from southern Ireland and grew up amid ample conflict, deliberately sought to shield their kids from the familial and economic uncertainties they experienced. Although my sister and I grew up in the '60s and early '70s, the focus in our home was on civic duties and responsibilities, not politics per se, and certainly not activism.

That said, both my parents acted on the basis of their moral convictions, and sometimes in surprising ways. My mother remained a Canadian citizen during more than forty years living in the United States, maintaining her green card through the Vietnam years as part of an exit strategy with and for an able-bodied boy child (i.e., me). She remained suspicious of the U.S. government, the Catholic Church, and most other mega institutions, finding her peace as an OB-GYN nurse and a children's advocate. My father, who grew up poor on the eastern Colorado prairies through the Dust Bowl, witnessed and experienced the terror of a Ku Klux Klan cross burning near his Irish Catholic family's home. He abhorred violence. But he hated bullies even more and was quick to intervene on their victims' behalf. I remember him confronting a man on a busy Denver sidewalk for slapping his little boy and telling the guy to pick on somebody his own size—a tough request, given that the bully weighed nearly 300 pounds (Papa weighed less than 150 pounds until he was 55).

If moving into Apache territory allowed me to find a focus for my latent activism, it was the romance I found there that made me stay. Love is the only word I know to explain why I spent so much time on and around the Tribe's lands—no fewer than 16 years between my initial field season as a first-year graduate student in 1984 and 2005, when I left to take my professor job. It was not the beautiful Apache people who romanced me, but their land. I spent six summers (1984–1989) as a member of the staff of the University of Arizona's field school at Grasshopper, on the rugged West End of tribal lands. After a first season of foreplay, I dove in, exploring on foot and mountain bike and inflatable kayak (and aircraft during fire seasons) every butte, mesa, and canyon. Through the later 1980s and continuing today, I have spent countless days on ardent quests for signs of previous lovers of mesas and precipitous places. I have tried to learn, first hand, why and how they made themselves at home in fortresses and cliff dwellings, searching for springs and stretches of entrenched canyons untouched by cattle and horses, looking for the best lunch spots and oldest foot trails and deepest swimming holes (Welch in Nicholas, Welch, and Yellowhorn 2008). But the epiphany was not just that I had fallen in love with a grand configuration of rocks and cacti and alligator junipers and coyotes but that I also shared this geophilia with Apaches. I don't know much about spirits, or whether the essence, or numen, of those uplands is particularly adept at occupying souls, but I do know that I found myself at home on Apache land. I also know I did not have much in common with Apaches until that happened. My life growing up in central Denver and going to college in upstate New York had few overlaps with most Apaches'. Walking Apache lands gave us common vocabulary, common ground, and then common cause. The hours I've passed in the shade of trees and the cabs of trucks talking with Apaches about places, especially ones that harbor remains of ancient lives, is time well spent.

Beyond discussing and visiting these places, documenting their contents and conditions, and assessing threats to their integrity, I have been honored to sometimes act on their behalf and on the behalf of Apaches who love them. I am proud to continue volunteering as an "archaeo-advocate," working to support Apache stewards.

So, my current answer to Ben's question: I work hard because I feel called by places and people to offer what help I can and because I can see and feel that this has made a positive difference.

———— ⱥⱥⱥ ————

I can't understand why people are frightened of new ideas. I'm frightened of the old ones.

—*John Cage*

Our activist focus in this and the next chapter (Ferris and Welch, this volume) is on transforming archaeology to reduce its destructive use of the archaeological record and to make the discipline more sustainable. We are concerned about the gap between, on the one hand, archaeology's lofty conservation goals and codified ethical principles, and on the other hand the realities of an archaeological practice that continues to consume the archaeological record at an unprecedented rate and scale. This gap is highlighted in the rhetoric that archaeologists use in extolling the importance of archaeology, in asserting that the tangible record of past human activity is part of the common heritage of humankind, in claiming that this re-cord—valuable, fragile, and irreplaceable—must be conserved, and in presuming that archaeologists are uniquely qualified for that stewardship duty. Archaeologists have been successful in capturing the public's imagination, and more importantly its financial support, in the context of both research grants and land use planning and development. In particular, archaeological requirements imposed on land altera-tion and development proponents by federal, state/provincial, and other regulatory conservation regimes are the driving force behind the staggering increase in cultural resource management (CRM). We think this expansion of archaeological mandates, especially as it is institutionalized in formulaic field research practices and reflected in incomplete data and object curation and in inattention to nonarchaeological values in cultural resources, is nearing a critical juncture. We join King (2002, 2009), Wheaton (2006) and others in calling for attention to inconsistencies between what archaeologists say archaeology is doing (i.e., conserving the archaeological record) and the consequences that the unprecedented rate and scale of harvesting the record is having, primarily within CRM practice. This contradiction, we argue, is making archaeology unsustainable.

Social psychologist Kurt Lewin (1952, n.p.) advised, "If you want to truly understand something, try to change it." We accept Lewin's challenge and offer means for transforming archaeology by analyzing and offering alternatives to that which limits its sustainability. This chapter expands on our activist commitments to preservation-focused and community-based archaeologies (Ferris 2003, 2004; Welch 2000; Welch et al. 2009; see Atalay 2012; Doelle 2012) and to knowledge creation, critical scrutiny, and action (Ferris 2000; see McGuire 2008). We begin by defining some implicit conceptions and framings in archaeology. We then review developments in North American archaeology that have led, since about 1960, to the entrenchment of what we term the *extractive-consumptive paradigm* in archaeological practice. Our last sections seek to inspire realignments among archaeological objectives and practice through applications of sustainable design concepts. Our ultimate objective, both through this writing and our careers more generally, is to boost the sustainability of our archaeologies and others'. Because archaeology occupies notably prominent and potent roles beyond the academy—in public education and local and regional land management—we think that boosting archaeology's sustainability cannot but also help to enhance social sustainability more broadly.

Whither the Enemy

For much of the nineteenth and twentieth centuries, the focus of archaeological practice has been on the extraction and consumption of the "things" of archaeology: the accumulation of objects, fragments, bits, remains, and their spatial contexts. These are then classified, analyzed, and stored away to facilitate and assure archaeological access to the past. The stuff of archaeology is the materials from and with which we build meaningful interpretations of culture histories, human behaviors, individual agencies, developmental patterns, and so on.

Over the last half century, this drive to accumulate has accelerated with the rise of commercial consultant archaeological practice, variably referred to as cultural heritage management (CHM), archaeological resource management (ARM), or cultural resource management (CRM). Borne of an urgency to document and recover the archaeological record threatened by looting or by the well-intentioned but no less destructive forces of land development and resource extraction, the desire to salvage, rescue, and recover the archaeological record to avoid loss in advance of development has emerged since 1960 as the primary preoccupation of archaeologists. This preoccupation, along with genuinely altruistic efforts to stop loss, has been greatly successful. Today, in many world regions and at many scales, States impose conservation laws, regulations, prohibitions, and programmatic conservation regimes on those who may, through their actions or inactions, cause the destruction of archaeological sites. This success, in turn, has created an economic and employment boom for archaeological practitioners, mostly beyond academic contexts, as archaeological services are increasingly required to be paid for by proponents who develop the land and thus may impact the record. Where such conservation regimes exist, CRM in the form of proponent-sponsored applied archaeology makes up 80 to 90 percent of practice and practitioners. At this point, it is common knowledge among many leading archaeologists that the rise and overwhelming dominance of commercial archaeology has changed the face and fabric of archaeological practice (e.g., Altschul and Patterson 2010; Messenger and Smith 2010; Schiffer and Gumerman 1977; Sebastian and Lipe 2009; Smith 2004; Willems and van der Dries 2007). Certainly in North America, ARM is *the* archaeology that the vast majority of professionals, students and the public experience day to day.

The logic that has guided the emergence of these conservation regimes has given birth to fully formed institutions—integrated systems of laws, policies, and organizations that exist to meet defined public interests in controlling access to and making use of the archaeological record. North American archaeologists have played a key role in establishing and tightening laws that recognize the public trust and common values embedded in the archaeological record yet ensure that the scientific values of archaeologists are given high priorities (Burley 1994; Ferris 2003; Lee 2006; McGimsey and Davis 1977, 1984; Williams 1976, 1980). By altruistically imploring the public to "save the past for the future," archaeologists have responded forcefully to physical threats to tangible cultural resources, especially looting and land modification (King 1998, 2008, 2002). Because of effective advocacy by archaeologists, federal, state, and provincial laws and regulations generally specify when land owners, land managers, and land modification proponents must sponsor CRM investigations; who is qualified to lead these investigations; what the standards are for archaeological data collection, reporting, and value determination; and how values of aesthetic, economic, historic, scientific, societal, and spiritual importance are to be assessed in this process.

These core functions illustrate the archaeocentric nature of institutional arrangements for managing the archaeological record. In North America and elsewhere, State permits to investigate or alter archaeological records can be held only by archaeologists. Other archaeologists review applications and reports then advise decision-makers about who should (and should not) hold permits or licenses. Most such permits and licenses require the appropriation and perpetual curation of collected materials (Ferris 1998; King 2000, 2008). And significantly, this process validates the archaeological extractive-consumptive paradigm, inherited from archaeology's long preoccupation with accumulation. In effect, archaeologists can be counted upon to insist that archaeological resource preservation is paramount, and at the same time to vigorously advocate for harvesting these resources, all the while claiming that scientific consumption is a close second to *in situ* conservation in the list of management preferences. While other environmental resource management practitioners mitigate impacts either by avoidance or replacement (i.e., tree planting, building a new fish run to bypass a dam), implicit in archaeological practice is the notion that extractive excavation and conversion to archaeologically meaningful values is a valid and socially meritorious replacement strategy.

This extractive-consumptive paradigm, then, undermines and discounts other values embedded in the archaeological record—notably social, spiritual, and heritage-based values held by nonarchaeologists (see Ferris and Welch, this volume). Archaeologists narrowly focus on the tangible things of the archaeological record—the scientific stuff of archaeological meaning making—as the singular social value of importance needing to be rescued from loss. As King (2002, 2009; 2011; cf. Smith 2006) has repeatedly pointed out, while in North America this institutional process is referred to by archaeologists as *cultural* resource management, supposedly encompassing the full spectra of tangible and intangible sociocultural heritage resources on the land to be managed, archaeologists in fact emphasize only that band of the spectra encompassing biophysical material remains deemed relevant to archaeology (Figure 5.1). CRM, as King argues, is a misnomer when it comes to most archaeological processes of resource management. Archaeocentric values have shifted the process from CRM, even while retaining this broader label, effectively rebranding CRM as contract archaeology. Archaeology driven by an extractive-consumptive paradigm to accumulate material is more accurately labelled archaeological resource management, or ARM. We distinguish, then, the practice of ARM and its focus on the portion of cultural resources of interest to archaeologists, from CRM, which encompasses a broader, more inclusive management of the full spectra of cultural resources, the veritable and variable sources and outflows—tangible and otherwise—of cultural identities and vitalities. CRM is concerned with the management of both tangible resources *and* intangible values tied to those materials. ARM is more narrowly concerned with those things, remains, places, and contexts that archaeologists seek to accumulate because they are specifically of value to archaeology and archaeological interpretation.

Important to these definitional distinctions is that although the archaeological record may be legitimately defined as all materials of interest to archaeologists, archaeologists are seldom the only ones interested in such materials. Indeed, as with the distinction between ore and metal, cultural resources become cultural heritage only as human groups "process" those resources by assigning them values, uses, and meanings. Concepts such as *value* and *significance,* which are commonly applied in ARM to mean "of value to archaeologists" and "the way archaeologists

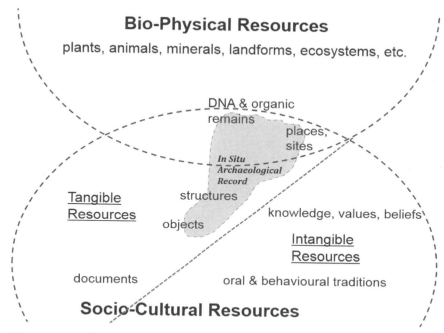

Figure 5.1 **The archaeological record of materials situated within broader, intersecting domains of biophysical and sociocultural resources.**

interpret the past" can and do have very different meanings for nonarchaeologists, especially members of descendant and place-based communities. For archaeologists, the materiality of the past has an "archaeological value"—both narrative and scientific—from which archaeological histories and inferences, as well as aspects of group identity and heritage, are derived (Ferris and Welch, this volume). But archaeological research is merely one of many ways by which cultural heritage is crafted using cultural resources (Welch et al. 2011). For example, under *The Burra Charter* (Australia ICOMOS 1999), scientific value is one of six overlapping values ascribed to cultural resources. We list the other five—aesthetic, economic, historical, societal, and spiritual—alphabetically to emphasize that different people at different times may ascribe different values and priorities to similar resources. Legitimate management of cultural resources, then, should entail deliberate and systematic consideration of desired futures based on the full spectrum of cultural resource values and relationships among those values, as well as the full spectrum of people holding those values.

Although understandably viewed in a positive light by many archaeologists, the dominance of archaeological approaches and methods in CRM—or rather the conversion of CRM to ARM in practice—raises numerous issues on disciplinary and societal levels. Management of tangible cultural resources that prioritizes or optimizes one value often necessarily discounts others. The obvious example is ARM's pursuit of scientific value, the most common result of which is transformation of loci of past behavior, first into archaeological sites and then, via extraction and consumption, into boxes of stuff and associated documentation. Those who understand that archaeological sites often contain much more than scientific values agree that value prioritization or balancing is best done case by case through significance assessments involving all who derive tangible or intangible benefits from the resources (Hardesty and Little 2000; New South Wales Heritage Branch 2009).

What unites archaeologists with practitioners of other fields engaged in the broader spectrum of CRM—ranging from natural and built heritage management to museum and tourism studies—is the conviction that cultural resources are valuable and deserve *management*. Our definition of *resource management*—guiding resource use and outcome decision making through processes and toward desired states (Lertzman 2009)—covers management goals ranging from absolute protection to utter destruction. In theory, management is value-neutral and apolitical, though in reality that condition ceases with the first management decision made, as practitioner agendas and biases are asserted (Lertzman 2009).

We see the biases in ARM practice, exported from archaeological sensibilities and inseparable from the extractive-consumptive paradigm, as transforming resources that are valued by many and varied publics and descendants into an archaeological record accessible almost exclusively to archaeologists. Driven logistically and financially by forces external to archaeology, ARM projects generally involve complex, dynamically negotiated entanglements of archaeological research, regional and project planning, archaeological heritage stewardship, professional ethics, and multiple contemporary pressures (Sebastian 2004; Sebastian and Lipe 2009). Specific complexity multipliers in ARM, all of which similarly confound much academic research, include negotiations to balance and satisfy:

1. Compliance with rules ranging from environmental and CRM laws to policies for workforce safety, cost accounting, and nondiscrimination;
2. Interests asserted by clients and by representatives of local, descendant, and peer research communities;
3. Expectations for research from the harvested archaeological record that adds value to previous studies;
4. Personal and professional needs, including livelihood, quality of life, job satisfaction, and so on; and
5. Conflicts among the previous as well as among affected communities, governments and jurisdictions, clients, other contractors, staff, and other stakeholders.

These multipliers point to the expertise—almost always experientially derived—ARM practitioners are required to apply in negotiating archaeological interests at the interface of client- and community-driven contexts (Altschul and Patterson 2010; Willems and van der Dries 2007). This negotiation almost uniformly consists of practitioners advancing an archaeological agenda (see Ferris and Welch, this volume) rather than seeking to balance the diversity of cultural resource values these regulatory regimes and external stakeholders may presume we are striving for. As such, most ARM is ready and able to harvest archaeological records, to accumulate objects and documentation accessible only to other archaeologists, and to advance scientific knowledge. ARM is seldom prepared or required to conserve and align nonarchaeological values and interests.

A vision of archaeology, explicitly including ARM, as one part of a broader CRM practice informed and inspired early visions of how to effectively conserve the archaeological record. Indeed, William Lipe's (1974) "A Conservation Model for American Archaeology" remains a vital conceptual and common-sense foundation for archaeological ethics and practice. Lipe's model includes disciplinary obligations to pursue conservation through (a) public education, (b) partnerships with local and descendant communities, (c) engagement in community and regional planning, (d) creation of parks and preserves, (e) proper curation of excavation records and collections, and (f) other efforts to boost the noncommodity values of the archaeological record. For Lipe (1974), the essential principle guiding archaeology to these worthy outcomes was to support mandated excavations in development contexts "only as a last resort," and discretionary (that is, academic) excavations "only when the data needs cannot be met from the available pool of sites requiring salvage" (Lipe 1974, 213, 1996).

In retrospect, Lipe's counsel appears Cassandra-like and overwhelmed by archaeology's growth and diversification over the last forty years. But that does not mean his vision for the broadly beneficial management of the archaeological record is no longer applicable. On the contrary, archaeologists have positioned the discipline both theoretically and politically to assist in the identification and optimization of the full spectrum of values embedded in cultural resources. More specifically, we think the potential for archaeology to effect meaningful change both within and beyond disciplinary boundaries will remain incomplete until archaeologists address intradisciplinary issues symptomatic of the extractive-consumptive paradigm underlying much of ARM and academic practice today. In the next section, we consider the consequences that linking the extractive-consumptive paradigm to land modification regimes is having for archaeology itself—the enemy that is us. We then explore sustainable design concepts as guides to transcending this extractive-consumptive paradigm, to reaffirming the conservation model for archaeology, to passing on to future generations a higher integrity and more diversely valued archaeological record, and to opening archaeology to greater participation in creating more sustainable societies.

Unanticipated Consequences of ARM's Success

ARM institutionalization has paved the way for unprecedented archaeological expansion and diversification. Growth has occurred in response to demands for professional services to facilitate compliance with heritage conservation and historic preservation statutes for land modification activities. Even without precise, region-specific data about how much of the archaeological record has been lost, either with or without systematic excavation, the trends are sobering. In the quarter century between 1982 and 2007, more than 16,723,553 square kilometers of "undeveloped" lands—encompassing everything from productive farmland to natural preserves, an area roughly the size of Illinois and New Jersey combined—was "developed," primarily through conversion to residential use (American Farmland Trust 2010). In Canada, where only about 0.5 percent of the land base is rated as prime farmland, more than 14,000 square kilometers were converted to residential use between 1971 and 2001 (Organic Agricultural Centre of Canada 2009). Losses of archaeological records are especially acute in and around metropolitan areas, often the same lands that attracted the preponderance of preindustrial settlement (e.g., Coleman and Williamson 1994). These impacts also fail to account for extensive resource extraction across the continent, including quarries, mining, forestry, and energy resource extraction, transportation, and refining. While substantial alterations to the landscapes that harbor archaeological records continue at elevated levels, capacities to preserve and protect lands and resources appear to be remaining level or declining.[1] A further irony is that, in the United States, the National Historic Preservation Act (NHPA) is more often triggered by land modification proposals located away from densely populated areas and extensive private land holdings, the rural zones where federal involvement is more pervasive. And although several provincial jurisdictions in Canada impose conservation requirements on private lands, the form of ARM nurtured in smaller municipal housing developments is often a race toward low bids and chronic whittling away at standards, at levels of documentation, and at the record itself (e.g., Ferris 2002, 2004; Williamson 2010). Although much more could be said about this broader consumption of land and the biosphere, the essential points are that both biophysical and sociocultural resources are being transformed; that the public benefits from these transformations, regionally and cumulatively, are untracked and uncertain; and that CRM and ARM increasingly prioritize the clearance of compliance requirements and the completion of land modifications rather than the creation and collectively beneficial mobilization of knowledge about cultural resources consumed in the name of "progress."

Institutional and industrial arrangements today embed ARM (and, thus, most of the archaeological profession by virtue of the overwhelming dominance of this form of practice) in commoditization initiatives. Archaeology's ranks, archaeologists' livelihoods, and archaeological repository collections have swelled because disciplinary leaders sounded public alarms regarding threats to archaeological records. As of 2013, no less than 75 percent of archaeological fieldwork worldwide is being done in ARM contexts. About 90 percent of all spending on archaeology in North America occurs via mandated ARM (Davis 2010, 194; see also ACRA 2013). These figures comport with Altschul and Patterson's (2010, Table 6) estimate that, for 2008, more than 80 percent of the 11,350 professional archaeologists in the United States worked in CRM and ARM contexts. The numbers for Canada outside of Quebec are similar (e.g., Ferris 2002; LaSalle and Hutchings 2012; Zorzin 2011).[2]

We think archaeology's unchecked growth imperils future prospects—that current ARM advancement of the extractive-consumptive paradigm is, in a word, unsustainable. Indeed, even as archaeology's extractive-consumptive paradigm reaches its zenith in terms of scale, it may have also reached its nadir in validity and viability. Although the conservation model remains a cornerstone of twenty-first century archaeological policy and ethics (Vitelli and Chanthaphonh 2006; Zimmerman, Vitelli, and Hollowell-Zimmer 2003), it is often difficult to discern in dominant practice. Even as archaeologists continue to advocate against external, unauthorized threats to the record, members of our profession often fail to recognize and advocate against those threats from within archaeological practice. Threats internal to archaeology include 1) lingering tendencies towards antiquarianism, especially preferences for ever more accumulation through excavation; 2) apparent incapacities to acknowledge, let alone grapple with, the global-scale curation crisis and degradation of amassed archaeological collections; 3) persistent divisions between ARM and academic practice, especially the lack of understanding that the bases for such divisions are largely irrelevant beyond the discipline; 4) workforce instability due to low and inconsistent wages in ARM and non-tenure-track academic jobs, both of which compromise quality of life and disciplinary commitments; 5) inconsistent, unprofessional, and commodity-oriented management of cultural resources and the consequences for practitioners' morale and job satisfaction; and 6) unrealized or lost collaborative opportunities with indigenous, descendant, local, and conservation communities in keeping with the conservation model.

Dominant ARM practice centers on exchanges of compliance with laws and regulations for a combination of money and exclusive, typically one-time-only, access to an archaeological record. In this mode, most archaeology amounts to little more than a minor cost of profit-driven land modification. Although many ARM practitioners retain heartfelt convictions that their knowledge and work are essential mediators between conservation and development, we think the convergence of legal, societal, personal, and disciplinary pressures in and on ARM has given rise to an actuality that, contrary to ethical coda, personal beliefs, and disciplinary aims, archaeologists now serve primarily as cogs in machines that overconsume and underdigest archaeological records. Our concerns with disconnects between ideal and actual practice are by no means limited to ARM. However, despite ongoing practical and conceptual innovations, as well as many examples of valiant efforts by ARM practitioners to operate independently from the extractive-consumptive juggernaut, ARM exists predominantly to enable and expand the reach of land modification.

In other words, most ARM fails to model the conservation model. Too many ARM research designs are out of synch with regional and theoretical developments. Too many contracts go to low bidders, notably those with underpaid and underqualified staff. Too many contracts encourage field methods that are rote and expeditious rather than context-sensitive. Too many seasoned practitioners are obliged by fierce competition among ARM firms to prioritize business development and report completions, leaving less time for direct participation in research or communicating results of findings. The same personnel, divorced from close connections with the fieldwork and analyses that attracted them to the discipline, often either "burn out" or bounce off salary ceilings. Too many collections of artifacts, samples, and field records are incompletely or inconsistently analyzed, entirely inaccessible, and not provided with appropriate physical and intellectual curation (Childs 1995; Childs and Sullivan 2004; Mullins 2013; Trimble and Marino 2003). Across most of North America the ARM "grey literature" remains difficult to access, use, or even learn about. This is due to either limited publication or, in some particularly lamentable cases, ARM client and practitioner determinations to retain control of research results as "commercially proprietary information." Financial support for follow-up analyses of excavated collections and publication of results in both research journals and outlets for nonarchaeologists is scarce, exacerbating the ARM-academic archaeology divide by limiting the availability and impact of ARM research results (Welch 2013). Finally, commitments by some archaeologists to cling to limited political power by insisting on the primacy of scientific values has hampered "natural" partnerships dedicated to site protection across academic and ARM practitioners, and among archaeologists and representatives of descendant and environmental communities. Each of these issues is attributable to imbalances between inflows of public and private ARM investments and outflows of bona fide public benefits. In sum, we question whether it is appropriate to prioritize scientific value in ARM and, more importantly, whether any values—aesthetic, economic, historic, societal, spiritual, or scientific—are accruing in proportion to the losses of archaeological records.

Applying Sustainability Principles to ARM

If there is good news amid these troubling trends it is the availability of sustainability principles and tools already proven useful in comparable domains of resource management. More often aspired to than achieved, sustainability is nonetheless applicable to conserving archaeological records in general and, more particularly, to building a discipline and business of archaeology that, by avoiding "irreversible commitments that constrain future generations" (Redman 2006), can improve intra- and extra-archaeological capacities to meet foreseeable future needs (see United Nations World Commission on Environment and Development 1987).

Intended to integrate practical reforms with more radical conceptual reorientations, sustainable design is grounded in understandings and preferences for global interdependence, environmental stewardship, social responsibility, and long-term economic viability (Clayton and Radcliffe 1996). Whether applied to facilities, institutions, organizations, or disciplines, sustainable design demands examinations of assumptions, preferences, and customs in terms of consequences for ecological and social systems at local, regional, and global scales. We found two sets of sustainable design concepts that hold promise for maximizing archaeological sustainability: the "Declaration of Interdependence for a Sustainable Future" (UIA/AIA 1993) and the "Principles of Sustainable Design" compiled by the U.S. National Park Service (1993).

We have integrated and adapted these suites of concepts into five hypothetical questions intended to inspire discussions about sustainability in archaeological policies, practices, and desired futures. In keeping with the radical mantra, "to change everything, start anywhere" (CrimethInc. 2012), we think it worth asking this question: What if archaeologists collectively committed to:

1. Considering the discipline and business of archaeology as subsidiaries of sociocultural and biophysical systems?
2. Prioritizing environmental and social sustainability in all decisions and actions?
3. Recognizing, assessing, and (where appropriate) interpreting archaeological records as reflections of previous quests for economic, social, and environmental sustainability?
4. Educating and learning from archaeological records, colleagues, clients, students, collaborators, and publics about the importance and application of sustainable design?
5. Expanding and enhancing methods and theories for *in situ* conservation and curation of archaeological records and elements thereof?

One pervasive archaeological assumption ripe for reconsideration in terms of sustainability is the widely accepted notion that the discipline and industry of archaeology are dependent upon intact archaeological records and archaeologists' access to these records for destructive excavations (see Lipe 1996). Treating archaeological records such as mineral ore bodies as finite and nonrenewable highlights the reality that there is no such thing as a sustainable consumptive use of archaeological records. Destruction at any level or rate will, given sufficient time, exhaust the resource. On the other hand, the nonrenewability assumption neglects the twin truths that living communities continuously create new archaeological records and simultaneously use existing records, along with other cultural resources, to craft contemporary meanings and values. This must not be mistaken for an argument favoring destructive use of any or all archaeological records; only a call for critical assessments of how archaeologists think and act in relation to other archaeological record shareholders.

Building upon the sustainable design questions and the possibility of renewability in archaeological records raises additional hypothetical questions: What if archaeologists recognized living communities, here in the present, as the quintessential cultural resources (that is, the wellsprings of culture, material and otherwise)? What if archaeologists acknowledged cultural resource shareholders, especially affiliated communities, as *de facto* resource managers and worked with them to set consensus management goals and to identify which elements of tangible cultural resources (i.e., not merely archaeological records) should be protected, which should be conservatively used, and which should be consumptively used or even ignored? (Welch, Riley, and Nixon 2009).

This realignment in priorities and values promises significant increases in the (a) political power of resource conservation coalitions; (b) scope and clientele of CRM; (c) range of innovative ARM practices and logics behind identifying, assessing, and mitigating harms to imperiled cultural resources; and (d) career satisfaction for CRM practitioners, especially through the addition of greater diversity and prospects for solidarity beyond disciplinary boundaries (see McGuire, this volume). Such shifts could reposition CRM and ARM as technical and facilitative leaders of broader communal values and preferences, blazing trails away from an extractive-consumptive model and toward an additive or servant culture of stewardship practice grounded in the conservation model (see Castañeda, this volume; McAnany, this volume; Ferris and Welch, this volume; See also Little and Zimmerman 2010).

Too ambitious? Utterly impractical? Maybe, but as Franklin D. Roosevelt (1946) said in 1934, "One thing is sure. We have to do something." Overconsumption and underdigestion of tangible cultural resources have placed archaeology on a collision course with disciplinary rhetoric and ethics. For those inclined toward more moderate-practical-reformist and less radical measures (for more on this distinction, see Castañeda, this volume; Clauss, this volume), our interpretation of Kloeckner's (2010) sustainability-focused scrutiny of hardrock mining provides six specific suggestions for boosting archaeological sustainability:

1. Think twice: Adopt an ARM variant of the precautionary approach (UNEP 1992) by placing the onus on the prospective destroyer of archaeological records to demonstrate that whatever harm is entailed by the proposed destruction will be counterbalanced by goods created.

2. Keep track: Account systematically, transparently, and cumulatively—beginning early in the project or program planning—for work completed, records consumed, goods produced, plans changed, mistakes made, and short- and long-term losses and enhancements in the values associated with affected archaeological records. It is especially easy to discount the cumulative impacts and unsustainability of ARM because governments and industries fail to keep tabs on the numbers of sites consumed, whether that consumption was accompanied by systematic study, whether the systematic study was published, and whether the publications have mattered—that is, whether the findings have contributed to or helped conserve aesthetic, economic, historical, societal, or spiritual values.

3. Watch your steps: Employ a life-cycle approach to tracking gains and losses in values associated with affected archaeological records through planning, implementation, and postimplementation project stages.
4. Just say "whoa!" Commit to making good decisions: If cumulative losses and impacts outbalance gains and benefits, reconsider project or program goals or plans. If a project or plan cannot be done without ethical compromises or unmitigated adverse effects to biophysical or sociocultural landscape elements, withdrawal may be the only professional option.
5. Close ranks: Boost oversight and limit access to archaeological records to archaeologists who continuously meet professional standards.
6. If you don't like the rules, change them: Amend legal, fiscal, and environmental policies to assure consistency with recommended practices and accepted ethical standards and other institutional arrangements, especially those grounded in the conservation model. Archaeologists have been effective lobbyists in the past and must continue to assert personal and professional interests in the protection and appropriate use of cultural resources.

Implementing these practical suggestions alone would narrow gaps between archaeology's aspirational policies and actual results. Taken together with the sustainable design principles, they provide a provisional framework for aligning existing assets and prevailing practices with disciplinary aspirations, policies, and ethics.

Sustaining a Nonrenewable Resource

One last hypothetical: What if one or several archaeological organizations adopted and acted strategically on a vision statement such as this: "Our professional ethics, training, and practices will create a more sustainable future"? Pondering archaeological participation in the increasingly urgent mandate to improve the sustainability of human ecosystems, Judge (2006, 107) wrote that if "archaeology can help define the proper relationship between humans and nature ... then we archaeologists will have paid our dues to society." Archaeologists have long promoted ourselves as gatherers and purveyors of wisdom and cautionary tales from the ancient past—discoverers of knowledge concerning how human communities have foundered by exceeding biophysical and sociopolitical parameters (Tainter 2006). Archaeologists constitute a reservoir of expertise pertinent to understanding and managing linked social and environmental systems across temporal and spatial dimensions (Hayashida 2005; Kirch 2005; van der Leeuw and Redman 2002). But except for the above-noted success in institutionalizing ARM practice, archaeologists have failed to meaningfully influence environmental policy (Nash 2011). Meanwhile, both the discipline and business of archaeology are operating without regard for obvious sustainability principles, the most apparent indicators of which are decimations of archaeological records and multiplications in curatorial burdens for excavated collections being passed on to future generations of both archaeologists and citizens.

Despite Nash's (2011) call on archaeologists to abandon the pretentious and thus far unfulfilled quest to help (re)build more sustainable societies, yielding is premature. Instead, we think archaeologists' failures to walk the talk of avoiding irrevocable resource commitments is one factor limiting our discipline's participation in broader conversations about what elements of biophysical and sociocultural heritage will be carried forward, and how to do so in a time of escalating global change. There will not likely be a better time than now for archaeologists to grasp that our discipline is a small but potent element of society, and society is a small but potent ecosystem subsidiary. We archaeologists have assigned ourselves majority shares of intellectual and management responsibilities for investigating and curating significant aspects of remote and underdocumented human and human-environment pasts. In asserting this leadership, archaeology has attracted and inspired significant public interest and support.

In these circumstances and with all these advantages and privileges, it would be a shame to squander archaeology's social license to operate, educate, and lead transformative thinking and acting. We encourage our colleagues to collaborate to move archaeology and public appreciation for archaeology beyond antiquarian fascinations with the oldest, rarest, and least known, and toward bold applications of accumulated knowledge, perspectives, and skills in pursuit of desired societal futures. We concur in the view that "[g]iven current concerns with restoration ecology, sustainable economies, and the role that indigenous knowledge can play in contemporary resource management, it is imperative that archaeologists get off the sidelines" (Lightfoot et al. 2013, 297). We aspire to an archaeology that places important roles in economic, land stewardship, and sociocultural processes. We think CRM is uniquely qualified and positioned to lead this pursuit, and in doing so to establish CRM as the primary dynamic loci in which archaeological research rubber hits the road of practical, social, political, and economic realities. This would vanquish residual notions of ARM as a sort of bastard stepchild of academic archaeology and reaffirm the pivotal role of the conservation model or its urgent and emergent successor: an archaeology of, by, and for sustainability and resilience.

―⟶∞∞⟵―

Considering Methods: Activism for Archaeologists: The An-Archaeologist Cookbook
John R. Welch

I suggest the time has come to harness a paradox. I think our notoriously reactionary disciplinary character distinguishes archaeologists as ready-made activists. Conservation-oriented perspectives and skill sets are invaluable additions, even to aggressively progressive activist discourse. Many archaeologists are experts at pushing the boundaries of the legal frameworks for environmental and cultural resource protection that are key issues in land modification and resource-extraction proposals. Most archaeologists have open minds about social and political formations, and how they can and do affect operational capacities and differential survivals of social groups. Many members of the public have positive regard for archaeologists, archaeological sites, and the prospect of learning from the past. This is important because these days, public opinion and associated politics, rather than moral principles or legal opinions, determine the outcomes of most activist campaigns.

Although archaeologists are not widely known as team players or joiners of causes beyond disciplinary boundaries, it is never too late to build new capacities and discover your inner activist. But where to begin? How do we get into the game? How about *The Anarchist Cookbook* (Powell 1971)? This hodgepodge of "recipes" for subversive action has been condemned by pretty much everyone: the FBI (Walker 2011), anarchists (CrimethInc. 2012), and even the author (Mieszkowski 2000). The only thing redemptive about this silly book is the title, which I have modified here to frame ten lessons from my experience (see Beach 2010). These double as a methodology for archaeological engagement with activism.

Taken together, the following principles offer archaeoactivists a framework for subverting dominant paradigms or just getting off the sidelines to make the world a little better:

1. Agree on campaign goal(s) and hold the focus. For example, an effort to save a place or archaeological site threatened by development may need to be deconstructed to identify the primary economic or political driver behind the threat, the legal basis that enables the threat, or the public or corporate decision-maker. Work "upstream" from the undesirable event or decision to maneuver the political, legal, or managerial flow around it.

2. Fight *for* something broadly desirable because it is often more satisfying and allows campaigners to set terms of reference and engagement. A campaign to save a beautiful and fascinating place is likely to be more effective than one framed primarily as a quest to stop a mine, road, or other change that brings benefits to others.

3. Insist on credibility and integrity in and among goals, methods, words, deeds, and so on. I once witnessed an otherwise solid campaign crumble because of a simple statistical error detected and publicized by the opposition. Nobody cares much about most campaign details until a mistake is exposed; from then on, that's all anybody seems to care about.

4. Build trust—the essential foundations for all relationships. Personal convictions, altruism, and lofty intentions are the coin of the activist realm and are among the proven bases for an effective campaign team. Leave the egotism and the profit- and status-driven motivations to the opposition. Use their hubris to crush them and showcase the virtue of opposition.

5. Build coalitions; eschew factions. Most campaigns require multiple partners; and campaigns involving cultural resources potentially entail, at a minimum, natural alliances among descendant or source communities, archaeologists, and environmentalists. Build and maintain allies by establishing common ground, leaving aside ancillary and past differences (refer to point 1). Insist on rigorously respectful interactions.

6. Commit to continuous critical review of goals, methods, capacities, and tactics. Feedback from all sources and campaign participants should be reviewed in terms of potentials to move the campaign forward. If feedback brings up a question that cannot be easily answered, a campaign improvement opportunity exists and should be addressed.

7. Craft resilience. The highest nail gets the hammer first. Altruists are often surprised by opposition intensity, sophistication (or blunt force), and persistence. Campaigns should prepare appropriate response plans, including lowering campaign profiles to absorb attacks without loss of core mission focus and operational capacities.

8. Follow your heart. The economic, political, and extra-campaign social benefits for activists are few and far between, so take satisfaction from the virtues of personal and campaign integrities, and successes large and small.

9. Be relentless, and better yet, victorious. At least for me, nothing spells success like an unequivocal defeat of a proposal for personal or corporate profit derived from the impairment or destruction of collectively owned biophysical or sociocultural heritage.

10. Celebrate your victories. Let the world know of your gratitude for the ascension of altruism and long-range thinking over greed and short-sighted pursuits of power.

I call on all archaeologists everywhere to step out of the shadows of past worlds, of academic limbo, and of fee-for-service thinking. Let our voices, deeply rooted in the sediments of yore, be heard in this world. Speak and act now on behalf of the places and traditions you know to be worthy bequests to the future!

NOTES

1. In recent years, governments such as Utah and Canada have used budget shortfalls as rationales for devolving public sector ARM capacities to project proponents and archaeologists (Kloor 2011; Lord 2012).

2. Similarly, more than half (54 percent) of the 13,130 professional members of the Geological Society of America (GSA) work in government or industry (http://www.geosociety.org/aboutus/documents/MbrDemographics.pdf); the more extraction-focused American Association of Petroleum Geologists has more than 30,000 members (http://www.aapg.org/member/insideaapg.cfm).

REFERENCES

Altschul, Jeffrey H., and Thomas C. Patterson. 2010. "Trends in Employment and Training in American Archaeology." In *Voices in American Archaeology,* edited by Wendy Ashmore, Dorothy Lippert, and Barbara J. Mills, 291–316. Washington, DC: Society for American Archaeology.

American Cultural Resources Association (ACRA). 2013. "Cultural Resources and Infrastructure in the United States," accessed June 10, 2013, http://acra-crm.org/associations/9221/files/ACRA%20Handout%20FINAL-revis4.pdf.

American Farmland Trust. 2010. "America Has Lost More than Twenty-Three Million Acres of Agricultural Land," accessed February 7, 2013, http://www.farmland.org/news/pressreleases/America-Has-Lost-23-million-acres-of-farmland.asp.

Atalay, Sonya. 2012. *Community-Based Archaeology: Research with, by, and for Indigenous and Local Communities.* Berkeley: University of California Press.

Austin Lounge Lizards. 1995. "Life is Hard, But Life is Hardest When You're Dumb." *Small Minds.* Austin, TX: Watermelon Records.

Australia ICOMOS. 1999. "The Burra Charter." Burwood: Australia ICOMOS, accessed January 20, 2013, http://australia.icomos.org/wp-content/uploads/BURRA_CHARTER.pdf.

Beach, Kaye. 2010. "10 Rules for Activists to Live By." AxXiom for Liberty, accessed May 20, 2013, http://axiomamuse.wordpress.com/2010/05/02/ten-rules-for-activists-to-live-by.

Burley, David V. 1994. "A Never Ending Story: Historical Developments in Canadian Archaeology and the Quest for Federal Heritage Legislation." *Canadian Journal of Archaeology* 18: 77-98.

Childs, S. Terry. 1995. "Curation Crisis: What's Being Done?" *Federal Archaeology* 7(4): 11–15.

Childs, S. Terry, and Lynne P. Sullivan. 2004. "Archaeological Stewardship: It's About Both Sites and Collections." In *Our Collective Responsibility: The Ethics and Practice of Archaeological Collections Stewardship,* edited by S. Terry Childs, 3–21. Washington, DC: Society for American Archaeology.

Clayton, Anthony M. H., and Nicholas J. Radcliffe. 1996. *Sustainability: A Systems Approach.* London: Earthscan.

Coleman, D., and R. Williamson. 1994. "Landscapes Past to Landscapes Future: Planning for Archaeological Resources." In *Great Lakes Archaeology and Paleoecology: Exploring Interdisciplinary Initiatives for the Nineties,* edited by R. MacDonald, 61–80. Ontario, Canada: Quaternary Sciences Institute, University of Waterloo.

CrimethInc. 2004. "Review: *Recipes for Disaster: An Anarchist Cookbook,*" accessed May 17, 2013, http://www.crimethinc.com/books/rfd.html.

———— 2012. "*Recipes for Disaster* Second Edition Arrives," accessed June 15, 2013, http://www.crimethinc.com/blog/2012/09/24/recipes-for-disaster-second-edition-arrives.

Davis, Hester A. 2010. "Heritage Resource Management in the United States." In *Cultural Heritage Management: A Global Perspective,* edited by Phyllis Mauch Messenger and George S. Smith, 188–198. Gainesville: University Press of Florida.

Doelle, William H. 2012. "What Is Preservation Archaeology?" *Archaeology Southwest Magazine* 26(1): 1–3.

Ferris, Neal. 1998. "'I Don't Think We're in Kansas Anymore . . . ': The Rise of the Archaeological Consulting Industry in Ontario." *Bringing Back the Past: Historical Perspectives on Canadian Archaeology*: 225–247.

————. 2000. "Current Issues in the Governance of Archaeology in Canada." *Canadian Journal of Archaeology* 24(2): 164–170.

————. 2002. "Where the Air Thins: The Rapid Rise of the Archaeological Consulting Industry in Ontario." *Revista de Arqueología Americana* 21: 53–88.

————. 2003. "Between Colonial and Indigenous Archaeologies: Legal and Extra-Legal Ownership of the Archaeological Past in North America." *Canadian Journal of Archaeology* 27: 154–190.

————. 2004. "Guess Who Sat Down to Dinner? Archaeology In Laws." In *An Upper Great Lakes Archaeological Odyssey: Essays in Honor of Charles E. Cleland,* edited by W. Lovis, 199–214. Detroit: Cranbrook Institute of Science, Wayne State University Press.

Hardesty, Donald, and Barbara Little. 2000. *Assessing Site Significance: A Guide for Archaeologists and Historians.* Lanham, MD: AltaMira Press.

Hayashida, Frances M. 2005. "Archaeology, Ecological History, and Conservation." *Annual Review of Anthropology* 34: 43–65.

International Union of Architects and American Institute of Architects (UIA/AIA). 1993. "Declaration of Interdependence for a Sustainable Future," accessed February 14, 2013, http://server.uia-architectes.org/texte/england/2aaf1.html.

Judge, W. James. 2006. "Conservation Archaeology and the Southwestern Anthropological Research Group." In *Tracking Ancient Footsteps: William D. Lipe's Contributions to Prehistory and Public Archaeology,* edited by R. G. Matson and Timothy A. Kohler, 97–108. Pullman: Washington State University Press.

King, Thomas F. 1998. "How the Archeologists Stole Culture: A Gap in American Environmental Impact Assessment and How to Fill it." *Environmental Impact Assessment Review* 18(2): 117–133.

————. 2000. *Federal Planning and Historic Places: The Section 106 Process.* Lanham, MD: AltaMira Press.

————. 2002. *Thinking about Cultural Resource Management: Essays from the Edge.* Lanham, MD: AltaMira Press.

————. 2008. *Cultural Resource Laws and Practice: An Introductory Guide.* 3rd ed. Lanham, MD: AltaMira Press.

————. 2009. *Our Unprotected Heritage: Whitewashing the Destruction of Our Cultural and Natural Environment.* Walnut Creek, CA: Left Coast Press.

————, ed. 2011. *A Companion to Cultural Resource Management.* Malden, MD: Wiley-Blackwell.

Kirch, Patrick V. 2005. "Archaeology and Global Change: The Holocene Record." *Annual Review of Environment and Resources* 30: 409–440.

Kloeckner, Jane. 2010. "Developing a Sustainable Hardrock Mining and Mineral Processing Industry: Environmental and Natural Resource Law for 21st Century People, Prosperity and the Planet." *Journal of Environmental Law and Litigation* 25: 123–188.

Kloor, Keith. 2011. "Firing of Utah Archaeologists Alarms Community." *Science Insider,* accessed February 13, 2013, http://news.sciencemag.org/scienceinsider/2011/06/firing-of-utah-archaeologists.html.

La Salle, Marina, and Rich Hutchings. 2012. "Commercial Archaeology in British Columbia." *The Midden* 44(2): 8–16.

Lee, Ronald F. 2006. "The Origins of the Antiquities Act." In *The Antiquities Act: A Century of American Archaeology, Historic Preservation and Nature Conservation,* edited by David

Harmon, Francis P. McManamon, and Dwight T. Pitcaithley, 15–34. Tucson: University of Arizona Press.

Lertzman, Kenneth P. 2009. "The Paradigm of Management, Management Systems, and Resource Stewardship." *Journal of Ethnobiology* 29(2): 339–358.

Lewin, Kurt Z. 1952. *Field Theory in Social Science: Selected Theoretical Papers,* edited by Dorwin Cartwright. London: Tavistock.

Lightfoot, Kent G., Rob Q. Cuthrell, Chuck J. Striplen, and Mark G. Hylkema. 2013. "Rethinking the Study of Landscape Management Practices Among Hunter-Gatherers in North America." *American Antiquity* 78(2): 285–301.

Lipe, William D. 1974. "A Conservation Model for American Archaeology." *The Kiva* 39(3–4): 213–245.

———. 1996. "In Defense of Digging: Archaeological Preservation as a Means, Not an End." *CRM* 19(7): 23–27.

Little, Barbara J., and Larry J. Zimmerman. 2010. "In the Public Interest: Creating a More Activist and Engaged Archaeology." In *Voices in American Archaeology,* edited by Wendy Ashmore, Dorothy Lippert, and Barbara J. Mills, 131–159. Washington, DC: Society for American Archaeology.

Lord, Ross. 2012. "Canada's Archaeologists Angry Over Budget Cuts." Canada Broadcasting Corporation (June 22, 2012), accessed February 13, 2013, http://www.globalnational. com/budget+blues/6442667014/story.html.

McGimsey, III, Charles R., and Hester A. Davis, eds. 1977. *The Management of Archeological Resources: The Airlie House Report.* Washington, DC: Society for American Archaeology.

———. 1984. "United States of America." In *Approaches to the Archaeological Heritage,* edited by Henry Cleere, 116–124. New York: Cambridge University Press.

McGuire, Randall H. 2008. *Archaeology as Political Action.* Berkeley: University of California Press.

Messenger, Phyllis Mauch, and George S. Smith, eds. 2010. *Cultural Heritage Management: A Global Perspective.* Gainesville: University Press of Florida.

Mieszkowski, Katharine. 2000 (September 18). "Blowing Up *The Anarchist Cookbook,*" accessed May 17, 2013, http://www.salon.com/2000/09/18/anarchy/.

Mullins, Paul. 2013 (May 28). "The Primal Fear: Historical Archaeology and De-Accessioning." President's Corner, Society for Historical Archaeology (May 28, 2013), accessed June 7, 2013, http://www.sha.org/blog/index.php/2013/05/the-primal-fear-historical-archaeology-and-de-accessioning/.

Nash, Stephen E. 2011. "Archaeology and Sustainability: Improbable Bedfellows." *Anthropology News* 52(7), accessed January 30, 2013, http://www.anthropology-news.org.

New South Wales Heritage Branch. 2009. "Assessing Significance for Historical Archaeological Sites and 'Relics.'" New South Wales, Australia Heritage Council, accessed January 30, 2013, http://www.environment.nsw.gov.au/resources/heritagebranch/heritage/ArchSignificance.pdf.

Nicholas, George P., J.R. Welch, and Eldon C. Yellowhorn. 2008 "Collaborative Encounters." In *Archaeological Practice: Engaging Descendant Communities,* edited by Chip Colwell-Chanthaphonh and T. J. Ferguson, pp. 273-298. Lanham, MD: AltaMira Press.

Organic Agricultural Centre of Canada. 2009. "Canada's Disappearing Farmland," accessed February 7, 2013, http://www.organicagcentre.ca/NewspaperArticles/na_disappearing_farmland_tb.asp.

Powell, William. 1971. *The Anarchist Cookbook*. New York: Lyle Stuart.

Redman, Charles. 2006. "Challenges of Implementing a University-Wide Sustainability Initiative: Lessons Being Learned from Arizona State." Tempe, AZ: Annual Meeting of the Association for the Advancement of Sustainability in Higher Education.

Roosevelt, Franklin Delano. 1946. "Personal Communication." In *The Roosevelt I Knew*, by Frances Perkins, Chapter 12, n.p. New York: Penguin Group.

Schiffer, M., and G. Gumerman, eds. 1977. *Conservation Archaeology: A Guide for Cultural Resource Management Studies*. New York: Academic Press.

Sebastian, Lynne. 2004. "Building a Graduate Curriculum for CRM Archaeology." *The SAA Archaeological Record* 6(5): 29, 35.Sebastian, Lynne, and William D. Lipe, eds. 2009. *Archaeology and Cultural Resource Management: Visions for the Future*. Santa Fe, NM: School for Advanced Research Press.

Smith, Laurajane. 2004. *Archaeological Theory and the Politics of Cultural Heritage*. London: Routledge.

———. 2006. *Uses of Heritage*. New York: Routledge.

Tainter, Joseph A. 2006. "Archaeology of Overshoot and Collapse." *Annual Review of Anthropology* 35: 59–74.

Trimble, Michael K., and Eugene A. Marino. 2003. "Archaeological Curation: An Ethical Imperative for the 21st Century." In *Ethical Issues in Archaeology*, edited by Larry J. Zimmerman, Karen D. Vitelli, and Julie Hollowell-Zimmer, 99–112. Lanham, MD: AltaMira Press.

United Nations World Commission on Environment and Development. 1987. "Report of the World Commission on Environment and Development: Our Common Future." Annex to United Nations General Assembly document A/42/427, accessed February 13, 2013, http://www.un-documents.net/wced-ocf.htm.

United Nations Environment Programme (UNEP). Conference on Environment and Development. 1992. "Rio Declaration on Environment and Development," accessed January 20, 2013, http://www.unep.org/Documents.multilingual/Default.asp?DocumentID=78&ArticleID=1163.

United States National Park Service. 1993. *Guiding Principles of Sustainable Design*. Denver, CO: Denver Service Center, National Park Service.

van der Leeuw, Sander, and Charles L. Redman. 2002. "Placing Archaeology at the Center of Socio-Natural Studies." *American Antiquity* 67(4): 597–605.

Vitelli, Karen D., and Chip Colwell-Chanthaphonh, eds. 2006. *Archaeological Ethics*, 2nd ed. Lanham, MD: AltaMira Press.

Walker, Jesse. 2011 (February 16). "The FBI on *The Anarchist Cookbook*," accessed May 17, 2013, http://reason.com/blog/2011/02/16/the-fbi-on-the-anarchist-cookb.

Welch, John R. 1997. "White Eyes' Lies and the Battle for Dzil Nchaa Si An." *American Indian Quarterly* 27(1): 75–109.

———. 2000. "The White Mountain Apache Tribe Heritage Program: Origins, Operations, and Challenges." In *Working Together: Native Americans and Archaeologists*, edited by Kurt E. Dongoske, Mark Aldenderfer, and Karen Doehner, 67–83. Washington, DC: Society for American Archaeology.

———. 2013. "Un-Silencing Kinishba." In *Kinishba Lost and Found: Mid-Century Excavations and Contemporary Perspectives*, edited by John R. Welch, 1–11. Arizona State Museum Archaeological Series 206. Tucson: University of Arizona.

Welch, John R., Mark K. Altaha, Karl A. Hoerig, and Ramon Riley. 2009. "Best Cultural Heritage Stewardship Practices by and for the White Mountain Apache Tribe." *Conservation and Management of Archaeological Sites* 11(2): 148–160.

Welch, John R., and Robert C. Brauchli. 2010. "'Subject to the Right of the Secretary of the Interior': The White Mountain Apache Reclamation of the Fort Apache and Theodore Roosevelt School Historic District." *Wicazo Sa Review* 25(1): 47–73.

Welch, John R., Dana Lepofsky, Megan Caldwell, Georgia Combes, and Craig Rust. 2011. "Treasure Bearers: Personal Foundations for Effective Leadership in Northern Coast Salish Heritage Stewardship." *Heritage and Society* 4(1): 83–114.

Welch, John R., Ramon Riley, and Michael V. Nixon. 2009. "Discretionary Desecration: American Indian Sacred Sites, Dzil Nchaa Si An (Mount Graham, Arizona), and Federal Agency Decision Making." *American Indian Culture and Research Journal* 33(4): 29–68.

Wheaton, Thomas. 2006. "Private Sector Archaeology: Part of the Problem or Part of the Solution?" In *Landscapes Under Pressure: Theory and Practice of Cultural Heritage Research and Preservation,* edited by L. Lonzy, 185–205. New York: Springer.

Willems, Willem, and Monique van der Dries, eds. 2007. *Quality Management in Archaeology.* Oxford, UK: Oxbow Books.

Williams, Sharon A. 1976. "Protection of the Canadian Cultural Heritage: The Cultural Property Export and Import Act." *Canadian Yearbook of International Law* 14: 292–306.

———. 1980. "Protection of Cultural Property: The Canadian Approach." *Arizona Law Review* 22: 737–751.

Williamson, Ronald F. 2010. "Planning for Ontario's Archaeological Past: Accomplishments and Continuing Challenges." *Revista de Arqueología Americana* 28: 7-45.

Zimmerman, Larry J., Karen D. Vitelli, and Julie Hollowell-Zimmer, eds. 2003. *Ethical Issues in Archaeology.* Lanham, MD: AltaMira Press.

Zorzin, Nicolas. 2011. "Contextualising Contract Archaeology in Quebec: Political-Economy and Economic Dependencies." *Archaeological Review from Cambridge* 26(1): 119–135.

Chapter 6

Working Class Archaeology

Randall H. McGuire

My grandfather, a union man, never understood why I wanted to be an archaeologist. He worked on a natural gas pipeline in northern Colorado. One afternoon in field school, he found me at the bottom of a deep stratigraphy trench, swinging a pick at the face of the ditch. A small shower of pebbles caused me to look up and see my grandfather. That next summer, I got my first paying job at the Arizona State Museum. My grandfather died without understanding my passion for archaeology. But he accepted it as honest work that would callous my hands and as a job that would earn me a living.

I shared my grandfather's appreciation of honest work. Archaeology's joining of intellectual and physical labor attracted me. Classes fulfilled my love of learning and of books. But, I also appreciated the camaraderie of field work and the physical and emotional feeling of well-being, material accomplishment, and deserved rest after a day of excavation.

My archaeology began as the heady days of the 1960s came to a close with protestors marching in the streets. My experiences during the Vietnam War led me to join the antiwar movement and to radical politics. I never took a course in radical theory, but rather learned my Marxism in the streets. Protestors also came into our labs and field sites. In 1972, American Indian Movement activists walked into an osteology laboratory at Colorado State University and demanded the return of a burial that I had excavated in field school the summer before.

When I finished my PhD, Ronald Reagan lived in the White House. Activism had become something I used to do in the streets and archaeology something I did in the university. At Binghamton University, I joined a community of radical scholars that helped me entwine my politics and my scholarship. Beyond Binghamton, I became involved with archaeologists, including Meg Conkey, Ian Hodder, Mark Leone, Robert Paynter and Martin

Transforming Archaeology: Activist Practices and Prospects, edited by Sonya Atalay, Lee Rains Clauss, Randall H. McGuire, and John R. Welch, 115–131. © 2014 Left Coast Press, Inc. All rights reserved.

Wobst, who were creating critical archaeologies. Indigenous activists Cecil Antone and Jan Hammil asked me to join in the struggle for repatriation. Along with Larry Zimmerman and others, I took up this struggle. We organized sessions and invited indigenous people to speak with archaeologists at the meetings of the Society for American Archaeology, the American Anthropological Association and the World Archaeology Congress. We also advocated within these associations for repatriation.

In 1990, NAGPRA made repatriation a reality, but did not immediately transform Native Americans and archaeologists. Indigenous archaeology would come later. Dean Saitta, Philip Duke, and I did not know how to do an activist archaeology of Native America in a context of colonialism, cultural difference, and exploitation. So we took up a new fight in support of workers' rights. Strikes usually leave little material evidence for archaeologists, but the burning of the strikers' tent camp during the Ludlow Massacre created an archaeological site. My grandfather had never understood my love of archaeology because archaeology had no relevance in his life. Now I had found a project that a good union man could relate to.

⸙

> Solidarity is not a matter of sentiment but a fact, cold and impassive as the granite foundations of a skyscraper. If the basic elements, identity of interest, clarity of vision, honesty of intent, and oneness of purpose, or any of these is lacking, all sentimental pleas for solidarity, and all other efforts to achieve it will be barren of results.
>
> —*Eugene V. Debs (1914, 534)*

My book, *Archaeology as Political Action* (McGuire 2008), argues that the intellectual tools for an activist, working class archaeology are praxis, craft, and class. I wield these tools as an archaeologist, as a scholar, and as a member of the United University Professions of New York State (AFL-CIO). My contract with the University of California Press stipulated that the book would be produced in a union shop. In the acknowledgment to the book, I thanked my union brothers and sisters of Graphics Communications International Union Local 898M, Binghamton, New York for the craft that they put into manufacturing the book. I insisted that the union bug of local 898M be displayed on the last page of the book. These were acts of solidarity (Figure 6.1). As Eugene Debs (1914) argued, class-based activism depends upon solidarity grounded in an identity of interest, clarity of vision, honesty of intent, and oneness of purpose. Such solidarity and activism are increasingly important in the contemporary world as concerted attacks from the right have eroded workers' rights and union membership (Durrenberger 2006; Fletcher 2012). *Archaeology as Political Action* was one of the last books produced by members of local 898M because the Maple-Vail Book Manufacturing Group closed down the Binghamton plant in October 2009.

In southern Colorado, the historical archaeology of the 1913–1914 Colorado Coal Field War offered us a stage for praxis and labor activism (Larkin and McGuire

Figure 6.1   Solidarity Banner at Ludlow Memorial Service. (Photo by Randall McGuire)

2009; Saitta 2007). It gave us a platform to build what Lee Clauss (this volume) has called transformative archaeology. Here, archaeologists of the Ludlow Collective joined in solidarity with unionized workers and studied class warfare to participate in modern day class struggle. In 1914, Colorado National Guard troops engaged in a pitched battle with striking coal miners at Ludlow, Colorado. The Guard fired two machine guns into a tent colony of strikers and their families, killing twenty of the camp's inhabitants. Two women and ten children died in a cellar beneath a burning tent, and another boy died with a National Guard bullet in his brain. Enraged by these events, the strikers launched a 10-day class war, torching company towns, dynamiting mines, and killing National Guard troops and company men. Finally, Federal troops appeared on the scene and restored order. In 1918, the United Mine Workers of America (UMW) purchased the site of the massacre and built a monument to the dead. Since then, the UMW has held an annual memorial service at the monument. We have done excavations at the site of the Ludlow Massacre and at the contemporary company town of Berwind. Our project has built archaeological praxis in collaboration and solidarity with the UMW. Our efforts address a variety of communities that include archaeologists, educators, and the children and grandchildren of the strikers. We address these audiences to engage in the broader discourses and practices about labor and labor rights in the United States. We primarily, however, serve the interests of the descendant community: unionized workers in southern Colorado. Our collaboration created a working class archaeology that differs from the tradition of archaeology as middle-class practice. Our archaeology joins working families in their struggle to hold back the erosion of their rights and dignity.

Building Collaboration

T. J. Ferguson (this volume) asks who invites and sanctions archaeologists to be advocates. In the mid-1990s, Phil Duke, Dean Saitta, and I planned the Archaeology of the Colorado Coal Field War Project as an activist archaeology in support of labor organization and working class rights. We knew that it needed to be a collaborative effort that involved us, the UMW, and unionized workers in southern Colorado. To that end, we spent nearly 2 years meeting people in the UMW at the national, regional, and local level to build support for our efforts and to design a plan for research. We learned much in the process of building collaboration, and two incidents were particularly instructive. They showed us that we should make no *a priori* presumptions about the utility of archaeology in contemporary life, and that our collaborators would look for that utility in terms of the relevance of our research for their struggle (Pyburn, this volume).

In 1996, Phil and Dean visited the UMW local in Trinidad. They arrived at a bad time: The Montana Power Company had just closed the last operating coal mine in southern Colorado. After hearing our proposal for archaeological field work at the Ludlow Memorial site, one newly unemployed coal miner told the two archaeologists that "all you need to know about Ludlow can be summed up in three words: they got fucked." The deep alienation and even hostility apparent in this statement revealed a class antagonism that rejected our intellectualization of the obvious.

In the same year, Dean and I visited the regional office of the UMW in Denver, Colorado. There we carefully explained our goals for the research and what impacts our excavations would have on the memorial grounds. A union professional listened attentively to what we had to say. After hearing us out, he said that "you have to understand that Ludlow is sacred ground to the UMW and there is one question that I have to ask you before we can approve you working there. Are you Republicans?" We paused, somewhat taken aback by the question, and then I said, "No, we are not Republicans; we are socialists." To which he replied, "Fine, as long as you are not Republicans." This interchange made it very clear that our project would be on sacred and very political ground where the union welcomed us only if our political agenda benefited the UMW.

Sonya Atalay (this volume) challenges archaeologists to use our theories and methods to address contemporary human issues. She maintains that an activist archaeology "matters to both the archaeologist and those they are working with; it aims to improve lives, and is often research they help define." The UMW made

Figure 6.2   Cecil Roberts, President of the UMW, discussing our exhibit with union members at the Ludlow memorial service. (Photo by Randall McGuire)

it clear to us from the beginning that our work mattered to them and that they would have a hand in defining it (Figure 6.2).

Praxis and Craft

Quetzil E. Castañeda (this volume) challenges us to examine the theory that we bring to a transformative archaeology. My colleagues, Phil Duke and Dean Saitta (2009), have argued that an activist, emancipatory, working class archaeology should not advance a hegemonic theory, but instead engage in a pragmatic epistemology. Such an epistemology entails a commitment to the struggles of other human beings rather than to polemics. A pragmatic perspective does not emphasize the fine points or elegance of theory, but rather what kind of action archaeology leads to in the real world. A theory of praxis, craft, and class has guided my archaeological activism and my attempts to do an archaeology that matters. I have found this theory a good guide, but others have followed different guides on different trails to effective activism. Praxis has no relevance or meaning in the abstract. It is only significant in its application. As Frederick Engels (1907, xv) noted, "The proof of the pudding is in the eating."

"Praxis" refers to the distinctively human capacity to consciously and creatively construct and change both the world and us (McGuire 2008, 38–42). The minimal definition of praxis is theoretically informed action. To engage in praxis, people must entertain concepts of possibility and change. Praxis becomes emancipatory when it advances the interests of the marginalized and the oppressed against the interests of the dominant. Praxis implies a process of gaining knowledge of the world, critiquing the world, and taking action to change the world. Praxis entails a complex dialectic between its three parts. Action without knowledge risks errors, failure, folly, and pernicious consequences. Yet, people make knowledge in social, cultural, and political contexts that effect and affect its creation, and we cannot know the world apart from this context. Through self-reflection or critique, people can evaluate what knowledge is worth creating; the fit of knowledge to our observations about the world; and the effects of social, cultural, and political forces on the making of that knowledge. Action flows from knowledge and critique, and action transforms the world, thus requiring continued knowledge creation and critique.

All archaeologists contribute to praxis, but few have engaged in activism. The vast majority of our colleagues seek to gain knowledge of the world, but often without critical reflection on the political content or importance of that knowledge. Critical and post-processual archaeologies argue that a dialogue between politically situated actors produces knowledge and seeks to understand that dialogue (Castañeda, this volume; Hodder 1999; Meskell and Preucel 2004). They usually embody a critique of the powerful and a desire to advocate for subaltern peoples. They engage in what Clauss (this volume) calls an internal activism. These archaeologies situate themselves in the academy where they seek to produce more sophisticated and analytically complex ways to understand the construction of knowledge. They focus on cultural representation as a dynamic political product that reflects the subject position of the scholar (Castañeda, this volume). At the extreme, authors advocate a radical multivocality that empowers all voices to speak, but leaves no truth that we can speak to power (Conklin 2003; McGuire 2008, 60–63).

Because activism functions in both academic and political worlds, it is fraught with contradictions, paradoxes, and tensions that do not exist in either empirical research or critique (Hale 2006). Activism does not fit neatly or comfortably with the usual goals of academic research or of cultural resource management (CRM) (Clauss, this volume; Ferris and Welch, this volume; Stottman, this volume; Welch and Ferris, this volume). Activist archaeologists have dual loyalties to both the academy and to the communities whose struggles they assist. The intellectual emphasis on innovation and the creation of knowledge contrasts with political struggles' demand for pragmatic and practical results. The criteria for evaluation differ in both contexts. Political struggles seek closure and resolution, whereas the academy rewards innovation and a constant redefinition of knowledge. Current theory in archaeology stresses the construction of identities and rejects essentialism; whereas in political struggle, people usually seek solidarity in essentialized identities. This leads some activists to embrace a notion of strategic essentialism that recognizes both the constructed nature of identity and the practical role of identity in political struggle (Clifford 1988, 2004; Gallivan et al. 2011). Activists also face challenges that post-processual critics do not. After all, by its very nature politics involves compromises that may be compromising to both the actors and researchers. How do activists transcend the simple sentimentality of doing good to decide whose interest to serve and what change to struggle for (Little 2010)? What do activists do when their archaeology does not support the political agenda to which they have committed themselves?

Intellectual activism is not just the application of science to struggle. It is instead a complex dialogue or dialectic between the academic and the political (Collins 2012). As Charles Hale (2006, 115) and Ferguson (this volume) note, scholarly activism straddles two intellectual worlds. Activists engage in cultural critique and must legitimate their knowledge in an academic setting at the same time that they invoke objective knowledge to serve political struggles. This requires activists to embrace the contradictions that the people they serve confront. This is not a comfortable or necessarily coherent position. This uneasy perspective may, however, lead to profoundly different knowledge and understandings than empiricism or critique.

Michael Shanks and I (Shanks and McGuire 1996) have argued that archaeology should be a craft that combats alienation by unifying hearts, hands, and minds. As a craft, archaeology entails a practice with a range of endeavors from the technical to the interpretative, and from the practical to the creative. As a craft, archaeology can be used to advance the interests of many communities. Archaeologists may interact with communities in many different ways, but collaboration is the surest route to effective activism. Collaboration requires cooperating social groups to assimilate their goals, interests, and practices in a dialogue that advances the interests of all groups involved in the collaboration (McAnany, this volume; Pyburn, this volume). As praxis, collaboration unifies knowledge, critique, and action to transform archaeologists' practice and the communities we work with. George Nicholas's (this volume) Indigenous Archaeology in British Columbia gives us an excellent example of this process. Archaeologists who enter into such a dialogue must give up some of their privilege. This authority should not be the privilege that comes from our craft (Atalay, this volume). If we do this, we cannot make a meaningful contribution to praxis. If we simply speak as the propagandists for political interests, why should anyone believe us? More importantly why should we believe ourselves? Rather, we should give up the programmatic privilege to exclusively define the questions, substance, and interpretations of our research. We also must politically position ourselves in support of the community(ies) that we serve. If we collaborate with the UMW, we cannot be Republicans.

Class

Class and class relations permeate all aspects of capitalist society, and as a part of that society, archaeology embodies these relations. It has also participated in the ideological myth that denies the importance of class in the United States (Durrenberger

2006). In an article in the Association of American University Professors' (AAUP) journal *Academe,* the archaeologist Michael Shott (2006) makes the point that the vast majority of archaeologists come from the middle and upper classes and they are oblivious to class issues. "Class is the whale in the living room whose stinking carcass polite academic society politely ignores" (2006).

Archaeology has typically served middle class interests. By middle class, I do not mean middle income but rather a structural position in contemporary class relations. In modern capitalism, the middle class are those individuals, such as managers, administrators, and professionals, who stand between the owners (or controllers) of the means of production, and the workers who do the labor of production. The work of the middle class is by and large intellectual labor, the application of formal knowledge or principles, commonly to tasks that working class individuals execute. Archaeology is part of the intellectual apparatus (things such as schools, books, magazines, organizations, and arts) that produces the symbolic capital (things such as esoteric knowledge, shared experience, certification, and social skills) that individuals need to be part of the middle class. Because it is set in the middle class, archaeology attracts primarily a middle class following and often does not appeal to working class audiences.

The Trinidad miner's exclamation that all we needed to understand about Ludlow was that "They got fucked" reflects a basic antagonism between the working and middle classes. Middle class education separates learning and doing. Middle class ideology puts a high value on the intellectual apparatus of capitalism, especially educational institutions, both because the middle class reproduces itself through this apparatus and because much of the class finds employment in it. Working class ideology tends to resent this apparatus as elitist, both because it hinders their own class mobility and because in the workplace their experience and skill are usually subservient to formal knowledge.

Castañeda (this volume) challenges us to take seriously the personal histories that bring us to activism and class-based notions of knowledge form part of my history. I was a studious child. My grandfather, who was a union worker on a gas line, and my uncle, who worked in a unionized cement plant, frequently admonished me not to elevate "book learning" above practical knowledge. They peppered dinnertime with stories of how a college-educated supervisor or engineer had directed them to do something by the book when their practical knowledge told them otherwise. In the stories, book learning always led to a bad end that their hands-on know-how would have prevented. Middle class individuals tend to value book learning, in contrast with the working class appreciation for knowledge based on experience (Braverman 1974, McGuire 2008, 102–104).

The dominance of middle class interests and ideologies in archaeology encourages archaeologists to see the middle class perspective as universal and to disdain other class interests and perceptions of the past (Jancius 2006; Shott 2006). Most archaeologists see their audience as broad and diverse. The limited studies that have been done of the constituency for archaeology suggest that this is not the case;

in fact, the middle class forms the primary audience for archaeology (for a review, see McGuire 2008, 106–108). The programs that archaeologists have developed to educate the public—exhibits, site tours, magazines, classes, and pamphlets—appeal more to middle class individuals who look to books and authorities for knowledge, and less to working class people who stress experience and practical know-how (Lareau 2003; Leonhardt 2005).

What Can Archaeology Do?

What then can an archaeology transformed by activism do to participate in the struggle for labor organization and working class rights? At Ludlow, we have sought to educate archaeology's traditional middle class constituency on how workers won their rights and to help unionized working families build solidarity for labor's struggle. In the first case, we embraced already-established educational methods, whereas solidarity building involves a more radical praxis.

In Wisconsin, the Republican governor and legislator of that state have stripped public employees of the right to collective bargaining. Even the traditional union stronghold of Michigan has recently become a right to work state. These acts have intensified current debates about the relevance of unions in the United States today (Fletcher 2012). The UMW had good reason to make sure that we were not Republicans. They embraced our project because we contributed to raising public awareness of the importance of unions. To this end, we developed interpretive signage at the site of the massacre, wrote a labor history curriculum for Colorado middle- and high schools, assembled a history trunk on the massacre to tour Denver schools, organized two teacher training institutes on the strike and massacre, and used the discoveries of our excavations to put the events of 1914 in the news again (CCFWP 2000; Duke and Saitta 2009; Larkin and McGuire 2009).

Our core message was simple: workers won their rights with blood. Capitalists did not freely give workers the rights that many take for granted today, such as the 40-hour week, respect in the workplace, union representation, health and retirement benefits, and a safe workplace. Instead, working people bought these rights with their lives and the lives of their children. The contemporary importance of this message is simple: Because capitalists did not freely give these rights and because workers won them only through great sacrifice, we must continue to struggle to keep them. Today, workers are losing this struggle (Fletcher 2012).

U.S. Department of Labor (2013) statistics reveal what workers are losing. As of 2012, only 11.3 percent of workers belonged to unions, down by 53 percent from 1973, when 24 percent of American workers belonged to unions. It is not a coincidence that between 1973 and 2011 real working class wages in the United States fell by 31 percent. Hundreds of thousands of U.S. workers share the experience of the unionized miners who lost their jobs at the Allen Mine in southern Colorado in 1996 and the unionized printers who lost their jobs at the Maple-Vail plant in

Binghamton in 2009. In addition, federal legislation passed in the last decade has seriously hampered the ability of unions to organize workers; and state governments in many states, including Wisconsin, Iowa, Indiana, and Ohio, seek to strip public workers of the right to collective bargaining (Fletcher 2012).

As the miner's comment "they got fucked" reveals, we do not need to educate unionized workers in southern Colorado about the horrible price that working families paid at Ludlow. Contrary to many discussions of archaeology and education, we do not need to interest working families in this past. It is a history already known and relevant to them. We can, however, use archaeology to struggle with working families to perpetuate knowledge, to construct meaningful histories for their communities, and to help build solidarity in labor's struggle. We do this by letting them set the agenda ("no Republicans") and by speaking to their experience—in a language that they can understand, in contexts that they inhabit, using means of communication familiar to them.

Many with right-wing interests in the United States want to forget or destroy the memory of the sacrifices that working families made for the rights we enjoy as workers today (Fletcher 2012). Labor's struggle occurs in the remembrance and forgetting of history, just as it does in courtrooms, on shop floors, and walking picket lines. Numerous people in southern Colorado told us that the UMW should let go of Ludlow and that we all should forget what happened there. Arguments against unions in the contemporary economy argue that laws now protect workers' rights and that unions should be forgotten with the past. Sometimes this forgetting takes a material turn. On May 3, 2003, someone used a sledgehammer to decapitate the granite miner and his wife on the Ludlow monument (Figure 6.3). For working families in southern Colorado, the symbolic violence of the beheadings summoned forth the real violence of the massacre of women and children at Ludlow (Saitta 2004). Appeals went out to union locals around the country, and in solidarity they donated funds to restore the monument (Figure 6.4).

We shared the remembrance of the sacrifices that working families made with the UMW (Duke and Saitta 2009). From 1996 to 2009, we made presentations on our research at the annual Ludlow memorial service and we are currently planning participation in memorials to celebrate the 100-year anniversary of the massacre. We developed a traveling exhibit that was sent to union halls around the country. The *United Mine Workers Journal* (UMW 1999) reported on our work and we published in an AFL-CIO–supported, popular, labor history journal (Walker 2000). We built a website that both the UMW and the AFL-CIO linked to their websites (CCFWP 2000). In 1998, when steelworkers from locals 2102 and 3267 in Pueblo, Colorado walked out to stop forced overtime, they made Ludlow a symbol of their struggle. We addressed strike rallies to reinforce the memory of Ludlow and attended union dinners in the steelworkers hall in Pueblo. They won their strike in 2004. At one memorial service, Yolanda Romero, the wife of a miner and then-president of the local union's women's auxiliary, commented on our work. She noted that the passing of the participants in the strike had severed the personal connections

Figure 6.3 The vandalized memorial to the Ludlow dead, 2003. (Photo by Randall McGuire)

Figure 6.4 The restored memorial to the Ludlow dead, 2005. (Photo by Randall McGuire)

Figure 6.5 Doll's head from a burned tent at the Ludlow Massacre site.
(Photo by Randall McGuire)

to the events and reduced them to the dry stuff of books. She found that our work remade that connection as we allowed her to touch the things that the strikers had held and to follow the path of the massacre on the ground (Figure 6.5). All these actions remember Ludlow.

Solidarity lies at the core of these actions. As Eugene Debs (1914, 534) noted, solidarity springs from "an identity of interest, clarity of vision, honesty of intent, and oneness of purpose." Remembering can lead to shared identity as working people see their contemporary interests and struggles as a continuation of the struggle at Ludlow (UMW 1999). Our public programs and support for the steelworkers' strike engaged us in shared experiences with working families that revealed to them the honesty of our intent. Through these experiences, we discovered common interests, developed a clear vision for action, and defined a shared purpose. Our actions built solidarity.

Solidarity is a unity of interests, purposes, or sympathies among members of a group. It produces a fellowship of responsibilities and interests. Building, maintaining, and advancing solidarity, especially in the context of practical politics, often require compromise and the putting aside of conflicting identities, interests, or goals. Unionized labor in southern Colorado tends to be highly patriotic, and coal miners often blame environmentalists for the decline in U.S. coal mining. Avid patriotism made some members of our collective uncomfortable. They came to understand, however, that it is primarily working people who join the military and die for our country. This patriotism did not come from right-wing politics but rather from the experience and sacrifice of fathers, mothers, brothers, sisters, sons, and daughters. The UMW consistently supports programs and legislation that would increase coal usage, principally in energy production. Archaeologists tend to be avid environmentalists, and members of the project often engaged in polite debate with union members over coal-fired energy. These discussions usually ended with an agreement to disagree, but we have found that solidarity with the UMW means that we must minimally not act in ways that compromise their interests.

I am reminded of an incident that occurred a few years ago at my university. A good friend, a paragon of the left on my campus and an officer in the Graduate Student Employee Union, approached me to sign a petition. The petition called for ending the university's use of coal to fire the campus power plant. He was quite surprised when I told him that I could not sign. I explained that I worked with coal miners. My research and collaboration with them has advanced my career. Despite the strong ecological reservations that I have about burning coal, I could not put my name on a petition calling for actions that would cost coal miners jobs.

Self-Reflection

Solidarity does not, however, mean that archaeologists should abandon our craft or our careful analytical evaluation of ourselves and the communities we work with. We cannot abandon our responsibility to "speak truth to power" (Conklin 2003), nor can an emancipatory archaeology ignore oppression by or within the communities that we collaborate with. We should constantly reflect on how these projects know the world and on the political goals that our work serves.

One of the most fascinating things about the Ludlow Project has been the stories. Even as the generations that experienced the massacre have passed away, family stories still link the people of southern Colorado to the 1913–1914 strike. Individuals have approached us in the field, at memorial services, and on the streets of Trinidad to generously share these stories with us. Some of the stories we cannot believe.

Many people have told us that the National Guard killed far more than 20 people at Ludlow. They firmly believe that the troops excavated a large trench in the middle of the tent colony and buried hundreds of bodies in it. Our tests, excavations, and analyses of photographs clearly show that no such trench existed within the Ludlow tent camp. We have applied our craft to the story, but our craft does not validate it. Some of our collaborators accepted our rebuttal of this story, whereas others simply took it as proof that the National Guard dug the mass grave somewhere else.

One of the women who died in the death pit at Ludlow was pregnant. Union people in contemporary southern Colorado widely believe that a National Guard soldier ripped open her belly and impaled the fetus on his bayonet. Our research does not support this story. Records of the armament issued to the Guard do not include bayonets, and in none of hundreds of photos do troops appear with bayonets. No contemporary accounts mention the incident. More conclusively, the county coroner performed an autopsy on the dead from the pit with a union representative present. The autopsy report explicitly states that none of the bodies from the pit bore wounds. British propaganda at the beginning of World War I (1914) spread tales of German soldier bayoneting pregnant Belgian women and ripping their fetuses out with the blade. We believe that people in southern Colorado heard this tales and then transferred it to the Ludlow Massacre.

Unions are human institutions and as such they can never be more than their members and leaders make them to be. They are not inherently just, noble, or equitable. I am proud to be a member of my union and the AFL-CIO and to be collaborating with the United Mine Workers. There have been other moments of history when I could not have said nor done these things. People may corrupt and weld unions as instruments of oppression as well as emancipation. We need to know this history, too. We should remember that on December 31, 1969, three hit men hired by UMW President W.A. Boyle entered the home of his rival, Joseph Yablonski. They killed Yablonski, his wife Margaret, and their 25-year-old daughter Charlotte as they slept. These events led to the formation of the Miners for Democracy Movement that brought democratic reform to the UMW. These reforms in the UMW were part of the larger movement for democratic unionism that transformed the labor movement at the end of the twentieth century. Maintaining democratic, inclusive unionism also requires struggle. Our praxis should contribute to the maintenance and advancement of democracy and inclusiveness for workers both without and within the union movement.

Effective activism requires a long-term commitment to the people and causes we work with and for. Our collaborators will question our honesty of intent if our support for their struggle ends with the publication of our book. Engaging in the struggle primarily to get our academic prizes demonstrates a lack of shared interest and common purpose with the communities we work with. As Patricia McAnany (this volume) notes, long-term commitments, by their very nature, bridge private and professional lives. A long-term commitment to activism should also lead scholars to assist in community interests beyond the craft of archaeology, archaeological questions, and the archaeologist's needs. In the United States today, Republicans have launched the most sustained and effective attack on workers' rights and unionism since the early decades of the twentieth century (Fletcher 2012; Meyerson 2011). Those of us who believe in these things need to fight this attack not only with trowels and whiskbrooms but also with a sustained commitment and political action at the local and national level. As Castañeda (this volume) urges us, we also need to critically reflect on our own complacency and place in these struggles.

I agree with Shott (2006) that the professoriate can be oblivious to class issues in their own lives. The turn of the twenty-first century has witnessed the creation of a proletariat of teaching assistants, adjuncts, and visiting faculty in the academe (McGuire and Walker 2008). Many of us with tenured or tenure track positions benefit and have actively aided in this creation. In contract archaeology, a similar proletarization has occurred with field techs and migrant project directors. An activist commitment to labor organization and workers' rights should include our own houses.

—∞—

Considering Methods: Picking Your Fight

Social activism involves more than just protesting or engaging in cultural critique. It is proactively organized work that seeks to improve peoples' welfare, to counterbalance perversion, to produce antidotes to human suffering, and to enhance human rights. A passion for reform and to transform the world drives this work. All social activists face the issue of how to source their passion and pick their fight. The fight needs be about something that you care about, something that is needed in the world, and something that you can affect. The fight should also have real benefit for people. The activist, however, must never make assumptions about what people need and want but rather enter into collaborative relationships that allow the communities we work with to define their own interests. As archaeological activists, we should pick a fight where we can effectively wield our craft. The archaeology of the Colorado Coal Field War of 1913–1914 project illustrates how activist-minded archaeologists may pick their fight.

"Never doubt that a small group of thoughtful committed people can change the world; indeed, it's the only thing that ever has." This quote, frequently attributed to Margaret Mead, makes a powerful case for activism (Bowman-Kruhm 2011, 176). Both the academe and cultural resource management, however, do not reward archaeologists for changing the world. Thus, the motivation for an activist archaeology must come from your own passion, and passion springs from something that you care deeply about. Labor rights and the Ludlow Massacre interested me because of my own working class roots, including ancestors involved in the strike and the desire to do archaeology that would be of relevance to my family. Union members easily related to my family background, my motivations, and my status as a union member.

Furthermore, understand that activism is pointless unless it addresses a needed change. The activist should consider both the need and the efficacy of activities to affect that need. Corporate interests are eroding workers' rights and attacking unions. These attacks spring from a monstrous lie: that politicians and corporations gave labor benefits and that workers no longer need unions. Our work at the Ludlow Massacre spoke truth to power, workers won their rights with blood. We communicated this truth to tourists and educators. This truth helped build solidarity among union members who visited us and interacted with us at memorial services.

The Ludlow Massacre created the perfect archaeological site: a short-term occupation destroyed by fire. Unlike most strikes and labor struggles, it left us a material record. We studied this record both to learn about the mundane lives of early twentieth-century working families and because our research made those lives real to modern working families. In 2003, I presented our research to striking steelworkers and their families in Pueblo, Colorado. Afterward, steelworkers shook my hand and thanked us for our efforts. Some of them gave me money, tens and twenties, to continue our research. I tried to give it back, but they would not take it.

Much of the literature in archaeology encourages us to present our data and interpretations to publics. It charges archaeologists to identify research questions, investigate these questions, and then present interpretations to the public. A transformative archaeology, however, requires that we do not assume what people need or want. Instead, we need an active process of collaboration that defines how our activism can meet their needs and wants. Collaboration implies a process whereby participating groups assimilate their goals, interests, and practices in a dialogue that advances the interests of all people involved in the collaboration. This process requires sustained action and long-term commitments that transcend the archaeological topic. Most importantly, collaboration requires that anyone involved in the process can say no.

At Ludlow, we did not assume what the community of unionized workers in southern Colorado needed or wanted. We engaged in almost 2 years of dialogue with the UMW before beginning the project. This dialogue had to overcome class differences and a skepticism that Indiana Jones had anything to say about labor's struggle. A member of the women's auxiliary who had taken archaeology classes and worked on digs helped us. Ultimately, we knew we had picked the right fight when our union collaborators embraced our help in their struggle.

REFERENCES

Bowman-Kruhm, Mary. 2011. *Margaret Mead: A Biography.* Amherst, NY: Prometheus Books.

Braverman, Harry. 1974. *Labor and Monopoly Capitalism: The Degradation of Work in the Twentieth Century.* New York: Monthly Review Press.

Clifford, James. 1988. "Identity in Mashpee." In *The Predicament of Culture: Twentieth-Century Ethnography, Literature, and Art,* edited by James Clifford, 277–348. Cambridge, MA: Harvard University Press.

———. 2004. Looking Several Ways: "Anthropology and Native Heritage in Alaska." *Current Anthropology* 45(26): 5–30.

Collins, Patricia Hill. 2012, *On Intellectual Activism.* Philadelphia: Temple University Press.

Colorado Coal Field War Project (CCFWP). 2000. Accessed June 13, 2013, http://www.du.edu/ludlow/index.html.

Conklin, Beth A. 2003. "Speaking Truth to Power." *Anthropology News* 44(7): 5.

Debs, Eugene V. 1914. "A Plea for Solidarity." *The International Socialist Review* 14: 534–538.

Duke, Philip and Dean Saitta. 2009. "Why We Dig: Archaeology, Ludlow and the Public." In *The Archaeology of Class War: The Colorado Coalfield Strike of 1913–1914,* edited by Karin Larkin and Randall H. McGuire, 351–361. Boulder: University of Colorado Press.

Durrenberger, Paul. 2006. "On the Invisibility of Class in America." *Anthropology News* 47(8): 9–10.

Engels, Frederick. 1907. *Socialism: Utopian and Scientific*. Chicago: Charles H. Kerr.

Fletcher, Bill Jr. 2012. *"They're Bankrupting Us!": And 20 Other Myths about Unions*. Boston: Beacon Press.

Gallivan, Martin, Danielle Moretti-Langholtz, and Buck Woodard. 2011. "Collaborative Archaeology and Native Empowerment: Collaborative Archaeology in Tidewater Virginia." *Historical Archaeology* 45(1): 10–23.

Hale, Charles. 2006. "Activist Research v. Cultural Critique: Indigenous Land Rights and the Contradictions of Politically Engaged Anthropology." *Cultural Anthropology* 21(1): 96–120.

Hodder, Ian. 1999. *The Archaeological Process: An Introduction*. Oxford, UK: Basil Blackwell.

Jancius, Angela. 2006. "Class in the Academy: Our Achilles' Heel." *Anthropology News* 47(8): 11–12.

Lareau, Annette. 2003. "Unequal Childhoods: Class, Race, and Family Life." Berkeley: University of California Press.

Larkin, Karen, and Randall H. McGuire, eds. 2009. *The Archaeology of Class War: The Colorado Coalfield Strike of 1913–1914*. Boulder: University of Colorado Press.

Leonhardt, David. 2005. "The College Drop Out Boom." In *Class Matters*, edited by B. Keller, 87–104. New York: Times Books.

Little, Barbara. 2010. "Epilogue: Changing the World with Archaeology." In *Archaeologists as Activists: Can Archaeology Change the World?*, edited by M. J. Stottman, 154–158. Tuscaloosa: University of Alabama Press.

McGuire, Randall H. 2008. *Archaeology as Political Action*. Berkeley: University of California Press.

McGuire, Randall H., and Mark Walker. 2008. "Class." In *Archaeology as Political Action*, by Randall H. McGuire, 98–139. Berkeley: University of California Press.

Meskell, Lynn, and Robert W. Preucel. 2004. "Politics." In *A Companion to Social Archaeology*, edited by Lynn Meskell and Robert W. Preucel, 315–334. Oxford, UK: Blackwell.

Meyerson, Harold. 2011. "The GOP's War on Labor Unions," *Washington Press*, accessed June 14, 2013, http://www.washingtonpost.com/opinions/the-gops-war-on-labor-unions/2011/12/01/gIQAvRGPIO_story.html.

Saitta, Dean. 2004. "Desecration at Ludlow." *New Labor Forum* 13: 84–87.

———. 2007. *The Archaeology of Collective Action*. Gainesville: University of Florida Press.

Shanks, Michael, and Randall H. McGuire. 1996. "The Craft of Archaeology." *American Antiquity* 61(1): 75–88.

Shott, Michael J. 2006. "How Liberal Arts Colleges Perpetuate Class Bias." *Academe* 92(5): 22–25.

United Mine Workers (UMW). 1999. "Lest We Forget: Ludlow Project Puts Massacre in Spotlight." *United Mine Workers Journal* (March–April): 12–13.

United States Department of Labor. 2013. "Statistics," accessed June 6, 2013, http://www.dol.gov/dol/topic/statistics/.

Walker, Mark. 2000. "Labor History at the Ground Level." *Labor's Heritage* 11: 60–75.

Chapter 7

Reconciling Inequalities in Archaeological Practice and Heritage Research

George P. Nicholas

How did a shy, introverted boy from New England who avoids confrontation become an activist (a term I'm uncomfortable with)? I'm not sure. I can certainly trace my development as an archaeologist—from a now-famous proclamation to my parents at the dinner table when I was 8, to field-school at Franklin Pierce College the summer after I graduated from high school, and so on. I find it more difficult to track this other trajectory.

In my high school years, I participated in protests against the Vietnam War, albeit within the confines of a small Connecticut town. I joined rallies, solicited signatures for petitions, and made an unsuccessful attempt to register with my draft board as a pacifist. But after the war had ended, I quietly went about my business as a student. Later, while working on my PhD at UMass-Amherst, I connected with Russ Handsman, who was then director of research at the American Indian Archaeological Institute (today, the Institute for American Indian Studies), in Washington, Connecticut. Together, we worked for several years at Robbins Swamp, which became the focus of my PhD research. It was through my involvement with Russ, Ann McMullen, Karen Cody Cooper, and others that my involvement with Native Americans began to develop. My relationship with Russ, a former student of Mark Leone, provided an interesting complement to my PhD committee at UMass-Amherst, with Dena Dincauze as my supervisor and Martin Wobst

Transforming Archaeology: Activist Practices and Prospects, edited by Sonya Atalay, Lee Rains Clauss, Randall H. McGuire, and John R. Welch, 133–158. © 2014 Left Coast Press, Inc. All rights reserved.

as a member—a heady mix of very different influences. Russ and Ann were pushing for innovative museum exhibits and public engagement, while Dena was setting high standards for the interpretation of Paleoindian sites, and Martin was involved with his critical assessment of archaeological theory and practice.

Immediately after completing my PhD, I found myself in Kamloops, British Columbia because my wife, Catherine Carlson, had accepted a faculty position at Thompson Rivers University. There I learned that Simon Fraser University (SFU) had, in partnership with the Secwepemc Cultural Education Society (SCES), recently opened a small campus on the Kamloops Indian Reserve. I soon after was teaching an Introduction to Archaeology course there, in the former residential school building. That soon led to a full-time position teaching as well as developing and directing the Indigenous Archaeology program from 1991 to 2005.

During my first semester, a young Tahltan woman told me that she could not complete an assignment for class. When I asked the reason, she replied, "Because my spirit helper left me." I first thought, "Well, that's one I haven't heard before," but then the proverbial light bulb went off, and I realized that this woman, identical in so many ways to students I taught elsewhere, was of a different culture with a very different worldview. And in that moment, I finally became an anthropologist.

My involvement with Secwepemc and other First Nations students and community members transformed me and led directly into my long-term engagement with indigenous peoples. For almost 25 years now, following the footsteps of such colleagues as Larry Zimmerman, T. J. Ferguson, Randy McGuire, and others, I have worked for a more representative and responsible practice in archaeology. This has been coupled with efforts to achieve a more critical understanding, both of the impact of archaeology upon descendant communities and of the promise of a postcolonial archaeology in which indigenous peoples benefit from and make decisions about their own heritage.

—∞∞∞—

Knowledge without action is not real knowledge.
—*Wang Yangming (1472–1529), cited in Taylor and Choy 2005, 76.*

In early 2011, I was on a panel facing the three commissioners of the Truth and Reconciliation Commission of Canada, in a room filled with hundreds of survivors of Indian Residential schools from throughout British Columbia (Figure 7.1). The commission was holding a forum in Vancouver on the creation of a national research center devoted to the massive amount of information that had been collected under its mandate, including survivor testimony, church records, and scholarly studies. They sought advice from survivors and indigenous organizations, and from archivists and scholars, as to what such a center might look like and how its goals might best be achieved. The commission invited me to provide information on community-based heritage research, as well as on indigenous intellectual property issues, the flow of knowledge and benefits, and the challenges of developing fair and equitable research practices.

Figure 7.1   2011 Truth and Reconciliation Commission Hearings, Vancouver, BC. (Photo by George Nicholas)

The residential school system in Canada began in the 1840s, with the last school closing in 1996. Over the course of 150 years, more than 150,000 First Nations, Métis, and Inuit children were taken from their families by the authorities and placed in government-funded, church-run residential schools (Castellano, Archibald, and De Gagné, 2008; Haig-Brown 1988). Comparable church-based or government-run programs existed in the United States and Australia. Although the original assimilationist policy to "kill the Indian in the child" somewhat softened, and some former students enjoyed their experience, many so-called survivors experienced physical, sexual, and psychological abuse that has resulted in lasting harm.

In that immense room, which smelled faintly of burning sweet grass, I reflected on what I was doing there, on what I—an archaeologist (and a non-indigenous one at that)—had to offer to the commissioners and especially to the thousands of individuals they represented. Indeed, was archaeology at all relevant to anyone there? This is a question that all of us in this volume have raised. Certainly much of my own work in the last 25 years has been aimed at redressing the legacy of colonialism by promoting an Indigenous archaeology, which seeks to expand archaeological practice and theory, and to assist in developing more equitable uses of cultural heritage. But how could an archaeology of any sort satisfy the needs of the hundreds of faces in front of me, whose lives have been irrevocably damaged by undisguised colonialism?

But sitting before the commission I realized that what had brought me to that event—and indeed shaped much of my career—was my connection to the Indian residential school system. This began in 1991, soon after moving to British Columbia from New England, when I taught an archaeology course in what was then a new and innovative postsecondary program on the Kamloops Indian Reserve that Simon Fraser University had recently developed with the Secwepemc Cultural Education Society. The classroom was in the former residential school where many of my students had actually gone to school years earlier. As I grew to know those students and earn their trust, some told me how they were punished by the priests for speaking *Secweptemctsin* and of frequently running away (see Jack 2005). I subsequently spent the next 15 years teaching in that program, during which time I began working in what would popularly become known as Indigenous archaeology (Figure 7.2).

What emerged early on in my encounter with those students and the many that followed was my rethinking of archaeology—a deep reevaluation of my aims within the discipline. This moved me well beyond the then-comfortable realm of the early postglacial land-use research that was (and still is) important to me (Nicholas 1988 to recognize that archaeology has to be more than the study of material culture and the lifeways it represents. I came to see that archaeological endeavors not only have to be methodologically sound but also representative, relevant, and responsible. In

Figure 7.2   The First Indigenous Archaeology Field School, 1991, Kamloops, BC. (left to right: Mel Symour, Steve Lawhead, Petrina Schooner, George Nicholas, Diane Biin, Dean Billy, Gladys Baptiste, Debbie Jules, Laurie Kennedy, John Jules, Percy Casper, Donna Dillman). (Photo by George Nicholas)

the process, three essential questions rose to prominence: Why do we do archaeology? For whom do we do it? And how best can it be done? They are a mantra for a more pragmatic and responsible archaeological practice. Or, as Anne Pyburn (2009) has stated, "Practicing archaeology as if it really matters."

Many will agree that archaeology must contribute to and must benefit descendant communities today to be credible, a point emphasized by Atalay, Clauss, and others in this volume. An honest engagement with those communities also has the capacity to transform us as practitioners and thus influence the kind of archaeology we do. This is especially so with approaches grounded in a more anthropological or ethnographic rationale that recognizes the colonial legacy of archaeology and/or foregrounds community needs, and that positions archaeology and ethnography in aid of the latter (e.g., Colwell-Chanthaphonh 2010; Hamilakis and Anagnostopoulos 2009; Hamilakis and Duke 2007; Hollowell and Nicholas 2008; Lydon and Rizvi 2010).

One striking commonality with our original Society for American Archaeology (SAA) conference session, reinforced by the Amerind Foundation session that followed, is how deeply (and necessarily) personal our presentations and discussions have been (e.g., Pyburn, this volume). Over the years, I've become increasingly aware of how privileged my life has been compared with many indigenous people with whom I work. I have also come to recognize that the prime beneficiaries of archaeological knowledge derived from a peoples' heritage are not the associated descendant communities, but the archaeologists themselves. My activism has thus aimed to promote a more equitable archaeology that acknowledges and respects different heritage values and legacies.

I have sought to do this in two ways. The first is through involvement in the realm of Indigenous archaeology. This endeavor has provided community members with the tools of archaeology to address their heritage-related needs and also challenged inequities in the political structure of archaeology and heritage in British Columbia and elsewhere. The second is as director and codeveloper of the Intellectual Property Issues in Cultural Heritage (IPinCH) Project, an international initiative that incorporates community-based participatory research and high-level analysis in pursuit of helping communities, scholars, and consumers resolve issues relating to the intangible aspects of cultural heritage and changing university research protocols. These two types of activism—trajectories that operate simultaneously at different scales—are discussed in this chapter: the first represents on-the-ground, community-centered/developed initiatives; the second represents a larger, meta-level engagement of the collective contributions of such initiatives with the world.

Indigenous Archaeology

Elsewhere I've discussed at length the premise and practice of Indigenous archaeology that can be characterized, in part, as "an expression of archaeological theory and practice in which the discipline intersects with indigenous values, knowledge, practices, ethics, and sensibilities, and through collaborative and community-originated or -directed projects, and related critical perspectives" (Nicholas 2008, 1660). This topic is today reasonably well known, so it requires only a brief introduction here. Its development over the past 20-plus years was, in part, influenced by feminist and Marxist archaeology, and by indigenous values and ways of knowing. Today, Indigenous archaeology has become a relatively familiar part of the archaeological landscape, but one that continues to be a touchstone for "spirited" discussion (e.g., McGhee 2009 vs. Colwell-Chanthaphonh et al. 2010; Croes 2010; Silliman 2010a; and Wilcox 2010).

Indigenous archaeology, as it first emerged, was very much about representation and participation. Although those themes still dominate, it is becoming broader in scope and more nuanced in its practice, and today's applications garner much attention in discussions of heritage management, stewardship, collaborative research practices, and postcoloniality, among other topics (see Atalay 2012; Murray 2011; Silliman 2010b). Praxis is central to the four realms that Indigenous archaeology currently operates in: reactive, interpretive, reflexive, and transformative (Nicholas and Watkins, 2014).

To date, Indigenous archaeology has largely focused on ensuring a place for descendant communities in the discovery and interpretation of *their* heritage, often though promoting working together and capacity building (e.g. Ferguson and Colwell-Chanthaphonh 2006; Davidson, Lovell-Jones, and Bancroft 1995; Klessert and Downer 1990). Most of my own efforts working with First Nations communities in Kamloops, British Columbia, emphasized the latter by offering a suite of classroom courses and field school–based training to provide indigenous students with the tools of archaeology to use as needed. The Indigenous Archaeology Program[1] (IAP) that I developed on the Kamloops Indian Reserve provided archaeological courses and/or field training to hundreds of First Nations students between 1991 and 2010, more than any other institution in Canada. It created opportunities for their involvement in heritage stewardship (Figure 7.3), policy-making, development of on-reserve permit systems, cultural sensitivity training in heritage research, land-use planning, and mentoring for high school students and archaeological training for teachers. Through its archaeology, ethnobotany, and language-immersion courses, the campus offered many opportunities for First Nations students to visit, or revisit, parts of their traditional territories and to work with elders. These elders were instrumental teachers and cultural advisors who introduced the IAP students to traditional knowledge that had been suppressed due to the language and cultural restrictions imposed by the residential school system and earlier Federal Indian policies.

The courses and practical training in archaeology assisted community members to identify more fully with their heritage by supplementing and expanding oral histories; and by giving them the tools to identify, recover, and interpret ancestral sites and the material culture contained therein. Importantly, from the start, the special connection of the people to their land was acknowledged by the program administrators in terms of jurisdiction,[2] decision making, and benefits flow. Students from the Kamloops program subsequently have pursued their interests in heritage in a variety of contexts, including

Figure 7.3   Nola Markey, former SCES-SFU Student (fourth from right) and an all-indigenous CRM crew, BC. (Photo courtesy of Nola Markey)

- as band council or committee members charged with making decisions on land-use planning (including archaeological overview assessments) for their communities;
- as archaeological permit holders, project managers, business managers, project directors, or crew members for cultural resource management companies working on local, national, and international projects;
- as managers, researchers, and field workers within First Nation cultural and/ or natural resource departments, involved in archaeological and environmental assessments that incorporate both Western science and traditional knowledge;
- as museum archivists and tour guides;
- as graduate students who have had the opportunity to teach at universities as sessional instructors; and
- as educators and instructors who have incorporated archaeology, ethnobotany, and language into the curriculum and teach at elementary, high school, and university levels (Nicholas and Markey 2014).

The SCES-SFU program represents one manifestation of Indigenous archaeology that addressed First Nations' concerns with heritage by providing First Nations members with the tools of archaeology that they could employ as CRM practioners, educators, or decision-makers. Over the course of 20 years, this initiative melded community values and recognition of sensitive and sacred places with scientific collection and preservation of archaeological materials, and has proved pivotal in educating future generations of both First Nations and the general public about First Nation histories, cultural identity, political perspectives, and social dynamics. It also served to inform industry (private and corporate) and government of the need to develop better relations and protocols with First Nations (Markey 2010). Although it closed in 2010, the program has left a lasting legacy in Secwepemc territory and has contributed to the greater involvement of indigenous involvement in archaeological practice throughout British Columbia.[3]

As descendant communities become archaeologically savvy and experienced, there is also the need for a fundamental reorientation of archaeology relative to the legacy of colonialism, the power differential that exists, issues of culture-based rights, and a host of other topics familiar in the postcolonial discourse (Appadurai 2002; Bhabha 1997; Kuper 2003; Minh-ha 1989; Said 1978). Collaborative heritage management initiatives that directly address local needs help to ensure that benefits flow to the descendant communities (Richland 2011; also see examples in Hamilakis and Anag-nostopoulos 2010; Lydon and Rizvi 2010; Silliman 2008). This is difficult to achieve, in part, because it requires that archaeologists give up some degree of control over the development and direction of a project. In addition, there may also a host of potential risks, especially to graduate students and young scholars associated with community-controlled projects.[4] However, the potential benefits may be substantial, especially when it comes to ensuring that archaeological and heritage-based projects are locally relevant (e.g., Castañeda and Matthews 2008; Ferguson and Colwell-Chanthanphonh 2006, Klassen 2013, McNiven 2010, Matsuda and Sadler 2010).

My involvement in working with, teaching, and learning from descendant communities in British Columbia represents a period of sustained activism on my part, but also, and perhaps more accurately, my being activated in the first place. As I became more aware of the significant inequalities in archaeology, and the lack of shared and respectful understanding of what constitutes "heritage," I resolved to make meaningful contributions. This would lead to my involvement with IPinCH, which starts from the premises of relevance and fair benefits exchange.

The IPinCH Project

Indigenous archaeology is very much concerned with the process of archaeology and with the achievement of a reasonable balance as just one goal (Nicholas 2008; Watkins 2005). In a relatively short time it has made considerable progress toward these goals. But what of the *products* of archaeology? Who controls, has access to, and benefits from these? How can a reasonable, fair, and equitable balance be achieved here? That is very much at the core of the IPinCH Project, a praxis-based academic initiative funded by Canada's Social Science and Humanities Research Council. This seven-year, international, multisectoral project explores intellectual property-related issues emerging within the realm of cultural heritage and their implications for theory, policy, and practice. The research team consists of more than fifty anthropologists, archaeologists, lawyers, ethicists, heritage museum specialists, and others from eight countries; and twenty-six community or organization partners. Many on the team, which include contributors to this volume, have had very long associations with indigenous communities and share IPinCH's strong commitment to training the next generation of scholars in collaborative research practices.

Over the course of the project (2008–2015), we have been working to document and analyze the diversity of principles, perspectives, and responses that arise from intellectual property issues related to cultural heritage. From this, we have compiled examples of good practice relating to (a) protocols for ethical heritage research, (b) access to museum records and other archives, (c) cultural tourism issues, (d) changing legal interpretations of cultural rights, and (e) international heritage protection efforts, among many other topics. Foundational to IPinCH is a critical theory approach that seeks to foster positive change in the lives of participants (including researchers) and encourages alteration of its course as it proceeds, based on feedback and critical reflection.

The project is organized into three major components: 1) a series of community-based research initiatives and case studies that investigate local intellectual property issues and the relationship between tangible and intangible heritage; 2) an online Knowledge Base that is both the repository of research results and a resource base available to others; and 3) eight thematic working groups (Appendix A) that develop initiatives in their respective areas (see Appendix B for one example). I focus here on how the community studies were designed to address community–identified heritage concerns and needs and to exemplify, as team member Sheila Greer has put it, "what happens when the community is in the driver's seat."

On-the-Ground Research

A community–based participatory research methodology in which the community develops the project drives our local research initiatives. We currently have fifteen community–based research initiatives in Canada, the United States, Kyrgyzstan, New Zealand, South Africa, and Australia (Appendix C), including special initiatives relating to the Ainu of northern Japan, the San of southern Africa, and others. In each case, the team is working to support and facilitate community interests and actions relative to their needs (Figure 7.4). At the same time, these projects have provided a means to improve the university research culture and infrastructure to be more accommodating of working with First Nations and with indigenous organizations and communities.

Community partners codevelop these initiatives and involve themselves in every facet—from the creation of research questions and research designs to conducting

Figure 7.4   Chief Wayne Christian (standing) and Secwepemc elders and spiritual leaders participating in an IPinCH-funded community project, November 2012. (Photo by George Nicholas)

the research, designing practical outputs, and reviewing reports before they can be released. IPinCH researchers act primarily as facilitators, reporters, and links to broader project objectives. Situated in different parts of the world, the studies address questions such as the following:

- "How do we establish protocols for outsiders who work with cultural sensitive sites or information?"
- "What guidelines should apply to knowledge produced from analyzing ancestral remains or sensitive cultural knowledge?"
- "How can we best collect and pass on knowledge about the land and lifeways for use in guiding future development policies and decisions?"
- "How do we protect, care for, and manage the sacred knowledge embodied in ancestral sites while also sharing their lessons in culturally appropriate ways with the public?"
- "How do we assure the protection and inclusion of our own cultural principles and ways of knowing in government consultations affecting our heritage?"

Protocols involving free and prior informed consent and confidentiality are in place from the start through negotiations with the community and incorporated into the requisite ethics reviews and funding transfer agreements for each IPinCH-funded initiative. Upon completion of each study, the community research team compiles a draft report and other materials derived from various activities (e.g., interviews, focus groups) and presents them to the community and/or tribal governance for review (with those entities having approved of the project in the first place). The host community or political organization thus has the opportunity to determine which research products and data can be released to the IPinCH team for analysis and dissemination, a process that ensures that no sensitive or secret/sacred information is released. In this way, the community retains or controls (i.e., "owns") the raw information collected and other research products.

This ground-up approach prioritizes community needs (see Atalay 2012) and ensures that the host community is the primary beneficiary of the research. This approach addresses some of the long-standing issues surrounding academic research relating to mistrust, unequal power, and loss of control over the process and products of research.

The point of describing the IPinCH Project here is that (a) collaborative projects such as this offer one means of redressing long-standing dissatisfaction of descendant communities because such projects help to restore *their* control over *their* heritage, and (b) the approach outlined here is revealing some of the many ways it is possible to enrich, not constrain, research by outsiders. True, we know that not all information collected in the IPinCH case studies will be released to the research team; indeed, we recognize that some privileged, sacred, or otherwise sensitive knowledge should not leave community control or be accessed by outsiders. But this turns out to be a relatively small amount of information. This is not without precedent. For their part, archaeologists generally do not publish site locations to protect that information, and researchers working in many other realms have generally sensible limitations on what they can or cannot do, as stipulated by ethics review, copyright, and other protective measures.

Detailed information about these studies and other components of this initiative are available on the IPinCH website (http://www.sfu.ca/ipinch) or described elsewhere (see *SAA Archaeological Record* 12(4), 2012).[5] However, to illustrate the nature of these projects, I provide brief descriptions of two of the community-based studies—one in New Zealand, the other Australia. I also discuss how these projects and others like them are effecting change in the university research administration.

The "Moriori Cultural Database, Chatham Islands, New Zealand"

The indigenous people of Rēkohu (Chatham Islands, New Zealand), the Moriori, have long desired a means of heritage protection that is relevant, respectful, and ethical. To this end, they have developed an IPinCH-funded, multilayer database that connects ongoing research on Moriori identity, cultural heritage protection, land

Figure 7.5   Recording *rākau momori* ("living tree carvings") with the use of hand-held 3D laser technology. (Photo courtesy of of Susan Thorpe and Maui Solomon)

use, and culturally sensitive resource management (Figure 7.5). Susan Thorpe and Maui Solomon, with Te Keke Tura Moriori, as part of the Hokotehi Moriori Trust, which represents all wherever they may be. The Hokotehi Moriori Trust serves to preserve, revive, and promote Moriori identity, culture, language, and heritage.

The Moriori cultural knowledge database was developed to record traditional knowledge and protect tangible and intangible heritage through appropriate protocols. The team grounded its creation in elder knowledge and traditional values and ensured that the Moriori controlled the research methodology and exclusively cared for the data and its uses. The database is now being used by Moriori to promote economic sustainability and inform land-use decisions for land and resource management that protect cultural heritage. An additional objective was a youth-focused Hokotehi mentorship program on knowledge recording and archaeological methods, which will help expand the documentation project in future years. Key activities have included

- Ongoing field studies with elders and youth by the case study team on Rēkohu (February 2010–present), which utilized an indigenous values–based methods and ethical framework;
- Two youth workshops in 2010 focusing on protecting material culture and the use of digital technology;
- Documentation of traditional knowledge about land and resource use with elders and landowners employing culturally appropriate software known as *Traditional Knowledge Revitalization Pathways* (http://www.tkrp.com.au);
- Partner-to-Partner presentation to the Yukon First Nations IPinCH case study (see Appendix B) to share experiences relating to project development and research methods, in addition to presentations in several IPinCH workshops and conferences;
- Workshops with Moriori youth that resulted in an exhibition in *Kopinga marae* (traditional meeting house) with *taonga* (ancestral objects) that have been returned to Moriori; and
- A training program for Moriori youth to record the knowledge of their elders.

"The Ngaut Ngaut Interpretive Project, Providing Culturally Sustainable Online Interpretive Content to the Public, South Australia"

Ngaut Ngaut is the traditional name of what is more familiarly known as Devon Downs, the first archaeological site to be scientifically excavated in Australia. Although this iconic site has long had a presence in the archaeological literature, its history and meaning to the traditional peoples of the area has been absent from both academic accounts and cultural tourism–related information. The Ngaut Ngaut Interpretive Project was designed to address the lack of culturally sustainable content for the public relating to this important heritage site, including such intangible values as cultural meanings and interpretations of rock art, dreamings, and oral histories (Figure 7.6). Amy Roberts (Flinders University), Isobelle Campbell, Chairperson, Mannum Aboriginal Community Association, Inc. (MACAI), and other members of MACAI—an IPinCH partner organization—developed the project.

Cultural tourism has become a point of connection between indigenous peoples and the larger world (e.g., Dallen 2007; Hinch and Butler 1996; Smith and Richards 2012; Tomaselli 2012). Many indigenous groups worldwide see it as an important opportunity to share aspects of their culture (or not) and to educate the public about their lifeways and history—on their own terms. There is also the potential for substantial economical and other benefits from such ventures (see McAnany, this volume; Stottman, this volume). Given that Ngaut Ngaut has long received much attention by archaeologists and tourists, the MACAI sought to engage with the visitors in meaningful ways. The The Ngaut Ngaut Interpretive Project, funded by IPinCH and other sources, sought to prepare:

> a suite of interpretive materials (for both off and on-site purposes) that would benefit the community's cultural tourism ventures as well as their aspirations to educate the public about Aboriginal culture and to foster greater cross-cultural understandings. The content of the signs, posters, and brochures specifically incorporated the many tangible and intangible aspects and values of this significant place … Indeed, whilst MACAI value the site's archaeological history and the physical evidence of the excavations, they also wanted the site's cultural importance to be presented to the public. In particular, they wanted to present to the public some of the cultural complexities relating to Ngaut Ngaut and to redress the standard, one-dimensional and arguably colonial archaeological story that exists in Australian textbooks (Roberts and MACAI 2012, 33).

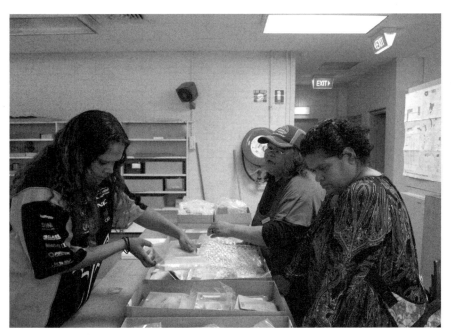

Figure 7.6   Isobelle Campbell, Ivy Campbell, and Anita Hunter looking at artifacts from the Ngaut Ngaut excavations. (Image courtesy of the South Australian Museum)

The team published *Ngaut Ngaut: An Interpretive Guide* (Roberts and MACAI 2012), a booklet now distributed by MACAI and the South Australian Department of Environment and Natural Resources and available in electronic form on the IPinCH website. Beyond these activities, the Ngaut Ngaut team is looking to develop new collaborative projects with other IPinCH team members and partner organizations, including the Ziibiwing Center of Anishinabe Culture and Lifeways of the Saginaw Chippewa Indian Tribe of Michigan, and the IPinCH Cultural Tourism Working Group. This reflects one of the much-anticipated aspects of this international project: the facilitation of connections between distant communities.

Improving University-Based Research

There are many different reasons for, and routes to, activism in archaeology, as evidenced in the contributions to this volume. In this chapter, I have focused on just two trajectories: one addressing the process of archaeology; the other its products. Beyond the political realm, engagement with indigenous and other descendant communities is on the rise not only in archaeology but also in the social sciences, public health, forestry, and other disciplines, and this has implications for the research process, especially in academic contexts.

Research is a major component of universities; it is a central part of their mandate to know the world and to ultimately use that knowledge to make the world better. Over the course of generations, universities have developed extensive policies and protocols to ensure responsibility in the research practice in terms of ethics reviews, funding transfers, and so on. The system is designed to encourage and expedite research projects both within and between institutions; the latter through memoranda of agreements and similar means. For the majority of research projects, the process operates like the proverbial "well-oiled-machine." But for nontraditional projects, especially those involving cross-cultural collaborations, community orientation, or involvement of indigenous organizations, there may be potential hurdles and risks (both perceived and actual). It might thus take substantial time and energy, working with multiple institutions (often transnationally), to get funds flowing and ethics reviews approved for a project.

This is frequently the case with community-engaged research, especially that involving indigenous peoples. In such instances, the direction for research may come from the heritage holders; community priorities may differ from those set by academic schedules; and tribal organizations reviewing research proposals may have limited human resources to devote in the face of more pressing needs. It also takes time to develop mutual understanding of needs, goals, methods, and outcomes, including data access, publishing, etc., and most especially to develop trust and respect—the foundation for successful partnerships (Atalay 2012; Nicholas et al. 2011).

Universities and funding agencies certainly see the need to promote and conduct research with indigenous peoples, but are generally naïve about what is required, and also heavily invested in the traditional research structure. This is what we have found with the case study component of the IPinCH Project. Recognition of the features noted above, plus a concern about benefits flow, have been the starting point for IPinCH's case studies, but these considerations have also been responsible for some of the delays we've encountered with getting projects underway. Some of the many challenges we have encountered include:

- IPinCH's primary funder encourages "outside the box" projects, yet the current Tri-Council Policy to which Canadian universities adhere is not ready to fully accommodate them, and the universities overseeing projects often have made a very conservative reading of those policies, and have stressed the importance of "protecting the grant holder" (in this case, me);
- Each IPinCH case study requires ethics review at three levels: by SFU, by other universities participating in that initiative, and by the community involved;
- We have encountered substantial difficulties in transferring relatively small amounts of funds (generally about $24,000) from the university to First Nations organizations, despite the latter often dealing with federal grants of hundreds of thousands of dollars; and
- Some participating universities have indicated concerns that their faculty don't own the research data (with IPinCH projects, the community does, releasing it, as appropriate, to the research team).

During the course of the first five years of the IPinCH project, we have literally spent hundreds of hours negotiating ethics agreements, funding transfers, intellectual property provisions, and more, with the university lawyer, financial services staff, and ethics office personnel. For its part, the university system has made considerable efforts to accommodate our nontraditional research projects within the confines of existing research parameters. In the end, we have been successful in getting our research projects through the system (albeit with considerable effort).

What's the point of this account relative to activism? It is simply that in the course of developing the IPinCH project and then in working with various university administrators and staff, we have not only challenged the research system, but have had some success reforming it. For example, in our first three proposals for funding, the SSHRC initially balked at our community-directed, bottom-up methodology (IPinCH 2007), but they eventually awarded us $2.5 million for the project; IPinCH responded to a call from Canada's Tri-Council Policy Statement (TCPS) for recommendations to improve research policies relating to indigenous peoples with a submission (IPinCH 2009) that contributed to TCPS2; and Simon Fraser University has made considerable improvements to the implementation of its research policies. Thus, IPinCH has been an active agent in promoting positive change by educating university administrators about the specific requirements of community-based research, which has contributed to changes in university research culture and to the Tri-Council's ethics policy. Somewhat ironically, in October 2013 the IPinCH project was the first recipient of SSHRC's prestigious Partnership Award for "its outstanding achievement in advancing research, research training or knowledge mobilization, or developing a new partnership approach to research ... It is awarded to a partnership that, through mutual co-operation and shared intellectual leadership and resources, has demonstrated impact and influence within and/or beyond the social sciences and humanities research community." This is one very clear measure of our impact upon this Canadian funding agency.

Taking Action

Can archaeologists change the world?—a question embedded in Stottman's (2010) edited volume *Archaeologists as Activists*. Archaeologists *have* changed the world, most often unintentionally, and not always for the better. The results of archaeological research, to cite just two examples, fanned German nationalism and contributed to conquest and genocide (Pringle 2006), and, more recently, challenged Native Americans as being the first peoples of the continent (Thomas 2001). But archaeologists *can* change the world in more positive ways by helping to restore connections to a history disrupted by colonialism, by helping to confront injustice, among other such efforts.

What I've learned first-hand is that for archaeology to have real value, action is needed. Whether prefixed by "Indigenous," "critical," "Marxist," "feminist," "public," or the like, archaeology requires constant input and direction for it to contribute in meaningful ways to contemporary society (Nicholas and Hollowell 2007). This includes the recognition that as practitioners (a) we need to loosen our control of the past—not in an "anything-goes" manner, but to recognize that heritage means different things to different people, most especially to the descendants of our research subjects; and (b) that in North America and other settler societies we have a responsibility to acknowledge the legacy of colonialism and otherwise confront and work to rectify the inequalities stemming from historical consequences and policies that have separated indigenous peoples from their heritage. At the same time, foregrounding communities' needs and values over those of outside researchers does not mean that archaeological initiatives are constrained, a point also taken up by in chapters by Atalay, Castañeda, Ferris, and Welch in this volume.

This volume makes a strong case, largely by example, for the need for a transformed archaeology and for an acknowledgment of the value of activism within archaeology. During our three days at the Amerind Foundation, we discussed the nature of "activist" archaeology, including what it was and what it wasn't (e.g., it's not "advocacy"). And during conversations about how to advance this discussion with others in the discipline, we agreed that we did not want to introduce yet another type of archaeology, but instead to demonstrate—more by action than word—how archaeology can be transformed to become more effective and satisfying in addressing the needs of descendant communities (see, respectively, chapters by Clauss,

McGuire, and Ferguson, this volume). I believe we should measure the value of such a "lower-case" activism by its effectiveness in meeting actual needs rather than as a "new" approach to showcase. This holds true for other approaches to heritage that are too often highlighted as special for *who* is doing the work (e.g., a Native American) rather than on the merit of the work and the innovative ideas presented.

Archaeology represents the intersection of different value systems, including those in which tangible and intangible heritage are indivisible and the nexus of different needs relating to heritage—one's own or someone else's. However, achieving a balance between these is seldom easy because archaeology is so frequently based in cross-cultural encounters with the descendants, whoever they are. Likewise, reconciliation has to be more than just saying "sorry." Instead, it requires that we change how we do things. For me, that means ensuring that heritage research is done in fair and equitable ways, and that indigenous peoples are the primary beneficiaries of their heritage.

The legacy of the Indian residential school transformed my life as an archaeologist and enabled me to work with residential school survivors and others to make archaeology more relevant to them—in a way, coming full circle.

Considering Methods: Funding

Projects designed to effect change are far more challenging to fund than those that simply perpetuate the status quo or are otherwise operating on familiar (i.e., safe) ground. This is especially so for initiatives that target the power imbalance that exists within archaeology and heritage-related realms. The IPinCH Project provides an example of some of the challenges faced in procuring major funding from organizations that support academic research.

We developed the IPinCH Project as an academic-based initiative to transform theory into action and then to use action to better inform our knowledge of the world and to effect positive change. Our funding is primarily through a $2.5 million grant from the Social Sciences and Humanities Research Council (SSHRC) of Canada, which provides support for this 7-year project; additional cash and in-kind contributions are provided by our team member institutions, partnering communities and organizations, and through other sources. The SSHRC grant we obtained through its Major Collaborative Research Initiatives program required a considerable investment in time and effort, especially because it took us four attempts to secure funding.

In 2004, Julie Hollowell, Kelly Bannister, and I submitted what would be the first of four Letters of Intent to SSHRC. In this process, a successful proposal led to an invitation to submit the full proposal and provided $20,000 in aid of its developments. The adjudication committee declined our first proposal, but strongly encouraged us to resubmit. We subsequently expanded the list of coinvestigators and collaborators, but more importantly refined our vision of the project and revised our methods accordingly (our last Letter of Intent in 2007 was 694 pages long). We were subsequently finalists for the next three attempts; each time, we prepared and submitted full proposals for review and also met with the SSHRC adjudication committee in Ottawa. In December 2007, the committee notified us that our proposal was accepted; IPinCH formally began in April 2008.

Why was securing funding from SSHRC so difficult, especially when the committee liked the project and it fit within SSHRC's targeted research themes? Although not privy to the deliberations of the grant adjudication committee, we eventually learned that some members found problematic the methods we were promoting to achieve our research goals. Instead of collecting information about intellectual property issues and then theorizing from there, we directed a significant portion of the budget to community–based participatory research, with considerable decision making placed directly in the hands of our research partners. We intentionally positioned these partners to codevelop the individual case studies, providing them with unfettered control over the products and the power to end the project at any time. In the end, we convinced the committee that not only was this methodologically sound but it was indeed also the only way we could achieve a meaningful research partnership that ensured that the community benefitted.

Developing the project structure, working with coinvestigators and partner organizations, preparing the four SSHRC proposals, and so on required a massive effort by many individuals. We had the benefit of many team members being supported by their institutions (i.e., our salaries paid) and also having already established long-term relationships with many of the indigenous communities and organizations we work with. In addition, the total of $60,000 we received from SSHRC over 3 years aided considerably in the development of the final proposal.

The amount of effort devoted to obtaining funding for IPinCH was draining, and the frustration of rejection was substantial, especially as we could not foresee that there would ever be a successful outcome. What kept us going? In part it was stubbornness, grounded in the belief that we *knew* what we were trying to do was important. There was also a strong sense of obligation to the various communities with whom many of us had been working and who had signed on to the project at the start. For them, and for all of us, this wasn't just an academic project, but an opportunity to make a real difference.

There are three important lessons to share regarding how we obtained funding for IPinCH. The first is to be persistent: it required four attempts to secure the funding, and the four letters of intent and three full proposals totaled literally years of hard work by many individuals. Second, one needs to match the research project to the most appropriate funding opportunities and to be aware of that organization's funding priorities. And finally, in pursuing this type of "high-risk" research (for which the outcome is unknown), the core team included many relatively well-established researchers who were able and willing to go out on a limb with this project. Their efforts and mentorship, in turn, now provide important opportunities to buffer the risk of this type of community-based research for younger scholars on the team who are seeking tenure or need to complete their theses and dissertations research while maintaining rigorous and high-quality standards.

Acknowledgments

I thank Lee Rains Clauss and Sonya Atalay for lighting the fire, and the other SAA session and the Amerind Foundation session participants—T. J. Ferguson, Quetzil E. Castañeda, Jay Stottman, Randy McGuire, Patricia McAnany, John Norder, Anne Pyburn, John Welch, and Neal Ferris—for adding fuel and fanning the flames; your ideas and encouragement have added much to this work. I am also grateful to Amy Roberts, Isobelle Campbell, Maui Solomon, Susan Thorpe, Nola Markey, and especially Lee Rains Clauss and Randy McGuire for reviewing this draft, and also to the IPinCH team for their many contributions.

NOTES

1. This was part of an innovative postsecondary program developed by the Secwepemc Cultural Education Society and Simon Fraser University (SCES-SFU). It began in 1989 and closed in 2010. See Ignace et al. 1996; Nicholas and Markey 2014 for more on this program.

2. This was made clear to me in 1991 when I met with the band council to discuss my request to develop a field school on the reserve. It allowed me to do so only on the provision that I did not apply for a permit from the B.C. Archaeology Branch. Although this could have severely hampered doing any further archaeology in the province, I agreed, believing that the Kamloops Band should have say over its own heritage.

3. A different but complementary approach is represented by the efforts of other First Nations in British Columbia to control their own affairs, as evidenced with the St'át'imc and Nlaka'pamux Nations (Klassen 2013).

4. For example, efforts to complete dissertation research and or to prepare publications in support of tenure may be adversely affected by a change in band council membership.

5. This thematic issue on collaborative research includes articles by IPinCH team members Ian Lilley, Natasha Lyons, George Nicholas, Amy Roberts, and Claire Smith.

REFERENCES

Appadurai, Arjun. 2002. "The Globalization of Archaeology and Heritage." *Journal of Social Archaeology* 1: 35–49.

Atalay, Sonya. 2012. *Community-Based Archaeology: Research with, for, and by Indigenous and Local Communities.* Berkeley: University of California Press.

Bhabha, Homi K. 1997. "Editor's Introduction: Minority Maneuvers and Unsettled Negotiations." *Critical Inquiry* 23(3): 431–459.

Castañeda, Quetzil E., and Christopher Matthews, eds. 2008. *Ethnographic Archaeologies: Reflections on Stakeholders and Archaeological Practices.* Lanham, MD: AltaMira Press.

Castellano, Marlene Brant, Linda Archibald, and Mike DeGagné. 2008. *From Truth to Reconciliation: Transforming the Legacy of Residential Schools.* Ottawa: Aboriginal Healing Foundation.

Colwell-Chanthaphonh, Chip. 2010. *Living Histories: Native Americans and Southwestern Archaeology.* Lanham, MD: AltaMira Press.

Colwell-Chanthaphonh, Chip, T. J. Ferguson, Dorothy Lippert, Randy H. McGuire, George P. Nicholas, Joe E. Watkins, and Larry J. Zimmerman. 2010. "The Premise and Promise of Indigenous Archaeology." *American Antiquity* 75(2): 228–238.

Croes, Dale. 2010. "Courage and Thoughtful Scholarship = Indigenous Archaeology Partnerships." *American Antiquity* 75(2): 211–216.

Dallen, Timothy, ed. 2007. *Managing Heritage and Cultural Tourism Resources: Critical Essays.* Aldershot, UK: Ashgate.

Davidson, Ian, Christine Lovell-Jones, and Robyne Bancroft, eds. 1995. *Archaeologists and Aborigines Working Together.* Hanover, NH: University of New England Press.

Ferguson, T. J., and Chip Colwell-Chanthaphonh, 2006. *History Is in the Land: Multitribal Vocal Traditions in Arizona's San Pedro Valley.* Tucson: University of Arizona Press.

Haig-Brown, Celia. 1988. *Resistance and Renewal: Surviving the Indian Residential School.* Vancouver: Tillacum Library.

Hamilakis, Yannis, and Aris Anagnostopoulos, eds. 2009. "Archaeological Ethnographies." *Public Archaeology* 8(2–3): 64–322.

Hamilakis, Yannis, and Phillip Duke, eds. 2007. *Archaeology and Capitalism: From Ethics to Politics.* Walnut Creek, CA: Left Coast Press.

Hinch, Thomas, and Richard Butler. 1996. "Indigenous Tourism: A Common Ground for Discussion." In *Tourism and Indigenous People,* edited by Thomas Hinch and Richard Butler, 3–19. London: International Thomson Business Press.

Hollowell, Julie, and George P. Nicholas. 2008. "A Critical Assessment of Uses of Ethnography in Archaeology." In *Ethnographic Archaeologies: Reflections on Stakeholders and Archaeological Practices,* edited by Q. Castañeda and C. Matthews, 63–94. Lanham, MD: AltaMira Press.

Ignace, Ronald, Marianne B. Ignace, Monique Layton, Hari Sharma, and J. Colin Yerbury. 1996. "Partners in Success: The Simon Fraser University and Secwepemc First Nations Studies Program." *Canadian Journal of University Continuing Education* 22 (2): 27–45.

Intellectual Property Issues in Cultural Heritage Project (IPinCH). 2007. "Intellectual Property Issues in Cultural Heritage: Theory, Practice, Policy, Ethics." Final Application for the Major Collaborative Research Initiative program of the Social Sciences and Humanities Research Council, Ottawa, accessed December 1, 2013, http://www.sfu.ca/ipinch/sites/default/files/page//project_description/MCRI2007FinalProposal.pdf.

_____. 2009. "IPinCH Steering Committee Comments on the Draft 2nd Edition of the Tri-Council Policy Statement: Ethical Conduct for Research Involving Humans," accessed December 1, 2013, http://www.sfu.ca/ipinch/outputs/reports/ipinch-steering-committee-comments-draft-2nd-edition-tri-council-policy-statement-et.

Jack, Agnes, ed. 2005. *Behind Closed Doors: Stories from the Kamloops Indian Residential School.* Penticton, Canada: Theytus Press.

Klassen, Michael. 2013. "Indigenous Heritage Stewardship and the Transformation of Ar-

chaeological Practice: Two Case Studies from the Mid-Fraser Region of British Columbia." PhD diss., Department of Archaeology, Simon Fraser University, Burnaby, Canada.

Klessert, Anthony L., and Alan S. Downer, eds. 1990. "Preservation on the Reservation: Native Americans, Native American Lands, and Archaeology." *Navajo Nation Papers in Anthropology* 26. Window Rock, AZ: Navajo Nation Historic Preservation Department.

Kuper, Adam. 2003. "The Return of the Native." *Current Anthropology* 44(3): 389–402.

Lydon, Jane, and Uzma Rizvi, eds. 2010. *Handbook of Postcolonial Archaeology*. Walnut Creek, CA: Left Coast Press.

Markey, Nola. 2010. "The 'Other' Accidental Archaeologist." In *Being and Becoming Indigenous Archaeologists,* edited by George Nicholas, 199–209. Walnut Creek, CA: Left Coast Press.

Matsuda, Akira, and Nigel Sadler, eds. 2010. "Making Archaeology More Inclusive." *Archaeologies* 6(3): 425–527.

McGhee, Robert. 2008. "Aboriginalism and the Problems of Indigenous Archaeology." *American Antiquity* 73(4): 579–598.

MacNiven, Ian. 2010. "(Re)Engaging with the (Un)Known: Collaboration, Indigenous Knowledge, and Reaffirming Aboriginal Identity in the Torres Strait Islands, Northeastern Australia." *Collaborative Anthropologies* 2: 33–64.

Minh-ha, Trinh. 1989. *Women, Native, Other: Writing Postcoloniality and Feminism*. Bloomington: Indiana University Press.

Murray, Tim. 2011. "Archaeologists and Indigenous People: A Maturing Relationship?" *Annual Review of Anthropology* 40(1): 363–381.

Nicholas, George. 1988. "Ecological Leveling: The Archaeology and Environmental Dynamics of Early Postglacial Land-Use." In *Holocene Human Ecology in Northeastern North America,* edited by G. P. Nicholas, 257–296. New York: Plenum Press.

———. 2008. "Native Peoples and Archaeology (Indigenous Archaeology)." In *The Encyclopedia of Archaeology,* edited by D. Pearsall, Vol. 3: 1660–1669. Oxford, UK: Elsevier.

Nicholas, George, and Julie Hollowell. 2007. "Ethical Challenges to a Postcolonial Archaeology." In *Archaeology and Capitalism: From Ethics to Politics,* edited by Y. Hamilakis and P. Duke, 59–82. Walnut Creek, CA: Left Coast Press.

Nicholas, George, and Nola Markey. 2014. "Secwepemc Cultural Education Society/Simon Fraser University (SCES-SFU) Indigenous Archaeology Program." In *Encyclopedia of Global Archaeology,* 6548–6550. New York: Springer.

Nicholas, George, Amy Roberts, David Schaepe, Joe Walkins, Lyn Leader-Elliot, and Susan Rowley. 2011. "A Consideration of Theory, Principles and Practice in Collaborative Archaeology." *Archaeological Review from Cambridge* 26(2): 11–30.

Nicholas, George, and Joe Watkins. 2014. "Indigenous Archaeologies in Archaeological Theory." *Encyclopedia of Global Archaeology,* 3777–3786. New York: Springer.

Pringle, Heather. 2006. *The Master Plan: Himmler's Scholars and the Holocaust*. New York: Hyperion.

Pyburn, Anne. 2009. "Practicing Archaeology: As If It Really Matters." In *Archaeological Ethnographies,* edited by Y. Hamilakis and A. Anagnostopoulos. *Public Archaeology* 8(2–3): 161–175.

Richland, Justin. 2011. "Beyond Listening: Lessons for Native/American Collaboration from the Creation of the Nakwatsvewat Institute." *American Indian Culture and Research Journal* 35(1): 101–111.

Roberts, Amy, and the Mannum Aboriginal Community Association. 2012. *Ngaut Ngaut: An*

Interpretive Guide, 1st ed. Nildottie, South Australia: Mannum Aboriginal Community Association, accessed November 30, 2013, http://www.sfu.ca/ipinch/sites/default/files/outputs/publication/nguat_ngaut_book_web_version.pdf.

Said, Edward. 1978. *Orientalism.* New York: Vintage.

Silliman, Stephen, ed. 2008. *Collaborating at the Trowel's Edge: Teaching and Learning in Indigenous Archaeology.* Tucson: University of Arizona Press.

———. 2010a. "The Value and Diversity of Indigenous Archaeology: A Response to McGhee." *American Antiquity* 75(2): 217–220.

———. 2010b. "Writing New Archaeological Narratives: Indigenous North America." In *Handbook of Postcolonial Archaeology,* edited by Jane Lydon and Uzma Z. Rizvi, 145–164. Walnut Creek, CA: Left Coast Press.

Smith, Melanie, and Greg Richards, eds. 2012. *The Routledge Handbook of Cultural Tourism.* New York: Routledge.

Stottman, Jay, ed. 2010 *Archaeologists as Activists: Can Archaeologists Change the World?* Tuscaloosa: University of Alabama Press.

Taylor, Rodney L., and Howard Yuen Fung Choy. 2005. *The Illustrated Encyclopedia of Confucianism,* Vol. 1. New York: Rosen Publishing.

Thomas, David Hurst. 2001. *Skull Wars: Kennewick Man, Archaeology, and the Battle for Native American Identity.* New York: Basic Books.

Tomaselli, Keyan, ed. 2012. *Cultural Tourism and Identity: Rethinking Indigeneity.* Boston: Leiden.

Watkins, Joe. 2005. "Through Wary Eyes: Indigenous Perspectives on Archaeology." *Annual Review of Anthropology* 34: 429–449.

Wilcox, Michael. 2010. "Saving Indigenous Peoples from Ourselves: Separate but Equal Archaeology is Not Scientific Archaeology." *American Antiquity* 75(2): 221–228.

Appendix A. IPinCH Working Groups

- Bioarchaeology, Genetics and IP
  Chair: Daryl Pullman, Alan Goodman, and Dorothy Lippert
- Collaboration, Relationships, and Case Studies
  Co-chairs: Larry Zimmerman and Brian Noble
- Commodifications of Cultural Heritage
  Co-chairs: Solen Roth and Sven Ouzman
- Community-Based Cultural Heritage Research
  Co-chairs: Kelly Bannister, Julie Hollowell, Ian Lilley, and John Welch
- Cultural Tourism
  Co-chairs: Lena Mortensen and Dave Schaepe
- Customary, Vernacular, and Legal Forms
  Co-chairs: Rosemary Coombe and Patricia Goff
- Digital Information Systems and Cultural Heritage
  Co-chairs: Eric Kansa and Sue Rowley
- IP and Research Ethics
  Co-chairs: Sonya Atalay and Alison Wylie

Appendix B. Example of IPinCH Working Group Mandate: Community-Based Cultural Heritage Research Working Group

Those pursuing community-based research need access to background information and case studies to help them think through the implications of their research overall and at each step of the research process.

Envisioned as a way to engage with and learn from the ongoing surge of writing on the principles and practices of community-based research (CBR), this working group is dedicated to gathering, creating, and making available guidance tailored to fieldwork or research that deals with cultural heritage issues. Rather than producing an academic volume, this working group will develop materials, in the form of a multi-authored constellation of contributions, that offer practice guidance. These will be free of academic jargon, and accessible to all those interested in intellectual property issues in cultural heritage.

Currently, the working group is drawing on feedback from team members at the 2011 IPinCH Midterm Conference to (1) understand what CBCH researchers would find useful, (2) identify, expand and categorize pertinent resources in the IPinCH Knowledge Base, and (3) contact contributors and draft content that can evolve "wikipedia style" using an internal online platform before being made public.

The goal is to create products that foster balanced and mutually beneficial relationships between academic and community researchers, build understanding about the scope and limitations of intellectual property laws, protect intellectual property in cultural heritage, and promote fair and culturally appropriate uses of intellectual property.

All IPinCH team members and others interested in creating or sharing practical guidance for community-based research on or relating to cultural heritage are encouraged to join or participate in this Working Group.

Appendix C. IPinCH Community-Based Initiatives and Case Studies

- "A Case of Access: Inuvialuit Engagement with the Smithsonian's MacFarlane Collection" (Northwest Territories, Canada)
  Team: Natasha Lyons, Kate Hennessy, Stephen Loring, Charles Arnold, Cathy Cockney, Mervin Joe, Albert Elias, James Pokiak, Maia Lepage, Inuvialuit Cultural Resource Centre, Arctic Studies Center, Parks Canada, Smithsonian Institution, and Prince of Wales Northern Heritage Centre
  Focus: Repatriation and restoration to community of knowledge from museum collections.
- "Education, Protection and Management of *ezhibiigaadek asin* (Sanilac Petroglyph Site)" (Michigan, USA)
  Team: Sonya Atalay, Shannon Martin, William Johnson, and Ziibiwing Center of Anishinabe Culture and Lifeways of the Saginaw Chippewa Indian Tribe of Michigan
  Focus: Co-management plan development with state of Michigan for petroglyphs and associated intangible values.
- "Cultural Tourism in Nunavik" (Quebec, Canada)
  Team: Daniel Gendron, Taqralik Partridge, Nancy Palliser, and Avataq Cultural Institute
  Focus: Protection of Inuit language and heritage in the context of cultural tourism.
- "Developing Policies and Protocols for the Culturally Sensitive Intellectual Properties of the Penobscot Nation of Maine" (Maine, USA)
  Team: Bonnie Newsom, Martin Wobst, Julie Woods, and Penobscot Historic Preservation Office
  Focus: Long-range stewardship plan and research protocols for tribal intellectual property.
- "Grassroots Heritage Resource Preservation and Management in Kyrgyzstan: Ethnicity, Nationalism and Heritage on a Human Scale" (Krygystan)
  Team: Anne Pyburn and Asipa Zhumabaeva vaz Tursunbaev, Momytbaev Yimadin Birnazarovich, Abakir Kalybekov, Kyrgyz Sacred Heritage Association and Uzgben State Museum
  Focus: Sustainable, culturally-appropriate, and community-embedded projects that address the preservation and educational use of intellectual property and cultural heritage.

- "Hokotehi Moriori Trust: Heritage Landscape Data Base" (Rehoku, New Zealand)
  Team: Maui Solomon and Partner Te Keke Tura Moriori (Moriori Identity Trust), in affiliation with the Hokotehi Moriori Trust and Kotuku Consultancy
  Focus: Database of traditional knowledge of cultural landscape that brings together elders and youth.
- "Secwepemc Territorial Authority—Honoring Ownership of Tangible / Intangible Culture" (British Columbia, Canada)
  Team: Arthur Manual and Brian Noble
  Focus: What do "cultural heritage" encounters look like if we fully accept and act upon the premise that Secwepemc peoples have economic, political, and legal authority within their territory.
- "The Journey Home—Guiding Intangible Knowledge Production in the Analysis of Ancestral Remains" (British Columbia, Canada)
  Team: Dave Schaepe, Sue Rowley, and Stó:lo Research and Resource Management Centre
  Focus: Developing protocols for outside researchers for study of acceptable methods of study of ancestral remains before reburied.
- "The Ngaut Ngaut Interpretive Project: Providing Culturally Sustainable Online Interpretive Content to the Public' (South Australia, Australia)
  Team: Amy Roberts, Isobelle Campbell, and the Mannum Aboriginal Community, Inc.
  Focus: Development of culturally sustainable interpretive content online for important heritage site through a community-based approach to interpretive materials
- "Treaty Relations as a Method of Resolving IP Issues" (British Columbia, Alberta, Saskatchewan, and Manitoba, Canada)
  Team: Michael Asch
  Focus: A study of the political relationship established between First Nations and Canada through historic, 19th-century treaties as a framework for resolution of outstanding intellectual property and heritage issues today.
- "Yukon First Nations Heritage Values and Heritage Resource Management" (Yukon, Canada)
  Team: Sheila Greer, Heather Jones, Paula Banks, Champagne & Aishihik First Nations Heritage, Carcross-Tagish First Nation Heritage, and Ta'an Kwäch'än Council
  Focus: Identify local conceptions of heritage values in aid of self-governing Yukon First Nations' management of their heritage resources.
- "The History and Contemporary Practices of the Hopi Cultural Preservation Office" (Arizona, USA)
  Team: Leigh J. Kuwanwiswma, Justin Richland, Susan Secakuku, and Stewart Koyiyumptewa
  Focus: An examination of the Hopi Cultural Preservation Office's navigation between radically different conceptualizations of Hopi cultural knowledge and those informing Euro-American interests.

Chapter 8

Transforming the Terms of Engagement between Archaeologists and Communities

A View from the Maya Region

Patricia A. McAnany

Although this expression sounds like an oxymoron, change is constant. The dynamism of life applies to the field of archaeology as well as careers of archaeologists. During the course of my participation in archaeology, I have witnessed profound change within the discipline as archaeology began to take context seriously; to restructure a formerly amicable relationship with artifact collectors; to adopt a proactive stance against looting and for conservation; and to respond to NAGPRA legislation and the empowering of Native American voices in reference to their past. In Maya archaeology—my area of expertise— a sea change occurred with the decipherment of Maya hieroglyphs and the implications of this new knowledge for temporally distant peoples formerly considered "prehistoric." Archaeologists were once thought to be eccentric antiquarians who studiously avoided social interaction, but in the twenty-first century, we find ourselves in the center of contentious issues of cultural heritage, practicing our profession amid heady questions regarding who owns the past and who benefits from it.

Transforming Archaeology: Activist Practices and Prospects, edited by Sonya Atalay, Lee Rains Clauss, Randall H. McGuire, and John R. Welch, 159–178. © 2014 Left Coast Press, Inc. All rights reserved.

My first introduction to the connection between descendant communities and archaeology came in 1977 at a state beach park on the island of Moloka'i, Hawai'i. Part of a group of enthusiastic undergraduates from the University of Hawai'i, Mānoa, I had flown to Molokai'i to meet with the 'Ohana—a Hawaiian word that means family and also is the name of an organization that worked to reverse the political and economic marginalization of the islands' descendant community. We (the students) had just received an undergraduate NSF grant under a currently mothballed program called Student-originated Studies. Our research design called for a multidisciplinary study of an ahupua'a (native Hawaiian land unit) called Wailau—a spectacularly beautiful valley on the windward side of Moloka'i. The valley contained lo'i (ponds for wetland taro production), irrigation canals, and dry-land terraces; and I was very excited to begin survey and mapping. We thought that our visit with the 'Ohana would be pro forma—a courtesy call before beginning our trek into the valley. We were dead wrong.

Many community members were strongly opposed to our study and very suspicious of our intentions. Some thought that powerful tourism interests were bankrolling our activities and that hotel construction inevitably would soon follow. Although our weekend of reconnaissance in Wailau Valley was not curtailed, soon afterward we received word from the 'Ohana that the valley was simply too dangerous and remote for us to successfully conduct our proposed study. Some members of the descendant community had seen no benefit to our proposed scientific research and had perceived it to be potentially deleterious to their carefully cultivated sovereignty on Moloka'i.

In retrospect, these failed negotiations were a harbinger of more to come—in Hawai'i and elsewhere—as indigenous peoples voiced objections over the asymmetrical terms of engagement with scientists of all stripes and colors. For archaeologists in general, and for me in particular, the demands of a new kind of dialogue resulted in a loss of innocence and a realization that investigating remains of the past does not exempt us from problems of the present. By avoiding dialogue about and sensitivity to the social and political issues that precondition our research, we flirt with the dangerous possibility of exacerbating existing inequalities. A dedication to elucidating the past cannot come at the expense of people in the present.

—◌◌◌—

Introduction

When U.S. soldiers fighting in the Iraq War returned home with artifacts in their duffel bags, top military brass—under pressure from the Department of Defense (DoD) Legacy Resource Management Program—launched an education campaign to change and codify the rules of engagement (ROE) for U.S. soldiers in reference to cultural heritage. By way of playing cards and other cultural awareness "products," the Legacy Program sought to sensitize soldiers to the value and vulnerability of things and places of the past (Figure 8.1). In the process, a new code of conduct was ushered in, and the rules of engagement were changed—at least officially.

Figure 8.1   Playing cards issued to soldiers in Iraq in an effort to change the Rules of Engagement (ROE) and to sensitize soldiers to the need for conservation of Iraqi cultural heritage. (Image prepared by P. A. McAnany)

In this paper, I advocate for a similar transformation in the terms of engagement (TOE) between archaeologists and communities. Such a change would affect not only how archaeologists relate to things and places of the past but also how we structure inquiry into the past, management of the past, and creation of narratives about the past. This consideration of engagement builds upon more than a decade of examination of the manner and methods by which archaeologists relate to communities, especially those proximate to sites of archaeological interest (see Pyburn 2003, among others).

One benefit of a transformation in TOE is the creation of "communities of practice" (Wenger, McDermott, and Snyder 2002, 4), in which research methods and results are generated by a broader base of participants. Within archaeology, Atalay (2012) has advocated for a similar approach—that of community-based participatory research; universities often call this approach engaged research or "3rd-sector science" (Schensul 2010). By whichever name it is called, transformed TOE open the process of knowledge production and expand the community for whom archaeology is relevant. Within this paper, I take the position that this transformation is critical to the continued vitality and relevance of archaeology.

Transforming the TOE is complicated because archaeology exists within a triadic network of archaeologists, communities, and places/objects of the past. The presence of additional interest groups (nation-states, tourists, collectors) and historical factors—like colonialism—also impinge upon what can be a very delicate relationship between archaeologists and communities. To illustrate how TOE transformation might occur and the challenges that it presents, I draw upon my involvement with cultural heritage programs in the Maya region (Figure 8.2). These examples provide support for the proposition that changing the terms of engagement is not a radical

Figure 8.2 The Maya Region showing the location of InHerit cultural heritage programs mentioned in the text. These initiatives were either conducted by InHerit in partnership with local organizations or funded by InHerit through small-grant competitions, specifically Community Heritage Grants (CHG) and Bi-Directional Knowledge Exchange Grants (BKE). (Map prepared by Sarah Rowe)

form of archaeology to be undertaken by a self-selected subset of practitioners, but rather a critical re-framing of mainstream archaeological practice that is necessary in order for the discipline to survive into the twenty-first century (Pyburn 2003; Silliman 2008, 21).

A critical part of a transformation in the TOE includes the realization that archaeologists have been looking for relevance "in all the wrong places." Rather than searching for relevance in weakly supported archaeological narratives that warn us not to repeat mistakes of the past (e.g., alleged "ecocide" committed by past peoples of Rapa Nui or the Maya region; *contra* Hunt and Lipo 2010; McAnany and Gallareta Negrón 2010), communities of practice create relevance through expansion and democratization of research communities. As I hope to demonstrate in this chapter, the past—and its conservation—has greater value to more people when they are directly involved in creating narratives about it. The creation of communities of practice, however, is not without critique. As I discuss at the end of this chapter, the ability to maintain the rigor of archaeology as a scientific pursuit when working with, by, and for communities is often questioned and scrutinized (Atalay, this volume; Ferris and Welch, this volume).

Looking for Relevance in All the Wrong Places

Commenting upon a series of papers dealing with alternative histories, Alison Wylie (1995, 262) observes that powerful and hegemonic paradigms are supported by a "preoccupation with artifacts and oral traditions as exotica or with large-scale evolutionary and ecological abstractions." As archaeologists, we like to ask questions about big problems that are relevant to the society in which we live. Today, these questions revolve around topics of environmental sustainability, competence of governmental structures, and the impact of martial conflict. Despite many sensational claims that Late Classic Maya societies were eco-cidal and lived in a state of perpetual warfare driven by incompetent rulers, scientifically robust data confirming these claims have been slow to materialize.

Decades ago, Richard Wilk (1985) noted that archaeological inferences about what happened in the ninth century Maya Lowlands closely parallel contemporary societal concerns, so this is not a new observation. Here, however, I focus on the impact of imposing contemporary societal perils onto the past in order to create what elsewhere has been called a "refracted mirror" (McAnany and Gallareta Negrón 2009:165) or "instrumental rationality" (Pyburn 2006, 4). In reference to the deep history of the U.S. Southwest, Mike Wilcox (2010) refers to these scenarios as the reverse engineering of social failure. For example, we might ask why the *abandonment* of an area—documented by archaeological techniques such as ceramic seriation and radiocarbon dating—is always interpreted as *failure* rather than *resilience* (Clauss, this volume). Nothing lasts forever, as Middleton (2012) notes, and archaeological theories of political cycles seem wedded intractably to presentist fears of ecological meltdown and gridlocked government. This interpretive perspective may seem academic, but invocation of sensationalist claims such as "total apocalyptic collapse" reverberate outside the walls of academia in ways that are coming back to haunt archaeologists.

"The haunting" to which I refer is the popular conflation of archaeological evidence for a ninth-century population drawdown in the southern lowlands with the myth of the Vanishing Indigene. Having encountered this specter on many occasions (particularly when delivering lectures to popular audiences), I still am astounded when a well-educated person comments that they were not aware that any Maya people still existed. How can you erase more than 5 million people living in the present? The conflation of ninth-century troubles with the colonial depredations and attempted ethnic erasure born of nineteenth and twentieth century nation-building becomes even worse when cross-threaded with the lack of access to archaeological information among descendant communities.

In 1995, while touring school children around the archaeological site of K'axob, a young Yukatek Maya girl asked me, "Why did all the Maya have to die?" She perceived the end of the Classic period in tragically apocalyptic terms akin to those proposed by some Maya archaeologists and, of course, by Mel Gibson whose movie bears that term in its title. She had no access to archaeological and historical information about the past—through school curricula or community programs—that would have given her insight into the resurgence of postclassic Maya polities or the painful erasure of political sovereignty wrought by colonization.

This type of collateral damage that results from both sensationalist interpretations of ecocide and a lack of meaningful engagement between archaeologists and communities weakens archaeology as a historical science. I am not suggesting that archaeologists propose only politically correct interpretations of the ninth-century time of troubles, either. I am advocating for better science and better modeling of how political change (and abandonment of place) occurs, and a retreat from the apocalyptic narratives that so pervade Judeo-Christian consciousness (see Restall and Amari 2011). Such research would attempt to go beyond today's societal concerns and generate a more precise way to think and talk about political change that is less about issuing a pass-fail report card on the past and more about understanding abandonment as a kind of agency that can be indicative of human resilience and persistence (McAnany and Yoffee 2010; Panich 2013).

Terms of Engagement:
Maya Communities, 2012 and Beyond

Many indigenous peoples in rural communities of the Maya region—whose homelands have been divided among the nation-states of Honduras, Guatemala, El Salvador, Belize, and México—are working very hard to take control of their past, present, and future (A. Cojtí Ren 2006; I. Cojtí Ren 2010; del Valle Escalante

2009; Gomez 2010; Montejo 2005). After a period of intense political and heritage alienation during colonial and nation-building times, there is renewed hope that a brighter future is possible. Although prophesized by some New Age seers as the end of time, many ethnically Maya peoples viewed the December 2012 seating of the new *bak'tun* (a period of about 400 years) in the old dynastic Long-Count Calendar as a critical turning point that marked a resurgence of political autonomy and social equality. A conference held in October of 2012 at UNC, Chapel Hill (http://www.maya2012.unc.edu) featured Maya intellectuals such as anthropologist Victor Montejo and poets Rosa Chavez and Briceida Cuevas Cob. They strongly voiced the hope that change is forthcoming. Archaeologists have an opportunity to play an active role in this positive change.

On the ground in the Maya region, change is also apparent. During the spring of 2011, while working out details of a collaborative archaeology project to be undertaken by UNC-Chapel Hill graduate student Claire Novotny on the community lands of Aguacate in southern Belize (Figure 8.2), I had an opportunity to speak with Pablo Mis—a Q'eqchi' leader and advocate of self-governance (Figure 8.3). He had just met with the district *alcaldes* (a title that is analogous to mayor) to distribute new (postcolonial) scrolls of office. A traditional symbol of authority, older scrolls bestowed authority from the Queen of England. The newer scrolls reference Judge Conteh's 2010 Supreme Court (of Belize) ruling that recognizes the land rights of Toledo Maya people. The new scroll also contains an image collage of Maya peoples with a stela in the background. When I asked Pablo what he felt about 2012, he said:

"For us it's not about catastrophe but about renewal. It's a time to reflect on the path we have walked. It is a positive time when Maya people are becoming actors—no longer passive. Many things are changing now. We want to embrace the change and channel it" (Pablo Mis, personal communication, 2011).

How does the political change that is afoot in parts of the Maya region relate to archaeology and more specifically to cultural heritage—how people view and value the past or conversely denigrate, destroy, or ignore it? For the past 7 years, my close colleagues and I have been working on this linkage and have deployed an array of programs designed to enrich the engagement of local communities with the past—to begin building communities of practice with descendant communities. These programs—especially the educational ones that introduce children living in rural communities to information about the past—are an effort to expand and reframe knowledge availability, a critical component of cultivating communities of practice (Wenger et al. 2002, 6).

Toward this end, I founded the Maya Area Cultural Heritage Initiative (MACHI), which was rebranded in 2011 as InHerit: Indigenous Heritage Passed to Present (http://www.in-herit.org). The initiatives are funded by private donors; the programs of InHerit operate through the University of North Carolina, Chapel Hill. In order to broaden the scope of heritage initiatives and to access funds more broadly, I also founded a 501(c)3 called The Alliance for Heritage Conservation.

Figure 8.3   Pablo Mis, a Q'eqchi' leader in southern Belize, unfurls a redesigned (postcolonial) scroll of office for *alcaldes* **of the Toledo District.** (Photo by Patricia A. McAnany; permission to print from Pablo Mis)

These organizations are very small, and in addition to me include a program manager, student volunteers, graduate-student affiliates, and partnering organizations locally based in the Maya region. Our *modus operandi* is strictly grassroots and we operate with very low overhead.

For instance, in western Honduras near the World Heritage site of Copán (Figure 8.2), we partnered initially with a local nongovernmental organization (NGO) called Arte Accion Copán Ruinas (AACR) and more recently with Asociación Copán. We designed a school enrichment program that would familiarize third- through fifth-grade students with the archaeology of nearby Copán and Ch'orti' heritage. Through Arte Accion, we trained local young adults to teach monthly workshops at schools within small Ch'orti' and Ladino communities (locally called *aldeas;* McAnany and Parks 2012). The three original teachers were diverse in terms of ethnic self-identities: Moises Mancia identified as Ch'orti'; Londin Velasquez initially identified as a Copaneco, but after the second year of teaching, began to identify as Ch'orti'. The third teacher, Elsa Morales, did not consider herself Ch'orti', although she is featured prominently on a Copán tourist brochure dressed in ethnic Ch'orti' clothing. With the help of the artwork of Carin Steen, the Director of AACR and cooperation of local schoolteachers, we designed and distributed workbooks for fourth–sixth grade children. For many children, it was the first book they ever owned.

The workbooks weave together threads of cultural heritage from the archaeological past of nearby Copán, discussing both archaeological conservation and the persistence of Ch'orti' identity, using Ch'orti' words whenever possible. The workbooks contain nine chapters that range widely over issues of agriculture (past and present) as well as presenting the dynastic sequence of Copán as depicted on the iconic Altar Q. Each teaching module includes an art exercise, such as making headdresses that resemble those worn by the sixteen rulers seated cross-legged around the four sides of Altar Q. The workbooks and the coloring books that are distributed to younger students explain what archaeologists do when they come to Copán. The goal is to encourage discussion of archaeology and also of site conservation and why such conservation might be of value to people today.

As Figure 8.4 illustrates, these ideas were communicated in the regional *lingua franca* (Spanish) as well as the local endangered language of Ch'orti' Mayan. The Copán area workshops are so popular with the children and teachers that we have held them continuously since 2007. Two of the students who attended the workshops went on to attend a 2012 international youth forum on cultural heritage in Spain. At the forum, they delivered a presentation on the world heritage site of Copán and what it means to them. The school enrichment program provided the students with an opportunity to think and learn about Copán, in effect to join a community of practice focused on issues of cultural heritage. In the process, the archaeological site of Copán acquired more meaning in their lives.

Newer InHerit and Alliance programs place more emphasis on community-initiated endeavors and on bidirectional knowledge exchange between archaeological projects and local communities. One of these projects, a heritage program that is

E pak'ab'ob' ke' uchyob' ch'en tyai b'ajxan turob' emayob' xe' uk'ab'ob' epak'ab'ob'
taka meyra ub'ijnusyajob' b'ajxan ub'isyob' xe tarum xi' uchyob' inte' mapa te' lugar.
Uchyob' e ch'en taka meyra te' kwidado twa' ma´chi ma'chachob' e patna'r ke' wa'r uchyob'.

*Las personas que excavan los sitios donde antes vivían los Mayas se
llaman arqueólogos. Primero miden el terreno y levantan un mapa del sitio.
Excavan con mucho cuidado para no dañar a los hallazgos.*

Figure 8.4 Page from a bilingual (Ch'orti' Mayan and Spanish) coloring book on Maya cultural heritage that was distributed to grade school students as part of a heritage enrichment program in the *aldeas* around Copán Ruinas, Honduras. (Artwork by Carin Steene)

entirely community-driven, involves mapping heritage features in the highlands of Guatemala. This GPS participatory mapping is based on a collaborative partnership with (a) the Riecken Foundation, which has built (with impressive local "buy-in") more than a dozen community libraries in the rural highlands and (b) five Tz'utujil-,

K'iché-, and Mam-speaking communities (Figure 8.2). Community mapping as a means of empowerment has produced positive results elsewhere (Gilmore & Young, 2012; Toledo Maya Cultural Council 1997, among others). We (MACHI, InHerit, and The Alliance) were interested in using it as a means of transforming the terms of engagement and building communities of practice in the Maya region.

We initiated conversations with the Riecken Foundation in 2011 about a potential partnership. Their community libraries housed computer terminals, a critical resource for downloading GPS coordinates. Representatives from the Foundation agreed to approach communities with libraries and ask if there was interest in the program. Initially, two communities were interested, and three more have joined since that time. As more communities with existing libraries express interest in the program, we have adopted a peer-transfer model. That is, veteran GPS users and mapmakers provide training for new communities as they join the program.

For communities that decided to map their heritage features (and more), access to GPS technology and complete control of the process from data collection to map production and distribution provide additional incentives. Produced maps have included thematic topics (locations of sacred sites, churches, or weavers' shops), and landscape and cultural features deemed important by community members. One community decided to map the boundaries of its community land and, toward that end, initiated discussion with neighboring groups to reach consensus on the demarcation of a boundary, particularly the stretch that bisected a forested *cerro* (large hill) that contains a summit shrine of great significance to both communities (Figure 8.5). Other participants decided to map lands that posed an environmental hazard and were prone to landslides. Another used the technology to document homes destroyed in the 2012 earthquake and by doing so expedited humanitarian assistance. The technology proved to be empowering in more ways than were originally anticipated.

During a site visit, InHerit Program Director Sarah Rowe asked why more of the region's archaeological features were not represented on the community maps. She was told that these features were of interest to communities, but mappers wanted training in site identification before documentation could begin. This answer reveals the lack of access to archaeological information that would allow communities to document precolonial places on their lands. This lack of access undergirds the bifurcation in local perspectives on heritage through much of the Maya region. Specifically, there is a strong connection with post-Hispanic places and a distancing from precolonial places, which are under the control of the nation-state. This dynamic changed when the Peace Accords of 1996—that ended a long civil war within Guatemala—guaranteed the right of indigenous Guatemalans to conduct ritual practice at sites of their ancestors. This right did not exist previously, and there was not much familiarity with places of deep history.

Tikal and Iximché, for instance, are part of an international heritage tourism business, and many local people could not afford the admission price. Now entrance is affordable for local people, and fire hearths have been built for prayers and offerings

Figure 8.5 Map of community boundaries prepared by a K'iche' community in consultation with surrounding communities as part of the joint InHerit/Riecken Foundation Community Mapping Project. Note the forested *cerro* (hill) bisected by a community boundary. Both communities maintain an important shrine on the hilltop. (K'iche' Community Mapping Project. Reproduced with permission)

at most large archaeological sites. Throughout the day, the hearths appear to be in constant use and thus are closing the distance between a people and their deep past. But smaller sites on community lands can go unnoticed and undocumented. As communities express interest in learning to identify and map precolonial places, InHerit has pledged to provide workshops to enable this important expansion of the heritage maps, although it poses issues in terms of information access for archaeologists. In terms of map-making and registration, communities completely control the products of their labor (McAnany et al. 2013). InHerit provides training, consultation, and equipment only. Sometimes, cultivating *communities of practice* requires acknowledging histories of inequality and establishing a basis for trust prior to promoting a research agenda.

In order to address the notion that Yukatek Maya communities do not identify with the archaeological past (Magnoni, Ardren, and Hutson 2007) and the reality of the acute heritage alienation experienced by many communities with limited voice in the management of places from their distant past, InHerit created a grant competition called *Community Heritage Conservation Grants*. During the first year of this program, Yukatek communities could apply directly for funds to be spent to increase awareness and protection of a heritage place—be it "natural" or humanly produced. During successive years, the competition has been expanded to include the entire Maya region. After three cycles of submissions and awards, it is clear that communities care a great deal about the past. They have proposed initiatives to refurbish old cemeteries and colonial buildings, care for neglected *cenotes* of Yucatán, and rekindle connections among youth to the *monte,* or forested areas, around communities, such as Motul, Yucatán (Figure 8.2).

These examples constitute only a small sample of the numerous indications that nonarchaeological communities desire to change the terms of engagement with archaeologists and to participate in a shared community of practice in reference to the past. What about archaeologists? Are we ready to change?

Terms of Engagement—Archaeologists

Changing the TOE among archaeologists working in the Maya region is a difficult task for a number of reasons. Archaeologists often profess to "have close friends" within the communities that provide field laborers, cooks, launderers, and house cleaners for archaeological projects, but this hierarchical relationship is very different from a collaborative community of practice in which community members and archaeologists share in the design and execution of field research. In an effort to balance the "playing field," InHerit implemented a grant competition called "Bidirectional Knowledge Exchange" (BKE) and solicited proposals from archaeologists working in the Maya region who were interested in changing the terms of engagement with communities.

In 2011, InHerit awarded a small grant to Scott Hutson to carry out a series of programs that engaged the northern Yukatek communities of Kancabel and Ucí (both located proximate to the site of an archaeological project) in a manner that was more intensive and collaborative than is typical of archaeological projects in the Maya lowlands (Hutson, Herrera, and Chi 2012; Figure 8.2). This program generated a synergy that culminated in a closing ceremony and presentation of fieldwork to local communities. The talk was presented by the young community members who had worked alongside archaeologists. At the last minute, the language in which the presentation was to be delivered changed from Spanish to Yukatek, allowing more community members (especially grandparents) to understand the content.

Hutson also requested funds to transport community members to Chichén Itzá. The World Heritage site is located only 100 km away, yet few community members had the opportunity or resources to make the trip. Yukatek Maya peoples have a complex and somewhat ambivalent relationship with the federally controlled archaeological sites of their distant past unless they receive income from guarding or grooming tourist sites or selling merchandise within or around the edges of sites (Breglia 2006; Castañeda 1996; Castañeda, this volume). Magnoni and colleagues (2007) have suggested that identities linked to ancestry do not provide a compelling narrative for Yukatek peoples whose identity—in rural towns at least—is strongly based upon relations to hard-won lands and *milpa* (fields). But as soon as Hutson's tour group approached El Castillo (the main pyramid of Chichén Itzá) and realized that visitors were no longer allowed to climb the staircase, they began to protest and suggest that they should be allowed to climb it because their ancestors built the pyramid. Heritage alienation, thus, would seem to be situational and not a fixed relationship with the past. History and Mexican nation-building in particular have clearly shaped the contours of indigenous identity. As archaeologists work to transform the terms of engagement with communities, history matters very much.

Additionally, although archaeologists have proclaimed themselves to be stewards of the past, in fact the best stewards are those whose lived existence is proximate to a place of heritage. Brent Woodfill, recipient of the 2012 Bidirectional Knowledge Exchange grant, strove to enable local stewardship by working closely with communities located near the endangered archaeological site of Salinas de los Nueves Cerros, a well-known inland salt-production locale in the Q'eqchí-speaking region of the Alta Verapaz, Guatemala (Figure 8.2). Woodfill initiated a dialogue about site conservation, and listened and responded to community needs such as the provision and installation of simple concrete piping to deliver potable water to rural dwellings. On the surface, the need for potable water—although of urgent humanitarian concern—may not appear to be linked to heritage conservation. But site stewardship with an eye to conservation is more difficult in a community in which potable water and other basic amenities are lacking. Many archaeologists working in developing countries (or rural parts of wealthy countries) balance site conservation with local development programs in an effort to empower people and to conserve archaeological sites.

Both of these bidirectional knowledge exchanges included a community facilitator who engaged daily with local communities and was responsible for the implementation of BKE initiatives. A project principal investigator generally is able to design BKE initiatives but does not have sufficient time in the field to implement them. Thus, successful cultivation of *communities of practice* requires expansion of field personnel to include a community liaison and a willingness to invest time and resources in building bridges. The two BKE examples provided here initiated partnerships and shifted the terms of engagement, a starting point for building communities of practice. Although in their infancy, the impact of such knowledge exchanges can be long-lived. For instance, a young Guatemalan member of the Salinas de los Nueves Cerros project—a talented illustrator—is now working toward a university degree. Change is constant but not instantaneous.

Building Communities of Practice While Improving Archaeological Rigor

During the 1990s, a subset of U.S. archaeologists—chafing from the Native American Graves Protection and Repatriation Act (NAGPRA) and perceived strictures on the pursuit of the past—argued that collaborative research (particularly with indigenous communities) would compromise the scientific integrity of archaeology (Clark 2000; McGhee 2008; *contra* Colwell-Chanthaphonh and Ferguson 2010; Pyburn 1999). The argument has a quasireligious sentiment in that it suggests nothing should impede the sacred "ah-hah" moment of staring into a cup of coffee and visualizing just the right theoretical approach, suitable analytical methods, and the perfect study area for a grant application. In reality, the research process is often more serendipitous than we care to admit. Generally, there are many theoretical pathways that can be followed; educational training often dictates (and restricts) methods selection; and analyses are limited by factors of preservation, time, finances, and permits. Furthermore, territorial landowners (who will not allow field work on their property) often play a large role in the delineation of a study area. So exactly what is being compromised by collaborative research other than the archaeological illusion that we control the pursuit of the past?

Clearly, there are many factors that shape archaeological research, and community participation is a positive rather than a negative factor. The triadic relationship in which archaeologists find themselves—in a dialogue with both contemporary communities and remains of the past—complicates a pursuit of the past in a way that is unique to historical disciplines. The extent to which local communities of practice may be constructible will vary from place to place and in certain parts of the world—such as the Maya region—it is difficult to disassociate the endeavor from larger issues of political and economic justice. This does not mean that the scientific integrity of archaeology has been compromised; only that archaeology has become a more humane discipline that is sensitized to history and to local narratives about the past (Colwell-Chanthaponh and Ferguson 2010).

Particularly in reference to the archaeology of indigenous America, the skill with which we navigate the intersection of archaeological science with traditional knowledge will determine the long-term sustainability of archaeology (Parks and McAnany 2011). In effect, transforming the terms of engagement has implications for practicing archaeology on a number of registers that include a more realistic assessment of the factors shaping archaeological research, an awareness of local histories and inequalities within which archaeological fieldwork takes place, and a willingness to engage with local communities as well as local knowledge and values. This final engagement—with local knowledge and values—is directly linked to conservation efforts, which many view as foundational to the continuation of archaeology as a scientific discipline. As archaeologists look ahead to a world that is increasingly and profoundly shaped (literally) by the terraforming capabilities of earth-moving bulldozers, we are confronted with the need for wider acceptance of conservation values within all sectors of society. Other scientific disciplines, such as conservation biology, have embraced the need for diglossic publication. That is, highly technical reports and journal articles that further the science of conservation biology among scientists, as well as more generally accessible articles in magazines or on Internet sites that communicate the how and why of conservation biology to a lay audience who increasingly want to be part of the dialogue. Gone are the days when archaeologists, as (asocial) social scientists, could molder away in forgotten labs in the basement of museums. The future of our discipline depends on our willingness and ability to communicate with a wider community that is both audience- and research- participant. On the academic side, this trajectory of change—which includes the ability to communicate research significance to more than one audience—needs to start at the level of graduate training and continue through tenure and promotion.

Conclusions

In this chapter, I have proposed that changing the terms of engagement between archaeologists and communities will create a more sustainable archaeology (Ferris and Welch, this volume; Welch and Ferris, this volume). The term "sustainable" is shaded with two meanings. First, a sustainable archaeology is a more inclusive discipline that embraces a participatory research paradigm and a more open architecture of inquiry and interpretation, particularly in reference to descendant communities. Second, with a broader base of participants who place value on remains of the past, it is more likely that the material remains upon which archaeology is based will be conserved. Embracing change also allows us to confront a central irony of our discipline—that we profess to study the long-term processes that create and maintain inequality, yet our research practices can reinforce inequality.

Considering Methods: Creating Communities of Practice

What methods are involved in the creation of communities of practice? Are there new ones to be learned, or is this change more akin to an altered state of mind (Clauss, this volume; Welch and Ferris, this volume)? In reality, the kind of change that is proposed throughout this book is about both method and perspective. Some archaeologists might be expert in the construction of communities of practice without a keen awareness of the theoretical underpinnings of such methodologies, whereas others might support the spirit of change while still employing traditional methods of archaeological inquiry. A nearly infinite number of permutations of transformational theory and practice are possible. Nonetheless, I have found in my practice that the adoption of certain methods does increase the probability that one can engage in building communities of practice. For instance, employment of a community liaison and consideration of a project's sustainability are central to the success of community-based archaeology.

For field-based projects, the presence of a community liaison, who can build bridges between communities and an archaeological project, is indispensible. Often an anthropologist with sociocultural training is sought to fill the liaison role, but there is a burgeoning group of young archaeologists who are equally conversant in community-based programs. A liaison helps to articulate the needs and desires of the community in reference to archaeological research and can clarify the limitations (funding, time, and so forth) faced by archaeological projects. Negotiating the terms of engagement happens through the community liaison, who plays an important role in managing expectations from both the archaeologists and the community.

Building communities of practice and enlarging participation in studying the past is predicated upon more dialogue with communities that have a vested interest in an archaeological site due to proximity or ancestry. Research partnerships cannot be built in the absence of shared knowledge about the substance, theory, and methods of archaeology. Archaeologists often confuse a lack of access to this knowledge with a lack of interest in the past. Although it is true that not everyone is a closet archaeologist, it is also true that one cannot place value on a process or place about which one has no knowledge or has not been engaged dialogically. For this reason, many archaeologists have invested in the design of workshops, special school programs, and other forms of public education. However, setting aside the problematic didactic structure of these endeavors (which can preclude rather than advance the formation of communities of practice), public education programs are expensive, time-consuming, and difficult to sustain.

For example, in the departments of Petén and Alta Verapaz, Guatemala (Figure 8.2), MACHI partnered with a local nonprofit, ProPetén, to script, record in both Spanish and Q'eqchi' languages, and broadcast on a number of radio stations a series of drama-filled stories about cultural heritage. The narratives, which were set in a fictitious rural community in the Petén, cultivated a loyal and enthusiastic audience. Unfortunately, the radio *novelas* were unsustainable because of the high and recurring expenses of production and broadcast. Our partners at ProPetén proposed that we incorporate relevant audio from the radio *novelas* into an ongoing grade school curriculum reform. The aim was to include, for the first time, precolonial Maya history, mathematics, astronomy, and indigenous languages into public education. In this way, a cultural heritage program that was novel but unsustainable became a vital part of a highly sustainable school curriculum. The lesson or *modus operandi* here is to allow programs—especially ones of educational enrichment—to change and gain greater utility. And, most importantly, as co-constituents of a community of practice, listen to and trust your partners who live "on location" to create sustainable programs.

In the end, transforming the terms of engagement may seem like an altruistic endeavor within archaeology. Hopefully, my foregoing discussion about the development of communities of practice will help to broaden this view. In my opinion, there is nothing altruistic about changing the terms of engagement between archaeologists and communities. For the reasons outlined in this chapter, this transformation within archaeology is not only the right thing to do but is also an important pathway toward the sustainability of the discipline and the conservation of tangible heritage.

Acknowledgments

I would like to acknowledge Shoshaunna Parks and Sarah Rowe for their insightful management of the MACHI and InHerit cultural heritage programs and our generous donors who believe in our vision and our ability to have an impact on "business as usual." To our many partnering organizations and collaborating archaeologists throughout the Maya region, *mil gracias!*

REFERENCES

Atalay, Sonya. 2012. *Community-based Archaeology: Research with, by, and for Indigenous and Local Communities.* Berkeley: University of California Press.

Breglia, Lisa. 2006. *Monumental Ambivalence: The Politics of Heritage.* Austin: University of Texas Press.

Castañeda, Quetzil E. 1996. *In the Museum of Maya Culture: Touring Chichén Itzá.* Minneapolis: University of Minnesota Press.

Clark, Geoffrey A. 2000. "NAGPRA: The Conflict between Science and Religion, and the Political Consequences." In *Working Together: Native Americans and Archaeologists,* edited by K. E. Dongoske, M. Aldenderfer, and K. Doehner, 85–90. Washington, DC: Society for American Archaeology.

Cojtí Ren, Avexnim. 2006. "Maya Archaeology and the Political and Cultural Identity of Contemporary Maya in Guatemala." *Archaeologies* 2(1): 8–19.

Cojtí Ren, Iyaxel Ixkan Anastasia. 2010. "The Experience of a Mayan Student." In *Being and Becoming Indigenous Archaeologists,* edited by G. P. Nicholas, 84–92. Walnut Creek, CA: Left Coast Press.

Colwell-Chanthaphonh, Chip, and T. J. Ferguson. 2010. "Intersecting Magisteria: Bridging Archaeological Science and Traditional Knowledge." *Journal of Social Archaeology* 10(3): 325–346.

del Valle Escalante, Emilio. 2009. *Maya Nationalisms and Postcolonial Challenges in Guatemala: Coloniality, Modernity, and Identity Politics.* Santa Fe, NM: School for Advanced Research.

Gilmore, Michael P., and Jason C. Young. 2012. "The Use of Participatory Mapping in Ethnobiological Research, Biocultural Conservation, and Community Empowerment: A Case Study from the Peruvian Amazon." *Journal of Ethnobiology* 32(1): 6–29.

Gomez, Felipe. 2010. "The Struggle for a Law on Sacred Sites in Guatemala." *Compas: Endogenous Development Magazine* 6: 26–29.

Hunt, Terry L., and Carl P. Lipo. 2010. "Ecological Catastrophe, Collapse, and the Myth of 'Ecocide' on Rapa Nui (Easter Island)." In *Questioning Collapse: Human Resilience, Ecological Vulnerability, and the Aftermath of Empire,* edited by P. A. McAnany and N. Yoffee, 21–44. New York: Cambridge University Press.

Hutson, Scott R., G. Can Herrera, and G. A. Chi. 2012. "Maya Heritage Entangled and Transformed." *International Journal of Heritage Studies* 19: 1–17.

Magnoni, Aline, Traci Ardren, and Scott Hutson. 2007. "Tourism in the Mundo Maya: Inventions and (Mis)Representations of Maya Identities and Heritage." *Archaeologies* 3(3): 353–383.

McAnany, Patricia A., and Tomás Gallareta Negrón. 2010. "Bellicose Rulers and Climatological Peril? Retrofitting 21st Century Woes on 8th Century Maya Society." In *Questioning Collapse: Human Resilience, Ecological Vulnerability, and the Aftermath of Empire,* edited by P. A. McAnany and N. Yoffee, 142–175. New York: Cambridge University Press.

McAnany, Patricia A., and Shoshaunna Parks. 2012. "Casualties of Heritage Distancing: Children, Ch'ortí Indigeneity, and the Copan Archaeoscape." *Current Anthropology* 53(1): 80–107.

McAnany, Patricia A., Sarah M. Rowe, Israel Quic Cholotio, Evelyn Caniz Menchú, and Jose Mendoza Quic. 2013. "Mapping Indigenous Self-Determination in Highland Guatemala." *International Journal of Applied Geospatial Research.* Accepted for publication.

McAnany, Patricia A., and Norman Yoffee. 2010. "Why We Question Collapse and Study Human Resilience, Ecological Vulnerability, and the Aftermath of Empire." In *Questioning Collapse: Human Resilience, Ecological Vulnerability, and the Aftermath of Empire,* edited by P. A. McAnany and N. Yoffee, 1–17. New York: Cambridge University Press.

McGhee, Robert. 2008. "Aboriginalism and the Problems of Indigenous Archaeology." *American Antiquity* 73(4): 579–597.

Middleton, Guy D. 2012. "Nothing Lasts Forever: Environmental Discourses on the Collapse of Past Societies." *Journal of Archaeological Research* 20: 257–307.

Montejo, Victor. 2005. *Maya Intellectual Renaissance: Identity, Representation, and Leadership.* Austin: University of Texas Press.

Panich, Lee. 2013. "Archaeologies of Persistence: Reconsidering the Legacies of Colonialism in Native North America." *American Antiquity* 78(1): 105–122.

Parks, Shoshaunna, and Patricia A. McAnany. 2011. "Heritage Rights and Global Sustainability via Maya Archaeology." *Anthropology News* 52(5): 27.

Pyburn, K. Anne. 1999. "Native American Religion versus Archaeological Science: A Pernicious Dichotomy Revisited." *Science and Engineering Ethics* 5: 355–366.

———. 2003. "Archaeology for a New Millennium: The Rules of Engagement." In *Archaeologists and Local Communities: Partners in Exploring the Past,* edited by L. Derry and M. Malloy, 167–184. Washington, DC: Society for American Archaeology.

———. 2006. "The Politics of Collapse." *Archaeologies* 2(1): 3–7.

Restall, Matthew, and Solari Amara. 2011. *2012 and the End of the World: The Western Roots of the Maya Apocalypse.* Lanham, MD: Rowman and Littlefield.

Schensul, Jean. 2010. "Engaged Universities, Community Based Research Organizations and Third Sector Science in a Global System." *Human Organization* 69(4): 307–320.

Silliman, Stephen W. 2008. "Collaborative Indigenous Archaeology: Troweling at the Edges, Eyeing the Center." In *Collaborating at the Trowel's Edge: Teaching and Learning in Indigenous Archaeology,* edited by S. W. Silliman, 1–21. Tucson: University of Arizona Press.

Toledo Maya Cultural Council. 1997. *Maya Atlas: the Struggle to Preserve Maya Land in Southern Belize.* Berkeley, CA: North Atlantic Books.

Wenger, Etienne, Richard McDermott, and William M. Snyder. 2002. *Cultivating Communities of Practice.* Cambridge, MA: Harvard Business School Press.

Wilcox, Michael. 2010. "Marketing Conquest and the Vanishing Indian: An Indigenous Response to Jared Diamond's Archaeology of the American Southwest." In *Questioning Collapse: Human Resilience, Ecological Vulnerability, and the Aftermath of Empire,* edited by P. A. McAnany and N. Yoffee, 113–141. New York: Cambridge University Press.

Wilk, Richard R. 1985. "The Ancient Maya and the Political Present." *Journal of Anthropological Research* 41(3): 307–326.

Wylie, Alison. 1995. "Alternative Histories: Epistemic Disunity and Political Integrity." In *Making Alternative Histories: the Practice of Archaeology and History in Non-Western Settings,* edited by P. R. Schmidt and T. C. Patterson, 255–272. Santa Fe, NM: School of American Research Press.

Chapter 9

From the Bottom Up
Transforming Communities with Public Archaeology

M. Jay Stottman

For those of us who see archaeology as being transformative, particular experiences in our careers helped create our desire to use archaeology as an agent of change. One such experience early in my career was responsible for showing me that archaeology, particularly in the cultural resource management (CRM) context, has an opportunity to do much more to benefit communities and to enact change.

My experience working on a large mitigation project for a CRM contract firm in one of Louisville's economically depressed neighborhoods struck a chord with me. It enlightened me to the realities of CRM archaeology and its public interest rhetoric. I was concerned with how the focus was centered entirely on satisfying a legal mandate, with no interest in how cultural resources articulate with the present-day community. The archaeological research was triggered by a government project to revitalize the neighborhood, but there was no attempt to integrate archaeology into this effort. As we dug and recovered pieces of a community's history inside the vacuum of cultural resource compliance, I became disillusioned about the hundreds of thousands of dollars that were reluctantly being spent to do archaeology so that city planners could be free to "revitalize" the community with new homes. Few from the community knew we were there, what we were doing, or why we were in their neighborhood.

Transforming Archaeology: Activist Practices and Prospects, edited by Sonya Atalay, Lee Rains Clauss, Randall H. McGuire, and John R. Welch, 179–196. © 2014 Left Coast Press, Inc. All rights reserved.

Having some experience in public archaeology, I understood that archaeology could do more than just recover information to save history in the public interest. I knew that public archaeology had the power to connect with communities. Furthermore, I saw the potential of CRM archaeology to be transformative because of the many opportunities that it affords archaeologists to come into contact with many publics and stakeholders (Ferris and Welch, this volume; McGhee and McDavid 2010).

Had that CRM archaeology project been developed within a transformative framework, we would have collaborated with the community to develop a public archaeology program that could have built community pride and strengthened identity through their participation in the archaeological process. Educational programs could have been created for local schools using archaeology and their community history as resources. The results of the project could have aided the struggling Kentucky African-American Heritage Center, which is housed in one of the buildings rehabilitated during the revitalization effort.

My experience enlightened me to the limitations of CRM archaeology as it was being practiced. At that moment, I knew that archaeology could be and do more for people in the present. Since then, I have worked as an activist to change the way we think about archaeology—from being just a means to collect and protect information to becoming a vehicle for change. I have seen that public archaeology can be more than just serving the public interest; it can be collaborative and empowering for communities. And, thus, I believe that the use of more public archaeology within CRM, as well as other archaeologies, has tremendous potential for transforming the communities in which we work.

Transformative Archaeology

Over the last ten years, archaeologists have been trying to define what many have sought to do or have been doing since the late 1980s: practice a transformative archaeology. During this time, we have seen a number of approaches that treat archaeology as a way to affect present-day people. We have seen the development of a civically engaged, collaborative, community, action, and redefined applied archaeology (Atalay 2012; Colwell-Chanthaphohn and Ferguson 2008; Derry and Malloy 2003; Little and Shackel 2007; Little and Zimmerman 2010; McGuire 2008; Sabloff 2008; Shackel and Chambers 2004). We have seen attempts to couch these approaches under the broader term of "activism" (Stottman 2010). However, bringing together these approaches within one term has been problematic because they are so diverse in their perspective, practice, and constituents. Thus, defining what we do and labeling has become futile (Atalay, this volume; Clauss, this volume). As described in the introduction, we discovered that although we all have similar goals, we cannot always apply our practices to all contexts, situations, or people; nor is there a one-size-fits-all terminology. For example, although the term and concept of "advocacy" is acceptable within present-day American communities, it is often problematic within indigenous communities. The people living in an American historic neighborhood may seek out an advocate to speak for them regarding the protection and use of their cultural heritage resources; in indigenous contexts, the colonial baggage of our field often creates tensions between Native Americans and archaeologists, making advocacy more nuanced and often difficult (Ferguson, this volume; Nicholas, this volume). Thus, we understand that what brings us all together is not a common terminology, but a desire to create change in and with archaeology. All the authors in this volume use archaeology to enact change and be transformative. Being civically engaged, collaborative, an advocate, or an activist are often understood as transformative actions and roles. However, public archaeology is perhaps overlooked and undervalued as another means by which archaeologists can be transformative.

Public Archaeology

Some form of public archaeology has been around almost as long as the field of archaeology, as some archaeologists sought to engage with lay people about archaeology through site tours and popular books. When McGimsey (1972) coined the term "public archaeology," archaeologists began to examine their relationship with the public, which consisted mainly of archaeologists operating through the state in the best interest of the public (Merriman 2004). However, over the last 20 years, public archaeology has developed to include many concepts and has become positioned as a subfield within archaeology that has theory, practice, and even its own journal (Merriman 2004; Jameson 1997, 2004; Little and Zimmerman 2010; Potter 1994). It has grown to include nearly all of archaeology's contact with nonarchaeologists, including not just public interest issues but also media relations, education, tourism, and outreach.

Because public archaeology is so broad in its scope and diverse in its practice, misconceptions about its innate capability to be collaborative and transformative have overshadowed its use to do so (Clauss, this volume). Perhaps due to the popularity of engaging with the public, many archaeologists have jumped blindly into public archaeology, leading to many criticisms about the value of this endeavor. Doing public archaeology for some simply means working for or through the government, or just inviting the public to their research project without any goals, methods, or understanding of the variety of publics that exist. Furthermore, public archaeology has traditionally been focused on archaeological literacy and stewardship for the sake of disciplinary self-preservation within difficult political climates. Thus, many public archaeology efforts are public interest–focused and employ a top-down approach in which the archaeologist initiates and controls all aspects of a program in the name of benefiting the public (Little and Zimmerman 2010). Unfortunately, these types of public archaeology tend to overshadow its potential to be transformative.

Some of the earliest attempts to use archaeology in a transformative way, however, took place with public archaeology. During the 1980s, as critical approaches to archaeology began to take root, the "Archaeology in the Public" program in Annapolis, Maryland sought to use archaeology to affect the present (Potter and Leone 1987; Potter 1994). The intent of the program was to create change through public archaeology: "Given that our ideas about the past are shaped largely by the present, the overriding goal of 'Archaeology in the Public' is to show people the ways that we strive to understand the past and therefore shape it, so that they may begin to take some responsibility for their own understanding of the past" (Potter and Leone 1987, 52). This effort represents one of the first attempts to consciously use archaeology to change people in the present, a main tenet of critical archaeology (McGuire, this volume; Leone, Potter, and Shackel 1987; Tilley 1989). In retrospect, Parker Potter, one of the creators of the program, did not think the program accomplished those goals, mainly because of a failure to fully understand and collaborate with their publics (1994, 234). Since then, public archaeology has developed beyond the top-down site tour approach to also include more collaborative and participatory approaches.

Applied anthropologist Erve Chambers observed that public archaeology is "participatory" and "collaborative" (Derry 2003, 185). Public archaeologists understand that the process of doing archaeology can be more meaningful to the public than the research they produce. Participation in the archaeological process also makes archaeology more intelligible to local communities, which, in turn, fosters better collaboration (Heckenberger 2008, 255). After all, the process of archaeology can be a means to directly involve and educate people in the discovery and experience of their past (Smardz and Smith 2000). And in order to better understand the variety of publics and their needs and wants, public archaeologists have become more collaborative. Some public archaeologists have taken a bottom-up approach by putting the goals of their publics on equal footing with traditional research goals (Cressey 2003; Little and Shackel 2007; Little and Zimmerman 2010; Shackel and Chambers 2004; Stottman 2010). Some public archaeologists collaborate with educators to develop educational materials and outreach programs that use archaeology to help them teach students about social studies, math, and science (Moe 2002; Jeppson 2010). They collaborate with communities to develop goals for their programs and to help address the issues that they face (Gadsby and Barnes 2010; Heckenberger 2008; McDavid 2010). Overall, although the goals and messages of most public archaeology programs still have a strong archaeological literacy and ethics component, there has been a growing emphasis on developing more collaborative and transformative goals. Such a public archaeology could help realize the goals of creating change in the present that was desired in Annapolis nearly 30 years ago.

Because being transformative is inherently public, what public archaeologists do and how they interact with communities provides a perspective that will allow transformative goals to be created and implemented during a project. Archaeology can be used to educate, develop heritage, and be a part of benefiting communities.

Transformative Public Archaeology

To demonstrate the transformative potential of public archaeology, I present two illustrative case studies. The Farnsley-Kaufman House and the Portland Wharf projects exemplify how public archaeology has grown beyond the typical top-down approaches to be collaborative, goal-oriented, and used as a vehicle to help benefit communities. Furthermore, they demonstrate that the process of doing archaeology has the capability to be a tool for change within communities. Whether we are asked to speak for communities or just to advocate for them in small ways, archaeologists, through public archaeology, can have a role in the transformation of communities.

Mystery at the Farnsley-Kaufman House

In 1996, an early nineteenth-century log barn at the Farnsley-Kaufman House located in southwestern Louisville, Kentucky was demolished to make way for a new middle school. The bulldozers were set on taking down the historic home and outbuildings before community outrage gave the remaining buildings a reprieve. The loss of the barn touched a nerve in a community that was primarily working class and had only recently been exposed to historic preservation with the restoration of the nearby Farnsley-Moremen House just 4 years prior. Preserving old houses was seen as something that took place only in the wealthier parts of town, in which the important buildings worthy of saving were located. But the community rallied around the Farnsley-Kaufman house to preserve a history that was equally as rich as any other in the city. Appalled by the possibility of having their history bulldozed, members of the local community and descendants of the Farnsley and Kaufman families banded together to preserve the remaining buildings. However, in order to accomplish this task, they had to find a new use for the house and convince the local school board not to demolish it.

Many of those who worked to stop the bulldozers were familiar with an archaeology–based school field trip program that I codeveloped at the Farnsley-Moremen House (Stahlgren and Stottman 2007). They asked me to convince the school board that the old house and property had educational value. Today, looming over the house is the brand-new Farnsley Middle School, which became one of the few schools in the state to have its own historic site. One of the keys to the preservation of the house was to demonstrate to the school board that the site was an asset and not a liability. The school board saw the site as an eyesore and potentially dangerous, whereas preservationists saw it as an educational resource. As one school board member put it, "We are not in the business of saving old buildings." However, they were responsible for educating our children and there was tremendous potential to use the Farnsley-Kaufman House to accomplish that. Everyone involved in the project understood that we had to make a connection to the school.

In 1998, a team of teachers from Farnsley Middle School and members of the community attended the Kentucky Resource Center for Heritage Education workshop to learn how to use the site as a heritage resource. This group determined that an archaeology education project with the school would be the first step. Such a project would have many benefits: the establishment of a link to the school, educating kids, providing important research about the property, and demonstrating the value of saving this piece of community history.

Working with teachers from the school and a grant from the Resource Center for Heritage Education, the Kentucky Archaeological Survey designed an educational archaeology project for 120 sixth graders. Through activities and lessons presented in the classroom, the children learned about the history of the site and the basic skills used in archaeology. They participated in all aspects of archaeological research, from research design to reporting the results. Weekly meetings with the teachers facilitated the use of archaeology as a hands-on example of concepts that were being taught in the classroom. Through the participation in the archaeology project, students learned applications of the scientific method, classification, grids, and the local history and culture of the people who lived and worked at the site. The students did everything that archaeologists do in the field: they excavated, sifted, and took notes and photographs (Figure 9.1). They worked in the lab by washing and

Figure 9.1 Students and teachers from Farnsley Middle School participate in an excavation at the Farnsley-Kaufman House with archaeologists from the Kentucky Archaeological Survey. (Photo by M. Jay Stottman)

Figure 9.2   Restoration work in the front porch area of the Farnsley-Kaufman house. (Photo by M. Jay Stottman)

cataloguing artifacts. The students even conducted analyses by creating a database for the artifacts and identified artifact patterns. Students also disseminated their findings by developing a PowerPoint presentation about the archaeology project that they presented to their school and to various preservation groups across the city. They also designed an exhibit about their project that was on display at the 1999 Kentucky State Fair.

Through the project, the students became invested in the work they were doing and in the house, as they became part of what was being saved. The archaeology project had research goals designed to help interpret the architecture of the house, so that it could be more accurately restored (Figure 9.2). The archaeological goals of the project were focused on the front porch of the house, which was removed many years before. Architectural historians working on the project did not know how many porches there had been over time, how big they were, or how they were constructed. The students not only helped to collect and process the archaeological data but they also helped us make interpretations about the front porch based on their findings. The archaeological research questions that we posed to them led to the naming of their exhibit "Mystery at the Farnsley-Kaufman House" because they really did see the porch as a mystery. To solve it, they used the clues that they collected and the skills they gained during the archaeological project. Using many of the wonderful ideas and interpretations that the students provided, we could determine that as many as three porches had existed in front of the house over time and we could provide their dimensions and construction type to the architectural historians.

We continued the archaeology program at the Farnsley-Kaufman House for 2 more years, focusing on surveying the entire property around the house and helping determine the foundation system originally used for the log portion of the house. Although archaeology is not always a part of the school programs conducted at the Farnsley-Kaufman House, it did provide a framework for the relationship that developed between the school, the Friends group, and the community. Architectural historians and historic preservation students from the University of Kentucky picked up where we left off as they worked with teachers and students to design an education program using the restoration of the house as a resource. Students from the school worked with the architectural historians much as they did with us to help with the interpretation, stabilization, and restoration of the house.

Like most projects, the educational programs conducted at the Farnsley-Kaufman House came to an end. Teachers and principals at the school came and went over the years, and archaeologists and architectural historians moved on to other projects. For nearly 15 years, the education project at the house was not funded and was inactive. However, its effect on the school, its students, its teachers, the community, and the site was not forgotten. So, did we change anything with our public archaeology program at the Farnsley-Kaufman House? Was it transformative? Like most public archaeologists, we like to think that we made a difference in that we helped students learn, helped a consistently low-performing school, and changed people's lives. We do know that the public archaeology conducted at the Farnsley-Kaufman House did change something. The house still stands among the truck traffic from the nearby industrial park, the service stations, billboards, and smokestacks from the nearby power plant as a reminder that this part of Louisville has history, too, and is important. The relationship of the Friends group to the school remains intact because school representatives sit on the Friends group board, and the group holds regular events and fundraisers at the school. Certainly, the project was transformative in helping to foster a relationship between this new school and the community. Because of this strong relationship, the school and the Friends group recently acquired funding to restore the historic landscape and they are eager to renew the archaeology education program in 2014.

This case study demonstrates that public archaeology need not be a superficial, top-down, do-good and feel-good activity for archaeologists. It reorients our perspective of archaeology from a focus on what we learn about the past being transformative to how we do it being even more so. Public archaeology programs such as these are a way to practice a transformative archaeology because they embody the qualities of what we do to be transformative, as described in the introduction of this volume. The Farnsley-Kaufman House archaeology project was a bottom-up program because community members invited me to help them preserve the house and establish a relationship with the school. It was collaborative because I worked with teachers to develop an educational program using archaeology that was conducive to what sixth graders were learning in class. I had regular meetings with the sixth grade teaching team to discuss what they were teaching in class and I found ways that archaeology could be used to demonstrate the concepts either in the field or the lab. It was goal oriented because we had traditional research goals to help aid the restoration of the house, but the community goals were equally important. We wanted to bring more attention to the site and the house's preservation, convince the school board that the house was an asset and not a liability, help create a relationship between the community and the school, make learning more interesting, instill a sense of ownership and meaning about the past in the students, and inspire them to use the skills they learn in school. Through public archaeology, I was able to use archaeology to be an advocate and activist, and to be transformative.

Transforming the Portland Wharf with Public Archaeology

Another case study in which public archaeology became an important element of a transformative archaeological project occurred at Portland Wharf. This particular project and the activist approach taken with its development have been extensively discussed in Prybylski and Stottman (2010). However, I want to discuss the importance of public archaeology in developing transformative archaeology within that context. Fresh off my experiences with the Farnsley-Kaufman House project, I found myself again being invited by a community to help them use archaeology for their benefit. The Portland neighborhood is currently one of Louisville's most economically depressed, a contrast with its history as an independent and prosperous town. The vestiges of the original town of Portland lie beneath the ground situated on the wrong side of the flood wall constructed in the 1940s to protect the community from the ravages of the Ohio River. Today, the Portland Wharf is now sixty acres of wooded scrub and meadow, cut off from the Portland community by the flood wall and an elevated interstate highway. Since the 1980s, this community has sought to reconnect with the river, the wharf that symbolized their early independence and prosperity, and their rich history (Figure 9.3).

The Portland Museum, a local history and cultural museum dedicated to the Portland community, began to examine ways in which the unused, forgotten land that was Portland's wharf could be reconnected to the community. The community felt that the rich archaeological deposits associated with the original Portland Wharf provided an opportunity to make some material connection to their past—a way for the community to remember and transform this useless landscape into one that

Figure 9.3   An archaeologist from the Kentucky Archaeological Survey uncovers the remains of a house at the Portland Wharf Park. (Photo by M. Jay Stottman)

is dedicated to and symbolizes Portland's rich past and identity. Thus, the Portland community has had the desire to use these resources to help transform the Portland Wharf landscape and their neighborhood. Neighborhood leaders thought that public archaeology could help achieve that goal by bringing publicity to their history, bringing people in, and changing negative perceptions of the neighborhood. Thus, the Portland community desired to create an archaeology and history park at the old Portland Wharf site, where people could learn about Portland's illustrious past and participate in the unearthing of its history through archaeology. Although the idea of the Portland Wharf heritage park was first conceived in the mid-1980s, it was not until the late 1990s that the site was designated a park by the City of Louisville, and the development of a master plan was initiated. I was brought in as a technical advisor on a community committee working with planners to examine what role archaeology—and more specifically, public archaeology—would play in the park.

Initially, the public archaeology envisioned by the neighborhood consisted of the sort of passive site tours that were common during the 1980s. But then we soon began to discuss incorporating some participatory excavation elements like those I had developed for other public sites, as well. As a result of the master planning process, which included many public meetings and design workshops, the park design included those passive elements of public archaeology such as signage informed by archaeological research and even a public viewing area for ongoing archaeological excavations. As part of the ongoing archaeological research at the park, a variety of participatory excavation and educational programs also would be developed, such as camps, field trips, public field experiences, and neighborhood volunteer opportunities. Although the development of the park presented a number of public archaeology opportunities, it was not known which programs would work best logistically for the site and achieve the goals of the neighborhood. Thus, prior to the implementation of the master plan, an assessment of the archaeological resources and some testing of public archaeology programs was conducted to determine which programs could best address community goals (Figure 9.4).

A park usage survey was conducted to measure how the park was being used, and various public programming strategies were tested. During our project, we kept tally of park visitors and used questionnaires to learn about who used the park, what people did there, archaeology's effect on users, and what kinds of public programming appealed to visitors the most. We tried to develop programming that accommodated a variety of people's interests and skills. We wanted to know

Figure 9.4   Public archaeology programs tested at the Portland Wharf included temporary interpretive signage and a participatory excavation. (Photo by M. Jay Stottman)

how long and how structured the programming should be. Also, what were the logistical problems with having a long-term active dig site open to weather, vandals, and flooding? Thinking about such issues beforehand and collecting data about particular types of programs allowed us to develop a public archaeology program at the park that would most effectively meet the community's goals.

In addition to better understanding the park and researching potential public archaeology programs, we heeded Parker Potter's (1994) call to better understand the community in which we were working. Although the master planning process was a public one that was designed to get input from a cross-section of the community, we really did not get a good understanding of the community's cultural dynamics. Because Portland is a community of nearly 4,000 people, developing a bottom-up collaborative approach to public archaeology was more challenging than our program at the Farnsley-Kaufman House. There were many more stakeholders than the teachers and preservationists I worked with at the Farnsley-Kaufman House. What we needed was a study of the current neighborhood population and a strategy for representing as much of the neighborhood as possible.

As discussed throughout this volume, to practice a truly transformative archaeology we have to be collaborative by first finding out what a community wants and needs. To do so, we will invariably and inevitably spend as much of our time working with present-day people as we do trying to learn about those in the past. Unfortunately, however, although archaeologists have become quite adept at researching past cultures, we are not usually trained to work with present-day cultures. Thus, our first reaction to doing public archaeology or collaborating with a community is to take a top-down approach, in which we treat people like the objects we find. As I and others have suggested elsewhere, archaeologists need to develop skills that will allow us to understand and collaborate with present-day communities to accomplish the transformative goals of our archaeology, such as those practiced by our cultural anthropology colleagues (Chambers 2004; Derry 2003; Stottman 2010). How do we know what a community wants and needs? How do we know that they think about archaeology and what it can do for them? How can we take a bottom-up and collaborative approach and develop transformative goals? To learn more about the Portland community, I adopted methods from my applied anthropology colleagues and conducted a rapid assessment as part of my dissertation research to get a snapshot of the community. I conducted interviews on a representative sample of people in the neighborhood to better understand perceptions of the neighborhood, their concepts of heritage, views of the park-planning process, attitudes toward the City of Louisville, attitudes toward neighborhood representatives such as the Portland Museum and the neighborhood association, the potential of archaeology, and a sense of neighborhood identity.

The information collected during the excavations, surveys, and interviews has helped determine the feasibility of developing a sustainable long-term public archaeology program at the Portland Wharf Park. It also helped identify some major logistical issues related to site security, access, facilities, and amenities. However, it also uncovered the complexity of Portland's identity and community stakeholders, and made us reexamine our role as archaeologists in the transformation of a community. Thus, the rather simplistic top-down approach to public archaeology, in which we just put our research on signs and allow people to dig up the Portland Wharf, does little to accomplish the goals of the neighborhood in a collaborative way. By better understanding the community via a bottom-up approach to public archaeology, we have been able to examine our effect on the transformation of the Portland Wharf landscape and ascertain whether our approaches are normalizing particular views and concepts of heritage. This project also demonstrates that public archaeology can be used in a transformative way, but that programs need to be collaborative, and we have to understand the communities in which we work.

Despite all the effort to understand the Portland community, be collaborative, and develop effective public archaeology programs that will transform the Portland Wharf, to date little has changed at the park and in the Portland neighborhood. There is a plan to transform the site into the heritage park that the people of Portland have so long desired, but that is all. It represents a dream and a promise that is unfulfilled and subject to political whims that are often out of the archaeologist's control. Although together with the Portland community we have used public archaeology to help create a master plan for a heritage park and developed public archaeology programs, we cannot and should not implement it on our own. A collaborative and transformative public archaeology is, by definition, dependent on others. Without the political will, funding, and help from the City of Louisville, the Portland Wharf Park master plan will never come to fruition. Thus, we must advocate for the project any way we can. In the case of Portland Wharf Park, I collaborated with the Portland Museum and local schools to conduct small public archaeology programs such as camps, field trips, and periodic special events at the park to keep the public interested in the project and to appeal to local politicians to implement the park master plan. Thus, when we do transformative archaeology, we often find ourselves becoming entwined in community causes and taking up a community's fight for justice or simply to get their projects implemented (McGuire, this volume).

Conclusions

The programs described in these two case studies were transformative because of a dedication to, and an implementation of, a community-first, collaborative approach. Both projects were designed to recognize and seek to understand the variety of publics and stakeholders within the communities they served. Public archaeology programs such as these provide a means to make archaeology and its process transformative. Not all public archaeology is created and practiced in the same way because there are many types and practices; however, with a bottom-up approach that seeks to understand and implement community goals in addition to archaeological goals, public archaeology can be one of many vehicles for a transformative archaeology. Although some may not consider their transformative projects to be public archaeology, such as other examples in this volume, I would argue that they are very much like the bottom-up and collaborative programs that public archaeologists conduct. Thus, the potential of public archaeology to be a vehicle for a transformative archaeology should not be ignored.

The two case studies I presented were transformative and collaborative largely because the communities that initiated the projects knew enough about archaeology to understand its potential to be used for their own benefit. Although public archaeology can be criticized for being largely concerned with increasing the public's archaeological literacy for our benefit, it is clear from these case studies that archaeology's power to be transformative is weaker without it. If the communities that we work with know very little about archaeology and its process, how can we collaborate with them to use archaeology for their benefit? Collaboration means that all parties need to have some basic knowledge of the issues or subjects at hand (Heckenberger 2008, 253). Otherwise, we place ourselves in a top position of the group power dynamic, where we have to assume complete control of a project that uses archaeology to be transformative in a top-down relationship. The more communities know about archaeology, the better able they will be to collaborate with archaeologists. Public archaeology thus plays an integral part in making publics more archaeologically literate, which will help foster more collaborative projects. The point is that not all public archaeology is transformative, but bottom-up, collaborative public projects and the work that public archaeologists do regarding archaeological literacy are important in our endeavor to make archaeology more transformative.

⟶ ⟶

Considering Methods

Evaluation and Assessment: Keys to Developing and Practicing a Collaborative and Transformative Archaeology

When it comes to collaborating with communities and practicing an archaeology that is transformative, we must use methods that will allow us to understand present-day people and we must evaluate our programs for their effectiveness in collaboration and achieving goals (Nicholas, Welch, and Yellowhorn 2008; Welch, Lepofsky, and Washington 2011). We really cannot know if we are being transformative if we do not evaluate. Evaluation has become important to public archaeology programs, especially those focused on education. Public archaeologists realized that it was important to know how effective their programs were at achieving education goals (Krupicz 2000; McNutt 2000). Thus, qualitative research methods and instruments such as rapid assessment procedures, questionnaires, surveys, evaluations, and interviews that are common in other fields have become an important part of some public archaeology programs (Brooks 2007; Gadsby and Chidester 2007; Moyer 2007). The two case studies discussed earlier in this chapter provide an opportunity to examine the importance of evaluating public archaeology programs in order to improve them and make them more collaborative and bottom-up in approach.

Although evaluation was not necessarily a part of the Farnsley-Kaufman House public archaeology program, it was modeled after other school-based educational public archaeology programs conducted by the Kentucky Archaeological Survey (KAS) that have been engaging in evaluation and assessment. KAS education coordinator Gwynn Henderson teamed with University of Kentucky education researcher Linda Levstik to conduct a study of fifth grade students who had participated in our public archaeology field trip program at Ashland, the Henry Clay Estate, and associated classroom lessons and activities (Henderson and Levstik 2004; Levstik, Henderson, and Schlarb 2003).

The evaluation consisted of interviews with the students to examine the effect of the program on the student's historical thinking and understanding of archaeology. The results noted that there was higher motivation and student interest in inquiry-based instruction and a development of a strong understanding of core historical and archaeological concepts. However, there also was development of misconceptions about those concepts. These results identified strengths in the program, such as the development of interest in history, as well as many weaknesses, such as confusing some students with the presentation of some materials. The study demonstrated that archaeology goals were too prominent, and that we needed to give equal attention to educational goals, suggesting that our programs need to be more bottom-up. Furthermore, we learned that we needed to better understand the students and their developmental and learning capabilities because we found that they developed many misconceptions from our overuse of analogies in presenting information. The evaluation provided information, which has helped us refine the goals for our school-based public archaeology programs and improve our practice by working with education professionals to see how archaeology can help kids learn more effectively.

Public archaeology test programs at the Portland Wharf site also were evaluated. The evaluations were conducted to determine whether public archaeology in the park could help accomplish the community goals of bringing more people into Portland, helping change negative perceptions about the neighborhood, and educating residents and nonresidents about the history of Portland. These programs encompassed a variety of programming types, including site signage, self-guided and guided tours, and participatory excavations.

To evaluate the test programs and participant experience, as well as collect feedback for future programs, we designed and administered an exit survey. The anonymous surveys collected basic demographic information about participants such as age group, residence zip code, and gender. We asked which type of program they participated in, their evaluation of the information presented, and how much time they spent at the site. We also asked questions about whether participating in the programs affected their understanding of Portland's history, their perception of the Portland neighborhood, and their desire to participate in future programs.

The results of the survey demonstrated that the programs did draw people from outside of Portland into the neighborhood for the first time. The programs did change perceptions of Portland for those from outside the neighborhood and helped Portland residents and nonresidents better understand the community's history. We also learned that participants were very enthusiastic about participating in future programs. Based on the results, we were able to better understand what kinds of public archaeology programs would work best at the park and address the goals of the community. The use of survey methods to evaluate our test programs at the Portland Wharf helped us develop a bottom-up approach to public archaeology and collaborate with the community.

These two examples demonstrate that evaluation is an integral part of any collaborative and public archaeology program with transformative goals. If the desired result of a project is to create change or transform, we must be able to assess it in a more rigorous and methodical way so that we can better collaborate, refine goals, and improve practice. To this end, public archaeologists are currently utilizing qualitative methods and collaborating with other fields to develop both a practice of, and mandate for, more evaluation.

Acknowledgments

I would like to thank Lee Rains Clauss and Sonya Atalay for organizing and inviting me to the SAA session and Amerind session on activist archaeology. I also would like to thank the editors of this volume and all the participants in the Amerind session for their insightful comments and discussions. I am grateful to the historical archaeology activist archaeologists who have pushed the discussion of activist archaeology in the many conference sessions and forums since 2004. I owe a great deal of gratitude to my colleagues at the Kentucky Archaeological Survey for their inspiration and dedication to public archaeology. Finally, I am indebted to my family, especially my wife Beth, without whom I would not be an activist archaeologist.

REFERENCES

Atalay, Sonya. 2012. *Community-Based Archaeology: Research with, by, and for Indigenous and Local Communities.* Berkeley: University of California Press.

Brooks, Meagan. 2007. "Reconnecting the Present with Its Past: The Doukhobor Pit House Public Archaeology Project." In *Archaeology as a Tool of Civic Engagement,* edited by Barbara J. Little and Paul A. Shackel, 203–222. Lanham, MD: AltaMira Press.

Chambers, Erve. 2004. "Epilogue: Archaeology, Heritage, and Public Endeavor." In *Places in Mind: Public Archaeology as Applied Anthropology,* edited by Paul A. Shackel and Erve Chambers, 193–216. New York: Routledge.

Colwell-Chanthaphohn, Chip, and T. J. Ferguson, eds. 2008. *Collaboration in Archaeological Practice: Engaging Descendant Communities.* Lanham, MD: AltaMira Press.

Cressey, Pamela. 2003. "Held in Trust: Community Archaeology in Alexandria." In *Archaeologists and Local Communities: Partners in Exploring the Past*, edited by Linda Derry and Maureen Malloy, 1–17. Washington, DC: Society for American Archaeology.

Derry, Linda. 2003. "Concluding Remarks." In *Archaeologists and Local Communities: Partners in Exploring the Past*, edited by Linda Derry and Maureen Malloy, 185–188. Washington, DC: Society for American Archaeology.

Derry, Linda, and Maureen Malloy, eds. 2003. *Archaeologists and Local Communities: Partners in Exploring the Past*. Washington, DC: Society for American Archaeology.

Gadsby, David A., and Jodi A. Barnes. 2010. "Activism as Archaeological Praxis: Engaging Communities with Archaeologies that Matter." In *Archaeologists as Activists: Can Archaeologists Change the World?*, edited by M. Jay Stottman, 48–62. Tuscaloosa: University of Alabama Press.

Gadsby, David, and Robert Chidester. 2007. "Heritage in Hampden: A Participatory Research Design for Public Archaeology in a Working Class Neighborhood, Baltimore, Maryland." In *Archaeology as a Tool of Civic Engagement*, edited by Barbara J. Little and Paul A. Shackel, 223–262. Lanham, MD: AltaMira Press.

Heckenberger, Michael J. 2008. "Entering the Agora: Archaeology, Conservation, and Indigenous Peoples in the Amazon." In *Collaboration in Archaeological Practice: Engaging Descendant Communities*, edited by Chip Colwell-Chanthaphonh and T. J. Ferguson, 243–272. Lanham, MD: AltaMira Press.

Henderson, A. Gwynn, and Linda S. Levstik. 2004. "What Do Children Learn When They Go on a Field Trip to Henry Clay's Estate?" *Forum Journal of the National Trust for Historic Preservation* 19(1): 39–47.

Jameson, John H. Jr. 1997. *Presenting Archaeology to the Public: Digging for Truths*. Lanham, MD: AltaMira Press.

———. 2004. "Public Archaeology in the United States." In *Public Archaeology*, edited by Nick Merriman, 21–58. New York: Routledge.

Jeppson, Patrice L. 2010. "Doing Our Homework: Reconsidering What Archaeology Has to Offer Schools." In *Archaeologists as Activists: Can Archaeologists Change the World?*, edited by M. Jay Stottman, 63–79. Tuscaloosa: University of Alabama Press.

Krupicz, Author E. 2000. "Be All You Can Be: Evaluating Archaeology Outreach Programs." Master's thesis, Department of Anthropology and Arkansas Archaeological Survey, University of Arkansas, Fayetteville.

Leone, Mark P., Parker B. Potter, and Paul A. Shackel. 1987. "Toward a Critical Archaeology." *Current Anthropology* 28(3): 283–302.

Levstik, Linda S., A. Gwynn Henderson, and Jennifer S. Schlarb. 2003. "Digging for Clues: An Archaeological Exploration of Historical Cognition." Paper presented at the Fifth Annual Meeting of the World Archaeological Congress, Washington, DC.

Little, Barbara J., and Paul A. Shackel, eds. 2007. *Archaeology as a Tool of Civic Engagement*. Lanham, MD: AltaMira Press.

Little, Barbara J., and Larry Zimmerman. 2010. "In the Public Interest: Creating a More Activist, Civically Engaged Archaeology." In *Voices in American Archaeology*, edited by Wendy Ashmore, Dorothy T. Lippert, and Barbara J. Mills, 131–159. Washington, DC: Society for American Archaeology.

McDavid, Carol. 2010. "Public Archaeology, Activism, and Racism: Rethinking the Heritage 'Product'." In *Archaeologists as Activists: Can Archaeologists Change the World?*, edited by M. Jay Stottman, 36–47. Tuscaloosa: University of Alabama Press.

McGhee, Fred L., and Carol McDavid. 2010. "Strategies of Practice: Implementing Post-colonial Critique, CRM, Public Archaeology and Advocacy." In *World Archaeological Congress (WAC) Handbook on Postcolonialism and Archaeology,* edited by Uzma Rizvi and Jane Lydon, 481–494. Walnut Creek, CA: Left Coast Press.

McGimsey, Charles R. III. 1972. *Public Archaeology.* New York: Seminar Press.

McGuire, Randall H. 2008. *Archaeology as Political Action.* Berkeley: University of California Press.

McNutt, Nan. 2000. "Assessing Archaeology Education: Five Guiding Questions." In *The Archaeology Education Handbook: Sharing the Past with Kids,* edited by Karolyn E. Smardz and Shelly Smith, 192–204. Lanham, MD: AltaMira Press.

Merriman, Nick, ed. 2004. *Public Archaeology.* New York: Routledge.

Moe, Jeanne M. 2002. "Project Archaeology: Putting the Intrigue of the Past in Public Educa-tion." In *Public Benefits of Archaeology,* edited by Barbara J. Little, 176–186. Gainesville: University Press of Florida.

Moyer, Teresa S. 2007. "Learning through Visitors: Exhibits as a Tool for Encouraging Civic Engagement through Archaeology. In *Archaeology as a Tool of Civic Engagement,* edited by Barbara J. Little and Paul A. Shackel, 263–278. Lanham, MD: AltaMira Press.

Nicholas, George P., John R. Welch, and Eldon C. Yellowhorn. 2008. "Collaborative En-counters." In *Collaboration in Archaeological Practice: Engaging Descendant Communities,* edited by Chip Colwell-Chanthaphonh and T. J. Ferguson, 273–298. Lanham, MD: AltaMira Press.

Potter, Parker B. Jr. 1994. *Public Archaeology in Annapolis.* Washington, DC: Smithsonian Press.

Potter, Parker B. Jr., and Mark P. Leone. 1987. "Archaeology in Public in Annapolis: Four Seasons, Six Sites, Seven Tours, and 32,000 Visitors." *American Archaeology* 6(1): 51–61.

Prybylski, Matthew, and M. Jay Stottman. 2010. "Reconnecting Community: Archaeology and Activism at the Portland Wharf." In *Archaeologists as Activists: Can Archaeologists Change the World?,* edited by M. Jay Stottman, 126–140. Tuscaloosa: University of Alabama Press.

Sabloff, Jeremy A. 2008. *Archaeology Matters: Action Archaeology in the Modern World.* Walnut Creek, CA: Left Coast Press.

Shackel, Paul A., and Erve J. Chambers, eds. 2004. *Places in Mind: Public Archaeology as Applied Anthropology.* New York: Routledge.

Smardz, Karolyn E., and Shelly Smith, eds. 2000. *The Archaeology Education Handbook: Sharing the Past with Kids.* Lanham, MD: AltaMira Press.

Stahlgren, Lori C., and M. Jay Stottman. 2007. "Voices from the Past: Changing the Culture of Historic House Museums with Archaeology." In *Archaeology as a Tool of Civic Engagement,* edited by Barbara J. Little and Paul A. Shackel, 131–150. Lanham, MD: AltaMira Press.

Stottman, M. Jay, ed. 2010. *Archaeologists as Activists: Can Archaeologists Change the World?* Tuscaloosa: University of Alabama Press.

Tilley, Christopher. 1989. "Archaeology as Sociopolitical Action in the Present." In *Critical Traditions in Contemporary Archaeology,* edited by V. Pinsky and A. Wylie, 104–116. Cambridge, UK: Cambridge University Press.

Welch, John R., Dana Lepofsky, and Michelle Washington. 2011. "Assessing Collaboration with the Sliammon First Nation in a Community-Based Heritage Research and Steward-ship Program." *Archaeological Review from Cambridge* 26(2): 171–190.

Chapter 10

Activating Archaeology

K. Anne Pyburn

I am Provost's Professor of Anthropology at Indiana University. I inherited an inclination to do fieldwork from my father who was a herpetologist, and my interest in human beings from my mother, who worked in social services. I have done cultural anthropological fieldwork in West Africa—in Ghana, Togo, and Burkina Faso—where I and my husband investigated why West Africans buy certain things and not others; and in Yemen, where I did a women-in-development project for USAID. I have done contract archaeology in the Western United States—in Texas, New Mexico, and Arizona; surveyed in South America (Peru); and directed excavations at ancient Maya sites in Belize, at Nohmul, on Albion Island, and at Chau Hiix. I am currently involved in a grassroots community preservation, cultural property, and education program in Kyrgyzstan. This somewhat eclectic career has given me a nonstandard perspective on archaeology, which I regard as generally entertaining and potentially useful, but find that it is often practiced as bad science that is wasteful of scarce resources, and irritating or even damaging to descendant and local communities.

Over the course of many field programs, I have witnessed a spectrum of unfortunate incidents between archaeologists and local communities. I have also observed a tendency for archaeologists to fail to notice the political implications of their research topics, which often focus on elite culture and regard the past as something superseded by superior cultures. Based on frustration with such practices, my research has tended to foreground underrepresented groups and run counter to received wisdom because I believe that science advances by disproof. My Maya research has focused on documenting ancient poor

Transforming Archaeology: Activist Practices and Prospects, edited by Sonya Atalay, Lee Rains Clauss, Randall H. McGuire, and John R. Welch, 197–213. © 2014 Left Coast Press, Inc. All rights reserved.

people who were thought not to have existed, successful agricultural strategies that counter popular beliefs about a Maya collapse, and evidence of a smallholder economy that provides a substantial pedigree for the sustainability of family farms, which undermines claims by modern agribusiness.

My personal experience of stereotyping and social injustice from working in a male-dominated discipline led me to challenge archaeologists' claims about the primordiality of the political and economic subordination of women. I worked with a group of students to document systematic bias in the reconstruction of the role of women in ancient civilizations. We showed how sketchy data viewed through a lens of preconception about women and based on an inadequate definition of civilization (or "complex society") resulted in an unsupported, reified, and essentialized picture of the past.

My commitment to the democratization of knowledge and to collaborative research led me to do a considerable amount of public outreach in Belize, where various community groups were kind to me and helped me pursue my research. Tourists, public officials, students, and teachers evinced interest in my work. I extended outreach efforts to include the promotion of tourism and the development of public pride in the incomparable archaeological heritage of Belize. I also made a sustained effort to explain what archaeology is and what archaeologists do so the public might see its potential utility. For the most part, my efforts along these lines were unsuccessful, as indicated by the fact that sites where I worked in Belize have fared poorly at the hands of the public since my departure.

I have taken a different approach to my work in Kyrgyzstan, as detailed in the following narrative. In short, rather than pursue an academic research design or a nonlocal preservationist agenda, I focus exclusively on the interests and needs of local groups. Thus far, I have done no archaeological research in Kyrgyzstan, but encouraging efforts to preserve and appreciate Kyrgyz heritage have sprung up at the local level among my Kyrgyz colleagues and friends who have generously tolerated my "help."

Barging In

It is often obvious where heritage is being lost or misused from the perspective of a person outside the context of the difficulties. It is usually less obvious how the situation can be improved, although casual observers often think they can help because they mistake the complexity of the situation. Although doing nothing is not necessarily more ethical than trying to do something and failing, it is daunting to try to figure out what to do to improve a situation that is having a bad effect on other people.

One of the primary lessons of colonialism is that interference is damaging to local groups and indigenous cultures, and that what outsiders think will help is often not at all helpful (Escobar 1997). Early anthropologists who conceived of culture as a closed system that adapted to an environment like an animal species over millennia of isolation thought that contact with outsiders disrupted the integration of traditional institutions and caused people to become dysfunctional and anomic. And colonial domination does indeed tend to be very destructive (Horvath 1972).

But the negative consequences of colonialism were not because the colonists disrupted the perfect synchrony of pristine cultural systems. Local and indigenous cultures and their participants can often benefit from outside resources, information, and help; in fact, cultural isolates are very rare circumstances, and peoples everywhere have always benefited from intercultural exchanges (Wolf 1982). The key difference lies in the attitude of the outsider. If you assume that your superior knowledge and experience prepares you to solve the problems of strangers, you would look good in a pith helmet. But if you begin by assuming that the people who have the problem know more about it than you do, and that they are capable of figuring out how to solve it if they are provided access to information and resources, you may be able to help.

I drew these conclusions from a series of experiences I have had over the past 30 years of working outside of my own homeland and culture, doing things that I hoped would have positive consequences for living people. Most of the time I was working in places in which I at least shared a language with people in the area. But in 2004, I found myself in the situation of being a complete outsider in a place where, despite my misgivings, it appeared that I might be able to offer some help.

Kyrgyz Case Study

Indiana University (IU) has had a long-term relationship with the American University of Central Asia (AUCA) in Kyrgyzstan, and because AUCA students and faculty all speak English, exchanges are not uncommon. In 2004, I met the chair of the Department of Ethnology and Archaeology at AUCA on one of her frequent visits to IU. We became friends, and she invited me to visit Kyrgyzstan. I agreed, thinking she was merely being polite, but was shortly contacted by a university administrator about planning my trip.

Although taken aback, I decided to go because, quite frankly, I was curious. All my archaeological expertise lies in the study of ancient America, and all the Postcolonial contexts I know well are places colonized by the Spanish and British. Postcolonial USSR promised to be something very different. In my experience, the best way to see your own biases is to take them to a new and unfamiliar place, where they will show up clearly against a new backdrop; about this, at least, I was proved correct.

Upon arriving in Kyrgyzstan, I was introduced to a very prominent and active Kyrgyz archaeologist who immediately welcomed me and did his best to integrate me into the local scholarly community, despite my linguistic inadequacy. He took me on several trips around the northern part of the country to see archaeological sites and to show me the places where he works. Our translator was amused by the fact that when archaeology was the topic, we did not need a translator. In fact, we understood each other better without her nonspecialist attempts to relay archaeological information between us.

I began to make some observations about things that seemed familiar from my own experiences. First, I observed that most archaeology was derived from the Russian system that was less about cultural resource management than cultural resource extraction. This was familiar from my experiences of Belize where colonial period British archaeologists routinely took artifacts home to England and practiced little or no site conservation. The only difference was that Kyrgyz independence is even newer, and Kyrgyz citizens generally seem to feel somewhat less antipathy toward their Russian colonizers than Belizeans feel for the British. But like Belizeans' British-influenced attitudes toward their heritage, Russian attitudes toward Kyrgyz heritage and its treatment were still largely intact among Kyrgyz citizens. In both countries, I have found that archaeology serves to verify essentialized ethnic political history, decorate museums, provide a backdrop that emphasizes the advances of the political present, blame the victims of Colonial domination for their plight, and privilege the perspective of cultural elites.

The history of Kyrgyzstan is long and complex, and Soviet historians construct it as a succession of battles among ethnic groups who wander across the landscape chasing and replacing their predecessors. In this context, archaeology serves to verify history and locate evidence of the ethnic succession, reifying the Soviet construction of ethnicity as inherited, unchanging until eradicated, and at least partly genetic. Local heritage either leads to or is replaced by the civilizing influence of the Soviet state.

Next I observed that Kyrgyzstan had no sites on the World Heritage list, very limited resources for public education, and no apparent national program for site protection. One person told me they thought it might be possible to buy an excavation permit from the president's wife. This was probably not true, but gives an indication of the dearth of information available to most Kyrgyz people about their nation's heritage resources. Further, although a certain amount of site destruction was taking place out of ignorance (people simply did not recognize that certain features in the landscape were archaeological sites), there appeared to be little looting because the art market was not yet available. However, I suspected that the government push for tourism would make that market available shortly.

This is the point where I began to see a break with my previous experience. Unlike Belize, Kyrgyzstan has been isolated from the developments of European-style social science, which are not necessarily less ethnocentric than Soviet social science, but different in some important ways. As an anthropological subfield, Western archaeology has begun to move away from the validation of ethnic boundaries and the authentication of particular political histories. Variations among cultures are seen to be as likely due to contact as to isolation because people signify social boundaries with their material culture and traditions when such distinctions are useful and dissolve them when they are not. Rather than seeing the past as a succession of pure races, it may be that tribal groups were rarely discrete either ethnically or genetically, and that splitting and amalgamation are as likely as clean replacements. In fact, it has been suggested that nomadic cultures are interrelated with settled societies in some important ways, even to the extent that some members of the family might be nomadic herders, whereas other members of the same family are urban dwellers, and most people are multilingual. This is certainly the case in the present day (Levi 2007).

Various newly independent and rapidly globalizing postcolonial nations are using archaeology, both to reify a national identity and to undermine the (usually condescending, if not pejorative) colonial view of the history and achievements of the local culture. Although useful in the global political arena, the promotion of an essentialist past is a two-edged sword that can empower or undermine the autonomy of indigenous groups. In Belize, for example, the deployment of Maya cultural symbols as emblematic of a multiethnic nation-state has actually undermined Maya sovereignty in that country and denied that the descendants of primordial Maya cultures have any particular rights to their land (Cultural Survival 2013).

In Kyrgyzstan, political insistence on the reification of a Hollywood-style, Genghis Khan-ish nomadic culture as the authentic origin of Kyrgyzstan at the expense of any of the other myriad cultures of the Silk Road has ominous implications. In particular, government characterization of ancient urbanism as Uzbek rather than Kyrgyz, and the rejection of the archaeology and preservation of ancient urban centers as relevant to Kyrgyzstan, parallel the political tensions between the language groups in the country (Liu 2012). Public attitudes toward archaeological heritage succumb to government propaganda to the extent that many educated people, including professionals in the tourist industry, told me that Kyrgyzstan does not really have much archaeology and no real monuments because "Nomads don't leave anything behind." And although Kyrgyz speakers maintain pride in their tribal heritage (the tradition of knowing tribal affiliations and the names of ancestors for seven generations is still common), the prevailing view is that the present-day Kyrgyz are not related to those who left the many kurgans, or burial mounds, that are densely scattered across the country.

Postcolonial critique by outsiders has tended to admonish the Kyrgyz for failing to embrace a multicultural heritage (Laruelle 2012), especially in light of recent anti-Uzbek violence, which is generally seen as related to the establishment of Kyrgyzstan as a postcolonial nation-state. Soviet colonialism allowed for a certain amount of ethnic continuity and fostered a degree of equality among language groups, at least insofar as possible under the weight of Soviet "civilizing" measures that stopped nomadism and enforced a secularized identity (İğmen 2012; Laruelle 2012). Although authorities differ in their analyses of the causes and ultimate consequences of Kyrgyz ethnic nationalism, Wachtel (2013, 972) notes that states "in which ethnic identity was subordinate to an abstract civic identity . . . ha(ve) never successfully occurred outside the Anglo-American world, and even there [they have] occurred primarily in those states (the USA, Canada, New Zealand, and Australia) in which the original inhabitants were almost completely eliminated and replaced by immigrants who could not claim deep historical ties to the land." His argument is that Kyrgyz suppression of Uzbek and other minorities is the strategy most likely to successfully result in a coherent democratic nation, citing other places where similar efforts have worked and not worked.

I have no quarrel with Wachtel's historical analysis or even the probability that his predictions are reasonable, but I do disagree that the suppression of minorities is the best and most rational and therefore the only likely path for Kyrgyzstan to take toward democracy. He proposes that when multiethnic nationalism failed after the Soviet "nanny state," people resorted to tribalism as a sort of "natural logic" (although he does not use exactly that phrase) because ethnic divisions had social if little political reality. I would argue that this "natural logic" is an artifact of Soviet reification of tribalism rather than a perpetuation of a precolonial reality and that pre-Soviet nomadic life (contrary to the constructions of Soviet ethnohistorians) was culturally diverse rather than simply multicultural, having less discrete and less rigid boundaries than those reified under Soviet domination. The colonial construction of ancient mobile cultures as inherently intolerant and hostile is not the only possible interpretation of available historical data.

Development anthropologists once believed that cultures must be helped through a series of technological steps toward complexity in order for economic development to succeed. Clearly, this model known as "appropriate technology" was an artifact of cultural evolutionary thinking that came directly from the same nineteenth-century philosophy that underlies Soviet concepts of ethnicity and "tribalism" (but see Dolukhanov 1995 for a more nuanced disciplinary history). According to the theory of appropriate technology you would replace a telegraph with a telephone land line, then a mobile phone, and eventually a cell phone so that people would be able to effectively incorporate new technology into their culture.

Anthropologists now know that this is not the way culture works; cultural change is not random, but it does not proceed according to a preset order of natural stages in a march toward one sort of civilization that enjoys superior technology. Within 10 years, people in Belize and many other countries went from having no phone to having a cell phone, with no steps in between. By the same token, the fact that other nations have become democracies after a period of genocide and oppression does not mean that all nations must make the same mistakes in order to develop. In fact, Wachtel's observation may provide an analytical tool to help avert similar disasters. Most relevant here is the idea that archaeology may be a source of alternate constructions and more complex histories than those promoted by colonial Soviet scholars of a previous generation. There are many ways to use the past to orient toward the future.

Archaeologists certainly do recognize a more complex past, and on my first trip to Bishkek, I learned that Japanese archaeologists were working with a UNESCO mission to investigate and consolidate a Buddhist monastery. This struck me as a problematic choice for the only significant heritage project in a Muslim nation. I visited this site recently and observed that a very expensive structure has been built to protect the site from the elements because it was left exposed after excavation.

But conservation efforts have failed because local people have recycled the attractive tiles used in the reconstruction, and the lack of upkeep has allowed the superstructure to deteriorate in such a way as to funnel water into the mud-brick structure rather than away from it. I was told that quite a few experts consulted on this consolidation, and that the cost was quite high, but there was apparently no discussion with the local population about their interest in preservation before the site was left in their keeping.

Later, I also learned that at least some people living in rural areas consider the kurgans (ancient burial mounds that dot the landscape) to be the remains of their ancestors. Their perspective is archaeologically accurate because the migrations into and out of the region of modern Kyrgyzstan are documented, and archaeological reconstruction supports continuity. However, continuity with the past was not promoted in Soviet schools, in which modernization superseded heritage identity, which was reified but also trivialized (İğmen 2012). Colonial powers do not benefit by emphasizing continuity in local heritage that might promote identity politics and strengthen ideas about indigenous rights.

So, to summarize my observations, or perhaps they are more appropriately characterized as my hypotheses about heritage in Kyrgyzstan: the state of preservation was poor, the level of public knowledge low, the probability of a rise in looting high, and the possibility of the archaeological reification of an imagined racially pure past used as a mechanism of political repression very real. The incident at Bamiyan also suggested that the selection of heritage sites for preservation by outsiders—such as the UNESCO interest in Buddhist temples—could trigger religious extremism.

Although problems from these alarming issues seemed imminent, it was obvious to me that solving them was not my business, and that Kyrgyz people might not see the same problems at all, or at least not see the ones I saw as the most pressing and significant. Still, I thought I might have some useful information. After all, although Kyrgyzstan is a very linked-in country, and the Internet is widespread, foreign ideas are reaching the older generation slowly. Access to information from Western sources is recent, and even when translated may still be culturally inaccessible.

Starting Small

My first thought was that it would probably be okay to ask people questions about their ideas about heritage, and then I might go on to see if people thought any of my experiences were interesting and whether I could share information that people might use. I began by talking to friends and expanded to informal groups who were willing to meet to talk about Kyrgyz heritage. More than once, people got tears in their eyes when I talked about heritage centers I have visited in other countries or asked about the conservation needs of their national museum.

People were so gratifyingly interested in the information I shared, or at least so incredibly nice, I was encouraged to think I could be useful. But just telling people how I do things or how I think things could or should be done still seemed really wrong. So the first thing I did was figure out a way to squeeze my regular field school budget to include my Kyrgyz colleague as a professional collaborator and guest. I invited him to join my field project in Belize to share my excavation methods and my teaching strategies, not as a perfect example, but well, just to share. He came to Belize with me and my crew for two months and appeared to have a great time. I certainly enjoyed having him.

Whether Kyrgyz archaeologists move toward recent Euro-American traditions in their excavation strategies is not for me to decide, and the factors involved in such professional choices are beyond my knowledge. By sharing my own project practices, I could offer information without insisting that a Western approach is the correct one for all circumstances. Its advantages and disadvantages could be observed firsthand, so my colleague could draw his own conclusions.

Whenever I asked people about Kyrgyz heritage or cultural property, they seemed very engaged, and when I discussed preservation with those who recognized the extent of Kyrgyzstan's archaeological record, they echoed my concerns. Because ordinary citizens seemed engaged with their heritage, I often mentioned community-based education and preservation programs I knew about, but such suggestions elicited the response "We would like to help you with your project." This was exactly what I did not want to do—convince Kyrgyz people to help me with my project to preserve their heritage. It was not my place to decide what their heritage should be or how it should be preserved.

In Belize today, a great deal of time is spent on recording and on consolidation of excavations, which mostly means careful backfilling. Backfilling was not practiced by either the British or early twentieth-century American excavators in Belize or according to Russian standards in Kyrgyzstan, so consolidation is a postcolonial practice in both contexts. I also have the luxury of specialists in the analysis of bone and lithic and ceramic artifacts, which means that rather than beginning with assumptions about gender roles and artifact function and chronology, received wisdom can be challenged. For example, without an osteologist, a skeleton buried with armor might be assumed to be male, but this assumption can be examined with the possibility of the discovery of unfamiliar gender associations, as has been suggested in Central Asia.

I also have students focused on particular aspects of the same project, all collaborating under a single research design. An extractive approach that emphasized finding objects for display and exemplification of predetermined features of the past does not require a replicable research design or the use of a set of hypotheses with test implications. But to discover unanticipated aspects of social process and cultural context, a reflexive and explicit scientific methodology is important. Archaeological research designs result in self-conscious methodologies and an awareness that decisions about excavation in natural levels, intensity of screening, sample fraction, and inclusion (or exclusion) of such data as fire-cracked rock, pollen, and phytolyths will affect the results of the investigation and the extent of what can be learned.

As my relationships with Kyrgyz people became stronger, I decided that to suggest the idea of community-based preservation projects, the best thing to do would be to show people—not just archaeologists—some examples. I asked my friends and colleagues to help me find the right people to bring to the United States to visit museums, and I asked the U.S. State Department to pay for it. Much to my shock, I got the money and brought 12 Kyrgyz citizens from various walks of life to the Midwestern United States for two weeks of talking and traveling to see how Americans are using their heritage.

We visited live action museums, small community storefront museums, and formal art and culture museums. We talked a lot about Kyrgyz heritage and American heritage, including a good bit about the horrible way the United States has treated indigenous people. In particular, I made sure to have information presented about the consequences of ethnic and cultural essentialism and denying people their right to maintain and value heritage in their own ways. To that end, I asked Sonya Atalay to find out whether members of the Ojibwe Nation on the Saginaw Chippewa Indian Tribe would meet with us.

The Ziibiwing Center of Anishinabe Culture and Lifeways agreed to host us, and we spent three days at the center in Mt. Pleasant, Michigan. It was one of the most enlightening and moving experiences of my life, beginning with the prayer of welcome that was spoken in Ojibwe, but translated through English into Kyrgyz by collaborating translators. It is difficult to explain how significant this was, but I can say that I observed that several Euro-Americans in the group had tears running down their faces as the words were spoken.

The Ojibwe were very generous with their time and resources, and invited us to dances, ceremonies, and their splendid museum at the Ziibiwing Center, in which they present their history and cultural heritage on their own terms. Visiting their casino brought forward Kyrgyz questions about authenticity. The idea that healthy cultures develop and change was a new concept, but a welcome alternative to the idea that to be traditional means being stuck in a premodern materially deprived past. If "real Indians" can have televisions, authentic nomads can have cell phones, and both groups can have access to good healthcare and education without "losing their culture."

During the two weeks of visiting museums and talking about heritage and cultural property and nationalism and authenticity, I became more confident in my ability to understand the interests and issues that were important to members of the group. The group was as varied as I could make it, including government representatives of the ministries of tourism and culture, public school teachers, archaeologists, museum curators, students, and village leaders. All the participants were Kyrgyz speakers, with one exception. I was able to include one Uzbek speaker from the south, who turned out to be a delightful companion and made it possible to keep the idea of a multicultural past evident throughout the trip. I also brought in American specialists in community mapping, educational programming, museum development, data management, and educational outreach, as well as community dignitaries and government employees with an interest in heritage.

It is important to note that the members of the project, although included because they had diverse backgrounds, were not a community nor did they necessarily represent communities in an ethnic or historical sense. Although the member of the ministry of tourism brought a perspective of a government official, he was not a representative of a community of government officials. Similarly, the teachers and agriculturalists are not representatives of a community. Communities are hard for outsiders to define; it is easy to mistake people who are interested in archaeology or in local development for a community, but chances are that such people constitute an *ad hoc* community that is likely to disappear unless some effort is made to create some infrastructure. In reality, everyone belongs to multiple communities, which are often in competition for labor and resources. Not all communities are equally important to their members (Pyburn 2007, 2009, 2011).

In this case, as a complete outsider, I felt it was not appropriate for me to try to define communities, but that this would be one of the outcomes of the project because constituencies would be identified by participants if they decided to pursue community-based projects. Although this seems less hegemonic, it makes it impossible to evaluate the success of the project overall because the impact of community activism has to be in evidence in the targeted community. At this point, I can enumerate only the actions taken by project members; eventually, a meaningful evaluation might be written by project members who became directors of their own projects. To date, the evidence I have is all biased and anecdotal.

Some members of the group from Kyrgyzstan knew each other, but not all, so interactions among the participants were interesting and sometimes very valuable. A wonderful lecture provided early in the trip by one of the Kyrgyz archaeologists in the group exposed the government representatives and tour company owners to the fact that the very elaborate heritage of Kyrgyzstan is echoed in the country's extensive archaeological record. They also learned that the creators of the visible heritage of Kyrgyz nomads—the people who built the burial mounds called kurgans—actually are ancestral to many contemporary Kyrgyz citizens. The mayor of the tiny village of Chap (also a project member) verified that many rural Kyrgyz know this and identify with this heritage.

Toward the end of the trip, I asked the group what they wanted to do for the final workshop that was to be held in Kyrgyzstan. I explained that although the grant would pay for it, the design of the meeting would be up to them. The discussion became animated, and to my delight, people forgot to translate for me for the first time during the trip. After considerable discussion, the outline of a program was explained to me, and I was asked to bring grant writing and museum display specialists to Kyrgyzstan to advise them on developing new programs. Being invited to "help them with their project" was one of the highlights of my life.

The final workshop began with a symposium in the Kyrgyz National Museum. Various dignitaries spoke about different aspects of Kyrgyz heritage. An Uzbek minister from Uzgen flew up especially for the occasion to emphasize the breadth of Kyrgyz heritage that is not always considered in the northern Kyrgyz-dominated areas. Cadets training for the police force, local academics, news reporters, and preservationists attended. A number of heritage enthusiasts whom I had not met, but who were known to the original participants, joined the group the next day when we toured several archaeological sites that were proposed as tourist destinations and possible foci of community involvement. One evening, after I went to bed, the group formed the Kyrgyz Sacred Heritage Association and elected our Uzbek-speaking member from southern Kyrgyzstan as president. He insisted he become joint president with a Kyrgyz-speaking village leader and preservationist from northern Kyrgyzstan. In a sense, with this action, participants constituted themselves as a "community." On the final day of the workshop and the last day of the project, we corralled as many translators as possible so that the grant and museum specialists could help with the design of projects that participants had begun to propose. By the end of a single day, thirteen grass roots projects were outlined, all of which were viable and promising. I went home to begin a search for more funding so the projects might be realized.

At present, two community museum startups, one teacher education program, one tourist development and preservation scheme, and one public education campaign have been funded by the Intellectual Property Issues in Cultural Heritage Project (IPinCH 2013), developed and funded by George Nicholas and Julie Hollowell (Nicholas, this volume). These projects all foreground the recognition and preservation of cultural property through grass roots involvement, and may serve as demonstration projects offering encouragement to other communities.

Although promoting these projects is exciting, even more important is the fact that members of the project have been involved in the creation of education campaigns and public outreach through posters, school presentations, and videos that have had no input from me whatsoever. Probably they would have arisen without my friendship, but my colleagues are kind enough to suggest that what I have shared with them has made a difference.

I write these lines just a few days after returning from Kyrgyzstan to deliver some resources and learn what people are doing. My colleague has published the first popular book on Kyrgyz archaeology, with a substantial section on preservation that highlights the programs developed by several project members. He has also produced an educational video about preservation that has already been shown on television. I was given a tour of the community museums developed in school classrooms by two project members. The Kyrgyz Sacred Heritage Association has been granted government approval and now has a Facebook page.

Two weeks ago, I visited Krasnaya Rechka (a.k.a. Navikat), the Buddhist site that UNESCO has worked to preserve (Levi-Strauss and Lin 2010). It is in sad shape. Millions of dollars were invested in expert consultation and consolidation measures. For a tiny fraction of that amount, a grass roots movement has been stimulated that has begun to enlist public interest in preservation. Already sites that were being damaged are now being protected. Preservation of a monument can never succeed with only outside support, no matter how generous. What must happen for preservation to succeed is a transformation that allows people to see local heritage with global eyes. Whether this vision results in preservation or destruction is not predetermined simply by exposing people to an outsider's view, but to me the important thing is that responsible archaeologists make sure people have the information they need to make informed decisions about their cultural property.

The new Kyrgyz preservation video begins with a traditional Kyrgyz saying that only a slave does not remember his ancestors. This is a powerful sentiment that evokes the Kyrgyz passion for freedom, which is symbolized in the iconography of the Kyrgyz flag.[1] But for me, it also means that the new impetus toward the preservation of heritage and pride in continuity with the past has indigenous roots. No one is creating community museums in response to pressure from me or simply as a result of the hegemonic forces of globalization.

I will continue to nourish Kyrgyz programs to the best of my ability, but the awareness has already been shared, and the blossoming concern and commitment for preservation and presentation of a broad complex heritage are out of my hands. What happens next in Kyrgyz archaeology and heritage is up to the citizens of that country. Perhaps I nudged the inevitable changes in the right direction, though I cannot truly say that what we have done is transformational, except perhaps in one sense. My experiences in Kyrgyzstan with friends, teachers, colleagues, and students with magnificent heritage sites, with optimistic universities and schools, have changed the way I understand the world and the way I see myself in it. The open-mindedness, graciousness, and warmth of the Kyrgyz people who have worked with me have given me a sense of possibility I have never had before.

⸺⸺⸺

Considering Methods: Regarding Methods for Inspiring and Guiding Activist Archaeologists

As all the chapters in this book demonstrate, there can be no single prescription for successful activism. Each project will have a unique cultural context as well as a locally specific goal. This is similar to the problem of research ethics: no single set of rules can serve all circumstances. And it is always possible to "follow the rules" and be unethical. Thus, it may be useful to regard ethics and activism as processes rather than procedures. It is not possible to teach someone to be an activist any more than you can teach someone to be ethical. But it is possible to share information about causes and consequences, to tell stories about successes and failures, and to encourage debate about alternative perspectives, so that when faced with real-world situations, a person who has "studied activism" is more likely to approach a desired outcome.

In that spirit, I provide the following list of considerations based on my experiences as an activist and economic development proponent. There will be disagreement and counter examples for all these pronouncements, but they are offered here as points of departure for discussion and campaign planning. I have derived these points from my experiences in collaborative archaeology that culminated in a situation where I was forced to decide how to proceed in a cultural context about which I understood very little.

Although these points can be useful to inform classroom discussion, I suggest approaching teaching collaboratively. Students have a tendency to take their teachers too seriously. In a classroom discussion, students should be encouraged to think of hypothetical examples in which the principle I delineate would apply, but also of counter examples in which my pronouncements would not be sufficient or perhaps not work at all. The key is to broaden perspectives without losing sight of the crucial fact that applications are always narrowly case specific.

Find the Experts

Archaeologists are used to getting help from specialists, whether faunal analysts, pollen analysts, and/or material type specialists (ceramic, lithic, ground stone, etc.). When it comes to community-based activism, I recommend a similar approach. Seek the assistance of an ethnographer or some sort of cultural anthropologist. And unless you have been specifically trained in these fields, resist the temptation to fill this specialist role. After all, the American delineation of archaeology as a subfield of anthropology does not qualify an archaeologist to be an ethnographer. But unless the goal is to shake up the profession by developing an ethnographic profile of the field (which is not a bad idea), an academic expert is not necessarily required. Community members are likely to be better versed in local issues of social justice (or, more likely, social injustice) than any outsider. So the first and foremost experts must be members of the group whose cause the archaeologist wants to promote. A cultural anthropologist or ethnographic specialist may be useful to help an outsider grasp the perspective of the local experts, but, generally speaking, most communities have a great deal of experience dealing with outsiders and are very capable of getting their message across to a sincere listener. In my opinion, the ethnographer may be most valuable for helping local community members understand the archaeologist/activist, who is likely much less skilled at cross-cultural communication. In fact, because the activist archaeologist is presenting herself as a potential resource, the first priority is for the community members to be able to understand who the archaeologist is and what she has to offer (and why she is offering it).

It is important that more than one expert opinion be included so that community members can make choices among options rather than follow the only path presented. For this reason, introducing communities to each other so people can communicate directly without having their experiences and recommendations translated through an outsider can be useful. I asked the Ojibwe for help so that my Kyrgyz friends would not only experience my own ideas about heritage but also because of the Ojibwe expertise in heritage development, management, and preservation.

In the classroom, I find that the best way to promote awareness of multiple perspectives and respect for competing types of expertise is to stage debates. Asking students or colleagues to take up the role of an expert on one side of an issue allows them to work deeply into a perspective that they might not ordinarily defend. The result is that even if they do not support the argument that they developed for the debate, they will have an intensified understanding of an alternative view and, almost invariably, more respect for it.

For example, assigning people to take the position of village elders, developers, tourist promoters, government officials, and archaeologists on each side of an issue, so that archaeologists will be mock-debating with archaeologists, and village leaders with village leaders, and so on has an immediate impact on understanding what it means to be an expert.

Mostly Listen

It is not helpful to insist on solving problems that people do not have. Sometimes people face difficulties they do not know about, but once the archaeologist has explained that she is concerned that heritage sites are vulnerable, or that research proving the ancestors were environmental wastrels might undermine local land rights claims, or that admitting cruise lines will destroy what the people on the ships want to see, it may be a good idea to step back and listen carefully. Although these are all potentially negative, they are not necessarily the worst things people face. A road to a health clinic may be more important than any other issue in communities in which infant mortality is high.

When UNESCO offered the Taliban money to conserve the Buddhas of Bamiyan, the Taliban asked for the money to feed hungry people. When the request was refused, the Buddhas were bombed. In the final analysis, few people would put conservation above their family's right to eat. Bombing the Buddhas didn't feed anyone, but the preservationists certainly afforded the Taliban a stage to make their point.

This means that activists for social justice have to put archaeology in second place, or else come up with very clever compromises that solve a combination of problems. In the classroom, I often challenge students to defend their scholarly inclinations and confront the fact that their use of scarce resources to "understand the past" may not seem very ethical to people who are economically deprived. I do not do this to be unkind, and I create a safe space in the classroom so that people's perspectives are respected. But thinking clearly and directly about economic realities and the privilege of a college education is necessary for developing a sound ethical foundation for a professional life. My students struggle with their answer, which will necessarily be a personal one. But the conversation plants the seeds of activism if they are not already present, and I find that most students are grateful to have the opportunity to discuss and share opinions about an issue that they have regarded as a personal demon.

Read A Lot

Clever strategies that enhance social justice and also preserve heritage sites and help feed people are not always easy to devise. Fortunately, there is a huge literature in applied anthropology that can be mined for ideas and examples of strategies that have worked. This literature is equally useful for finding examples of programs that did not work, which is invaluable when the activist plan is headed for unseen obstacles that other do-gooders have already hit. There is no need to drain your budget on a scheme that could be fixed or scrapped via the lessons learned from other people's experiences.

Human Organization is a great journal to become familiar with, along with some of the new journals more specifically directed at activism-oriented archaeological projects, such as *Public Archaeology*. If you are working outside the United States, there is likely to be gray literature associated with the missions of various nongovernmental organizations (NGOs) that are active where you want to work. Such organizations are often eager to share their reports and recommendations. When I worked in Yemen, in order to "find my feet" I got permission to move into the Fulbright residence that was full of active researchers involved in current projects. They happily shared their experiences with me and helped me analyze my findings, thereby broadening the expertise that went into my efforts, while familiarizing me with the immediate conditions in the country.

I have a set of priorities about disciplinary literature that I try to instill in my students. They include an admonition to read the authors who disagree with you; always read diverse authors (women must appear in the bibliography; if the research is about Bolivia, something published by a Bolivian should be read, etc.); seek out "gray literature"; assume that someone else has already had the same idea you have and find their work; and if you want to use an idea from an article by Ian Hodder that Hodder derived from Marx, read Marx.

Worry About Power

College professors and heritage management specialists who practice archaeology for a living do not think of themselves as rich because most of us know we could make more money with less education if we plied a different trade. Consequently, it often seems like the archaeologist can relate to an impoverished community on equal ground. In fact, to do otherwise seems disrespectful. But few archaeologists have experienced firsthand the worst sorts of social injustice, and the life chances of a person with a college degree are not comparable with those of someone who does not always have enough to eat (two categories of people that rarely overlap). In these unequal power dynamics, the person on top may not see how their status is influencing their communication with the people they want to help.

Because you have money and power through your professional credentials and connections, you represent both an opportunity and a threat to local people—especially those who live in strained economic circumstances. They cannot afford not to flatter and follow you, so try very hard not to lead. Whenever possible, make sure that credit for the success of activist efforts falls on the community participants. On the other hand, if the government responds negatively to your activism, be ready to put responsibility on the shoulders of participants who can afford to leave town—most notably, yourself.

Being paid or backed by a government can create a similar dynamic. Even being part of a well-established archaeology project that has wide visibility can silence local dissent, especially if the project provides local jobs. Governments are often not enthusiastic about giving voice to their disgruntled citizens, and those citizens usually are aware of the fact.

On the other hand, in local communities or any group with a genuinely demo-cratically elected leadership, the leaders can be the best people to start with; if the community does not like the way the resources that you bring are being used, they have recourse via elections. And village leaders are aware of where their authority originates.

Americans are especially uncomfortable acknowledging their class privileges and are often shocked to be told that they may unwittingly take advantage of local people by using power they do not know they possess. I have experienced this with both young students and senior colleagues. In general, it is easier to warn people away from unequal relationships before they begin than to try to extract them once the asymmetry has been established. So I emphasize discussions about power in my classes and tend to be very directive when working with inexperienced colleagues.

Do Not Be Confused by Star Trek

By definition, an activist is trying to affect the lives of real people. This is a sobering if not downright frightening proposition, and has to be taken seriously. But it is equally important to beware of the opposite, apathetic tendency to hang back and not interfere in situations where an outsider really can help. The "Prime Directive" does not apply to the real world.

A nonlocal activist is likely being judged in relation to other outsiders, some of whom may have behaved badly while others may have been immensely popular and wielded considerable resources. Either way, it is reasonable that people mis-trust visitors or have unrealistic expectations, so it is crucial to be clear about who you are, why you are there, what you can offer, and what is beyond your scope.

In my classes, I ask students to think honestly about what they might have to offer a community suffering from some sort of social injustice. I do this not only to inject realism into their future plans but also to suggest some new possibilities to consider when they select their classes for the next year.

NOTE

1. The Kyrgyz flag design is a golden circle with two crossed lines on a red background. It represents what is seen through the top of a yurt when the roof is opened.

REFERENCES

Cultural Survival. 2013. "Belize: Our Life, Our Lands—Respect Maya Land Rights," accessed November 28, 2013, http://www.culturalsurvival.org/take-action/belize.

Dolukhanov, Pavel M. 1995. "Archaeology in Russia and Its Impact on Archaeological Theory." In *Theory in Archaeology, A World Perspective,* edited by Peter Ucko, 327–342. London and New York: Routledge.

Escobar, Antonio. 1997. "Anthropology and Development." *International Social Science Journal* (49): 497–515.

Horvath, Ronald J. 1972. "A Definition of Colonialism." *Current Anthropology* 13(1): 45–57.

İğmen, Ali. 2012. *Speaking Soviet with an Accent: Culture and Power in Kyrgyzstan.* Pittsburgh, PA: University of Pittsburgh Press.

IPinCH: Intellectual Property Issues in Cultural Heritage. 2013. Project website, accessed November 28, 2013, http://www.sfu.ca/ipinch/.

Laruelle, Marlène. 2012. "The Paradigm of Nationalism in Kyrgyzstan: Evolving Narrative, the Sovereignty Issue, and Political Agenda." *Communist and Post-Communist Studies* 45(1–2): 39–49.

Levi, Scott. 2007. "Turks and Tajiks in Central Asian History." In *Everyday Life in Central Asia: Past and Present,* edited by Jeff Sahadeo and Russell Zanka, 15–31. Bloomington: Indiana University Press.

Levi-Strauss, Laurent, and Roland Lin. 2010. "Safeguarding Silk Road Sites in Central Asia." In *Conservation of Ancient Sites on the Silk Road,* edited by Neville Agnew, 56–61. Los Angeles: Getty Conservation Institute.

Liu, Morgan Y. 2012. *Under Solomon's Throne: Uzbek Visions of Renewal in Osh.* Pittsburgh, PA: University of Pittsburgh Press.

Pyburn, Anne. 2007. "Archaeology as Activism." In *Cultural Heritage and Human Rights,* edited by H. Silverman and H. F. Ruggles, 172–183. NY: Springer.

———. 2009. "Practicing Archaeology: As If It Really Matters." In *Archaeological Ethnographies,* edited by Y. Hamilakis and A. Anagnostopoulos. *Public Archaeology* 8(2–3): 161–175.

———. 2011. "Engaged Archaeology: Whose Community? Which Public?" In *Global Public Archaeology,* edited by Akira Matsuda and Katsu Okamura, 29–41. New York: Springer.

Wachtel, Andrew. 2013. "Kyrgyzstan Between Democratization and Ethnic Intolerance." *Nationalities Papers: The Journal of Nationalism and Ethnicity* 41(6): 971–986.

Wolf, Eric. 1982. *Europe and the People Without History.* Los Angeles: University of California Press.

Chapter 11

Beyond Archaeological Agendas

In the Service of a Sustainable Archaeology

Neal Ferris and John R. Welch

Neal Ferris

The challenge for me in outlining a personal biography that explores how I came to activist archaeology is that I don't think I can point to any eureka moments, either deciding to be an archaeologist or an activist. For me, archaeology was something I discovered in university, embraced as much for the community it gave me as for the intellectual excitement it offered. Through that connection, I found my own competencies and capabilities, a social milieu and language, humor, passion, righteous indignation, and a livelihood and occupation that I continue to feel privileged to be a part of. And from archaeology I have met many people who would become colleagues; friends; and in one special instance, my love—leading to the family I am fortunate to have today. Archaeology, in effect, is really who I am.

That personal dimension to how archaeology operates for/is me means that the practice I follow is infused with who I am, including those political and social leanings formed in the social liberalism, humanism, and relativism of the 1970s. They included a tendency toward earnest convictions, a belief in the social contract, and fair play. No doubt tedious to those around me at the time, I recall early on having a strong conviction that what we do as archaeologists must be accountable beyond ourselves and our discipline, and that

Transforming Archaeology: Activist Practices and Prospects, edited by Sonya Atalay, Lee Rains Clauss, Randall H. McGuire, and John R. Welch, 215–237. © 2014 Left Coast Press, Inc. All rights reserved.

those who consume the archaeological record (and environment) have a societal obligation to ensure that those impacts are mitigated.

That earnest and naive view would be heavily tempered over 20 years I spent working in government as a regulatory archaeologist, reviewing the continually accumulating output of archaeology for southern Ontario and living in the borderland between archaeology and broader society. Over that time, I met and interacted with a handful or two of truly inspirational people; an endless number of decent, good people; a few handfuls of people genuinely incompetent at what they do; and less than a handful of truly hurtful persons. I saw plenty conflicting and contested opinions; beliefs, biases and prejudices; as well as the consequences of the gap between intent and action. I saw people wield power and process to effect good and withhold doing so for venal self-interest or cowardice. I met people caught up in the conservation of archaeology that were indifferent or disdainful, respectful or resentful, sorrowful or angry, but mostly just trying to address the requirement/job/task at hand. I found myself sitting across a table from people crying tearfully over the loss of their home because of the cost of archaeology, or over the disrespect to the bones of ancestors by archaeologists, or over the loss of their archaeological livelihood by the actions of other archaeologists. I argued with people over more that had to be done, or less; yelled at people and was yelled at; and was called every possible good and bad pronoun in the book. I helped people get their development projects approved, helped others stop development projects, and helped people find peace and the cemeteries of their direct ancestors they had fought so long and hard to have recognized and protected. I provided opinion and information that helped judges, arbitrators, hearing officers, politicians, First Nations, and government negotiators try and balance contested values. I also helped enforce requirements to protect the past that clearly harmed, emotionally or financially, people living in the present. I also sometimes found myself requiring bad archaeology to be done or bad logic to govern outcomes, simply because it was easier to follow the process than to act alternatively. I saw both the good effect of good intentions and good legislation, and many train wrecks brought on by good intentions and good legislation. And through it all, I met endless numbers of people genuinely in awe of the material record they were handling; speechless over a personal connection they found with people from generations or millennia ago; or ecstatic over their introduction to, and pursuit of, the past and archaeology.

So for me, if activism is a dimension of the archaeology I do, it is because my entire experiential life as an archaeologist really was not about the stuff left behind in the past, but about the many different people in the present I've met, worked with, helped, failed to help, and variously combated or supported over my career as first a government archaeologist and now as an academic. Researching the archaeological record, to me, has always been secondary to that primary dimension, and humanity, of "doing" archaeology through my interactions with those I meet along the path. And while I joke that I "retired" when I left government to take a job in a university, in truth the primacy of archaeology as engagement with people, helping and being helped, continues, only with more of an educational and mentoring bent, and less of a regulatory one.

I guess the key point I underscore is that archaeology is a fascinating pursuit, but it is a pursuit done now, in the present, and so it obviously is consequential primarily for *people in the present. People, not things, should be what matters in our archaeology. But sometimes our collective passion for the stuff of archaeology—be it stone scrapers, clay pots, animal or plant remains, or stains in the ground—might confuse us as to priorities. If there is one thing I've learned, and if there is an activism in what I do, it is that it always needs to be the person, not the scraper, that our archaeology and our activism is on behalf of. Realizing this is a bit like putting toothpaste back in the tube: once you realize archaeology isn't about scraper metrics, it will never again go back to being about scraper metrics.*

———— ∞ ————

As archaeology advances into the twenty-first century, being able to conceive of it as a single, all-inclusive discipline is much more challenging. This is readily evident in the diversity of what is presented as archaeology at any national or international meeting or basic Google-framed topical search. Ranging from inventory, description and historical narrative, cultural systems analysis, material science, relational actor networks, interpretive relativity, or inclusive multivocality, a definitional cohesiveness to what archaeology "is" seems stretched beyond tolerance.

Whether this is good or bad is debatable, but the epistemological questioning that arises from these differences is substantial. Intellectual gulfs between the schools and types of archaeology make it difficult to imagine the hard-core normative cultural historian, processualist objective truth builder, neo-Darwinian materialist, and relative inclusivist ever being able to work together to develop consensual interpretations of the material past, much less offer them for public use or benefit. We also suspect that the concept of "activism" across this spectrum will mean very different things; and for at least some, activism in archaeology will mean stoutly defending intellectual freedoms, objective truth seeking, and a vision of archaeology as the material domain of archaeologists that cannot brook, let alone accommodate, alternative ways of knowing the past because they threaten core archaeological orthodoxies (e.g., McGhee 2004, 2008, 2010).

If this was the full spectrum of the ontology that fell under the broad rubric of "archaeology," our discussion of activist practices would focus on countering that disciplinary exclusionism, and enabling and translating archaeology into a history of relevance to the societies we are a part of, in our role as educators and storytellers of this deep past, by recovering, revising, and providing access to long-term histories that otherwise tend to be marginalized from dominant colonial narratives. But the irony is that this diverse and fractured academic archaeological intellectual spectrum is just a small part of an even more diversified range of archaeologies. As discussed in Welch and Ferris (this volume), today individuals who self-identify as archaeologists and undertake archaeologically oriented work across North America overwhelmingly operate outside of the academy and within the applied contexts of cultural resource management (CRM), or, more properly, archaeological resource management (ARM; see Welch and Ferris for an explanation of the distinction).

By "applied contexts," we are referring to forms of archaeology occurring in a borderland where practice meets and interacts with broader social interests and engagements with the material remains of the archaeological record (Ferris 2004). This applied practice encompasses federal, state/provincial, municipal, and First Nations regulators and information managers; museum, K–12, and community education specialists; and, most prominently of all, private, for-hire consultant ARM practitioners. In this latter category, commercial enterprise ranges from self-shingled, spare bedroom operations, to medium-sized corporate organizations, to embedded divisions within national or international engineering or development firms, to hybrid commercial/research foundations. Each of these operations meet, fail to meet, or exceed, on a daily basis, state-, professional-, societal-, and personally regulated ethical expectations of conduct (e.g., Breternitz 2004; Everill 2007, 2009; Ferris 2002, 2007; Glørstad and Kallhovd 2013; Metcalf and Moses 2011).

Welch and Ferris (this volume) review the nature, form, and historical development of ARM practice—that narrowly defined commercial management of archaeologically relevant material heritage—and the development and current status quo of a practice based on an extractive-consumptive paradigm modelled on cultural historical imperatives to harvest archaeological data for the sake of "saving" the record for archaeology. As a distinct entity, it is also fair to say that ARM practice encompasses at least as broad a range of intellectual and methodological diversities as can be found in the academy. They are also interwoven with a diversity of corporate, client-driven, and bureaucratic conventions, predilections, and pressures that tend to impinge on ARM practitioners' capacity to research, make available, or share their findings, and to affect their livelihood and work satisfaction in a plethora of ways not typically negotiated by those of us in the academy (e.g., Altschul and Patterson 2010; Barker 2010; Ferris 1998; Fitting 1984; Wheaton 2006; Whittlesey and Reid 2004). In short, once the diversity of ARM practices are included under the heading of archaeology, any sense of this practice as a unified whole is stretched far beyond any singular definition.

The Archaeologist's Agenda

While fundamental differences across the academic and applied spectrum of what it means to be "doing archaeology" are readily recognized by those of us within archaeology, this distinction is typically only poorly understood and largely irrelevant beyond archaeology. This is the case whether referring to generic "person on the street" publics or to those individuals who, by dint of regulatory requirement, landowner happenstance, or personal or community identity, find themselves interacting with archaeologists (e.g., Birch 2006; Skeates 2000). From this outside standpoint looking in, archaeologists all "do" archaeology. This external appearance of homogeneity is a challenge for archaeological nuance and intellectual distinction to negotiate, if for no other reason than it means we rarely present a common voice or unified vision externally. It is also a challenge to an activist or transformative archaeology because the diverse internal conceptions of what archaeology should be activist about generates the need for continual rear-guard reactive reparations (e.g., responding to McGhee [2008] as not representing the views of all). This, by the way, is also the daily existence of most ARM practitioners, for whom oral histories of ethical lapses and profit-driven expediencies by colleagues circulate both within the industry and widely beyond archaeology among external groups regulating, purchasing, collaborating with, or opposing that practice (e.g., Ferris 1998, 2007; Williamson 2010). Despite the valiant efforts of individual ARM archaeologists, a chronic personal dimension of an ethical and transformative ARM practice can often be a continual apologia for the behavior and choices of other ARM archaeologists.

The common, external-to-archaeology appearance of what archaeology is and does is not mere masking of complexity. We would argue that it also reveals core commonalities that are present across diverse archaeological belief systems, perhaps more evident to outsiders than to us. Certainly archaeology, and especially the rise of ARM as the means of managing the common wealth that is archaeology as regulated by the State and paid for by development proponents, has been extremely effective over the past century at framing the discipline, on the basis of these core commonalities, as *the* primary expert authority when it comes to the material record (Ferris 2003; Smith 2004; Watkins 2000). This common face to archaeological belief systems is also reinforced through the use of idiosyncratic and specialized technical jargon not accessible to outsiders (Ferris 1999). It is further shaped by the shared mystique and bonding internal to archaeology that arises from the privations and experiential excitement of fieldwork. On this latter point, although archaeology does allow outsiders various behind-the-scenes fieldwork experiences in the form of field schools and public programming, this rarely reflects the true day-to-day of archaeology, especially in ARM, so it only reinforces popular generalizing tropes about what "real" archaeology is about (e.g., Chirikure and Pwiti 2008; Everill 2009; Everill and Young 2011; Faulkner 2000; Ferris 1999; Holtorf 2005, 2007).

Most central to this external common understanding of what archaeology is, and the basis for validating archaeology as expert arbiter of the archaeological record, is the general invocation by archaeologists of archaeology as science. We don't mean science as a methodology or science in the strictly positivistic sense of its use, but rather science as that contemporary western societal touchstone to authority, validating Western thought, and affirming modern faith (e.g., McMullin 1992; Shapin 1982). Archaeology as science has been invoked for decades—both internally and to various publics—in asserting the accuracy and authenticity of the ways archaeologists come to know the past (e.g., Criado-Boado 2001; Pruitt 2011; Wylie 2002; see also Rathje, Shanks, and Witmore [2013] for many examples of how validation of archaeology through science claims are variously articulated by archaeologists). We do not want to rehash the intellectual wars within archaeology that have tended to pivot around how science-like one's archaeology is versus another. Instead, we underscore the point that from within archaeological sensibilities

(Shanks 2012) and extending across the many internal iterations of how archaeology makes meaning, there is a strong, albeit circular belief that as archaeology comes to know the material past through science, archaeology is the right way to know that past. So if scientific archaeology, through the careful analysis and comparison of material remains and their contexts, comes to know the past beyond living memory or written documents, and differently from oral histories or mythologies, then from a Western perspective, of course, there must be an essential accuracy or "truthiness" to that archaeological way of knowing.

Framing what archaeologists do as science serves as more than just personal validation—though that is a very important disposition strongly assumed in archaeological culture—it also is a key driver behind the imperative to conserve and manage the archaeological record from other forms of loss. Specifically, archaeologists continually advocate for stronger and more encompassing forms of regulated conservation because of their strong conviction that the scientific value of the record will be lost if land alterations occur without archaeological documentation. Faith in scientific value also underlies claims that warehousing the massive accumulated output of the extraction-consumption ethos in ARM will, eventually and somehow, contribute to advancing our science-based knowledge about the past.

Although many archaeologists internally hold passionate convictions that archaeological loss must be avoided, the rhetorical claim we advance externally to society, especially around conservation and management of the record, tends to be less that loss will impinge on our ability to do archaeology and harm to our scientific prerogative, and more that such loss deprives all of humanity from knowing and appreciating our common human heritage. In other words, digging up or bulldozing material things into nonarchaeologically relevant locales, soil heaps, or debris is a loss for everyone. Value in the record is preserved through the avoidance of such loss, assumed by archaeologists to be a readily recognizable truth in society. And by that logic, avoiding loss is therefore the responsibility of all society to work toward, which is a key explicit principle operating within state-based conservation regimes (Carman 2005b).

This belief by archaeologists that the loss of the record is bad for everyone, not just for archaeologists wanting to study that record, is indeed readily recognizable externally—not as a universal truth, but as one of a number of core convictions we archaeologists hold. These convictions make up a deeper doctrine archaeologists advance that asserts archaeology is done for the greater good of society by expanding our knowledge of the past on behalf of all humanity, and that archaeologists are the stewards or guardians of the archaeological record. This doctrine is recognizable beyond archaeology because archaeologists vigorously and continually advocate these views to nonarchaeologists and to the next generations of academic, applied, and ARM archaeologists (e.g., McCarthy and Brummitt 2013). This belief system, or *habitus,* of the archaeological self sustains the certainty that archaeology is the sole rigorous means of extracting meaning/truth from the material remains of past life to provide explanation/understanding into ancient human behavior/lived life.

The stuff of archaeology allows archaeology, uniquely, to access the past, especially more ancient pasts, in a manner no one else can or should even try. And its interpretations arise from a strict adherence to archaeology as a science, constrained by tangible though fragmentary data, in order to generate substantiated knowledge. In effect, what the invoking of archaeology as science does is to validate, as much for internal consumption as for external consumers of archaeology, this way of knowing as the exclusively correct and authorized way to access and use the material past.

From the standpoint of someone external to archaeology, we can perhaps envision a bit of the hubris they might infer from this internal framing of the archaeological belief that although others might contribute interesting insights about ancient times or be able to dig up the material remains of the past, they cannot offer authorized or valid meanings from that record because those narratives arise from outside the parameters that archaeology authenticates as being correct. This disposition of the archaeologist's *habitus* is a deeply ingrained orthodoxy that sustains a consistent call from across archaeology to recover the material record before it is destroyed. This conviction drives the extractive-consumptive imperative in ARM. It is the basis for why practitioners frame ARM as more altruistic than self-serving, and why it is only "natural" to expect the State to require various land developers to pay hundreds of millions of dollars per annum worldwide recovering soon-to-be destroyed parts of the record. As well, framing the archaeological record as having value only from within archaeological sensibilities also validates and is validated by the conviction that archaeologists are the intellectual and moral stewards for a record under siege by development and other forms of nonarchaeological consumption. These beliefs, in effect, give rise to what we refer to here as the *archaeologist's agenda*: that internal set of rationales and motivations that lead archaeologists to engage with broader societal values and activities that archaeologists perceive as threatening to their personal interest in and concern for the archaeological record. This is the agenda archaeologists then bring with them to the borderland, where applied practice plays out and engages with broader society. And it is out here that the archaeologist's agenda is then operationalized within the thousands of contexts and decisions made on a daily basis within ARM.

A Heritage Beyond Archaeological Agendas

Although the archaeological agenda thrives internally within archaeological discourse, and drives broader advocacy from the academy and professional organizations, it was really only when that agenda became institutionalized within the State, through the incorporation of statutes and regulations, that this agenda began to adopt a State-sanctioned authorized voice and definition to conservation (e.g., Carman 2012; Ferris 1998; Schiffer and Gumerman 1977; Skeates 2000; Smith 2004, 2006). Over the last half century, archaeology's success has meant that State-legislated conservation regimes now capture the essence and many of the particulars of the archaeologist's agenda. They include sites routinely treated as valuable resources to manage in land-use planning through proponent-pay requirements in law. Conservation regimes also formally regulate and certify (through licenses/permits) the individuals who can do archaeology, privileging these members of society from everyone else who is deemed unqualified and therefore under law prohibited from doing archaeology. Archaeology's institutionalization also provides for the imposition of archaeology-centric standards of documentation and interpretation, provisions for the warehousing of material, and so forth.

In governance contexts, the archaeologist's agenda is seldom articulated baldly as servicing the needs of archaeologists, however. Instead, it is translated into a conservation imperative that speaks to conserving the common heritage of all people. Indeed, ARM statutes, regulations, policies, and programs typically embed archaeology as one component of a broader cultural heritage of value to be known and appreciated (Dent 2012; Messenger and Smith 2010). But this cultural heritage conserved on behalf of broader society is not directly and self-evidently present within the collections of stone, fired clay, bone, and plant remains found on the land. So the motive for conservation encompasses not so much the things that archaeology documents, but more the *meanings* this detritus enables by way of archaeological interpretation.

This distinction is critical to understanding how embedded the archaeologist's agenda is in conservation regimes, and to understanding how archaeologists "create" heritage value in society. Notably, the heritage value of the archaeological record emerges less from the stuff found doing archaeology, and more from the intangible ways in which archaeologists create narratives of the past that then ascribe heritage values to those things—much the way Stonehenge is a world heritage site, not an odd accumulation of rocks at a particular locality. This tangible-thing-to-intangible-heritage-value is a conversion process seen endlessly in the report recommendations submitted by ARM practitioners and then used by the State and development proponents to confirm a property can be "cleared" of any archaeological values. It is also seen more casually in the countless interactions between archaeologists and members of the public when these individuals bring objects they have found to the archaeologist. These objects usually are carried in to that meeting carefully boxed and wrapped protectively. The individual then gently removes the item and offers it up to the archaeologist for identification and confirmation of value. That person subsequently either leaves the encounter with the archaeologist carrying those objects safely boxed up again (the archaeologist "confirms" the object is an artifact) or empty-handed, with packaging and object usually left in a waste bin (the archaeologist "confirms" that the object is not an artifact). The object itself has not changed; only the intangible value of the object as heritage has changed on the archaeologist's say-so.

Despite this process of instilling heritage meaning into things through archaeological interpretation, most legislative regimes tend to imply that the objects of archaeology themselves are of inherent value. So here in legislation is a blurring of potential archaeological value with actual heritage value, but not in the sense of integrating two distinct concepts. Rather, these concepts are simply made synonymous through the regulatory embodiment of the archaeologist's agenda to conserve the material record in order to enable archaeological study. This can be seen in the regulatory stipulations that govern archaeology (as opposed to other forms of heritage such as buildings, landscapes, stories, folk traditions, etc.). Typical provisions include permitting archaeologists access to recover and remove the archaeological record from the landscape through excavation while prohibiting collecting or looting, providing methodological particulars for how artifacts are to be recovered and documented, and acknowledging archaeological interpretation and scientific analysis as the means for determining societal significance and value (e.g., Carman 2002, 2005a; King 1998, 2011; Smith 2004). Ironically, the regulatory intertwining of archaeology *as* heritage means that, by dint of being regulated and licensed, commercial archaeologists often also manage and make decisions around other unregulated forms of heritage as *de facto* heritage managers licensed by the State. ARM firms can diversify their expertise to manage this broader heritage, (e.g., Polk 2013), although the degree to which this is done successfully is perhaps more abstract than actual (e.g., King 2002, 2009).

The translation of the archaeologist's agenda into cultural heritage statute and regulation has been less a calculated stratagem and more the inability of many archaeologists to disentangle their own belief system from the broader concept of heritage in their efforts to advocate for archaeological conservation. But although "heritage" as a social value may thematically overlap with archaeological ways of making meaning from the material remains of the past, it is not the same thing. Heritage is a set of intangible values that functions as a process engaging the contemporary with pasts that are self-referential, defined differently by different groups, encompassing a range of tangible and intangible manifestations that extend far beyond the traditional purview of archaeology, and whose values and meanings are continually being revised and contested (e.g., Harrison 2012; Harvey 2008; Schofield 2008; Silverman 2011; Smith, Messenger, and Soderland 2010; West 2010).

Especially in ARM discourse, the notion that heritage is something that encompasses archaeological things and values within a much wider and revising conception of the role of the past in the present is difficult to parse out from the notion of archaeology as having heritage value solely because of its value to archaeologists and their ways of knowing the past. For example, pleas in archaeology for engaging the public and to promote the value of archaeological conservation in society (e.g., Crass 2009; Everill and Young 2011; McManamon 2000) are often framed as critical to securing a necessary broader societal relevance for this valuable heritage resource. The thinking implied in these pleas is that by doing this often and forcefully enough, the public will finally "get it" and come to fully support archaeologists and their efforts to conserve archaeology for archaeology's sake. But the core conceit of the archaeologist's agenda remains embedded in this thinking; that is, that public heritage value emerges only when the archaeologist has unfettered access to this record under threat, in order to interpretatively translate the record into meaning for archaeologists. Nonarchaeologists just need to understand how important this is for them, too, and so get behind what archaeologists want.

The problem that tends to elude such communication campaigns to advance the archaeologist's agenda is that while the logic of archaeology equalling heritage makes common sense to archaeologists, other members of society who meet up with us in this borderland do not usually arrive wanting to access archaeology or the material record (site looters excepted) the way archaeologists do. And while archaeologists may believe that archaeology is the only way to correctly know the ancient past, heritage values do not arise from a simple translation of archaeological ways of knowing into contemporary understandings of heritage. In reality, self-evident truths in archaeology are really only contested opinions of variable worth within broader, contemporary social relevances (e.g., Harrison 2008; Holtorf 2010; Kojan 2008).

Especially in ARM practice, the societal engagement that archaeology participates in is defined not by archaeology, but by the broader concept of cultural heritage as being of value in society, and as such articulating a social contract for managing that public resource captured in legislation. Critically, external-to-archaeology agents involved in cultural heritage management are contesting differing values of worth because there are spectra of contemporary interests intersecting the material of archaeology found on lands to be altered for the purposes of resource profit, development, and social infrastructure growth. Broadly speaking, the values playing out over the archaeological record (as they also play out over environmentally sensitive areas) include economic, political, social, and personal. These values are weighted against either the loss or the preservation of archaeological remains. While these contested values are typically mitigated by the archaeologist's agenda that aligns removal in advance of development with an archaeological desire to recover the record for archaeology's sake, letting archaeologists in to dig up a site does not necessarily balance other nonarchaeological cultural heritage values associated with those locales. In fact, the ARM extractive-consumptive paradigm tends to exclude those other heritage values that are supposed to be accounted for in conservation regimes.

Importantly, while conservation regimes emphasize the material of archaeology as the aim of archaeological resource management, archaeological sites and remains really become part of that cultural heritage of broad social relevance envisaged in law only after diverse perspectives access and engage with the archaeological record *beyond* archaeology and the archaeologist's agenda (e.g., Carman 2009; Skeates 2000; Smith 2006; Smith and Waterton 2009, 2012). Indeed, when we step out from behind our own particular interests, assumptions, and biases as archaeologists, it should be readily evident that it is the people and communities today who draw meaning, identity, vitality, and even sustenance from heritage places and things that are *the* cultural resources of greatest importance in cultural heritage management regimes. Not surprisingly, it is these people who are most immediately threatened by the loss of heritage places and things meaningful to them.

Because archaeological practice today so overwhelmingly occurs in commercial, State-regulated contexts, it is from within this setting that the contestation of archaeology as cultural heritage beyond the archaeologist's agenda emerges most clearly. And even though ARM practice can be crippled by persistent tendencies toward unreflexive normative assumptions, commercial expediencies, cultural historical sensibilities, and scientific prerogatives (Allen 2011; Cumberpatch and Roberts 2011; King 2009), contestation in ARM typically plays out beyond these internal-to-practice issues. This is because internal-to-archaeology concerns are largely irrelevant to the broader competing societal values, capitalistic profits, and State and economic imperatives that surround and enable growth and development of scarce resources and infrastructure. This forum of land-use development inherently operates within a milieu of contestation, negotiation, and differentially weighted decision making around competing values and worth. The insertion of the archaeologist's agenda into this process simply makes archaeology part of that contestation, inviting challenges from those who pay for the conservation of the record and from those who draw value, meaning, and connection from that record, over what archaeology is and what worth it has in society. And because it is in this context of contested heritage and ARM practice that archaeologists often act as agents for the State in assigning, amplifying, and silencing voices over archaeology (Ferris 2003), it is also here that the consequences of archaeological belief systems and conceptions of the archaeological record have the most impact, while also experiencing the most overt challenges to core internal archaeological orthodoxies (Ferris 2004, 2007).

Those challenges continually threaten conventional ARM practice and also invite it to be something other than it has been. Specifically, these challenges demand ARM practice be other than the harvesting and accumulating of the material record for the exclusive use of archaeologists under what externally can appear to be little more than a self-serving pretext of advancing knowledge while colluding in the commodification and consumption of urban and rural cultural heritage places, spaces, and landscapes. Thus, the transformative turn in ARM, at its core, needs to be about conceptually shifting practice away from archaeological agendas and extractive-consumptive paradigms, to acknowledging and servicing the spectra of contemporary contested values that converge where heritage is made and carried forward.

In the Service of Sustainable Archaeologies

There is a lot of sympathy beyond archaeology for the archaeologist's desire to avoid the destruction of archaeological sites. This is reflected in the proliferation of ARM statutes, inventories of protected sites, public outcries over examples of such destruction, and various crowd-sourced efforts to purchase or protect specific locales. That goodwill tends to be anchored to the perceived "greater good" that archaeological conservation has been framed as addressing. However, the staggering scale of ARM globally, the harvested record left in various states of access and care, the endless oral histories within ARM of incompetency for profit, all suggest that ARM is less about the "greater good" and more about the consumption of the material past for personal and professional benefit (Ferris 2007; King 2009; LaSalle and Hutchings 2012; Zorzin 2011). And because ARM is so massively the face of archaeology in society today, as attitudes go for this applied practice, so they go for all forms of archaeology.

Importantly, however, the status quo in archaeology is changing regardless of whether archaeologists act. State priorities are shifting to more directly address cultural heritage beyond archaeological agendas. This is especially the case as descendant groups and other publics engage the State directly to participate in the decision making and outcomes of archaeological practice, react to the inaccessibility of the accumulated record amassed by ARM, and seek to bypass archaeologists who are perceived to be gatekeepers to their heritage. This trend in governance is part of broader social developments in Western societies that emerged in the last part of the twentieth century (e.g., Niezen 2003), as well as a response to increasing challenges to any notion that a public trust is the exclusive purview of the group that directly benefits financially and professionally from their authority over publically managed resources and spaces (environmental, cultural, etc.). Moreover, from the State's perspective, the call by First Nations and other groups to have a role, or even the primary role, in managing and deciding outcomes for the archaeological heritage is a relatively easy "give" in the complex and ongoing mediation of issues of sovereignty, fiduciary responsibility, and autonomy. As such, these demands increasingly are being met by the State as proscribed best practices or even regulatory requirements, especially in Canada (e.g., Dent 2012; Klassen, Budwa, and Reimer/Yumks 2009; Williamson 2010).

So a transformative ARM practice necessarily will include the abandonment of the extractive-consumptive paradigm, either proactively or consequentially, as a result of heritage forces in society redefining the range of values and motivations driving management and conservation. And this change in turn can empower the emergence of a *sustainable archaeology*, situating the archaeologist not as authorized voice and arbiter of heritage advancing the archaeologist's agenda, but as servant to the other many complementary and competing values that come to bear over contested heritage in society. This transformation toward a sustainable archaeology also requires paradigmatic change to both the intent and the rationale to doing archaeology. Indeed, within ARM contexts, this change is already occurring, where the ability to effectively service broader social needs is becoming an essential part of the ARM industry's toolkit of good commercial practices.

Sustainable archaeological practice situates the archaeologist exactly within the nexus of those contesting contemporary social values that play out over the archaeological cultural heritage (Carman 2005b; Harrison 2008; Skeates 2000). This is also the place where most ARM decision making; negotiation; and mediation of value, expediency, and documentation occurs. And this engagement with the wider world means that on a daily basis, ARM generally has to operate as a dynamic negotiation of diverse values and conceptions of archaeology and heritage. Chronic second guessing by diverse clients and communities lays bare the conceits of status quo archaeological agendas, challenges core orthodoxies, and makes overt those dispositions within the archaeologist's *habitus* that in other settings, such as academic forms of practice, are far less frequently or forcefully challenged to justify internal "way the world works" logics. So it is perhaps not so surprising to suggest that the shift toward a transformative and sustainable archaeological practice and ethos emerges most forcefully from ARM.

For example, ARM practitioners regularly have to defend and continually revise their reasoning over the particulars of archaeology in response to developers' complaints over costs and from State regulatory oversight that only really requires archaeological conservation be done, not necessarily done well (Ferris 1999, 2004). ARM practitioners also have to respond meaningfully to frequent First Nations queries about why and for what purpose archaeologists dig up so many sites to allow lands to be developed. Even more challenging, ARM practitioners are increasingly called on to investigate, on behalf of descendant groups, the places and issues of community importance that are not conventionally archaeological in nature, but nonetheless encompass intangible values and locales of importance to these communities. In these contexts, ARM is employed not by development proponents needing the archaeological heritage to be moved out of the way, but by clients who ask the ARM practitioner to advise on and resolve issues of importance to the community, without care for or consideration of archaeologist sensibilities or values. These client-based needs force the archaeologist to see archaeology beyond the internal archaeologist's standpoint, to service a new kind of client expectation just to get the job done.

Servicing this broader relevance for nonconventional ARM clients situates applied practitioners beyond archaeology as conventionally defined within archaeology. Decision and meaning making here occur entirely in an interactive, sometimes collaborative, sometimes combative frame in which the ARM archaeologist services certain societal needs simply to further the client's interests. Although this accommodation is often a source of frustration for practitioners, who decry that their work is no longer about the archaeology (Ferris 2007), there is no question that in these contexts the applied practitioner's essential role has shifted from scientist and material manager to facilitator in the service of extra-to-archaeology needs and interests. As that role continues to expand as a result of regulatory reconfigurations seeking to better meet broader and newly emerging social values, ARM increasingly finds itself sustaining a business model that is not really about extraction and consumption at all, but about accommodation, mediation, and resolution over contested issues of heritage. There is a real capacity in this newer day-to-day reality of archaeology beyond the academy to allow archaeologists to reconceptualize themselves as something altogether different through a heterodox—rather

228 — Neal Ferris and John R. Welch

than orthodox—engagement that transforms applied archaeology into something more (not less) and active beyond archaeological sensibilities. In other words, the escalating and differing forms of service that ARM practitioners are expected to deliver are providing practical and conceptual foundations for a transformative and sustainable archaeology.

This shift toward a sustainable archaeology in applied practice ultimately enables a more activist practice that is fundamentally about mediating the economic, social, and governmental power and processes of dominant societal forces with those underpowered or marginal communities that nonetheless access societal power structures through archaeology, heritage, and identity (e.g., King 2009; McGuire 2008). This was evident in 2006 and 2007 during Ferris' role as a civil servant when he was required to participate in a Nation-to-Nation negotiation between the Haudenausee Iroquois First Nation, Canada, and Ontario over what ostensibly was an issue of a developer's housing subdivision being built on land that the Haudenausee saw as part of an unresolved land claim (DeVries 2011). Archaeology was identified as a specific topic requiring discussion at a relatively minor side table, which also would address restoring and beautifying the property. But archaeological discussions at this technical side table often encompassed much broader social issues, such as educational curriculum reform to redress colonial legacies, as well as issues of sovereignty, land title, and ownership of the past as socially and politically relevant to those who can and cannot speak for First Nations in the present. As well, this side table sustained an ongoing discourse and narrative that framed the role of the archaeologist in society as being either a naïve puppet or colluding partner in State suppression of aboriginal pasts and presents, and archaeological ways of knowing as being wholly irrelevant and fictional to community identity as a heritage of value in the twenty-first century. This "inconsequential" side table also nearly caused the breakdown of the entire State-to-State negotiation process over the Crown's nonresponse and attempt to play down an archaeological reassessment of the property that concluded the earlier ARM work conducted on the lands in dispute failed to "properly" conserve the archaeological record.

Another example that might have ended differently had archaeology been more in the service of broader social values relates to the tragic death of a Kettle Point Anishnabeg protester at Ipperwash Provincial Park in 1995 by Ontario provincial police. This dispute was in part triggered by the First Nations' claim (proven true years later) that the park held an historic community cemetery that had been impacted and covered over by parking lot construction earlier in the twentieth century. In the legislature, the Crown categorically denied that assertion (Edwards 2001, 249; Linden 2007), citing an early 1970s provincial archaeological survey of the park that failed to find any "archaeological resources." But that earlier study simply assumed that previous land disturbances would have destroyed any present archaeological remains, so it did not use methodologies to confirm what might have still been intact under sand dunes or graded deposits because the archaeologists were certain there would be nothing of any archaeological "value" left. Neither did the study undertake the historical research that would have readily confirmed a historic indigenous cemetery existed in the park.

Whether that archaeological study was or was not adequate is not really the point. Had provincial archaeological oversight or the archaeological community itself clearly and publicly cautioned the State (in lieu of internal grumbling) that the earlier archaeological investigation might not have been thorough, the public debate and issue could well have shifted from State denials of a cemetery and indigenous claims of heritage value for the land, to how or should the State redress or move past its earlier authorized but perhaps flawed archaeological investigation. Although the reputation and competency of ARM practice and government oversight would have been put under a critical spotlight, it surely would have been less consequential than actual outcomes. It is troubling to think that had the debate shifted the dispute away from issues of an "unjustified" occupation to the government's failure to properly manage cultural heritage, perhaps the circumstances that led to the death of Dudley George could have been avoided.

The transformation that arises from servicing the extra-to-archaeological interests of ARM clients can initially feel to the practitioner as not activist at all, or only accidental and arising from simply resolving the particular needs of a project in order to move on to the next one. But over time, these context-specific approaches have built up both a toolkit of best practices (e.g., community monitors, engagement/consultation, accommodating differential values and solutions, etc.) as well as a conceptual logic that, for both archaeologists and nonarchaeologists alike, leave material inventory and description far behind in the need to address social values and resolve points of conflict to achieve effective and consensual resolution. This also fosters a further evolution of ARM toward that statutory and socially acknowledged ideal of needing to service an inclusive cultural heritage of all, not solely the intellectual curiosity and possessive hoarding of the archaeologist.

Concluding Comments

Although the status quo in ARM is not sustainable, it could be argued that there has never really been a status quo to this continually revising practice, as it matures and finds its way in broader society and beyond the assumptions and biases of archaeology. This includes slowly leaving previous tendencies behind, notably normative, cultural historical sensibilities that valued accumulation for accumulation's sake—a sensibility that exploded into an extractive-consumptive paradigm once conservation and recovery of the record was deemed effective at countering development impacts. What is beginning to emerge across ARM practice instead is a more sustainable archaeology, focused on the servicing of contemporary community interests in the values and meanings of heritage, and on discovering ways to act and engage the world through archaeological heritage and beyond legislated mandates.

Being in the service of and engaging archaeology within the broader social arena of contested cultural heritage values necessarily reimagines the archaeologist as less the authorized voice of the State and holder of exclusive access to the archaeological record, and more the social servant of those forces in society that play out over the archaeological heritage. This loss of exclusive "ownership" and control of the material record, and the necessary accommodation of and deference to nonarchaeological values, can be seen as a threat to archaeology by some in applied or academic practice, in much the same way that dispositions previously beneath awareness and made overt can trigger orthodox retrenchment rather than heterodox engagement and change. But this is a misplaced anxiety because the loss of exclusive power enables archaeology to be sustainable beyond current excesses, and makes archaeology more relevant through the servicing of contested heritage values, including those of groups otherwise marginalized from dominant social discourses and histories. Amplifying previously silenced voices in archaeology validates significant heritage, their ties to the archaeological record, and even the need for conservation regimes. A sustainable practice is thus essential to service contested values and is essential to delivering a responsible, effective commercial model sustaining the ARM industry past extractive-consumptive paradigms.

Moreover, given the massively disproportionate scale of applied archaeology in relation to academic archaeology practiced globally, and the reality that ARM is the form of practice that most nonarchaeological interests will interact with, the emergence of a sustainable archaeology in the service of broader societal values within ARM will, over time, also require academic forms of practice to transform in similar ways. An obvious critical point is that academic, value-added research needs to be much more primarily directed toward the massive accumulated output of ARM activities. And the corollary to this point is that site excavation and accumulation of the record purely in pursuit of intellectual curiosities is no longer really viable and needs to be curtailed. There is neither the need nor the ethical imperative to pursue "archaeological knowledge" on intact and unthreatened sites, given the scale of publicly and privately financed data recovery occurring globally and largely left unexamined. Although the case can certainly be made for investigating particular sites that can advance methodological, theoretical, or heritage knowledge, making the case beforehand to communities that would be affected by those investigations (local and descendant) ensures community consent and proper commitments to following up and sharing results. Excavating solely for intellectual curiosity without consideration of interests beyond archaeology has left a staggeringly long legacy of sites consumed and collections left unusable. To continue this legacy with nothing more than good intent and scholarly career advancement as the motivation is the ethical equivalent of bloated expense claims or international corporate tax sheltering: allowable by the letter of the laws written by and serviced for such people and entities, but morally stretching social justifications.

That being said, we need to underscore that we do not feel we are advancing anything like a radical prognosis for archaeology here. Building the capacity of a transformative, sustainable archaeology in the service of broader social values has been underway for a long time, informally by many individual ARM and academic practitioners. This trend is seen in the emergence of academic research foci directed toward the implications and consequences of contemporary archaeological practice in society today, and in revisions to regulatory frameworks that are now more inclusive and multivocal in intent. Critically, it is important to note that the loss of exclusive control over setting research priorities and heritage values does not mean a loss of advancing knowledge, as has been decried by more orthodox colleagues since before the emergence of the Native American Graves Protection and Repatriation Act (NAGPRA) more than 2 decades ago. Instead, practitioners of a sustainable archaeology explore the many and various research opportunities they find within the spaces created in servicing archaeology beyond the archaeologist's agenda. These are robust undertakings, both theoretically and methodologically, that arise from research questions and the documented material record that community interactions and ARM practice enable. Indeed, the publication record and funded research programs of the many contributors to this volume are ample testament to this fact.

While the dominant paradigm in archaeology continues to be deconstructed, sustainable archaeology in the service of broader societal interests and values injects a social relevance into the practice that 2 centuries of exclusionist, cultural, historical, or science-like approaches failed to achieve. Ultimately, the empowerment—the activism—that sustainable archaeology promotes at the overlap between material pasts, cultural heritages, and societal relevances contributes to the demise of the legacies of colonial and imperial pasts and to shared commitments to transcend the legacies of our forebears and benefactors that continue to resonate across so much of our collective world.

Considering Methods: Methodology for a Sustainable Archaeology

Critical underpinnings to sustainable archaeology include embracing sustainable design principles (Welch and Ferris, this volume) that respond to unsustainable policies and practices, and recognizing that it is past time for current generations of archaeologists to take responsibility for our values and practices, rather than shifting the consequences of unsustainability onto subsequent generations. We employ these principles here to outline steps to (a) prolong indefinitely archaeology's vitality; (b) maximize archaeology's benefits and minimize adverse effects; (c) recognize that all archaeology is part of the greater enterprise of cultural heritage conservation; (d) affirm a dedication to prioritizing service to society over intradisciplinary needs and interests; (e) promote the application of sustainable design principles in archaeological decision making; and (f) shift archaeological discourse toward active quests for alignment among values and interests shared by practitioners, descendant communities, and broader societal domains.

Sustainable archaeology adopts one of the simplest sustainable design principles to facilitate a paradigm shift away from current extractive-consumptive practices: "reduce, reuse, and recycle." Adapted for archaeology, this tripartite protocol could be recast as "reduce, reuse, and reimagine." "Reduce" means avoiding excavation and adding to the amassed holdings generated by archaeological site harvesting. Making ARM about avoidance wherever possible is consistent with both environmental conservation and most descendant community preferences. So if we can reduce—or rather, preserve heritage places—except where conservation imperatives or community preferences direct us otherwise, then the job is done.

Although reducing consumption facilitates a sustainable record, "reuse" fosters sustainable archaeologies by redirecting research toward that record and output of archaeological material accumulation. It integrates academic and ARM practice, and also enhances the values of commercially harvested material while also validating "preserve the past for the future" rhetoric in conservation regimes.

The third principle of a sustainable archaeology seeks to "reimagine" archaeological practice, leaving behind archaeological values and sensibilities in favor of being in the service of broader social values. This principle requires the acknowledgment and balancing of the spectra of societal values embedded in archaeological sites and objects, and the recognition that archaeological value is just one of those value systems, neither better nor worse than any other. As such, a sustainable archaeology is, at its core, about conceptually shifting practice from pursuing archaeological agendas to servicing the full spectrum of values that converge where heritage is made and carried forward. This shift in practice entails embracing consultation and collaboration; distinguishing archaeological from societal agendas; and assisting in the mediation of contestation that arises, especially in applied contexts, by providing technical expertise and disinterested opinion that all sides can use to seek resolution. Moreover, reimagining accommodates nonarchaeological interpretations and conceptions of the past, without undermining the unique way archaeologists come to know the past. This accommodation reveals how the process of archaeological knowledge making can variously be strengthened through multivocality, or can diverge from epistemologies that differentially emphasize contextual, temporal, material, and phenomenological engagements with the archaeological record. Likewise, archaeologists have traditionally been gatekeepers to understandings (archaeological and nonarchaeological) of the record through specialized jargon and material classification. Reimagining seeks ways to facilitate access beyond those technical constraints—for example, through the use of variable ontologies, visuals, and languages in databases and informational platforms (e.g., one example of that re-imagining is taking form at Sustainable Archaeology: www.sustainablearchaeology.org). The aim is to enable independent access to and engagement with the material record directly and as a means to create alternative, nonarchaeological understandings of the past arising from outside archaeological sensibilities; not to counter or "weaken" archaeological interpretive frameworks, but to make space for and acknowledge those other-than-archaeological ways of knowing the past that already exist in today's society.

What a sustainable archaeology achieves is the construction of bridges and comanagement collaborations between archaeologists, descendant groups, and others in society that come together over the archaeological heritage of a region. This necessarily resituates the role of archaeologist and fulfills the archaeologist's social contract with the societies we are a part of (explicitly articulated through regulatory regimes and State-sanctioned privileges granted to archaeologists, as well as implied as a result of the costs imposed on those who impact the archaeological record), while affording the practice of archaeology a broader relevance that serves to sustain the practice onto the next generations of practitioners.

REFERENCES

Allen, Harry. 2011. "The Crisis in 21st Century Archaeological Heritage Management." In *Bridging the Divide: Indigenous Communities and Archaeology into the 21st Century,* edited by Caroline Phillips and Harry Allen, 157–180. Walnut Creek, CA: Left Coast Press.

Altschul, Jeffrey H., and Thomas C. Patterson. 2010. "Trends in Employment and Training in American Archaeology." In *Voices in American Archaeology,* edited by Wendy Ashmore, Dorothy T. Lippert, and Barbara J. Mills, 291–316. Washington, DC: Society for American Archaeology Press.

Barker, P. 2010. "The Process Made Me Do It: Or, Would a Reasonably Intelligent Person Agree that CRM is Reasonably Intelligent?" In *Archaeology and Cultural Resource Management,* edited by Lynne Sebastian and William Lipe, 65–90. Santa Fe, NM: SAR Press.

Birch, Jennifer. 2006. "Public Archaeology and the Cultural Resource Management Industry in Southern Ontario." Master's thesis, Department of Sociology and Anthropology, Carleton University, Ottawa, Canada.

Breternitz, Cory Dale. 2004. "Growing Up with CRM in the Southwest: A Personal Account of the Evolution of CRM from Campus to Corporation." In *From Campus to Corporation: The Emergence of Contract Archaeology in the Southwestern United States,* edited by Heidi Roberts, Richard Ahlstrom, and Barbara Roth, 51–58. Washington, DC: Society for American Archaeology Press.

Carman, John. 2002. *Archaeology and Heritage: An Introduction.* London: Continuum Press.

———. 2005a. "Good Citizens and Sound Economics: The Trajectory of Archaeology in Britain from 'Heritage' to 'Resource.'" In *Heritage of Value, Archaeology of Renown,* edited by Clay Mathers, Timothy Darvill, and Barbara Little, 43–57. Gainesville: University Press of Florida.

———. 2005b. *Against Cultural Property: Archaeology, Heritage and Ownership.* Oxford, UK: Duckworth Publishers.

———. 2009. "Where the Value Lies: The Importance of Materiality to the Immaterial." In *Taking Archaeology Out of Heritage,* edited by E. Waterton and L. Smith, 192–208. Newcastle, UK: Cambridge Scholars' Publishing.

———. 2012. "Towards an International Comparative History of Archaeological Heritage

Management." In *The Oxford Handbook of Public Archaeology,* edited by Robin Skeates, Carol McDavid, and John Carman. Oxford, UK: Oxford University Press.

Chirikure, Shadreck, and Gilbert Pwiti. 2008. "Community Involvement in Archaeology and Cultural Heritage Management." *Current Anthropology* 49: 467–485.

Crass, David Colin. 2009. "The Crisis in Communication: Still with Us?" In *Archaeology and Cultural Resource Management,* edited by Lynne Sebastian and William Lipe, 253–282. Santa Fe, NM: SAR Press.

Criado-Boado, Felipe. 2001. "Problems, Functions and Conditions of Archaeological Knowledge." *Journal of Social Archaeology* 1: 126–146.

Cumberpatch, Chris, and Howell M. Roberts. 2011. "Life in the Archaeological Marketplace." In *Archaeology in Society: Its Relevance in the Modern World,* edited by Marcy Rockman and Joe Flatman, 23–44. New York: Springer.

Dent, Joshua. 2012. *Past Tents: Temporal Themes and Patterns of Provincial Archaeological Governance in British Columbia and Ontario.* Master's thesis, Department of Anthropology, University of Western Ontario, London, Ontario.

DeVries, Laura. 2011. *Conflict in Caledonia: Aboriginal Land Rights and the Rule of Law.* Vancouver: University of British Columbia Press.

Edwards, Peter. 2001. *One Dead Indian: The Premier, the Police, and the Ipperwash Crisis.* Toronto: Stoddart.

Everill, Paul. 2007. "British Commercial Archaeology: Antiquarians and Labourers; Developers and Diggers." In *Archaeology and Capitalism: From Ethics to Politics,* edited by Yannis Hamilakis and Philip Duke, 119–136. Walnut Creek, CA: Left Coast Press.

———. 2009. *The Invisible Diggers: A Study of Commercial Archaeology in the UK.* Oxford, UK: Oxbow Books.

Everill, Paul, and Peter A. Young. 2011. "Archaeological Working Conditions and Public Perception." In *Archaeology in Society: Its Relevance in the Modern World,* edited by Marcy Rockman and Joe Flatman, 57–64. New York: Springer.

Faulkner, Neil. 2000. "Archaeology from Below." *Public Archaeology* 1: 21–33.

Ferris, Neal. 1998. "I Don't Think We're in Kansas Anymore . . . : The Rise of the Archaeological Consulting Industry in Ontario." In *Bringing Back the Past: Historical Perspectives on Canadian Archaeology,* edited by P. Smith and D. Mitchell, 225–247. Mercury Series, Archaeological Survey of Canada Paper 158. Ottawa: Museum of Civilization.

———. 1999. "What's in a Name? The Implications of Archaeological Terminology Used in Nonarchaeological Contexts." In *Taming the Taxonomy: Towards a New Understanding of Great Lakes Archaeology,* edited by R. Williamson and C. Watts, 111–121. Toronto: Eastendbooks.

———. 2002. "Where the Air Thins: The Rapid Rise of the Archaeological Consulting Industry in Ontario." *Revista de Arqueología Americana* 21: 53–88.

———. 2003. "Between Colonial and Indigenous Archaeologies: Legal and Extra-Legal Ownership of the Archaeological Past in North America." *Canadian Journal of Archaeology* 27: 154–190.

———. 2004. "Guess Who Sat Down to Dinner? Archaeology In Laws." In *An Upper Great Lakes Archaeological Odyssey: Essays in Honor of Charles E. Cleland,* edited by William A. Lovis, 199–214. Detroit: Cranbrook Institute of Science, Wayne State University Press.

———. 2007. "Always Fluid: Government Policy Making and Standards of Practice in Ontario Archaeological Resource Management." In *Quality Management in Archaeology,* edited by W. Willems and M. van der Dries, 78–99. Oxford, UK: Oxbow Books.

Fitting, James E. 1984. Economics and Archaeology. In *Ethics and Values in Archaeology,* edited by Ernestine Green, 117–122. New York: Free Press.

Glørstad, Hakon, and Karl Kallhovd. 2013. "The Allure of Bureaucracy: Cultural Heritage Management and the Universities in Norway." In *Heritage in the Context of Globalization: Europe and the Americas,* edited by Peter F. Biehl and Christopher Prescott, 19–27. London: Springer.

Harrison, Rodney. 2008. "Politics of the Past: Conflict in the Use of Heritage in the Modern World." In *The Heritage Reader,* edited by Graham Fairclough, Rodney Harrison, John H. Jameson Jr., and John Schofield, 177–190. London: Routledge.

———. 2012. *Heritage: Critical Approaches.* London: Routledge.

Harvey, David. 2008. "The History of Heritage." In *The Ashgate Research Companion to Heritage and Identity,* edited by Brian Graham and Peter Howard, 19–36. Aldershot, UK: Ashgate Publishing.

Holtorf, Cornelius. 2005. *From Stonehenge to Las Vegas: Archaeology as Popular Culture.* Lanham, MD: AltaMira Press.

———. 2007. "Can You Hear Me at the Back? Archaeology, Communication and Society." *European Journal of Archaeology* 10: 149–165.

———. 2010. "Heritage Values in Contemporary Popular Culture." In *Heritage Values in Contemporary Society,* edited by George S. Smith, Phyllis Mauch Messenger, and Hilary A. Soderland, 43–54. Walnut Creek, CA: Left Coast Press.

King, Thomas F. 1998. "How the Archeologists Stole Culture: A Gap in American Environmental Impact Assessment and What to Do About It." *Environmental Impact Assessment Review* 18: 117–133.

———. 2002. *Thinking about Cultural Resource Management: Essays from the Edge.* Langham, MD: AltaMira Press.

———. 2009. *Our Unprotected Heritage: Whitewashing the Destruction of Our Cultural and Natural Environment.* Walnut Creek, CA: Left Coast Press.

———. 2011. "Cultural Resource Laws: The Legal Melange." In *A Companion to Cultural Resource Management,* edited by Thomas F. King, 405–419. Malden, MD: Wiley-Blackwell.

Klassen, Michael, Rick Budwa, and Rudy Reimer/Yumks. 2009. "First Nations, Forestry, and the Transformation of Archaeological Practice in British Columbia, Canada." *Heritage Management* 2: 199–238.

Kojan, David. 2008. "Paths of Power and Politics: Historical Narratives at the Bolivian Site of Tiwanaku." In *Evaluating Multiple Narratives: Beyond Nationalist, Colonialist, Imperialist Archaeologies,* edited by Junko Habu, Claire Fawcett, and John M. Matsunaga, 69–85. New York: Springer.

La Salle, Marina, and Rich Hutchings. 2012. "Commercial Archaeology in British Columbia." *The Midden* 44(2): 8–16.

Linden, Hon. Sidney B. 2007. *Report of the Ipperwash Inquiry.* Toronto: Ontario Ministry of the Attorney General, Queen's Printer for Ontario.

McCarthy, John P., and Aaron Brummitt. 2013. "Archaeology in the 'Real World': The Training-Practice Disconnect in North American Consulting Archaeology." In *Training and Practice for Modern Day Archaeologists,* edited by John H. Jameson and James Eogan, 145–151. New York: Springer.

McGhee, Robert. 2004. "Between Racism and Romanticism, Scientism and Spiritualism: The Dilemmas of New World Archaeology." In *Archaeology on the Edge: New Perspectives from the Northern Plains,* edited by Brian Kooyman and Jane Kelley, 13–22. Occasional Paper Number 4. Calgary: Canadian Archaeological Association.

———. 2008. "Aboriginalism and the Problems of Indigenous Archaeology." *American Antiquity* 73: 579–598.

———. 2010. "Of Strawmen, Herrings, and Frustrated Expectations." *American Antiquity* 75: 239–243.

McGuire, Randall H. 2008. *Archaeology as Political Action.* Berkeley: University of California Press.

McManamon, Francis. 2000. "Archaeological Messages and Messengers." *Public Archaeology* 1: 5–22.

McMullin, Ernan, ed. 1992. *The Social Dimensions of Science.* Notre Dame, IN: Notre Dame University Press.

Messenger, P., and G. Smith, eds. 2010. *Cultural Heritage Management: A Global Perspective.* Gainesville: University Press of Florida.

Metcalf, Michael, and Jim Moses. 2011. "Building an Archaeological Business." In *Archaeology in Society: Its Relevance in the Modern World,* edited by M. Rockman and J. Flatman, 89–96. New York: Springer.

Niezen, Ronald. 2003. *The Origins of Indigenism: Human Rights and the Politics of Identity.* Berkeley: University of California Press.

Polk, Michael R. 2013. "Resource Transformation: The History and Status of the Cultural Resource Management Industry in the United States." In *Training and Practice for Modern Day Archaeologists,* edited by John H. Jameson and James Eogan, 131–144. New York: Springer.

Pruitt, Tera. 2011. *Authority and the Production of Knowledge in Archaeology.* PhD diss., Department of Archaeology, University of Cambridge, Cambridge, UK.

Rathje, William L., Michael Shanks, and Christopher Witmore, eds. 2013. *Archaeology in the Making: Conversations through a Discipline.* New York: Routledge.

Schiffer, Michael B., and George J. Gumerman, eds. 1977. *Conservation Archaeology: A Guide for Cultural Resource Management Studies.* New York: Academic Press.

Schofield, John. 2008. "Heritage Management, Theory and Practice." In *The Heritage Reader,* edited by Graham Fairclough, Rodney Harrison, John H. Jameson, Jr., and John Schofield, 15–30. London: Routledge.

Shanks, Michael. 2012. *The Archaeological Imagination.* Walnut Creek, CA: Left Coast Press.

Shapin, Steve. 1982. "History of Science and its Sociological Reconstructions." *History of Science* 20: 157–211.

Silverman, Helaine. 2011. "Contested Cultural Heritage: A Selected Historiography." In *Contested Cultural Heritage: Religion, Nationalism, Erasure, and Exclusion in a Global World,* edited by H. Silverman, 1–49. New York: Springer.

Skeates, Robin. 2000. *Debating the Archaeological Heritage.* London: Duckworth.

Smith, George, Phyllis Mauch Messenger, and Hillary A. Soderland, eds. 2010. *Heritage Values in Contemporary Society.* Walnut Creek, CA: Left Coast Press.

Smith, Laurajane. 2004. *Archaeological Theory and the Politics of Cultural Heritage.* London: Routledge.

———. 2006. *The Uses of Heritage.* London: Routledge.

Smith, Laurajane, and Emma Waterton. 2009. "There Is No Such Thing as Heritage." In *Taking Archaeology Out of Heritage,* edited by E. Waterton and L. Smith, 10–27. Newcastle, UK: Cambridge Scholars' Publishing.

———. 2012. "Constrained by Commonsense: The Authorized Heritage Discourse in

Contemporary Debates." In *The Oxford Handbook of Public Archaeology,* edited by Robin Skeates, Carol McDavid, and John Carman. Oxford, UK: Oxford University Press.

Watkins, Joe. 2000. *Indigenous Archaeology: American Indian Values and Scientific Practice.* Langham, MD: AltaMira Press.

West, Suzie, ed. 2010. *Understanding Heritage in Practice.* Manchester UK: Manchester University Press.

Wheaton, Thomas. 2006. "Private Sector Archaeology: Part of the Problem or Part of the Solution?" In *Landscapes Under Pressure: Theory and Practice of Cultural Heritage Research and Preservation,* edited by Ludomir R. Lonzy, 185–205. New York: Springer.

Whittlesey, Stephanie, and J. Jefferson Reid. 2004. "Money for Nothing: Ethical Issues in Contemporary Cultural Resource Management." In *From Campus to Corporation: The Emergence of Contract Archaeology in the Southwestern United States,* edited by Heidi Roberts, Richard Ahlstrom, and Barbara Roth, 114–126. Washington, DC: Society for American Archaeology Press.

Williamson, Ronald F. 2010. "Planning for Ontario's Archaeological Past: Accomplishments and Continuing Challenges." *Revista de Arqueología Americana* 28: 7–45.

Wylie, Alison. 2002. *Thinking from Things: Essays in the Philosophy of Archaeology.* Berkeley: University of California Press.

Zorzin, Nicolas. 2011. "Contextualising Contract Archaeology in Quebec: Political-Economy and Economic Dependencies." *Archaeological Review from Cambridge* 26(1): 119–135.

Chapter 12

Archaeologists as Activists, Advocates, and Expert Witnesses

T. J. Ferguson

In different phases of my career, I've been variously characterized as an activist, an advocate, and an expert witness. After being trained as an anthropological archaeologist during graduate work that led to a Master's degree at the University of Arizona in the 1970s, my first professional employment was as an archaeologist for the Pueblo of Zuni in New Mexico. During the 6 years I worked for the tribe, most of which was spent as Tribal Archaeologist, I served as an advocate for the tribe in the field of historic preservation. I advised the Zuni Tribal Council on matters relating to archaeology and cultural resources management, and I was often asked to be a spokesman in public settings, articulating the tribe's position on various matters. This was an exciting beginning to my career, and I was fortunate to work with tribal leaders who understood how archaeology and ethnography could be productively used as tools to attain tribal goals.

The opportunity to live in an Indian Pueblo community and work daily with tribal members taught me that archaeological sites and material culture have a powerful effect on living people. I came to realize that even if I did not personally understand or subscribe to tribal values and beliefs, I had to respect the unknown forces and spiritual power associated with ancestral sites and remains. My attitude about the propriety of archaeological fieldwork, especially the excavation of human remains, was profoundly shaped by how those activities affected my friends and tribal colleagues in the pueblo.

I learned that some human remains need to be excavated to protect them from land-disturbing projects—but those remains need to be immediately reburied after documentation

Transforming Archaeology: Activist Practices and Prospects, edited by Sonya Atalay, Lee Rains Clauss, Randall H. McGuire, and John R. Welch, 239–253. © 2014 Left Coast Press, Inc. All rights reserved.

239

to respect the dead and their living descendants. I assisted the tribe in applying the state of New Mexico indigent burial statutes to prevent the sale of ancient human remains at an auction in Santa Fe, an activity that many of my peers in archaeology perceived as activism. At the time, however, I saw this as fulfilling the Zuni Governor's admonition that all people should be treated the same, and if the remains of white people were not sold at auction and were reburied after archaeological excavation, Indian remains should be treated with the same respect (Ferguson 1982). The Tribal Council asked me to provide technical assistance to tribal religious leaders interested in recovering sacred artifacts that had been wrongfully removed from tribal lands, and some people also viewed this as activism (Merrill, Ladd, and Ferguson 1993). I was given an opportunity to record Zuni sacred sites in the tribe's aboriginal area for documentation of a land claim against the United States (Ferguson and Hart 1985). By the time I left Zuni and returned to graduate school at the University of New Mexico, my interests had broadened from conventional archaeology to ethnographic research of what we now refer to as traditional cultural properties and cultural landscapes.

During a second stint in graduate school, I continued to work as an archaeologist on land claims research for the Zuni Tribe (Ferguson 1995). During this period, I made a transition from working as an advocate to undertaking research as an expert witness, and from working as an activist to providing information to clients who then used that information to advance their interests without my further involvement. I came to view myself as an applied anthropologist specializing in the archaeological and ethnographic interpretation of settlement patterns and material culture, with a particular focus on serving the needs of indigenous communities. This work is intellectually challenging, and providing research services when requested to do so rather than working as an overt agent of social or cultural change satisfies me.

After earning a Master's of Community and Regional Planning and a PhD in anthropology at the University of New Mexico, I worked for a nonprofit educational corporation for 8 years and then started a series of companies to conduct research needed for implementation of the National Historic Preservation Act (NHPA) and the Native American Graves Protection and Repatriation Act (NAGPRA). In 2007, I was invited to join the faculty of the Department of Anthropology at the University of Arizona as a Professor of Practice, an untenured position that brings people working in the private sector into the university to share with students what they've learned about their field of study. In 2012, I was granted tenure as a full professor, with responsibilities for teaching and editing a publication series. My position now entails half-time work in the University of Arizona's School of Anthropology, allowing me time to pursue additional scholarly interests through a research company I operate in Tucson, Arizona. My practice is currently focused on investigation of traditional cultural properties, repatriation, and expert witness research needed for litigation of land and water rights (Ferguson 2004; Kuwanwisiwma and Ferguson 2009).

Key Questions

As the chapters in this volume amply demonstrate, archaeology is practiced in a social context. It's encouraging to see archaeologists address social issues such as environmental justice, intellectual property, sustainability, labor organization, and economic development. In writing about these issues, the authors in this volume raise key questions:

- What are "activist" and "transformative" archaeologies?
- Who invites or sanctions archaeologists to act as advocates?
- Can uninvited or naive activist archaeology reduce the sovereignty of indigenous groups or create other problems?
- What is the role of expert witnesses in relation to advocates?
- Do all archaeologists need to engage in transformative archaeology?
- Is good research the foundation of effective activism?

I address these questions in relation to the ideas presented in various chapters by reflecting on the work I've done over the course of my career.

What Are Activist and Transformative Archaeologies?

The authors in this volume underwent a semantic and conceptual shift in characterizing the archaeology they aspire to develop. At our original gathering at an annual meeting of the Society for American Archaeology, the discourse was phrased in terms of "activist archaeology." At the end of several days of brainstorming at the Amerind Foundation, the frame of reference shifted to "transformative archaeology."

In Chapter 3 (this volume), Atalay defines activist archaeology as doing research in dialogue, collaboration, and alliance with communities on topics that affect the lives of community members. Some, but not all, of these communities are engaged in struggles against oppression. Atalay argues that "activist archaeology" is not the same as "applied archaeology" because it involves a practice of democratizing knowledge rather than simply using it. I think this is a somewhat false dichotomy, however, because applied archaeology can also involve democratizing knowledge. For Atalay, activist archaeology is a way of "doing science," a particular form of practice that critiques the process of knowledge production, deconstructs it, and then reclaims it. In her work, a community-based participatory research model offers a methodology for doing archaeology in a manner that benefits communities. Atalay explains that many communities want archaeological research to be scientifically rigorous because painstaking scholarship respects the corresponding care exercised in the indigenous production and dissemination of traditional knowledge. That is true, and I would add that many indigenous communities want scientifically rigorous research because that is what is needed to apply this research most effectively in managerial and legal contexts.

After struggling with the conceptual and methodological basis of activist archaeology, the contributors to this volume came to focus on how archaeology can positively transform the lives of the people we study (Atalay and others, Chapter 1, this volume). In the process of working toward that goal, archaeology will also transform itself as a scholarly discipline that promotes capacity building in indigenous and local communities, and politically empowers those communities in the restoration and revitalization of their cultural and environmental environments. Transformative archaeology is thus a two-edged sword, changing the lives of the people we study and how we study those people. And as Pyburn (Chapter 10, this volume) observes, this type of archaeology sometimes transforms the archaeologist as much as the community in which the research is being conducted.

As Clauss (Chapter 2, this volume) explains, the move from activist to transformative archaeology came, in part, from dissatisfaction with archaeological discourse that conflates consultation with true collaboration. Clauss calls for a revolutionary archaeology that seeks to "change the internalities of our practice—our most fundamental understandings of what archaeology can, and therefore should, be." This revolutionary archaeology blurs the boundaries between academic and applied paradigms as it seeks to serve community-based needs.

Welch and Ferris (Chapter 5, this volume) examine archaeology as an instrument of State power conjoined with the interests of archaeologists in perpetuating a livelihood based on extracting and using the material remnants of the past. They outline what they characterize as an "extractive-consumptive paradigm" that governs how the state exercises control over the archaeological record. Ferris and Welch (Chapter 11, this volume) call for a "sustainable archaeology" that situates the role of archaeologists as servants of contemporary cultural heritage. This sustainable archaeology, which they assert is broader than our current conception of applied archaeology, is predicated on the principles of avoidance, integration, and innovative thinking that incorporate indigenous perspectives. They call for an archaeology that helps marginalized groups secure a voice for themselves through the validation of heritage tied to archaeological remains managed within conservation regimes. In doing this, they say, sustainable archaeology is activism because it empowers people with social interests and values that transcend the conventional goals of our discipline. I agree, but I question whether the activism in this equation comes primarily from the archaeologists involved in this work or from the marginalized groups that use the information that those archaeologists provide.

Nicholas (Chapter 7, this volume) implicitly defines activist archaeology as indigenous archaeology aimed at redressing the legacy of colonialism by expanding practice and theory to develop equitable uses of cultural heritage. He argues that archaeology has to be more than the study of material culture and the lifeways it represents, a perspective that has the capacity to transform us. As Nicholas describes, the Intellectual Property Issues in Cultural Heritage (IPinCH) project is forging the way for establishing new protocols for working with indigenous communities, protocols that entail our loosening control over representing the past, acknowledging our colonial past, and foregrounding indigenous values to strike a new balance.

Stottman (Chapter 9, this volume) tells us that activist archaeology is an agent of change, and something that can be intentionally and consciously used for advocacy.

Archaeology can be more than a tool to pursue the past; it can also be used to change the present and future. More than anyone else in the volume, Stottman urges archaeologists to be advocates for the communities in which they work. He concludes that evaluation is essential to an activist archaeology as a method that allows us to gauge whether collaborative research is effective in attaining transformative goals. Critical evaluation enables goals to be refined and archaeological practice to be improved.

As he has in the past, McGuire (Chapter 6, this volume) today points out that activist working class archaeology is based on praxis, craft, and class. The Colorado Coal Field Project exemplifies how they are put into action. McGuire's union brothers and sisters taught him to not make *a priori* presumptions about the utility of archaeology in contemporary life. Instead, McGuire argues, collaborators will find that utility in terms of the relevance of archaeological research for their own struggles. Implicit in McGuire's approach is that first and always we need to do good archaeology; from that comes the utility of research for other groups. As McGuire observes, if we simply speak as the propagandists for political interests, why should anyone believe us? This holds true for work with indigenous communities as well as unionists. Of course, in McGuire's work the ability to do good politically-informed archaeology goes hand-in-hand with what others are calling community-based participatory research, where research subjects help structure the questions that are asked and the methods used to answer them.

One implication of the chapters in this volume is that that activist and transformative archaeology must go beyond public education or ideological critique; it demands collective, radical, and social action against structural inequalities in contemporary society. At its core, these chapters suggest that activism should work to change contemporary power relationships to attain solutions for pressing social issues. One way to foster this change is by constructing unpopular or subversive narratives related to heritage preservation. In this volume, subversive narratives are entailed in the archaeological study of indigenous use of land and resources seen in the work of Atalay, the search for equity in intellectual property issues promoted by Nicholas, the sustainable archaeology espoused by Welch and Ferris, the indigenous educational programs promoted by McAnany, the situated activism and ethnographic archaeology of Castañeda, the community-based projects undertaken by Stottman, and the investigation of labor struggles by McGuire. All these narratives subvert the status quo and champion the interest of marginalized or underrepresented communities.

Who Invites or Sanctions Archaeologists to Act as Advocates?

An advocate is someone who advises another party and speaks for them to advance their interests. The quintessential advocate is an attorney who represents a client by speaking for that party in legal proceedings and advising the client on courses of action. The principles of archaeological ethics espoused by the Society of American Archaeology (SAA) exhort archaeologists to exercise stewardship responsibilities by acting as "advocates for the archaeological record" (Lynott and Wylie 1995). However, advocating for a living person or community is different from speaking on behalf of the insensate archaeological record. Who invites or sanctions archaeologists to act as advocates to speak for them and advise them about archaeological issues? When archaeologists act as self-appointed advocates, do they silence or reduce the voice of the people or communities they are championing? Advocating for conservation of the archaeological record *per se* and advocating for community values relating to the archaeological record require a careful balance.

A clear invitation or sanction for advocacy is provided by communities who hire archaeologists as cultural resource managers or tribal historic preservation officers (THPOs), in which part of the job description is to provide advice and speak for the community. These cultural resource managers and THPOs are authorized to represent the community when dealing with external groups. My own work as an advocate in the early stages of my career was based in this type of relationship. As a tribal employee in the era before NAGPRA was passed, I was sent to the State Historic Preservation Officer (SHPO)'s office in Santa Fe to argue that unmarked Native American graves should receive the same treatment as marked graves in consecrated cemeteries. This was the position of the Zuni Tribal Council and one I came to personally agree with. Similarly, at the request of Zuni civil and religious leaders, I contacted museums in my role as Tribal Archaeologist to inquire about the ritual objects in their collections, and I was asked to serve as an amanuensis to explain Zuni beliefs and values related to sacred objects and the need for their repatriation (Ferguson, Anyon, and Ladd 2000). When my employment with the Pueblo of Zuni ended, however, I intentionally made a transition from speaking for the Zuni to working in the background to undertake the research that tribal leaders needed in order to speak for themselves.

Ferris and Welch (Chapter 11, this volume) note that cultural resource management (CRM) archaeologists, or "applied practitioners," can become "accidental" activists when a descendant group hires them to investigate places or issues of community importance. I think that in that situation, the relationship between research and advocacy needs to be defined and controlled by the community so archaeologists don't overstep their bounds.

To be sure, the archaeological research needed for CRM is time consuming and often requires considerable effort that goes beyond compensation for the work. In many cases, committing oneself to undertaking good CRM research by, for, or with indigenous communities provides a way to advance a transformative agenda. This is true even when an archaeologist eschews being an advocate and simply submits research results to a community that then uses the research to further its own political or social agenda without the further involvement of the archaeologist. In this situation, the archaeologist is more like a tool used by the community than an actor in the political system.

Archaeologists not directly employed by a community with well-defined job descriptions or contracts may be sanctioned as advocates in other ways. The questions a community asks about what an archaeologist can do for the community may be interpreted as a request for an individual to serve as an advocate to empower traditional community values and knowledge in the face of challenging social and political circumstances. Inherent in the community-based participatory research that Atalay (2012, and Chapter 3, this volume) espouses is the notion that communities are full participants in research, and this participation invites or sanctions the involvement of archaeologists as advocates.

All these forms of advocacy are based on a community hiring an archaeologist or working with an archaeologist to establish a relationship of trust based on long-term interaction. Incumbent on archaeologists is developing a clear sense of when they should speak for a community and when a community should speak for itself. This understanding needs to be continually negotiated and reaffirmed so that when roles change, archaeologists continue to act in the best interest of the community.

Can Uninvited or Naive Activist Archaeology Reduce the Sovereignty of Indigenous Groups or Create Other Problems?

When archaeologists act as self-appointed advocates for Native American communities, they run the risk of diminishing or silencing the voice of those communities and reducing their sovereign right to speak for themselves through their own community members or employees. I once observed a situation involving the mitigation of adverse effects on a shrine where a CRM archaeologist, with the best of intentions, represented the views of the tribal members on his field crew to governmental agencies. The unintended result was that the agencies then did not undertake formal government-to-government consultation with the tribe's designated historic preservation official. This unsolicited advocacy, however well intentioned, thus worked to diminish tribal sovereignty by foreclosing on the tribe's opportunity to engage in the decision making process.

In the United States, the political status and rights of indigenous communities are well defined, and Indian tribes have the right and ability to speak on their own behalf. If these tribes want archaeologists to speak for them, they hire or sanction them to do so. The ethical situation in other countries, in which indigenous communities have fewer political rights and fewer forums to voice their concerns, is less clear.

Archaeological research may have unintended consequences that run counter to the ontological and epistemological frameworks of indigenous communities. Concepts of heritage as differentially defined by archaeologists and indigenous peoples can lead to social and environmental injustices if cultural and natural resources are not seen as inextricably linked aspects of heritage. The extraction of traditional environmental knowledge and its use in co-management can commodify knowledge, alienate it from the associated community, and result in managerial decisions that don't necessarily resonate with indigenous values.

If archaeological relevance is naively construed as framing archaeological explanation in terms of the shifting social concerns of our time, as McAnany (Chapter 8, this volume) points out, archaeologists who do not understand the power that an archaeologically constructed past can have may alienate people from their history. Monolithic conceptions of past and present populations can be harmful to modern groups, so McAnany calls for better science and modeling to offset the theoretical fashion of explaining the Maya in terms of contemporary social concerns. In this case, an activist archaeology helps redress the bad science that has gone before. By actively pursuing educational programs with indigenous communities, McAnany demonstrates how powerful archaeological knowledge can be when it is used to bear witness to the past in a manner that benefits contemporary Maya people.

While Stottman (Chapter 9, this volume) provides a strong call for archaeologists to serve as advocates, he also recognizes that activist archaeology is risky, subject to unintended consequences and unresolved conflicts. To this I'll add that being an advocate can be tricky because it does not always entail helping communities struggling in opposition to the oppressive forces of colonial or neoliberal institutions of the dominant society. Sometimes activist archaeology involves championing one community over another. I think we need to tread carefully when our activist work benefits one indigenous or local community and hurts another at the same time. An example of this is adjudicating land claims and water rights when multiple tribes are parties to the litigation. Sometimes land and water are taken from one tribe and awarded to another. Serving as an advocate for one tribe may mean you are effectively opposing another tribe, and this creates thorny ethical and intellectual issues that need careful consideration to ensure objective scholarship (Washburn 1989).

What Is the Role of Expert Witnesses in Relation to Advocates?

Communities sometimes need expert witnesses in addition to advocates in legal proceedings. They do not need an archaeologist to advise them or speak for them; they need a scholar with the education, training, skill, and experience in the specialized field of archaeology to answer specific questions relating to historical issues involving heritage sites, repatriation, land use, and other issues. Unlike fact witnesses, who can recite facts or events relating to only a particular case, expert witnesses can present an opinion about facts or evidence that is within the scope of their scientific, technical, or scholarly expertise (Gormley 1955).

The role of archaeologists and other anthropologists serving as expert witnesses was firmly established during the Indian Claims Commission between 1946 and 1970 (Rosen 1977; Dobyns 1978), and has continued on other land and water rights cases since then (Feldman 1980; Hart 1995). Ideally, the service of an expert witness is grounded in objectivity and scholarship that is explicitly not advocacy, and is not biased toward finding only the results that a client desires (Stewart 1979). Good expert witnesses reach the same conclusions based on the same facts, whether they testified for a plaintiff or a defendant. In the Southwest, one archaeologist who attained this ideal was Florence Hawley Ellis (Ellis 1974a, 1974b, 1974c, 1974d). She variously testified for tribes as plaintiffs and the Department of Justice as the defendant, and the scope and nature of her conclusions were notably consistent regardless of her client.

Participating in litigation as an expert witness requires substantial investments of time, resources, and commitment. It can be viewed as a form of activism in which a scholar provides answers to questions posed by a client, but does not assume an activist's desire to direct social or political change. The advocates in legal proceedings are the attorneys who advise clients and speak for them in court proceedings. Expert witnesses might be part of a litigation team, but the key elements of their work and how it is conducted are distinct from advocacy. In litigation, justice is derived from the interplay of the legal system rather the individual actions of a scholar.

Serving as an expert witness is both difficult and rewarding. Litigation is an adversarial process, and the scrutiny of research offered as testimony typically far exceeds that of the academic peer review process. This scrutiny generally produces better scholarship. A substantial amount of time is needed for research, preparing written testimony, and preparing to testify orally in a courtroom. The time spent in serving a community as an expert witness takes away from other scholarly activities that provide more immediate academic rewards. Publication of expert testimony is often delayed for years or decades until legal proceedings are concluded. Judicial decisions using expert testimony are rendered using legal standards rather than scholarly reasoning, and this creates intellectual problems for some witnesses (Miller 2011; Rosen 1979). These issues aside, expert witnesses are often gratified when they meet high scholarly standards in their research, and their clients and the courts find their work useful in seeking justice.

Do All Archaeologists Need to Engage in Activist and Transformative Archaeology?

It is unrealistic to think that we can personally commit to a never-ending activist project within the realities of our archaeological careers. All projects must come to an end, and many projects cannot be sustained in an ever-changing political context. Although some archaeologists can be activists all the time, all archaeologists should work to transform archaeology some of the time. Archaeologists need to understand the parameters and potential of activist approaches in specific contexts. Activist and transformative archaeologies are predicated on long-term collaboration with communities. This engagement often extends beyond the time frame of a specific project and to issues that transcend archaeology *per se*.

Stottman (personal communication, 2011) has also observed that activist archaeology has had a decidedly academic overtone, and he raises the question whether
contract archaeologists and SHPOs can also be activist archaeologists. Ferris and
Welch (Chapter 11, this volume) provide one answer to this question in the form of
sustainable archaeology. Ultimately, the answer to this question is still unfolding, and
it depends in part on the semantics of labeling or branding the type of archaeology
one does. However, as many of the participants at the Amerind symposium agreed,
we don't need a label to do activist and transformative archaeologies.

Is Good Research the Foundation of Effective Activism?

There is universal agreement that an activist and transformative archaeology—
however it is conceived—needs to be built on the foundation of good research
that meets high scholarly standards (Atalay, this volume; Hale 2001). If any kind
of archaeology fails to meet scholarly standards, it risks being reduced to propaganda or one-sided argumentation based on selective data and biased conclusions.

Choices for How to Advance an Activist Agenda

A key issue for transformative archaeology is whether individual archaeologists
decide to pursue indigenous issues by explicitly working to produce structural
changes in society or by working through existing bureaucratic structures. Some
participants in the Amerind symposium argued that transformative archaeologies
should seek structural change to attain social justice. Alternately, however, some
of us choose to work through existing bureaucratic structures because that is the
strategy of the communities that hire us to do research. In this mode, the goal is
to produce good scholarship that provides the high-quality information needed
for legal, political, and bureaucratic processes, and we are willing to then leave
the remaining work to indigenous and state politicians (Henriksen 2003). In this
way, we seek to avoid the danger of speaking on behalf of a people rather than
expanding the capacity of the people to speak on their own behalf.

   In this chapter, I have developed a position in which an archaeologist can be fully
engaged in actively helping a community through good research that is not framed
as advocacy. The community poses questions that can be answered with archaeological research. An archaeologist then commits the time and resources needed to
develop answers to the community's questions. After presenting that research to
the community, the archaeologist then stands back while the community uses the
information provided to it to advance its interests. This strategy of activism builds
community capacity and respects tribal sovereignty.

   In the final analysis, there are many paths to fully engaged, activist, and transformative archaeologies. The path that archaeologists choose to take should be

determined by their personal philosophy of social justice in relation to the political needs and sovereign rights of local communities and indigenous groups. Ultimately, activist archaeology provides a toolkit or pragmatic framework to accomplish a variety of goals, including political, social, and environmental justice. As such, transformative archaeologies need to tack between archaeology, ethnography, heritage, research, management, legal proceedings, and social justice.

Conclusion

My final comment on activist and transformative archaeology is that 90 percent of archaeological research is now done outside universities. We need to infuse CRM and other forms of applied practice with the ideas about activism, advocacy, and expert witness testimony that are incubating in academic discourse. Furthermore, to nurture transformative archaeologies in the future, we need to train students on how to conduct collaborative archaeology in an ethical manner, and we need to support our activist colleagues in their work during all stages of their careers, whether that work be in CRM or academia. We need to appropriately value and recognize the results of transformative archaeologies in both commercial archaeology and the university tenure process. If we do this, archaeologists working toward beneficial social and environmental change by providing services relevant to the needs of indigenous and local communities can help make the world a better place for everyone.

———∽———

Considering Methods: A Methodological Road Map

First and foremost, activist archaeological research requires the same fundamental methods as any other archaeological study. A well-thought-out research design, reliable field observations, appropriate analytical techniques, reasoned interpretation, and clearly written narrative summaries that communicate findings are key to successful research. Inasmuch as most activist archaeology entails research with one or more living communities, an understanding of the theory and methods of community-based participatory research is essential (Atalay 2012). Watkins and Ferguson (2005) provide practical suggestions for working with and working for communities, especially indigenous communities. Ultimately, community-based research necessitates developing long-term working relationships built on mutual trust, and this takes years to develop. Archaeologists interested in pursuing an activist agenda must be prepared to commit themselves to sustained interaction with the communities with which they are involved. Decisions about research in indigenous and local communities often take substantial time, and archaeologists need patience during this process. Archaeologists must be willing to work collaboratively at the pace of the community.

The research questions that are asked in activist research, the archaeological methods used to answer those questions, and the rights to disseminate research results need to be carefully negotiated at the outset of research, and sometimes periodically reconsidered with community involvement as the work unfolds. Many indigenous communities are concerned about protecting their traditional intellectual property, and archaeologists engaged in activist research should be willing to enter into research contracts and ethical agreements wherein communities explicitly own the intellectual property created by research, and archaeologists need to obtain approval from the community to publish their findings. Archaeologists need to be prepared to turn over their field notes, photographs, and other work products to communities if that is asked of them as a condition of research. I primarily work with Indian tribes, and most of them contractually own my work products but allow me to retain copies of notes and photographs for use in long-term research. The tribes I work for generally support publication of research results after appropriate review because that dissemination of knowledge increases the credibility of their heritage programs and builds a knowledge base that is useful in future tribal endeavors.

On long-term projects, activist archaeologists should seek to build community capacity, training community members and working with them as research participants in carrying out research tasks. The full engagement of the community is often a key to a successful research project. Activist archaeologists, especially those working in indigenous communities, should be concerned with process as much as product. Although efficacy of process is more difficult to measure than research products such as the growth of archaeological databases or the number of publications, in many indigenous communities the personal experiences of the research participants are communicated to other community members, and this ultimately is as effective a means of dissemination of knowledge as the scientific publications and technical reports produced by archaeologists. When planning how knowledge will be shared with community members, designing some products for community members in addition to academic publications is advisable. Popularly written pamphlets, poster displays, copies of videos showing interviews or tribal representatives doing fieldwork, and public meetings where results are discussed orally generally have more impact in a community than journal articles and books published by university and commercial presses.

Archaeologists working as expert witnesses should carefully define their role with their client at the outset of their work. They should only agree to undertake research and testify in cases where they have knowledge about the issues being litigated and pertinent data to offer. The adversarial research entailed in litigation involves a higher standard than most academic research. You can expect opposing parties to closely examine your work and assess every reference that is cited in a written report to determine whether it actually states what you assert. You should welcome this scrutiny because it produces better scholarship.

As you conduct research for expert testimony, you often need to obtain copies of everything you cite, and it is advisable to cite to specific pages rather than entire books or long articles. You need to keep records of the scholarly sources you reviewed in your research that are used to form opinions while keeping in mind that everything you write is discoverable. In writing expert testimony, it is important to write clearly using scientific concepts but not obfuscating with unnecessary jargon. You need to be ready to define all the terms you use and to pay attention to language. In a legal setting, words don't always mean what they mean in anthropological discourse. For example, archaeologists generally use the term "abandonment" to denote that sites are no longer inhabited. In legal discourse, however, that term means that all rights and claims to property have been relinquished, without vesting ownership in another person and with no intention of reclaiming rights in the future (Colwell-Chanthaphonh and Ferguson 2006). The term "abandonment" is thus problematical because many tribes have ancestral sites that are no longer inhabited, but those tribes still claim ownership or rights to these ancestral places.

In rebutting the testimony of experts retained by other parties in a case, it is important not to reduce your objection to *ad hominem* attacks; you need to specifically address the issues at hand. In some legal cases, anthropologists and other expert witnesses develop a personal enmity that lasts throughout their careers; in other cases, opposing witnesses can offer differing opinions in court and then go out to dinner as friends and colleagues because their disagreements are intellectual and evidentiary, not personal.

The ethics of testifying as an expert witness include scientific integrity, safeguarding objectivity, maintaining appropriate professional relationships with other litigation participants, and differentiating between personal opinions and scientific fact (Eaton and Kalman 1994). It is important for expert witnesses to have a strong foundation of professional training and experience relevant to the issues they are testifying about, good communication skills, and appropriate demeanor. Expert witnesses need to be prepared for cross-examination by offering considered opinions that have a basis in fact and the established methodology of archaeology.

I've been fortunate to work for a series of clients who have hired attorneys who shape their legal theory in relation to the facts presented in the objective research of their experts. I've never been asked to change my findings to fit the needs of a case. It is important for expert witnesses to realize that each expert on a litigation team is limited in the conclusions they can make on the basis of their discipline, and that other experts using other disciplines may be able to provide other relevant conclusions. Ultimately, the client's attorney may be able to use the entire body of the expert testimony to make conclusions that a single expert could not make on the basis of a single discipline. Expert witnesses need to understand how scholarly work is used in legal proceedings, and accept the fact that the decisions reached by a court are based in legal concepts that may differ from scholarly conventions. It is imperative to have a clear understanding and willingness to contribute opinions based on archaeology and anthropology and, at the same time, to recognize that the final decision of the court will not be based solely on your testimony.

REFERENCES

Atalay, Sonya. 2012. *Community-Based Archaeology; Research with, by, and for Indigenous and Local Communities.* Berkeley: University of California Press.

Colwell-Chanthaphonh, Chip, and T. J. Ferguson. 2006. "Rethinking Abandonment in Archaeological Contexts." *The SAA Archaeological Record* 6(1): 37–41.

Dobyns, Henry F. 1978. "Taking the Witness Stand." In *Applied Anthropology in America,* edited by E. M. Eddy and W. L. Partridge, 261–274. New York: Columbia University Press.

Eaton, David L., and David Kalman. 1994. "Scientists in the Courtroom: Basic Pointers for the Expert Scientific Witness." *Environmental Health Perspectives* 102(8): 668–672.

Ellis, Florence Hawley. 1974a. "Anthropology of Laguna Pueblo Land Claims." In *American Indian Ethnohistory: Pueblo Indians III,* edited by David Agee Horr. New York: Garland Publishing.

———. 1974b. "Archaeologic and Ethnologic Data: Acoma-Laguna Land Claims." In *American Indian Ethnohistory: Pueblo Indians II,* edited by David Agee Horr. New York: Garland Publishing.

———. 1974c. "The Hopi: Their History and Use of Lands." In *American Indian Ethnohistory: Hopi Indians,* edited by David Agee Horr. New York: Garland Publishing.

———. 1974d. "An Anthropological Study of the Navajo Indians." In *American Indian Ethnohistory: Navajo Indians I,* edited by David Agee Horr. New York: Garland Publishing.

Feldman, Kerry D. 1980. "Ethnohistory and the Anthropologist as Expert Witness in Legal Disputes: A Southwestern Alaska Case." *Journal of Anthropological Research* 36(2): 245–257.

Ferguson, T. J. 1982. "Application of New Mexico State Dead Body and Indigent Burial Statutes to a Prehistoric Mummified Body." In *American Indian Concerns with Historic Preservation in New Mexico,* edited by Barbara Holmes, 45–51. Albuquerque: New Mexico Archaeological Council.

———. 1995. "An Anthropological Perspective on Zuni Land Use." In *Zuni and the Courts,* edited by E. Richard Hart, 103–120. Lawrence: University Press of Kansas.

———. 2004. "Academic, Legal, and Political Contexts of Social Identity and Cultural Affiliation Research in the Southwest." In *Identity, Feasting, and the Archaeology of the Greater Southwest,* edited by Barbara J. Mills, 27–41. Boulder: University Press of Colorado.

Ferguson, T. J., Roger Anyon, and Edmund J. Ladd. 2000. "Repatriation at the Pueblo of Zuni: Diverse Solutions to Complex Problems." In *Repatriation Reader,* edited by Devon A. Mihesuah, 239–265. Lincoln: University of Nebraska Press.

Ferguson, T. J., and E. Richard Hart. 1985. *A Zuni Atlas.* Norman: University of Oklahoma Press.

Gormley, Donald C. 1955. "The Role of the Expert Witness." *Ethnohistory* 2(4): 326–346.

Hale, Charles R. 2001. "What is Activist Research?" *Social Science Research Council* 2(1–2): 13–15.

Hart, E. Richard, ed. 1995. *Zuni and the Courts.* Lawrence: University Press of Kansas.

Henriksen, George. 2003. "Consultancy and Advocacy as Radical Anthropology." *Social Analysis* 47(1): 116–123.

Kuwanwisiwma, Leigh J., and T. J. Ferguson. 2009. "Hopitutskwa and Ang Kuktota: The Role of Archaeological Sites in Defining Hopi Cultural Landscapes." In *The Archaeology of Meaningful Places,* edited by Brenda J. Bowser and María Nieves Zedeño, 90–106. Salt Lake City: University of Utah Press.

Lynott, Mark J., and Alison Wylie. 1995. "Stewardship: The Central Principle of Archaeological Ethics." In *Ethics in American Archaeology: Challenges for the 1990s.* Washington, DC: Society for American Archaeology.

Merrill, William L., Edmund J. Ladd, and T. J. Ferguson. 1993. "The Return of the Ahayu:da: Lessons for Repatriation from Zuni Pueblo and the Smithsonian Institution." *Current Anthropology* 34(5): 523–567.

Miller, Bruce Granville. 2011. *Oral History on Trial: Recognizing Aboriginal Narratives in the Courts.* Vancouver: University of British Columbia Press.

Rosen, Lawrence. 1977. "The Anthropologist as Expert Witness." *American Anthropologist* 79: 555–578.

———. 1979. "Response to Stewart." *American Anthropologist* 80(1): 111–112.

Stewart, Omer C. 1979. "An Expert Witness Answers Rosen." *American Anthropologist* 81(1): 108–111.

Washburn, Wilcomb E. 1989. "Anthropological Advocacy in the Hopi-Navajo Land Dispute." *American Anthropologist* 91(3): 738–743.

Watkins, Joe, and T. J. Ferguson. 2005. "Working with and Working for Indigenous Communities." In *Handbook of Archaeological Methods,* edited by Christopher Chippendale and Herbert Maschner, 1372–1406. Lanham, MD: AltaMira Press.

Index

Academe, 47, 67, 122, 230

Academic vs. CRM archaeology, 93, 95, 101–103

Action research, 48, 50

Activism, activists, and activist archaeology, 8, 10–13, 15, 18–20, 30, 34–36, 38–40, 45–55, 62–71, 73–78, 92–94, 106–108, 115–116, 119–121, 123, 128–130, 133, 137, 140, 147–150, 180–181, 187, 194, 198, 206, 208–212, 215–217, 219, 228–229, 231, 239–243, 246–250
  Challenges for Activist Ethnography workshop, 50
  Depoliticizing, 76
  Four-part typology of, 62
  Future needs in activist archaeology, 52
  Professional, 63, 64
  Public (*See* Public archaeology)
  Scholarship, 50–52, 55, 63, 75, 76
  Vocational, 62, 64–65, 67, 68, 69, 71, 76–77

Advocacy, advocates, and expert witnesses, 9, 35–36, 38–40, 64–65, 73, 92–93, 95, 118, 120, 149, 243–247, 249–251

AFL-CIO, 116, 124, 127, 165, 180–181, 183, 187, 239–251, 259

Africa, 197

Ainu, 141

Allen Mine, 123

Alienation, 16

Althusser, Louis, 67
  notion of interpellation, 67

American Anthropological Association, 14, 47, 55, 116
  AAA Anthropology and Environment Society, 47
  Engagement blog of, 47

American Indian Archaeological Institute (Institute for American Indian Studies), 133

American Indian Movement, 115

American University in Central Asia, 199–208, 209

Amerind Foundation, 15, 16, 22, 50, 137, 149, 152, 194, 241, 248

Anarchism and *The Anarchist Cookbook*, 107

Ancestral human remains, 46, 54, 142, 158

Annapolis, Maryland, 182, 188

Antiquarianism, 31, 101, 159

Antone, Cecil, 116

Apaches, 38, 90–93

Arab Spring, 51

Archaeological Resource Management (*See* Cultural resource management)

Archaeology:
  Action and applied, 33, 36, 240
  American, 204, 209
  As historiography, 66
  Benefits of, 13
  Civically engaged, 30–33, 162 (*See also* Engagement)
  Collaborative, community, engaged, and participatory, 11, 13, 30–31, 33–34, 36, 68, 73, 79, 140, 165, 168, 174, 180, 190, 191, 192, 194, 209, 248–249
  Conflict in (*See* Conflict)
  Conservation model in, 99, 101–106
  Craft of, 14, 19, 116, 119, 120–121, 127–129, 243
  Critical, 8, 10–11, 16, 36, 120, 149, 182
  Equitable practices in, 134–135, 137, 150

Ethnography in (*See* Cultural anthropology)

Excavation in, 8, 84, 96, 99–103, 115, 117–118, 123, 127, 145, 146, 184, 188–190, 197, 204, 223, 230, 232, 239–240

Employment, jobs, and careers in, 18–20, 29, 39, 49, 66–68, 95, 100–101, 104, 115, 127, 179, 197, 216, 239, 244–249, 251

Ethics in (*See* Ethics)

Feminist (*See* Feminism)

Inequalities in, 140, 149, 160, 170, 173–174

Japanese, 202

Land use and land rights issues in, 16, 81, 93–95, 100–101, 107, 136, 138–139, 144–145, 165, 169–173, 200–202, 210, 218–229, 240, 246

Marxist, 36, 138, 149, 243

Maya (*See* Maya)

Niche approaches to, 8, 14, 33, 34

Political, governmental, and public policy issues in, 8–9, 11–13, 17, 19, 30–31, 35, 37, 39, 47, 61–88, 98, 102, 104–108, 115–130, 140, 160–175, 191, 197–208, 215–233, 242–249

Postcolonial, 33, 134, 138, 140, 165, 199, 201, 204

Post-processual, 33, 68, 120–121

Public trust, 9, 11, 95, 226

Public (*See* Public archaeology)

Russian, 200–201

Service-oriented, 20, 30–36, 64–65, 73–77, 215–232, 249

Social and sociological context, roles, and dimensions of, 14, 16, 63, 80–81

Transformation, transformed, and transformative, 32–33, 35–38, 162, 174–175

Tribal (*See* Indigenous)

Archaeological site loss, avoidance and impact reduction, 95–96, 100–101, 103–104, 108, 179, 183, 200, 208, 220, 225, 239, 245 (*See also* Looting)

Archaeological site values other than

scientific, 96–98 (*See also* Intangible values)

Archaeologists as Activists, 149

Archaeology as Political Action, 116

Architecture and historic structures and buildings, 29, 83, 92, 134, 171, 180, 183–186, 202–203, 223

Arizona, 91, 158, 197, 240

Arizona State Museum, 115, 260

Arte Accion Copán Ruinas (AACR), 167

Asociación Copán, 167

Association of American University Professors, 122

Atalay, Sonya, 12, 35, 45–46, 70, 86, 118, 137, 149, 152, 156–157, 162, 194, 205, 241, 243, 245, 259

Austin Lounge Lizards, 91

Australia, 135, 141, 143, 145, 158, 201

Authenticity, 205

bak'tun, 165

Bamiyan, Afghanistan, 203, 210

Bannister, Kelly, 150, 156

Bannister, Robert, 72

Belgium, 128

Belize, 35, 164–165, 197, 198, 200, 201, 202, 204

Berwind, Colorado, 117

Bidirectional knowledge exchange, 162, 167, 171–172

Binghamton, New York, 116, 124

Binghamton University, 115

Bishkek, 202

Boas, Franz, 75, 77

Bolivia, 211

Boyle, W. A., 128

British Columbia, Canada, 35, 121, 134–140, 158, 260

British Propaganda, 128

Bourdieu, Pierre, 64

Concept of specific intellectual, 64–66, 71

Buddhist sites, 202–203, 207, 210

Burkina Faso, 197

Burra Charter, 97

Bush, Vannevar, 74, 75

Cage, John, 93

Calhoun, Craig, 46, 52, 55, 71, 75, 77

Campbell, Isobelle, 145, 152, 158

Campus Compact Program, 47

Canada, 17, 100–101, 134–135, 138, 141, 148, 150, 157–158, 201, 226, 228

Capacity building, 14, 17, 19, 39, 138, 242

Capitalism, 12, 66, 121–123, 225

Carlson, Catherine, 134

Carnegie Foundation for the Advancement of Teaching, 47

Carnegie Institution of Washington (CIW), 72, 74–75

Castañeda, Quetzil E., 10, 49, 119, 122, 128, 149, 152, 243

Çatalhöyük, Turkey, 45–46

Catholic Church, 92

Chambers, Erve, 36, 182,

Chatham Islands, 143

Chau Hux, 197

Chavez, Rosa, 165

Chichén Itzá, 171–172

Chilam Balam, 62

Chomsky, Noam, 65

Ch'orti', 167–168

Class and class relations in archaeology, 9, 116, 117–118, 119, 121–123, 128–129

Clauss, Lee Rains, 29–30, 78, 86, 117, 120, 137, 152, 194, 242, 259

Cherokee, 38

Cob, Bricieda Cuevas, 165

Collaboration, cooperation and collaborators, 10, 13, 16, 30–31, 34–39, 45–48, 51, 56, 62–63, 68, 73, 79–80, 84, 86, 106, 117–119, 121, 127, 128, 130, 138, 140–141, 143, 147, 151–152, 156, 165, 167–168, 171, 173, 180–183, 187, 190–194, 198, 204–205, 209, 219, 227, 232–233, 241–243, 247, 249

Collecting, collections, curation, and collection crisis, 84, 94–96, 99–103, 106, 140, 143, 157, 159, 162, 222–223, 230, 244, 259–260

Colonial Williamsburg, 188

Colonialism and colonization, 10, 69, 116, 135, 140, 146, 149, 162, 164–165, 198–200, 203, 213, 242

Neocolonialism, neocolonialist, 34

post-colonial, 201, 204, 204

Colorado, 92–93, 116–118, 123, 124, 126–128, 130

Colorado Coal Field War, 116–117, 243

Archaeology of, 118, 129

Ludlow Massacre, 116–117, 122–130

Ludlow Memorial, 117–118, 124–125

Colorado State University, 115

Common heritage of humankind, 9, 93, 220, 222

Community, complexity of, 16

"Communities of practice," 162–167, 170–175

Community-based, -oriented, -centered archaeology and research, 10–20, 13, 30–40, 45–51, 53–57, 68, 76, 79, 94, 99, 101, 103, 121, 128, 134, 137–143, 146–152, 156–158, 160, 162, 168–175, 179–194, 197–198, 204–212, 227–232, 239–250, 259–260

Community-Based Participatory Research (CBPR), 48–49, 53, 54, 56, 137, 141, 151, 162, 241, 243, 245, 249

Community liaison, 172, 174–175, 244

Compliance, regulatory, 13, 35, 98, 100, 101, 179, 259

Confidentiality, 39–40, 143

Conflict, 16, 69–70, 73–75, 98, 163, 216, 229

Conkey, Meg, 115

Conservation regimes, 93, 95, 106, 16, 163, 167, 172–175, 203, 220–232, 242

Consultants and consultancies, 84, 94, 203, 207, 218

Consultation, as distinct from collaboration, 30, 34, 170, 229, 232, 242, 245

Contemporary protest movements, archaeology of, 51

Cooper, Karen Cody, 133

Cooperation (*See* Collaboration)

Copán, 167–168

Craven, Christa, 50

Cultural anthropology and ethnography, 35, 50–51, 61–63, 66, 69, 71, 76, 79, 81–86, 137, 190, 197, 209, 239–240, 243, 249

Cultural heritage management (*See* Cultural resource management)

Cultural resource management (CRM), 8–9, 13, 15, 19, 35, 94–106, 120, 128, 129, 216–232, 244, 245, 249

Distinct from archaeological resource management, 95–96

Heritage issues in, 9, 12, 17, 30, 45–46, 64, 75–76, 96–98, 134–150, 155–159, 160–175, 197–198, 200–209, 218–232

Historical and institutional development of, 94–95

Current Anthropology, 47

Curriculum, 35, 139, 164, 175

Davis, Dána-Ain, 50

Decolonization and decolonized approaches, 11, 30, 66, 77

Debs, Eugene V., 116, 126

Democracy and democratized practice, 17, 34, 36, 47, 52, 53, 163, 198

Denver, Colorado, 92–93, 118, 123

Descendant communities (*See also* Indigenous), 15, 30, 35, 46, 97, 98, 99, 101, 102, 108, 118, 134, 137–140, 143, 147–150, 160, 164–165, 174, 197, 230, 232, 233

Devon Downs, 145

Digital media, digital technologies, 49, 84, 145, 156

Dincauze, Dina, 133

Disenfranchise and disenfranchisement, 9–10, 12, 30, 39, 54–55, 65

DuBois, W.E.B., 70

Duke, Philip, 116, 118, 119

Dust Bowl, 92

Eastern Band of Cherokee, 40

Ecocide and ecocidal, 163–164

Education (*See* Public archaeology)

Einstein, Albert, 30

Ellis, Florence Hawley, 247

El Salvador, 164

Engaged scholar (scholarship) and learning economies, 12, 45, 47, 49, 53, 65, 73, 147, 162

Engagement, rules of and terms of, 159–160, 162, 164–165, 169–175

Engels, Frederick, 119

Environmental justice, 16, 241, 249

Epistemic injustice, 12, 34, 39, 54

Epistemological politics, 66

Equity, 17, 243

Essentialism, 11, 120, 201, 205

Ethics (professional and research), 9, 11, 14–15, 20, 31, 35–39, 46, 53, 61–63, 66–68, 71, 73–84, 93, 98–101, 104–105, 138, 141, 143, 145, 147–148, 182, 198, 208, 210, 218–219, 230, 244–246, 249–251

Ethnicity, 200–202, 203, 205

Ethnobotany, 138–139

Ethnography (*See* cultural anthropology)

Evaluation and assessment issues and methods, 13–14, 57, 73, 75, 108, 120, 127, 141, 156, 192–194, 206, 243

Expert Witness (*See* Advocacy, advocates, and expert witnesses)

Extractive-consumptive paradigm, 9, 35, 94, 96, 98–99, 101, 104, 218, 220–221, 224–227, 229–230, 230, 242

Facebook, 207

Farnsley-Kaufman House, Louisville, Kentucky, 183–187, 190, 193

Feminism and feminists, 11, 36, 50, 53–54, 66, 68, 70, 72–73, 138, 149, 198

Ferguson, T. J., 35, 118, 121, 134, 152, 239–240, 249

Ferris, Neal, 9, 149, 152, 215–218, 228, 242–244, 248

Field school and schools, 61, 69, 92, 115, 133, 136, 138, 152, 204, 219

Flint Stone Street site, 54

Fortmann, Louise, 54

Fort Apache and Theodore Roosevelt School National Historic Landmark, Arizona, 91–92

Foucault, Michel, 64
Franklin Pierce College, 133
Fricker, Miranda, 12, 34
Fulbright, 45, 211

Gatekeeping, 9, 12, 232
George, Dudley, 229
Gender and gender identity, 9, 16, 70, 85,
    193, 198, 204
Genghis Kahn, 201
Geophilia, 92–93
Germany, German soldiers, 8, 12, 128, 149
Ghana, 197
Globalization and global issues, 10, 13, 16,
    18, 52, 65, 76, 101–103, 106, 201,
    208, 226, 230
Google, 217
Graduate Students Employee Union, 127
Graphics Communications International
    Union, 116
Great Britain, 199, 200
Greer, Sheila, 141, 158
Guatemala, 61, 164, 168–169, 172, 175
    Civil war in, 61
    Petén, 175
    Alta Verapaz, 175

Haber, Alejandro, 36–37
Habitus, 220–221, 227
Hale, Charles, 12, 36, 47–48, 50–55, 66,
    70, 121
Hammil, Jan, 116
Hand-heart-mind thinking, 19
Handsman, Russ, 133
Haraway, Donna, 54, 66
Harrison, Faye, 50
Harvard University, 53
Haudenau (*See* Iroquois First Nation, 228)
Hegemonic knowledge systems, 13
Henderson, John, 61
Heritage (*See* Cultural resource
    management)
Heritage Resource Management (HRM)
    (*See* Cultural resource management)
Historic preservation, 29, 30
Hodder, Ian, 115, 211
Hollowell, Julie, 150, 156, 207

Holtorf, Cornelius, 12
Honduras, 61, 164, 167–168
Horvath, Agnes, 32
Human Organization, 211
Human and ancestral remains, human
    bones, 46, 54, 92, 142, 158, 216,
    239, 240
Hutson, Scott, 171–172

Identity construction and maintenance,
    39, 167, 171–172
Inadvertent discovery of human remains, 54
Indian Claims Commission, 246
Indiana, 124
Indiana Jones, 130
Indiana University, 53, 62, 197, 199
Indigenous Archaeology and Indigenous,
    tribal and First Nations people and
    issues in archaeology, 8, 11, 13, 15,
    17, 30–36, 45–46, 53–57, 68, 70–73,
    79, 91–92, 98, 101, 106, 116, 121,
    134–152, 157–158, 160, 164–175,
    180–181, 198–208, 216, 227–229,
    239–251, 259–260
Indigenous Heritage Passed to Present
    (InHerit), 162, 165, 167, 169–171, 176
Intangible values in cultural resources,
    80, 96–98, 137, 141, 145–146, 150,
    157–158, 222–223, 227
Intellectual property, 17, 35, 40, 134, 141,
    148, 151, 156–158, 241, 243, 250
Intellectual Property Issues in Cultural
    Heritage (IPinCH) Project, 137,
    140–152, 156–158, 207, 242, 260
Intersubjectivity of research, 11
Inuit, 135, 157
Iowa, 124
Ipperwash Provincial Park, Ontario, 228
Iraq War, 160
Irish heritage, 92
Iximché, 169

Japan, 141, 202
Jingoism, 74–75

Kamloops Indian Reserve, 134, 136, 138,
    152

Kancabel, 171
Kentucky African-American Heritage Center, 180
Kentucky Archaeological Survey, 184
Kentucky Resource Center for Heritage Education, 183
Kettle Point Anishnabeg, 228
K'iche', 170
King, Thomas F., 94, 96
Kloeckner, Jane, 104
Knowledge mobilization, dissemination, 9, 13, 17, 57, 149, 241, 250
Knowledge production, egalitarian and reciprocal, 55
Krasnaya Rechka, 207
Ku Klux Klan, 92
Kurgans, 201, 203, 206
Kyrgyz Sacred Heritage Association, 207
Kyrgyzstan, 35, 141, 157, 197–209

Ladino, 167
Landscapes (cultural and historical), 16, 30, 46, 62, 86, 93, 96, 105, 142, 158, 160, 169–171, 186–188, 191, 193, 200–203, 223, 225, 240
Land Claims, 240, 246
Language immersion, 138
Leone, Mark, 67, 115, 133
Lewin, Kurt, 94
Life-cycle approach, 105
Little, Barbara, 18
Lilley, Ian, 152, 156
Liminal, *limina,* liminality, 31–33, 37
    as a fixed or permanent state, 32–34, 38
Lipe, William D., 99
Looting, 94–95, 159, 200, 203, 223–224
Louisville, Kentucky, 179–194
Ludlow Collective, 117
Ludlow Massacre (*See* Colorado Coal Field War)
Lutz, John, 52
Lyons, Natasha, 152, 157

Magnoni, Aline, 172
Management (*See* Resource management)
Mancia, Moises, 167
Manhattan Project, 74

Mannum Aboriginal Community Association, Inc. (MACAI), 145–147, 158
Maple-Vail Book Manufacturing Group, 116, 123–124
Markey, Nola, 152
Marxism, 11, 36, 68, 70, 72–73, 115, 138, 149, 211, 260
Materialism and materiality, 32, 80, 97, 217
Maya Area Cultural Heritage Initiative (MACHI), 165, 169, 175–176
Maya region and peoples, 61, 159, 162–173, 175–176, 197–198, 201, 246 (*See also* Yukatek)
McAnany, Patricia, 34, 128, 152, 159–160, 243, 246
McGhee, Robert, 11
McGuire, Randall H., 134, 152, 243
McMullen, Ann, 133
Mead, Margaret, 129
Métis, 135
México, 164
Michigan, 56, 123, 147, 157, 205
Middleton, Guy, 163
Midewiwin, 54
Mignolo, Walter, 76
Miners for Democracy, 128
Mis, Pablo, 165
Moloka'i, Hawai'i, 160
Montana Power Company, 118
Montejo, Victor, 165
Montt, Rios, 61
Morales, Elsa, 167
Moralism, 62
Moriori, 143–145
    Cultural Database, 143, 145, 158
    Hokotehi Moriori Trust 144, 158
    mentorship program, 145
    Te Keke Tura Moriori, 144, 158
Morley, Sylvanus, 75
Mt. Pleasant, Michigan, 205
Multiple narratives, 14
Multivocality, 11, 36, 120, 217, 232
Museums and museum studies, 98, 138–139, 141, 157, 174, 187, 190–191, 200, 203, 205–208, 218, 244

NAGPRA (Native American Graves

Protection and Repatriation Act), 30, 56, 75, 92, 116, 157, 159, 172, 231, 240, 244, 246, 259

Nalda, Enrique, 7, 8

National Association of Tribal Historic Preservation Officers (NATHPO), 55

National Congress of American Indians Policy Research Center, 53

National Science Foundation, 74

Nationalism, 12, 62, 69, 74, 96, 149, 157, 201–202, 205

Nazi, Germany, 12, 74

NHPA (National Historic Preservation Act), 30, 240

Neis, Barbara, 52

Neo-Darwinism, 217

New England, 134, 136

New Mexico, 197, 239, 240

New Zealand, 141, 143, 201

NGOs, 211

Nicholas, George, 35, 121, 133–134, 136, 207, 242, 243

Ngaut Ngaut Interpretive Project, 145–147, 158

Nohmul, 197

Norder, John, 152

Novotny, Claire, 165

Nuvamsa, Ben, 91–92

Objectivity, 45, 47–50, 52–55, 67, 247, 251

Occupy Wall Street, 51

'Ohana, 160

Ohio, 124

Ohio River, 187

Ojibwe Nation, 45, 205, 209

Okazawa-Rey, Margo, 50

Osteology, 204

Ontario, Canada, 216–217, 228,

Panameno, Rebecca, 7, 8

Paradigmatic shift, change, 67, 68, 226

Parks and protected areas, 99, 160, 188–194, 207, 225, 228–229

Parks, Shoshaunna, 176

Participatory Action Research (PAR), 36, 48, 68

Participatory planning, 56–57

Partnerships, 37–38, 147, 168–169, 172, 175

Paynter, Robert, 115

Peru, 197

Places (*See* Landscapes)

Pomo, 38

Portland and Portland Wharf, Kentucky, 183, 187–194

Positioned objectivity, 54–55

Positivism, 45

  Neopositivism, 75

  Strategic duality to deconstruct, 53

  Reclaiming, 53

Postmodernism, 11

Potter, Parker, 182, 190

Pragmatism and pragmatic epistemology, 10, 72, 119–120, 137, 249

Presidents' Declaration on the Civic Responsibility of Higher Education, 47

Praxis, 15, 37, 116–121, 123, 128, 138, 140, 243,

Pro bono work (in law and medicine), 65

ProPetén, 175

Protocols, 46, 54, 143, 145, 147, 157, 158, 242

Public archaeology, benefits, education, non-academic audiences, 13, 30, 33, 49, 52, 64–65, 68, 93–100, 102–103, 106–107, 123, 126, 130, 134, 140, 142, 145–147, 149, 158, 165–166, 175, 179–194, 198, 200, 204–207, 211, 217–219, 222–226, 239, 243, 260

Pueblo, Colorado, 124, 130

Pyburn, K. Anne, 137, 242, 152, 157

Q'eqchi', 165, 172, 175

Rathje, William L., 219

Reagan, Ronald, 115

Reflexivity, 7, 18, 32, 36, 71, 81

Reform, 32, 37

  as distinct from revolution, 32, 37–38

Rekohu, New Zealand, 145, 158

Relativism, 8, 55, 215

Repatriation (*See* NAGPRA)
Republicans, 118, 121, 123, 124, 128
Research, sociohistorical dimensions of, 80–81
Residential schools, 134–138, 150
Resilience, 106, 108, 163–164
Resource management, defined, 98
Respect, 17–18, 30, 35, 39, 108, 123, 147, 240
Revitalization, cultural, 30, 39
Revolution (*See* Reform)
Riecken Foundation, 168–170
Robbins Swamp, 133
Roberts, Amy, 145, 152, 158
Roberts, Cecil, 119
Rogers, Will, 30
Rohr, Richard, 31
Romero, Yolando, 124–126
Rowe, Sarah, 169, 176

Sacred areas, objects, and knowledge, 31, 46, 92, 118, 140, 142–143, 157, 169, 173, 207, 240, 244
Said, Edward, 65
Saginaw Chippewa Indian Tribe of Michigan, 53, 147, 157, 205
Saitta, Dean, 116, 118, 119, 260
Salinas de los Nueves Cerros, 172
Sanilac petroglyphs, 54–55, 56, 157
Santa Fe, New Mexico, 240, 244
Schiller, Glick, 63
Schmidt, Peter, 8
Secwepemc and Secwepemc Cultural Education Society (SCES), 134, 136, 139, 140, 142, 152, 158
Self-reflexivity, 32, 36
Science
    Authority and rigor in, 12–13, 163, 172
    Ethical mandates of, 77–80
    Situated nature of, 11
    Transform values of, 77
    Value-free, 72, 75
Shanks, Michael, 121, 219
Sherwood Valley Rancheria of Pomo, 40
Shott, Michael, 122, 128
Silk Road, 201
Simon Fraser University, 134, 136, 139, 148, 152, 260

Situated knowledge, 54, 66, 71, 76,
Smith, Claire, 152
Social inequality, social justice, 16, 17, 36–37, 46, 49–50, 63–63, 70, 76, 78, 209–212, 248–249
    political and economic, 173
Social Science and Humanities Research Council of Canada (SSHRC), 46, 141, 148–151
Social relevance, 14, 31, 33, 38, 163, 224, 231
Society for American Archaeology (SAA), 9, 14, 15, 55, 73, 81, 116, 137, 143, 241, 244
Solidarity, 16, 104, 116–117, 120, 123–127, 129
Solomon, Maui, 144, 152, 158
South Africa, 141
South Australian Department of Environment and Natural Resources, 147
Sovereignty, 17, 30, 39, 160, 164, 201, 226, 228, 241, 245–246, 248, 259
Spain, 199
Star Trek, 212
State Historic Preservation Officer, 244, 248
Steelworkers, 124, 126, 130
Steen, Carin, 167–168
STEM learning, 48
Stereotypes, 11
Stewardship, 9, 36, 73, 93, 98, 103–104, 106, 138, 157, 172, 181, 244, 259–260
Stottman, M. Jay, 35, 149, 152, 179–180, 187, 242–243, 246, 248
Stump, Daryl, 11, 17
Subaltern groups, 11, 120
Subjectivity, 62, 67, 72
Sudbury, Julia, 50
Sustainable design, 94, 103–106
Sustainability, 9, 18, 20, 35, 45, 93–106, 145, 157–158, 163, 173–175, 190, 198, 225–233, 241–243, 248
    defined, 102
Szakolczai, Arpad, 32–33

Tax, Sol, 36
Taliban, 210

Tennyson, Lord Alfred, 33
The Alliance for Heritage Conservation,
    165, 167, 169
Texas, 197
Theoretical Archaeology Group (TAG), 51
Thomassen, Bjørn, 32
Thompson Rivers University, 134
Thorpe, Susan, 144, 152
Tikal, 169
Tourism and tourists, 46, 62, 65, 69,
    98, 129, 141, 145–147, 156–157,
    160, 162, 167, 169, 171, 181, 198,
    200–201, 205–207, 210
*Traditional Knowledge Revitalization
    Pathways*, 145
Transforming archaeology collective,
    14–15
Tribal Historic Preservation Officers, 244
Tribalism, 202
Trinidad, Colorado, 118, 122, 127
Trust, 17, 40, 107, 170, 175, 245, 249
Truth and Reconciliation Commission of
    Canada, 134–135
Tucson, Arizona, 240
Turner, Victor, 32

Ucí, 171
Union of Soviet Socialist Republics (USSR),
    199, 200–201, 202, 203
United Mine Workers' Journal, 124
United Mine Workers of America (UMW),
    117–119,121, 123, 124,127, 128,
    130
United Nations Declaration on the Rights
    of Indigenous Peoples, 17
United Nations Educational, Scientific, and
    Cultural Organization (UNESCO), 46,
    202, 203, 207, 210
    World Heritage Sites, 200
United States of America and U. S.
    government, 12, 17, 34–35, 72, 74,
    92, 100–101, 118, 121, 135, 141,
    160, 197, 201–205, 211–212, 240,
    245
United States Agency for International
    Development (USAID), 197
United States Bureau of Indian Affairs, 91

United States Department of Justice, 247
United States Department of Labor,
    123–124
United States Department of Defense, 160
United States Indian Land Claims
    Commission, 246
United States National Historic
    Preservation Act, 30, 100, 240
United States National Park Service, 103
United States State Department, 205
United University Professions, 116
Universal truths, 46, 73, 74, 76, 220
Universalism, 71, 73, 76
University of Arizona, 239–240, 259–260
    archaeological field school at
        Grasshopper, 92
University of California Press, 116
University of Hawai'i-Manoa, 160
University of Kentucky, 186, 193
University of Massachusetts-Amherst, 133
University of Michigan, 53
University of New Mexico, 240
University of North Carolina-Chapel Hill,
    165
Uzbek, 201–202, 205, 206, 207
Uzgen, Kyrgyzstan, 206

van Gennep, Arnold, 32
van Willigen, John, 36
Velasquez, Londin, 167
Victory Circle, in participatory planning,
    56
Vietnam War, 92, 115
Volunteers, 64–65, 93, 167, 189

Wachtel, Andrew, 201–202
Wailau, Moloka'i, 160
Watkins, Joe, 249
Weber, Max, 71–72, 74
Welch, John R., 9, 35, 50, 86, 91–94, 149,
    152, 156, 217–218, 242–244, 248,
    260
Western thought, science, traditions, 139,
    200, 203–204, 219–220, 226
Witmore, Christopher, 219
Wobst, Martin, 116, 133, 157
Wisconsin, 123–124

Wheaton, Thomas R., 94
White Mountain Apache Tribe, 40, 91–93, 259
Wilcox, Michael, 163
Wilk, Richard, 163
Woodfill, Brent, 172
Woodward, Ralph, 75
World Archaeological Congress, 14, 55, 79, 80, 116
World War I and II, 72, 74–75, 128
Wydra, Harald, 32
Wylie, Alison, 163

Yablonski, Joseph, Margaret and Charlotte, 128
Yangming, Wang, 134
Yemen, 197, 211
Yucatán, 171
Yukatek, 170–172

Ziibiwing Center of Anishinabe Culture and Lifeways, 147, 157, 205
Zimmerman, Larry, 9, 116, 134, 156
Zinn, Howard, 12
Zuni Pueblo, 239–240, 244

About the Editors

Sonya Atalay is an Assistant Professor of Anthropology at the University of Massachusetts Amherst. She received her MA and PhD from the University of California, Berkeley and received postdoctoral funding from the National Science Foundation and the Ford Foundation. Atalay's primary research interests are related to engaged anthropology—particularly the use of community-based research methodologies, intellectual property in relation to indigenous cultural heritage, and research ethics and protocols when working with indigenous communities. She has served on and chaired committees within the American Anthropological Association and the Society for American Archaeology, and served two terms as a member for the Native American Graves Protection and Repatriation Act Review Committee. Her recent book, *Community-based Archaeology: Research with, by and for Indigenous and Local Communities* (2012, University of California Press) provides theoretical discussions and methodological guidance on conducting community based participatory archaeology and cultural heritage research.

Lee Rains Clauss is an archaeologist and advocate for Native American communities' sovereignty and stewardship of cultural resources. She has 15 years of experience in historic preservation law and federal regulatory compliance, with a broad theoretical and technical background that also includes architectural history, Tribal heritage management, curation, and community-based participatory research. Her degrees include a BS in Historic Preservation from Southeast Missouri State University and an MA in Anthropology with an emphasis in Applied Archaeology from Northern Arizona University. Clauss currently works as a consultant for the Sherwood Valley Rancheria of Pomo's Tribal Historic Preservation Office (THPO) in California. She was previously employed as the Historic Preservation Specialist for the Eastern Band of Cherokee Indians in North Carolina, a THPO intern/assistant for the White Mountain Apache in Arizona, and a curation and NAGPRA fellow for the US Army Corps of Engineers Mandatory Center of Expertise for the Curation and Management of Archaeological Collections (MCX-CMAC). Clauss also teaches courses in Archaeology, Cultural Anthropology, Native American History and Culture, and Tribal and Ethnic Religions. Clauss is actively involved in professional service and currently serves as the chair of the Society for American Archaeology Government Affairs Committee.

Randall H. McGuire is a Distinguished Professor of Anthropology at Binghamton University in Binghamton, New York. He received his BA from the University of Texas and his MA and PhD from the University of Arizona. He has taught at the

Universitat Autònoma de Barcelona and at the Esquela Nacional de Antropología y Historia in México City. He has published extensively on Marxist theory and Indigenous archaeology. From 1996 to 2007, he and Dean Saitta of the University of Denver directed the Archaeology of the Colorado Coal Field War, 1913-1914 project near Trinidad, Colorado. He has worked with Elisa Villalpando of the Centro INAH, Sonora for 29 years investigating the Trincheras Tradition of northern Sonora, México. The Spanish summary of their excavations at Cerro de Trincheras, *Entre Muros de Piedra,* was published in Hermosillo, Sonora in 2010. The full site report on the excavations was published by the Arizona State Museum in 2011. His latest books include *Archaeology as Political Action, The Archaeology of Class War* with Karin Larkin, and *Ideologies in Archaeology* with Reinhard Bernbeck. He recently published "Steel Walls and Picket Fences: Rematerializing the U.S.–Mexican Border in Ambos Nogales" in *American Anthropologist* (2013, 115(3):466–480). His webpage is http://bingweb.binghamton.edu/~rmcguire/index.html.

John R. Welch is a Canada research chair and associate professor, jointly appointed in the Department of Archaeology and School of Resource and Environmental Management, Simon Fraser University, British Columbia, Canada. He received his AB from Hamilton College and his MA and PhD from the University of Arizona. Welch is an applied archaeologist with research, teaching, and outreach commitments that center on collaborations with indigenous nations in projects at the interface of anthropology, resource management, and cultural perpetuation. Since the mid-1980s, Welch has facilitated partnerships with the White Mountain Apache and other tribes in upland Arizona and First Nations in coastal British Columbia. Against a backdrop of ongoing reassessments of what to conserve in the face of global change, Welch facilitates the mobilization of indigenous knowledge and the advancement of indigenous community and broader public agendas for stewardship of sociocultural and biophysical legacies. He is a member of the steering committee for the Intellectual Property issues in Cultural Heritage Project (http://www.sfu.ca/ipinch/). *Kinishba Lost and Found,* a 2013 book Welch edited on legacy collections from Kinishba Ruins National Historic Landmark, was published in 2013 by the Arizona State Museum. Welch's faculty page is at http://www.rem.sfu.ca/people/faculty/welch/.

green press
INITIATIVE